Studies in Media Management

AMERICAN MAGAZINES

for the 1980s

To my wife, Myrtle,
and our children: Marie, Bill, and Alice
Who together have made my life worthwhile

Library of Congress Cataloging in Publication Data
Taft, William H. (William Howard), 1915 Oct. 24—
American magazines for the 1980s.

(Studies in media management)   Bibliography: p.
Includes index.
1. American periodicals. I. Title. II. Series.
PN4877.T26 1982   070.5'72'0973   82-6207
ISBN 0-8038-0496-2 (pbk.)   AACR2

Published simultaneously in Canada by
Saunders of Toronto Ltd., Markham, Ontario

Printed in the United States of America

Contents

Introduction

Few businesses in America are as fluid as the magazine industry. Millions of Americans read magazines each day, often unaware of their long history of publication or, on the other hand, more recent appearance. Americans continue to visit their newsstands (and supermarkets) as they do their weekly shopping and there purchase magazines by the thousands. Some of our magazines appeal to enormous groups of readers; the majority, however, are to more limited numbers in specialized interest areas.

Magazines will celebrate the 250th anniversary of their existence in America in 1991. No one can hazard a guess about how many periodicals have appeared here since Andrew Bradford and Ben Franklin started the nation's first magazines in 1741. Debates continue about a suitable definition for a magazine and there are more debates over how many are published in America at the present time.

A complete history of American magazines is impossible. The late Frank Luther Mott devoted five volumes in his Pulitzer Prize-winning study of the nation's magazines, yet at the time of his death he had reached only to the 1930s.

Obviously this volume makes no pretense at providing information about *all* magazines. It seeks to present a panoramic view of today's magazine industry, offering bits and pieces with occasionally larger bits of information about as many publications as space allows. Indeed, one could fill these pages merely by *listing* today's magazines without comments.

This study also attempts to awaken the general public to the complex magazine world with its thousands of publications regularly seeking sufficient audiences to supply the needed revenue from advertising and subscriptions for

7

survival. The emphasis throughout is on those publications that carry advertisements, eliminating additional thousands of periodicals issued by clubs, societies, associations and others.

Lesser attention is directed toward the editors and publishers as individuals. The magazine world, as noted, is too mobile; many of these individuals shift from publication to publication. Another major problem would be the selection of these leaders. Certainly another book could be written on the Who's Who in the magazine world.

Special thanks to my colleagues on the University of Missouri School of Journalism faculty and to the 12,000 students who listened to me discuss journalism history during a 35-year career. Dr. Don Ranly, who directs the Missouri magazine program, deserves special thanks for his advice and encouragement.

Thanks to the Research Council of the University of Missouri-Columbia for funds that assisted in several trips to confer with publishers and to visit their operations.

Thanks, too, to Russell F. Neale, Al Lichtenberg and Jim Moore at Hastings House for their concern with this project and their assistance in helping me bring it all together.

Obviously such a long, tedious project could never have been completed without the encouragement and cooperation of my wife. For more than five years she was surrounded by magazines, books, articles, term papers, books, and Xerox prints while her husband attempted to bring order out of chaos.

WILLIAM H. TAFT
University of Missouri-Columbia

Spring 1981

Acknowledgments

No study of the American magazine scene could be accomplished without serious attention to a group of media-orientated periodicals. In an industry that changes daily, these periodicals provide readers with necessary data and pro vide historians with significant material to produce such books as this. The material used from each source has been fully documented in the footnotes.

Special thanks to the following periodicals for permission to quote from their issues:

Advertising Age, with special attention to its valuable supplements; *AD-WEEK; Editor & Publisher,* since many newspaper owners also own magazines; *Folio,* creator of the significant Folio 400 and the interpretator of numerous topics of concern to all those in the industry; *Gallagher Report,* for its statistical accounts; *Madison Avenue,* with its emphasis on national advertising and its interviews with magazine leaders; *Magazine Age,* a newcomer for advertisers and agencies; *Media Industry Newsletter,* with its weekly update of the industry; *Marketing & Media Decisions; IPDA Profit Way* and Council for Periodical Distributors Assn. *News* for data on distribution; and *Publishers Weekly.*

In several instances articles from these periodicals were copyrighted by their authors and thanks to David P. Forsyth, John D. Klingel, Frank Romano, Henry Turner, and others for the opportunity to quote from their comments.

Cooperation also came generously from the Magazine Publishers Association, American Business Press, Inc., and other associations with more specialized interests.

In the majority of the references, only limited quotes or material were used. However, footnotes provide references to these sources so readers may probe deeper into selected topics than space permitted us to cover here.

A number of publishers granted permission to use their material with specific requirements for acknowledgment, as noted in the following instances.

Caroline Bird, "Gadfly of Medicine," *Esquire* (February 1956) Copyright © 1956 by Esquire Publishing Inc. Used by permission of the magazine.

Edward Bok, "Return of the Business Woman," *Ladies' Home Journal* (March 1900) Copyright © 1900 by LHJ Publishing Inc. Reprinted with permission of *Ladies' Home Journal*.

J. W. Click and Russell Baird, *Magazine Editing and Production.* Copyright © by Wm. C. Brown. (Dubuque, Iowa, 1979). Reprinted with permission.

Edwin Diamond, "Take a Great Editor, Add Great Writers, Throw Caution to the Wind," *NEXT* (January–February 1981, Volume 2, Number 1) Copyright by Litton Magazines, Inc. Published by Next Publishing Company.

Lana Ellis, sketch of Helen Gurley Brown, (December 6, 1970) *Louisville Courier-Journal,* Copyright © 1970.

Robert T. Elson, *The World of Time Inc: The Intimate History of a Publishing Enterprise, 1941–1960.* Copyright © 1973 by Time Inc. (New York: Atheneum, 1973). Reprinted with permission of Atheneum Publishers.

Nora Ephron, "People Magazine," *Scribble Scribble: Notes on the Media.* Copyright © Alfred A. Knopf, Inc. (New York, 1978).

Otto Friedrich, "There are oo Trees in Russia," *Harper's* (October 1964). Permission granted by author.

Jay S. Harris, ed., *TV GUIDE, The First 25 Years.* Simon & Schuster, Inc., (New York, 1978). Reprinted by permission of copyright owner, Triangle Publications, Inc.

How and Why People Buy Magazines. Completed by Lieberman Research Inc. of New York (1977). Reprinted by permission of Publishers Clearing House, Port Washington, N.Y.

"John H. Johnson of *Ebony,*" *Nation's Business* (April 1974). Copyright © 1974 by *Nation's Business,* Chamber of Commerce of the United States.

John H. Johnson, "Failure is a word I don't accept," interview, *Harvard Business Review* (March–April 1976). Reprinted by permission.

Dow Jones & Company, Inc., for permission to quote from the *Wall Street Journal.* Items identified in footnotes are copyrighted © by Dow Jones & Company, Inc., for dates indicated. All rights reserved.

Journalism Quarterly, publication of the Association for Education in Journalism, for permission to quote from the following articles: Ben L. Moon, "City Magazines, Past & Present," (Winter 1970); Paul Hirsch, "An Analysis of *Ebony,*" (Summer 1968); and Edward Smith and Gilbert Fowler Jr., "The Status of Magazine Group Ownership," (Autumn 1979).

James B. Kobak, "The Bright Future of the Magazine Industry," *Magazine,* Progressive Graphics, Inc., Oregon, Ill.

"Introducing . . ." editor's comments, *People* (March 4, 1974). Copyright © 1974 by People Weekly.

Profits Way, publication of the International Periodical Distributors Association, for permission to use the following references: "Personality journalism: selling magazines for you," (May/June 1979); "Take off with the science fiction category," (November/December 1979); "Those sensational tabloids sales," (November/December 1979); and "A publication marketing strategy for the 1980s," (May/June 1980).

"How J. I. Rodale Founded PREVENTION," *Prevention* (June 1975). Reprinted by special permission from *Prevention* Magazine, Copyright © June, 1975, by Rodale Press, Emmaus, Pa.

"Scandal sheet or media pacesetter?" *Kansas City Star* (January 25, 1981). By permission of The Kansas City Star Company, Copyright © 1981.

Michael Andrew Scully, "Would Mother Jones Buy 'Mother Jones' "? *The Public Interest* (Fall 1978). Copyright © 1978 by National Affairs, Inc.

"Taking the Measure of Magazine Audience," *The New York Times* (February 3, 1981). Copyright © 1981 by The New York Times Company. Reprinted by permission.

The following references from *TIME* were reprinted by permission from Time, The Weekly Newsmagazine; Copyright Time Inc. in years indicated. Letter from the Publisher (May 10, 1963); "Hang-up at *Harper's,*" (March 15, 1971); "Spokesman for Conservatism," (July 10, 1964); "The *Atlantic* Makes Waves," (October 12, 1970); "Woman Power," (March 30, 1970); "Skin Trouble," (September 22, 1975); "The *New Yorker* Turns Fifty," (March 3, 1975); and "Exodus at *Quest,*" (January 12, 1981).

Chris Welles, "Can Mass Magazines Survive?" *Columbia Journalism Review* (July/August 1971). Reprinted by permission of author.

"What every marketer should know about women," *Harvard Business Review* (May–June 1978). Reprinted by permission.

Theodore H. White, *In Search of History.* Harper & Row, Publishers, Inc. (New York, 1978).

Nancy Yoshihara, "Women's Magazine Dilemma: Who Are They For?" (December 23, 1979). Copyright, © 1979 by *Los Angeles Times.* Reprinted by permission.

The following from *U.S. News & World Report,* copyright © in year indicated by U.S. News & World Report, Inc.; "Why Postal Service Faces Bleak Future," (December 1, 1980); Special Section: "Challenges of the '80s," (October 15, 1979); and "Printing by Computer: A USN&WR Gamble Pays Off," (September 5, 1977).

AMERICAN MAGAZINES
for the 1980s

The AMERICAN MAGAZINE

OR

A MONTHLY VIEW OF

The Political State

OF THE BRITISH COLONIES:

For JANUARY, 1740-1.

To be Continued Monthly.

Containing,

I An ABSTRACT of the Proceedings of the *Assembly* of NEW JERSEY, in Relation to HIS MAJESTY's Instructions, for furnishing Provisions, for the Troops directed to be raised there, and sent from thence against the *Spanish West-Indies.*

II A DESCRIPTION of PENNSYLVANIA, in Answer to a Misrepresentation of it, in the DRAPER's Letters.

III. An ABSTRACT of the Dispute between the Governor and Assembly of PENNSYLVANIA, on the Subject of *Defence.*

IV. EXTRACTS from the Proceedings of the MARYLAND-ASSEMBLY, with an Account of the Controversy between the Upper and Lower House of that Province

V. REMARKS on the MARYLAND Government, and Constitution.

VI CHARACTERS of the WORTHIES at *Stowe*, the Right Hon. the Lord Cobham.

PHILADELPHIA: Printed and Sold by ANDREW BRADFORD: (Price One Shilling *Pennsylvania* Currency, or Eight Pence Sterling.) Of whom may be had singly, The PLAN of this Magazine, lately published in the *American Mercury,* which is now Reprinted with Alterations and Additions. (Price Three-Pence *Pennsylvania* Money.)

THE
GENERAL MAGAZINE,
AND
Historical Chronicle,

For all the *British* Plantations in *America.*

[To be Continued Monthly.]

JANUARY 1741.

ICH   DIEN

VOL. I.

PHILADELPHIA:
Printed and Sold by B. FRANKLIN.

1

The Stage Is Set

IT ALL BEGAN during a weekend in 1741.

Within four days, two enterprising Philadelphia newspaper publishers offered their customers a new product in America—the colonies' first magazines. Andrew Bradford's *The American Magazine, or a Monthly View of the Political State of the British Colonies,* won over Benjamin Franklin's *The General Magazine, and Historical Chronicle, For all the British Plantations in America.* A wordy and lengthy editorial battle had been waged for several months by these longtime competitors, each promising readers of their newspapers that his new magazine would arrive "next week" or "soon."

Bradford's success on Friday, Feb. 13, 1741, was short-lived. His *American Magazine,* the first of several to bear this title, survived for only three issues. Franklin's *General Magazine* had better success, continuing for six months. Obviously the British Colonies were not ready for such home-produced periodicals. Weekly newspapers furnished sufficient news for their limited audiences, while the better educated and financially secure citizens obtained books and periodicals from England.[1]*

The nation's most famous printer-statesman previously had convinced his Philadelphia followers that he was the more knowledgeable in what they wanted to read than was Bradford. Franklin's newspaper, the *Pennsylvania Gazette,* had outclassed the older publisher's efforts, *The American Weekly Mercury.* Franklin, who learned the printing trade initially in his native Boston, had refined the craft through study in England. Early he became aware of the more successful British periodicals such as the *Tatler* and the *Spectator,* using them

* Footnote references are arranged, Chapter by Chapter, in a separate section of this book beginning on page 349.

as models to improve his own style. Although these two early magazines indicated a desire to become publications for the masses, as indicated by their long sub-titles, neither reached its objective.

Bradford's magazine may have failed because it lacked variety, being loaded with proceedings from the four-state area of New York, New Jersey, Maryland, and Pennsylvania. Obviously, readers were not so concerned about what their legislative bodies were doing as Bradford had believed. His only illustration was on the title page, a cut representing the Philadelphia waterfront. The three-month career of the *American Magazine* provides an indication of how unprofitable the publication had been.

Franklin also featured a large woodcut on the title page, described by Frank Luther Mott as "the coronet of the Prince of Wales, adorned by its three large plumes and the motto *Ich Dien.*" [2] Franklin also paid attention to proceedings of the state assemblies as well as those of Parliament. However, he informed readers of a greater variety of topics, such as new books, complete sermons and other religious news, poetry from English and American sources. The business-minded Franklin paid considerable attention to the raging currency problems and to the activities and opinions of the Rev. George Whitefield, a prominent revivalist of the times. Franklin liked Whitefield, yet opened his magazine to the minister's critics, which prompted considerable letter writing on the part of the colonists. Being the better printer, Franklin turned out a more attractive periodical, one of more value to historians today than to readers in 1741. Today we tend to give it more attention than Franklin apparently felt the magazine deserved—he failed to mention it in his *Autobiography*.

Obviously, neither printer had to worry about the circulation numbers game that have highlighted more recent years in the history of American magazines. Nor did they have such competition as today's publishers for the readers' interest—no radio, television, daily newspapers, or other American periodicals.

Magazines as we know them today had to wait for high-speed presses and improved transportation systems to reach a broader market in contrast to the newspapers, which depended more on the local surroundings for their success. With a nationwide market that the magazines eventually obtained, they could attract the advertising needed for financial security. It is interesting, however, to observe an exception to this trend today, with the advent of numerous city and regional periodicals with their objective to serve a limited audience.

Nearly 250 years later, the advent of two newcomers to the magazine field would create little excitement. Americans find their wants satisfied as publishers offer solutions via their printed pages for a multitude of needs, desires, and hopes for their millions of readers. All age groups, all areas of the nation, and all interests—serious and otherwise—appear satisfied today. Should any group find itself without a periodical of its own, someone certainly will start a magazine with all the fanfare of a bicentennial celebration.

Magazines since the 19th Century have helped to bring about social, economic, and political reform in America. According to historian Dr. Theodore

Peterson, of the University of Illinois, magazines also place issues and events into perspective, foster "a sense of national community," provide low cost entertainment while offering an inexpensive method for instruction in the art of daily living, and serve as an "educator in man's cultural heritage." Although many of the pioneer magazines failed to live to graceful maturity, Peterson notes that: "In America the magazine occupied the place in reading habits that the book did in some other countries, and never before in history had a medium devoted primarily to subjects other than news reached so vast an audience." And Peterson added, "one of the most reassuring strengths of magazines was their variety of entertainment, information, and ideas. Their variety arose from their selectivity of audience," a situation that gained momentum in the post-World War II era.[3]

From a period of beginning that covered roughly 50 years, 1741–1794, the industry moved into the era of nationalism, 1794–1825. During the earliest era Bradford and Franklin were followed by Rogers and Fowle's *American Magazine and Historical Review,* H. H. Brackenridge's *United States Magazine,* Mathew Carey's *American Museum,* Isaiah Thomas' *Massachusetts Magazine,* and others. The nationalism period was highlighted by the start, in 1815, of the *North American Review and Miscellaneous Journal.*

A period of expansion occurred between 1825 and 1850, when the *Saturday Evening Post* arrived, as well as *Godey's Lady's Book, Knickerbocker Magazine, Southern Literary Messenger, Graham's,* and others. The years between 1850 and 1865 have been described as the period of politics and war. In 1850, *Harper's New Monthly Magazine* appeared, followed seven years later by the *Atlantic Monthly.* From the end of the Civil War until 1890, the golden era occurred. Edwin Godkin established the *Nation* in 1865 and in 1870 *Scribner's Monthly* arrived. *Frank Leslie's Magazine* followed in 1876 and Cyrus H. K. Curtis, who had made the *Saturday Evening Post* and *Country Gentleman* well known, started the *Ladies' Home Journal* in 1883.

McClure's, Everybody's, Munsey's, and *Cosmopolitan* were all part of the muckrakers' era, 1890–1914. And after World War I, the news-pictures dominated the era, with such newcomers as *Time, Fortune, Esquire, Reader's Digest, Newsweek, U. S. News & World Report, Life, Look,* and hundreds of other periodicals. Such tremendous growth continued after World War II. In the 1980s this trend toward specialization continued, moving to a state of "specialization within specialization" as the market becomes dissected into more minute elements. Mott also considered the period of 1880 to 1902 one of advertising development, which no doubt made possible the golden era noted by others. And he would have to consider the post-World War II years as another period of tremendous expansion in advertising.

Mechanical Growth Significant

The earlier decades were highlighted by the significant role played by outstanding editors and publishers, much as the 19th Century newspaper world was marked by the personal journalism of such leaders as Horace Greeley, James Gordon Bennett, Joseph Pulitzer, William Randolph Hearst, E. W. Scripps, and others. Some magazine publishers included their names on their publications, including S. S. McClure and Frank A. Munsey, as well as Louis A. Godey, whose *Godey's Lady's Book* provided the stage for many of today's leading publications for women. Cyrus H. K. Curtis made his publishing house the nation's leader through his choice of excellent editors, such as Edward W. Bok and George Horace Lorimer. Growth continued through the years in advertising revenues, readership surveys and research, standardization of page sizes and in the technology necessary for the printing and distribution of publications. Such advances continue today at a more torrid pace. Neither Franklin nor Bradford would recognize the immense printing establishments that produce the millions of copies of magazines each day in America.

Theodore H. White, noted historian of presidential elections, considers the 1890s to be the time when all the elements merged to place the magazine in a position of dominance in this nation.

> The halftone photoengraving process permitted inexpensive photographic reproduction for a national population, which, though literate, was for the most part repelled by unbroken blocks of type on the printed page.
>
> The high-speed rotary press, another device, was perfected—presses which could spit out millions of copies a day. And most effectively, by the 1890s that giant device, the national railroad net, was completed from coast to coast, border to border. A manufacturer could deliver stoves, pianos, beds, furniture and, soon, automobiles to one national market—if only a way could be found to reach the entire national market . . .

White thought about a situation that existed in the last century and continues to exist: "No local newspaper could reach from Maine to California; no New York or Washington newspaper could reach, as did Paris and London papers, half the country's reading population." White also believes that 1940 can be recognized as the date "magazines had become the dominant political medium of this nation. No greater demonstration of media authority has been exhibited in our time than when three East Coast magazine publishers forced the nomination of Wendell Willkie on the Republican Party in 1940—the publishers of *Life* and *Time, Look,* and the *Saturday Evening Post.*" [4]

The expansion of the magazine world has never been easy. Publishers have always encountered hurdles to conquer. Peterson notes that the development of the automobile after World War I threatened to put everyone on the open road, thus taking away available time previously devoted to reading. [5] When the radio appeared in the mid-1920s it, too, threatened not only the magazine business but also the newspaper industry. After World War II a similar threat, apparently more serious and more lasting, came with the tremendous growth of television. Of these major competitive factors, television has brought about more changes in the magazines, changes that will continue to be highlighted throughout the 1980s. Roland Wolseley observed that "it took years before advertisers were convinced that magazines might be weaker quantitatively but could prove considerable strength qualitatively."[6]

While these outside invasions moved through their novelty stages magazines survived to reach new plateaus by adjusting to readers' interests and desires, as well as their needs. For example, when the economic picture darkened, publishers came forth with more how-to-do-it magazines to assist home owners and others make necessary repairs and adjustments in their living conditions. And during recent years, with a better educated nation, with the people possessing more financial security, and with more leisure time for the pursuit of hobbies and interests, magazines have developed by the hundreds to cash in on such opportunities.

What Is a Magazine?

Another magazine historian, Pulitzer Prize winner Frank Luther Mott, started his study beyond Bradford and Franklin, returning to England and *The London Gentleman's Magazine* of 1731. According to Mott and others this was the first to use "magazine" in its title, a word derived from the French "magasin," which originally meant "storehouse." Many pioneer American publications were considered "miscellanies," conveying this storehouse connotation with their collection of odds and ends designed to attract all members of the family.

The Gentleman's Magazine was designed "to give a Monthly View of all the News-Papers (which of late are so multiplied as to render it impossible, unless a Man makes it a Business, to consult them all) and in the next Place, we shall join therewith some other Matters of Use or Amusement that will be communicated to us." Thus did the publisher, Edward Cave, prepare the public for *The Gentleman's Magazine.* He was 250 years ahead of today's publications, yet his thoughts are reflected in what we read today, as he promised readers his magazine would "constantly exhibit Essays on various Subjects for Entertainment, and all the rest, occasionally oblige their Readers with Matters of Publick Concern, communicated to the World by Persons of Capacity, through their Means; so that they are become the chief Channels of Amusement and Intelligence. But being then only loose Papers, uncertainly scatter'd about, it often happens that many things deserving Attention, contained in them, are only seen by Accident, and others not sufficiently publish'd or preserved for universal Benefit and Information."[7]

Other terms have been associated with magazines. In one sense at least all magazines are *publications,* while within the industry they are labeled *books,* a term that will be avoided here to prevent confusion. *Review* has long been associated with magazines, as has *journal,* which originally was applied to diurnal or daily, reflecting a daily record or account of official transactions. Mott, a stickler for details in his studies of American magazines and newspapers, defined a magazine as "a bound pamphlet issued more or less regularly and containing a variety of reading matter." Little remains today of any distinction in the use of periodical, review, journal, book, or magazine. Periodicals such as *National Enquirer* and *Parade* are considered magazines by some although they are more like newspapers in appearance and format. They tend to emphasize magazine-oriented content, however. Possibly one could fall back on Alexander Pope's 1743 definition of magazines as "Upstart collections of dullness, folly and so on" without any reference to size, content, or what have you.[8] But could we call them dull today? Certainly not.

WHY PEOPLE READ MAGAZINES

Whatever we decide to term magazines apparently has had no effect upon the readers, who continue to purchase millions of copies daily. This consumer demand continues to increase despite setbacks in the general economy. The purchasing public may shift from time to time, from the young to the old, or from the mass audiences to the specialized minorities but the overall total revenues continue upward.

In a national study of the consumer market for magazines by the Lieberman Research, Inc., of New York, for Publishers Clearing House, these five major points were stressed:

First, magazine buying is a widespread phenomenon, but a relatively small proportion of the population accounts for a disproportionately high percentage of magazines sold. This study noted that three out of four adults buy magazines in the course of a year. However, heavy magazine buyers—those who buy nine or more different titles a year—account for one-fifth of the adult population but represent about three-fifths of all magazines purchased.

Second, the magazine-buyer market is fluid—not static. As this book will note, the top three magazines in America (*TV Guide, Reader's Digest,* and *National Geographic*) continue to hold their circulation leadership. However, the Lieberman study found that three out of ten magazine buyers report they are reading more magazines now than five years ago, yet the same number report they are reading fewer magazines. Thus a fluid arena.

Third, the magazine industry is doing a good job of attracting younger people but it may be alienating and losing some older people. Lieberman notes that the 18–34 age group has been raised in an age of television, yet they are favorably disposed toward magazines. Older persons, many in retirement and affected directly by the high rate of inflation, have become more sensitive to price increases and are buying fewer magazines. One might also observe that many senior citizens, with leisure time, seek magazine reading rooms in public libraries for more economical reading conditions.

Fourth, both demographically and psychographically, magazine buyers as a whole—and particularly heavy magazine buyers—constitute an upscale, contemporary, confident segment of the population. Traditionally, magazines have attracted the more affluent, better educated audiences. Many older Americans can recall the "status symbol" that magazines held in their homes. Such publications were placed in the living room where visitors could see them. They were saved, often bound in annual volumes. Lieberman added that magazine buyers are more community-oriented and more willing to experiment than non-buyers, who often suffer from a sense of social isolation and social alienation. The study reveals "there is something about magazine buying which is associated with having a contemporary, active, outgoing orientation."

Fifth, magazine buying is not only related to demographics but it also is linked with people's basic reading orientations. Obviously, magazine buyers enjoy reading more than non-buyers. And the study observed that those who read faster are more likely to be magazine readers than those who admit to being slow readers.[9]

This study also reviewed the role of magazines, finding that basically this has not changed through the years. For example, "There are just as many people who turn to magazines primarily for information." And today's publications rate better in the information function than in the entertainment function. "People regard magazines as an excellent way of keeping abreast of trends, keeping informed about new products, and securing information about individual and special interests and activities such as hobbies, decorating, family care and fashion." Here, obviously, is the influence of specialization. However, the interviewees considered radio and television better for entertainment.

While recognizing that magazines have changed in the past five years, the interviewed subjects disagreed as to whether the changes were for the better or for worse. The pros believed they were "more informative, more open, and more honest and truthful," while the cons claimed "too much advertising and too much nudity/sex." The pros tended to be in the younger generation. The opposition came mostly from older people, a situation not too unexpected in today's society.

Among other significant conclusions or implications were these:

> The state of the magazine buyer market—insofar as consumer demand for magazines is concerned—appears to be good.
>
> The magazine buyers tend to have a more outgoing, optimistic, contemporary orientation. These positive psychographics appear to go beyond demographics alone.
>
> While parents encourage their teenagers to read newspapers and books, teenagers themselves cite magazines as their favorite reading material.

EARLY 70S INFLUENCE 80S

Chris Welles, a former editor of *Life* and a commentator on the magazine scene, raised a significant question as the 70s opened: Can mass magazines survive? Writing in the *Columbia Journalism Review,* Welles' concern was well-founded, since his study centered on the future of *Life* and *Look,* two of the nation's circulation leaders in the last decade.[10]

Life's circulation in 1971 was 7,110,000, down from its 1969 peak of

8,548,500. Its gross advertising revenues were slightly under $110 million, down $32 million in a year and well below the peak of nearly $170 million in 1966. At the time of its death in 1972, *Life*'s actions confirmed what many had been saying—the mass magazine was dead. Meanwhile, the *Media Industry Newsletter* noted this about the mass market:

> It is not that the market for mass national magazines has dissipated; it's that the mass national magazines have dissipated their editorial vitality. The fault did not lie with the editor but with the management either for not permitting the editor to run freely or for not getting the kind of editors that would compel readers to turn to *Life* each week in the face of overwhelming distractions of competing media. It's management palsy that withers mass magazines—in fact, any magazine.[11]

Welles raised other questions about the mass magazines and their future. Quoting media leaders, he observed the problems of magazine identity, the image before the advertisers and their agencies. He placed some responsibility for this confused picture on the advertisers who "have responded to the decline in mass tastes with an extensive proliferation of products, some entirely new, some differentiated versions of old products. Each of the products appeals to specific types of persons. Advertising agencies have directed research toward 'demographics'—the specific characteristics of different media audiences."

The attention to demographics expanded in the 70s and continues to be significant in the picture during the 80s. This represented a change of directions from the 60s, when *Life, Look* and others sought massive circulations in their competitive war with television. This trend was reversed in the 70s, when magazines turned to specific but limited audiences, a concept that continues into the 80s.

Some readers felt that *Life, Look, Saturday Evening Post,* and a few others were hesitant to recognize this trend toward specialization. However, other publishers had moved to "highly particularized intellectual, vocational, and avocational interests," according to Welles, who cited Helen Gurley Brown and her revitalized *Cosmopolitan,* Clay Felker and the *New York,* and dozens of others. Welles was correct in his prediction concerning the possible death of *Life* and *Look*. Both died and both were revived, with mixed results. *Life* is still around, but as a monthly, not a weekly. *Look* is gone again.

The individual reader still held the key in the early Seventies, according to Roland E. Wolseley.[12] He thought "that decisions by entrepreneurs to face realities for the sake of survival" influenced others. Magazines suffered temporarily during the rebellious 60s when students found the "Establishment" periodicals lacking in material of their interest. The "liberated" women and their struggle for women's rights resulted not only in significant changes within their publications but in the establishment of a all-new breed of magazine. This new tone in American periodicals started to sound in the 60s, according to Wolseley, when more freedom of expression appeared, making it possible to cover subjects formerly considered inappropriate for widely circulated periodicals. Meanwhile, the New Journalism of Tom Wolfe, Jimmy Breslin, Gay Talese, Truman Capote, Norman Mailer, and others also helped to influence the content of American magazines.

SPECIAL INTEREST TREND CONTINUES

Though many associate specialization with a new trend in recent years, this idea really has been around for decades. A review of the Bradford and Franklin publications, as noted earlier, indicate their basic appeal was to the political concerns of their readers, although both realized the need to attract other readers through a variety of topics. Possibly only the *degree* of specialization is new. Bob Donath, writing for *Advertising Age* in the mid-70s, noted that this trend had succeeded in moving consumer magazines away from their head-to-head battle with the television industry. More attention was directed to local and regional advertisers, who could be attracted to the many new demographic splits now offered by magazines. This was one way to solve the declining advertising revenue scare. "Faced with burdensome postal rate increases, publishers are trimming paper weights, seeking more newsstand distribution, and experimenting with alternative subscription delivery methods," Donath added. On a more optimistic note in 1974, Katharine Graham, of *Newsweek* and the Washington *Post,* said, "Magazines are in many ways the ideal medium for serious treatment of the major issues of our day."[13]

"Look What TV's Doing for Magazines" headlined the *Christian Science Monitor* on Feb. 27, 1974. Although television had shocked the magazine industry in the early 50s, a reversal of this trend appeared in the mid-70s. "We're seeing a second revolution in print," claimed Robert M. Goshorn, of the Magazine Publishers Association. He was quoted as saying, "The resurgence of magazines lies in the fact that television can only whet an interest for information. Magazines give depth of perspective, interpretation, and reflection." Goshorn also observed that "All the long-term trends—higher education, higher incomes, the knowledge explosion, a more complex world—all of them point toward more magazines. The need to know has never been greater. It is second only to tomorrow's need to know."

Magazines profited tremendously from the Bicentennial bonanza. John Peter, writing in *Folio,* noted the unusualness of this situation: "Nobody had a scoop on the idea. It was out there for everybody. It didn't come in a rush. Everybody should have had time to think and plan. The Bicentennial was an editorial Olympics with the premium on imagination and execution."[14] Among those that produced historical editions were *Time, Newsweek, U.S. News & World Report, Saturday Evening Post, AIA Journal, American Artist, New York Times Magazine, Think* (IBM), *National Geographic, Design News, Dun's Review, Atlas,* and *Fortune.* Each, in its own way, approached the topic from a specialized point of view, appropriate for its readership. Some publications objected to another special issue, questioning the return in advertising revenues in proportion to the special production costs. Some felt the theme had been overworked, although many felt the reading public expected magazines to prepare something special for the occasion. The *Saturday Evening Post,* for example, capitalized on its long history by reprinting stories and illustrations culled from its issues during the two centuries, with stories from Ben Franklin to George S. Patton. Pictures also were reproduced from the massive illustration collections of Norman Rockwell and J. C. Leyendecker.

How Many Magazines?

Since there appears to be no single acceptance as to what a magazine is, researchers have difficulty in determining how many periodicals exist today. In the "Folio 400" study (noted later), the magazine considered only those with a minimum frequency of four times a year. It also used a broader base than some sources do, including inflight publications, Sunday newspaper supplements, and others such as *Barron's* and *Rolling Stone* even though they are printed on newsprint. Listings from the Standard Rate and Data *Consumer and Farm Magazines* and *Business Publication* rate books also are used. From its database, *Folio* had 10,665 active publications, including 5,464 trade and 4,801 consumer magazines, plus the "Folio 400," which includes 267 consumer and 133 trade periodicals.

Folio recognized the difficulties one encounters in defining publications under a specific classification. For example, it noted that the highly successful *Smithsonian* could appropriately appear in the general interest humanities market as well as in the general interest science market. And *Black Enterprise* could be listed under both consumer and business headings.

In an earlier study, James L. C. Ford estimated there were 17,000 public relations magazines designed for specific audiences. Ford, however, included leaflets inserted with utility bills. A figure of 9,000 to 10,000 appears more reasonable, according to the International Association of Business Communicators. These publications are internal, external, or a combination of the two.[15]

Similar confusion is admitted by J. W. Click and Russell Baird, in their *Magazine Editing and Production.*[16] They conclude that: "Mere figures cannot convey the magnitude of an industry so diverse as the magazine industry." The *Ayer Directory of Publications,* which includes publications "required by the general advertiser or the public" will list approximately 9,500 magazines, high school, and local church papers. None of the latter will be included in this study.

The *Standard Periodical Directory* provides the most massive listing, with more than 62,000 United States and Canadian periodicals included. Newsletters, college yearbooks, shopping guides, and public relations magazines are included.

The monthly *Business Publication Rate and Data* book contains material concerning some 2,600 periodicals, including those that are issued by associations. There are nearly 180 classifications, with Medical and Surgical the largest, having some 300 publications. Since SRDS lists only publications that carry advertisements, obviously there are hundreds of others that are not included.[17]

There are more than 200 publications directed to the agricultural industry, including many regional and state-oriented magazines. The specialization goes deep, i.e., dairy, field crops, soil management, livestock, breeds, fruit, nuts, vegetables, and on and on. The leaders, *Progressive Farmer* and *Successful Farmer,* seek a broader appeal though some degree of specialization appears in their articles and departments.

The Audit Bureau of Circulation has the most accurate listing for the major publications, including consumer, farm and business categories. However, there are some periodicals that do not have their circulation audited, since they do not solicit advertising. These include *Consumer Reports, Guideposts, Highlights for Children, Decision, Arizona Highways, Sesame Street,* and others.

OPENING OF THE 80S

The "Folio 400," termed "the first comprehensive magazine industry revenue study ever undertaken," set the statistical stage for the opening of the 80s. *Folio* labels itself "The magazine for magazine management" and proves its leading role in this area through this special contribution to the industry. *Folio* was established in 1972 and informs the public of new periodicals as well as data concerning those that fail. Records of new starts are easier to maintain; for obvious reasons, publishers are reluctant to announce their failures, preferring to depart in silence. Researchers find *Folio* an excellent source for the past, present and future status of magazines, with articles involving all stages of production, from the creation of an idea and the selection of a title to the final delivery to the consumers.

Although many readers may be more concerned with magazines' new visual appearances, or the contents, or special appeals for how-to-do-it fanatics, publishers are more aware of the significance of advertising and circulation revenues as the major factors in determining the future for their periodicals.

The "Folio 400," which soon should reach the status in the magazine world that the "Fortune 500" has in the business world, involves an annual in-depth, lengthy probe of more than 10,000 magazines and 6,000 publishing companies. Such a study as *Folio* initially presented in January, 1980, on a test basis, had never been attempted before. By September, 1980, *Folio* had refined its research and then presented its account of the magazine world through 1979.

THE TOP 10 BY CATEGORIES

The "Folio 400" project examines "each magazine on an individual basis, and painstaking care was used to estimate each magazine's revenue streams." All sources of income are examined, from subscriptions, newsstand sales, and advertising, although ancillary revenues are not included. By studying these revenue streams, Folio 400 tells us what consumers and companies spend each year. Magazines tend to have varied subscription rate structures and a few vary their publishing frequency from the norm, such as *Family Circle* and *Woman's Day* that add issues during high-advertising seasons. Of value to the general public seeking an over-all picture of the magazine industry are these Folio 400 highlights for 1980 presented in the September, 1981, *Folio* by a research staff under the direction of Jay Walker.

Gross revenue of these 400 magazines reached $8,300,000,000 for 1980, up 7.7% over 1979. Of this total, $7,500,000,000 went to the 273 consumer magazines with their massive circulations and $843,000,000 to the 127 trade publications. This was the first year that consumer circulation revenues ($3.77 billion) outpaced advertising revenues ($3.72.)

In addition to the 400, *Folio* estimated another $728,000,000 for 4,925 consumer magazines and $1,760,000,000 for 5,505 trade magazines not included in the top 400.

Thus *Folio* estimated $10,830,000,000 volume for 10,830 active periodicals on January 1, 1981. Although the top 400 represent only 4 per cent of the total magazines, they do represent 77 per cent of the industry's dollars. Publications to be considered in the Folio 400 must generate a minimum dollar volume of approximately $3 million.

In its initial study, *Folio* warned that profitability cannot be decided solely by these figures because of "the difficulty in accurately researching cost factors for any individual magazine."

Some problem of understanding among readers might develop over the inclusion of Sunday newspaper supplements and national tabloids. Folio 400 considers these as part of its goal to present the broadest picture possible of this industry. Many of these sensational tabloids, such as *National Enquirer, The Star,* and *Globe,* deal with magazine-type stories and compete for the customers' dollars on the same markets, especially the supermarkets. *Family Weekly* and *Parade* are circulation leaders reaching across the nation through hundreds of our Sunday newspapers. In recent years a number of Sunday magazine supplements prepared by newspapers have reached major status in circulation and advertising revenues, such as the *New York Times Magazine.* These as well as other factors must be considered by any historian of the magazine industry. *Folio* spent eight months of research efforts and $130,000 to prepare its initial report in 1979.

Highlights from the Folio 400 study include the following condensations for 1980. In total revenue, the Top Ten were:

1. TV Guide	$613,850,000
2. Time	346,623,000
3. Reader's Digest	261,205,000
4. Newsweek	256,805,000
5. Playboy	199,279,000
6. People	198,502,000
7. Sports Illustrated	196,183,000
8. Woman's Day	163,455,000
9. Better Homes & Gardens	162,909,000
10. Penthouse	162,542,000

With the exception of *People,* these magazines have been around for many years. The weekly and Sunday tabloid markets are represented by *Parade,* with $135,899,000 for No. 15, and *National Enquirer,* with $124,510,000 for No. 16.

The Top Ten consumer magazines with their estimated average circulation for 1980 included:

1. Parade	21,644,000
2. TV Guide	18,426,194
3. Reader's Digest	18,045,968
4. Family Weekly	12,366,269
5. National Geographic	10,560,885
6. Better Homes & Gardens	8,055,040
7. Woman's Day	7,661,274
8. Family Circle	7,443,306
9. Modern Maturity	6,748,925
10. McCall's	6,237,176

Another approach to the circulation battle is to separate the weeklies from the monthlies. Here are the Top Ten in each:

(Weeklies)		(Monthlies)	
1. Parade	21,644,000	Reader's Digest	18,045,968
2. TV Guide	18,426,194	National Geographic	10,560,885
3. Family Weekly	12,366,269	Better Homes & Gardens	8,055,040
4. National Enquirer	5,032,486	Woman's Day	7,661,274
5. Time	4,407,928	Family Circle	7,443,306
6. The Star	3,444,669	Modern Maturity	6,748,925
7. Newsweek	2,958,397	McCall's	6,237,176
8. People	2,407,501	Ladies' Home Journal	5,502,232
9. Sports Illustrated	2,304,570	Playboy	5,378,818
10. New York News Mag.	2,125,156	Good Housekeeping	5,214,891

For the business-minded reader, total advertising revenue reveals a somewhat similar picture. As expected, those with the higher circulation records

tend to be among those with high advertising income. The only newcomer is
Business Week.

1.	TV Guide	$239,468,000
2.	Time	214,139,000
3.	Newsweek	175,049,000
4.	Parade	135,899,000
5.	Business Week	129,554,000
6.	Sports Illustrated	123,052,000
7.	People	102,138,000
8.	Woman's Day	95,347,000
9.	Reader's Digest	94,056,000
10.	Better Homes & Gardens	94,004,000

When one studies the leaders among consumer magazines in total advertising
pages, other newcomers are welcomed. *Business Week*, with 4,941 pages, led
the Top Ten, followed by the *New York Times Magazine*, 4,398; *The New
Yorker*, 4,223; *Linn's Stamp News*, 4,222; *TV Guide*, 3,747; *People*, 3,275;
Newsweek, 3,098; *Los Angeles Times Home Magazine*, 2,828; *Washington Post
Magazine*, 2,772; and *Interior Design*, 2,741.

Reader's Digest, with 16,849,086, continues its long-time leadership in
the subscription race, followed by *National Geographic*, 10,557,463; *Better
Homes & Gardens*, 7,350,829; *TV Guide*, 6,966,151; *Modern Maturity*,
6,748,925; *McCall's*, 5,467,521; *Ladies' Home Journal*, 4,539,054; *Time*,
4,116,443; *Redbook*, 3,473,585; and *Good Housekeeping*, 3,420,056.

On the other hand, *TV Guide* continues its domination of newsstand rev-
enues, with $238,369,000, followed by *Penthouse*, $129,179,000; *National
Enquirer*, $94,436,000; *Playboy*, $91,498,000; *People*, $81,820,000; *Family
Circle*, $71,999,000; *The Star*, $68,944,000; *Woman's Day*, $67,497,000;
Hustler, $53,397,000; and *Cosmopolitan*, $50,467,000.

Newsstand sales are dominated by *TV Guide, Woman's Day, Family Circle, National Enquirer, Penthouse, The Star, Playboy, Cosmopolitan, People*,
and *Good Housekeeping*.

With this definitive, clear-cut profile of the national magazine audience
and industry by *Folio* for the start of the 80s, one can better speculate concerning what's ahead, a decade that will furnish the real test for the business. This
will be a time when "the magazine business will be tough, unyielding and
unforgiving for those who make mistakes, and richly rewarding for those who
have mastered their craft," according to *Folio* executive editor, Barbara Love.[18]

Riding a peak of prosperity, with record growth in advertising and circulation, magazine leaders approached the 80s through varicolored glasses. Some
were optimistic; others were more guarded. Would periodicals be successful in
maintaining the growth pattern set as the 70s ended? For example, Magazine
Publishers Association members annually review the industry and peer into the
future, usually with mixed reactions, as seen in the 1979 Bermuda conven-

tion.[19] Industry growth of about 13 per cent a year for the early 80s was seen by Robert J. Coen, of McCann-Erickson, a longtime statistical expert for the media world. This growth, however, would be below the 20-plus per cent recorded for the last three years of the 70s. There were signs, too, of "shrinking revenue and profit margins."

There were some signs that magazine start-ups were on the decline as the 70s ended. Investors found other places for their funds, especially when interest rates remained so high. To some, the gamble they viewed in backing a new magazine wasn't sufficient to offset the security of the money market. Nevertheless, a study by N. W. Ayer's media department suggested; "The 1980s will be a time of growth for the magazine industry. The number of new titles being introduced each year is truly amazing. One would not be surprised to see the number of magazines launched exceed 500 each year."[20]

MAGAZINE ASSOCIATIONS

Activities within the magazine world are directed by a number of associations. Whether trade or professional, these groups bring their members together to seek solutions to mutual problems and to present a uniform front in legislative campaigns. Likewise, they seek more advertising for their members; promote the advancement of technical skills and equipment; pursue more favorable postal rates; and strive for formalized ethical procedures to protect their clients. The magazine industry, as noted previously, is diverse and complicated, yet there are some similarities within these associations.

Magazine Publishers Association

Best known is the Magazine Publishers Association, founded in 1919. Representing consumer magazines, the MPA operates on an annual budget of $2.5 million with headquarters in New York and offices in Washington. Its endeavors are varied, from answering inquiries through the Information Center to seeking a halt in the increasing postal rates, which have moved up more than 400% since the Postal Reorganization Act of 1970.

In advertising, MPA works with other groups, including the National Newspaper Association and the American Newspaper Publishers Association in "defending the rights of various industries to advertise and to include the cost as a legitimate expense item." This has involved institutional messages in media and debates with Federal regulatory agencies.[21]

MPA members participate in management and editorial conferences designed to improve the finished product for the benefit of the readers. The Legal Affairs Committee concerns itself with the Copyright Law, trends in libel laws, and problems with privacy, antitrust and trade regulations, both in force and anticipated. Both the Paper and Production Committees have continuous assignments as their titles suggest. The Membership Committee has added many American and foreign publishers to the association's roll in recent years: Its

MPA Congressional Reception (This one is 1980 with then Speaker of the House Thomas "Tip" O'Neill)

MPA "Magazine Day" in Detroit

MPA Seminars

1980 Henry Johnson Fisher 'Publisher of the Year' Award Recipient of Award onstage: George H. Allen, CBS Publications

MPA Seminars

MPA "Magazine Days" sponsored throughout the country—this one in Detroit.

MPA Board of Directors meet with the President of the United States

Ruth Whitney, editor in chief of Glamour, accepts a 1981 National Magazine Award for general excellence, from Osborn Elliott, dean of the Columbia University Graduate School of Journalism. (Awards are sponsored by American Society of Magazine Editors—ASME—with a grant from MPA and administered by Columbia.)

MPA Seminars

Media Credit Association provides frequent bulletins that involve associations and data from advertising agencies, reports of name changes, mergers, delinquents, and the like.

An affiliated group, the American Society of Magazine Editors, was established in 1963 with more than 225 editors now represented. This group sponsors the annual National Magazine Awards, administered by the Columbia University Graduate School of Journalism. It also sponsors an Internship Program each summer for students as well as an annual Education Seminar for journalism professors.

MPA has sponsored research through its Publishers Information Bureau and the Opinion Research Corporation. The first in this series to measure the public's involvement with media was made in 1972, the second in 1975, and the third in 1979. Future studies are projected. These studies examine magazines and television "in terms of the degree to which people discuss editorial programming—an article or feature, documentary film or sporting event—and the advertising." Also studied is the relationship between "talking about" and "doing something about" advertising content.

Alternate delivery systems and computer services are typical of the many topics discussed in seminars. Customer complaints and inquiries are handled by MPA. Newsletters appear regularly reporting results of the group's efforts in advertising, circulation, and research.

MPA's Media Imperatives campaign, started in 1976, continues through messages in trade publications and in visual presentations to concerned groups. In a series of ads, this Media Imperatives concept was said to be capable of achieving three goals:

1. It can show you (the advertiser) how many of your prime prospects are Television Imperatives and how many are Magazine Imperatives. (The first category is big on television and not so big on magazines. The second group is the reverse).
2. It can tell how many of your prime prospects are missed entirely by your current media plan.
3. It can help you reach more of your prime prospects by defining a more efficient balance between television and magazines.

And in another message, MPA notes: "A magazine is a different proposition. It doesn't disappear before the reader's eyes. It waits for him to come back to the same magazine and the same ad."

Media Imperatives has been termed the best selling vehicle ever utilized by magazines by the leading trade periodicals, *Folio, Marketing and Media Decisions,* and *Madison Avenue*.[22] One indication of its success has been the shift by the Television Advertising Bureau from newspapers to magazines as its prime competitive target.

Other services are provided as needs arise. On occasion some services are abolished, such as the Field Selling Information Service in 1979. This had been started a decade earlier to protect both the subscriber and the publisher against unethical salesmen and agencies.

MPA's longtime president, Stephen E. Kelly, died in 1978 and was succeeded by former *Reader's Digest* executive, Kent Rhodes. Kelly had correctly visualized the 70s when he predicted in 1969, "the second great revolution in advertising—the return to print."[23] A Steve Kelly award for creativity in magazine advertising has been established in his honor.

American Business Press Inc.

Another extremely active organization is the American Business Press Inc., an outgrowth of the 1906 Federation of Trade Press Association, which later became the Associated Business Publications. In 1940 free-circulation publications founded the National Business Papers Association and in 1948 this became the National Business Association, including both free and audited magazines. In 1965 these were merged into the present group, headquartered in New York.

Today it is the association of publishers of specialized business periodicals, also known as trade papers, business papers, or trade and technical journals. In its 1977 report on contest winners for its Jesse H. Neal Editorial Achievement awards (established in 1945), ABP noted: "No single medium covers so wide a range of editorial topics as does the business press . . . covers every subject of major interest to all of business, industry, the profession."

Of the estimated 2,400 business publications some 20 per cent belong to ABP. All members must have audited circulations by an independent, tripartite auditing bureau, be independently owned and taxpaying, and agree to abide by ABP's Code of Publishing Practice. (See Appendix). Recognized auditing firms are the Audit Bureau of Circulation and the Business Publications Audit. Publishing companies rather than individual magazines belong to ABP.

ABP spreads the message about specialized publishing activities not only to the magazine world but to students and others studying journalism. Within the industry, ABP sponsors meetings, forums, seminars, and workshops. Newsletters, bulletins and reports concern cost, compensation, benefits, production, circulation, and other topics of interest to members. Probably no single force has done more to upgrade the editorial content of member publications. The Neal Award, for example, recognizes the results of this effort. Another recognition is the Crain Award for a Distinguished Editorial Career in the business press. For others there is the Advertising to Bureau and Industry competition as well as special studies, such as "An Evaluation of 1,100 Research Studies on the Effectiveness of Industrial Advertising."

In serving as an information center for the medium, ABP seeks to "foster greater awareness of quality publications." In Washington, ABP represents the unified voice of the business press in debates over postal rates, copyright pro-

BETTER PUBLIC RELATIONS

An ABP Guide for Business Press Publishers

Libel: An ABP Practical Guide

BY FAUSTIN F. JEHLE, P. C.

THE ABP CODE OF PROFESSIONAL RESEARCH ETHICS AND PRACTICES

2   *THE CASE FOR REPEATS*

ABP ACCOUNTING REFERENCE GUIDE FOR BUSINESS PUBLICATIONS

Editorial Excellence 1981

The

Guidelines to Editorial Performance

ABP CODE OF PUBLISHING PRACTICE

HOW MUCH DOES NO ADVERTISING COST ?

tection, tax benefits granted some association and society publications, and other legal affairs.

One of ABP's major contributions to the industry is its Code of Publishing Practice. In explaining its code, ABP has detailed methodology for research so that four major components will be served: respondents, advertisers, research staff conducting the studies, and the professional community at large.

According to ABP, more than 63 million Americans receive business publications, with more than 1,100,000 pages of advertising included each year. More than 75 per cent of these publications are printed by offset, providing greater flexibility for the advertisers.

Business Publications Audit of Circulation Inc.

"Comparability" appears to be the keynote for the operation of the Business Publications Audit of Circulation, Inc. Such a need crops up frequently, as noted at their 1979 convention when a speaker said, "A computer needs comparable data or it gets mean and ugly." If magazines fail to fit into a recognized category, they should be known as NEC (not elsewhere categorized), according to Al Ries, of Ries Cappiello Colwell.[24]

The BPA developed from the Controlled Circulation Audit, a group organized in 1931 after the Audit Bureau of Circulation decided to review only publications with paid circulations. The controlled circulation publications suddenly found themselves out in the cold.

In 1953, CCA became the Business Publications Audit, noting that "the business press . . . is substantially different from the other three classes of print media audited by ABC which are basically consumer oriented. The press run of business publications are usually smaller. The audience can be determined by the business or professional activities of the recipients, and the page rates are in line with the smaller print runs."[25]

After World War II expansion became the keynote in this area. As BPA president Thomas J. Campbell noted, the electronics industry came into its own after 1945, along with the plastics and aerospace industries. From its original 39 members, the group increased to 370 in 1950 and to 720 in 1979. By 1981 the group expects to have 1,000 members.

A publication declares itself in one of the 200 primary markets represented by BPA. Thus BPA can rightfully claim that it "is an effective forum where the buyer and the seller meet to agree on what questions the seller should answer and how that data should be compiled." In other words, the goal is comparability. Marketing data gathered by BPA seek to serve this group.

BPA will shift to a computerized data processing system in 1982 to shorten the time needed to process publication reports.

BPA also operates its Selected Market Audit Division to handle publications other than business oriented, such as United Air Lines' *Mainliner* and *Holiday Inn Companion*. BPA provides an audit service for attendance at trade shows as a sidelight.

Control of BPA rests with a 21-member Board of Directors, representing equally advertisers, agencies, and publications.

International Association of Business Communicators

One of the industry's fastest growing groups is the International Association of Business Communicators. A professional organization, IABC reached a membership high of 5,000 in 1978 and, as the new decade opened, it included 6,500 writers, editors, audio-visual specialists, and managers. They are organized into some 100 chapters in the United States, Canada, Mexico, and England.

IABC members produce magazines for employe communications, internal and external. They represent a growing area, with special attention from educational institutions. The *IABC Journal,* published quarterly, offers suggestions for beginners in the business as well as veteran communicators as they all seek to improve their communication assignments. There also is the *IABC News.*

In the 1930s there was the American Association of Industrial Editors and in the next decade the International Council of Industrial Editors. These merged in 1970 into the IABC.

Members are provided a wide range of services, including IABC's popular reference library with its idea files on more than 200 topics. These files, which are loaned to members, include guidelines from other members about problems, issues, and situations they encounter. Seminars, symposiums, and workshops are conducted, while the IABC International Conference is designed for beginners, intermediate and more experienced communicators. In-depth surveys are conducted, such as Profile/79 which summarized jobs, salaries, and other data supplied by members.

IABC's first venture into book publishing brought national recognition, with 50,000 copies sold. *Without Bias: A Guidebook for Nondiscriminatory Communication* discusses the elimination of bias from written, visual and spoken communication. The survey noted that the typical communicator is a woman, 32 to 35, with a journalism degree. Women account for 55 per cent of the IABC membership. This person, employed by an organization for six years with the last three as an editor, reports to a public relations manager. She works for a manufacturing firm employing from 1,000 to 3,000 workers. Communicators' salaries have passed a $20,000 average, although the disparity between male and female pay levels continues.

IABC members serve an audience estimated at 460 million. They seek to service the "needs, interests and goals" of workers and members, and at the same time educate top management to the significance of communication.

IABC President Rae Leaper said, "Organizations of all types have recognized just how vital communication is to their well-being. The broadening scope of communication—and its great visibility—has strengthened IABC's role." The Gold Quill Awards of Excellence and Awards of Merit recognize the leaders.[26]

American Society of Association Executives

Of special concern is the Communication Section of the American Society of Association Executives (ASAE). This group, established in 1975, had more than 1,200 members by early 1981.

Members of ASAE spend more than $300 million on printing, typesetting, artwork and graphics, and thus many are vitually concerned with the magazine industry. Individuals in the Communication Section include writers, editors, public relations managers, communication directors, and others. They publish magazines, journals, newsletters, and prepare audiovisual and public relations programs for nonprofit organizations.

The ASAE publishes a monthly magazine, *Editors' News,* and sponsors its annual Gold Circle Awards in 12 categories, from Total Communication Programs to magazines, newsletters, and annual reports. Publication evaluation programs, workshops, and research studies also are conducted by the Communication Section.

The ASAE Communication Section believes that "without communication nothing would be accomplished . . . Communication is the success ingredient that is vital to all associations."

Association of Area Business Publications

> We're not going to cry any tears because the giant business publications are king of the mountains. We're content to bask in their long shadow and go about our business of delivering an audience that slips through the fingers of the giants.
> We're the Association of Area Business Publications.

With that introduction, AABP presents itself to the trade world, seeking advertising for its 50-member group and their publications that represent a combined circulation in excess of 700,000.

Members include publications that are organized for profit. Non-profit periodicals, newsletters, house organs, and similar publications are excluded. Member publications are primarily interested in the broad comprehensive business news and analysis of a region or an area, rather than the highly specialized, such as real estate listings, buyer arrivals, or financial transactions such as bankruptcies, incorporations, and the like.

The audience for AABP members consists basically of owners, partners, officers, trustees, corporate executives and middle management in a specific area. Their audiences are documented and the circulation is audited. The strength of the organization is obvious by its membership, not by a single publication. This is a growing field, with similar publications appearing regularly. Such magazines are not designed to replace the *Wall Street Journal, Forbes,* or *Fortune.* They have many of the advantages noted under city magazines.

Within the AABP framework are such publications as *Chicago Business,*

Dallas/Fort Worth Business, Hawaii Business, Indiana Business & Industry, New England Business, Pacific Business News, and others.

Industrial Communication Council

Communication managers, consultants, and educators from industry, government, universities, and non-profit organizations formed the Industrial Communication Council in 1955.

Today the 250 members of ICC share their knowledge and experience through mailings, meetings, conferences, and seminars.

In addition, the Council publishes the *ICC Newsletter,* a membership directory, special reports and books, such as *Case Studies in Organizational Communication* and *Beyond Communication.* This New York-based organization seeks to improve communications with employees, customers, stockholders, governments, educators and the general public.

Other Allied Associations

Since the magazine industry is so diverse, there are many associations that affect its operations, directly or indirectly.

The Association of Second Class Mail Publishers is the only national group devoted exclusively to the interests of paid-circulation publications. It seeks to maintain reasonable and equitable postal rates and, to achieve this, the association participates in hearings before Congress. The group also seeks to improve the processing and delivery of second-class mail publications and to help members with their other problems.

ASCMP publishes a *Monthly News Bulletin* and *Postal Alerts* that cover current and upcoming legislature proceedings and other matters. Seminars, clinics, and roundtables are helpful for an exchange of ideas. Annually it grants the Henry T. Zwirner Memorial Award to the individual who has contributed the most to the paid-circulation concept of periodical publishing.

Fulfillment Management Association Inc. is an individual membership, professional organization for those devoted to selling or servicing, by mail, large and small segments of the public and special interest groups. FMA was founded in 1948 to handle problems with subscribers, direct response inquiry programs, fund raising supervision, marketing service, and other related projects.

Personnel come from consumer magazines, newspapers, book clubs, trade magazines, and other areas. Each year FMA grants the Lee C. Williams Award to honor the memory of the fulfillment manager of Hearst Magazines. The FMA "recognizes that computers and equipment aside, the key to fulfillment is good management."

The American Society of Magazine Photographers, founded in 1944, has more than 2,200 members involved in print, film, tape, from documentary and photojournalism to industrial and advertising photography.

ASMP publishes *Professional Business Practices in Photography* which is concerned with contractual questions. The *ASMP Book 1981* is an excellent source book for buyers of editorial and advertising photography. It offers several awards and citations, including the photographer of the year, and, from time to time, technical and achievement awards and others that give special recognition for outstanding work. Its Honor Roll reads like a Who's Who in American photography.

Magazine & Paperback Marketing Institute is a trade association funded by the publishing industry. It represents the mass media marketplace for magazines and paperbacks and their sales within chain store operations.

MPMI works with the Family Reading Centers within these stores. The group collects sales data, coordinates approved title lists, consults on proper placement of fixtures, coordinates marketing programs. Through newsletters, marketing bulletins and other materials MPMI seeks to improve its members' goals. Its research tells about the variety of outlets, magazine and book sales, average sales, and similar data helpful to members.

American Society of Business Press Editors is devoted to the interests and advancement of the editor and the business press. Members are primarily editors, professionals of all levels. Services and benefits include the *Editor's Notebook,* a loose-leaf project with useful ideas; the *Monthly Newsletter, Salary Survey,* and book reviews. Professional seminars and the Annual Editors' Conference also help members. Local chapters operate across America. Awards are granted for Excellence-in-Graphics Competition.

The *Committee of Small Magazine Editors and Publishers* was formed in 1967 as a non-profit, international association of more than 1,200 editors and publishers. Members include poets, writers, researchers, librarians, publishers, editors, and printers. The group publishes *The Independent Publisher* monthly and conducts annual conferences.

American Institute of Graphic Arts is involved in a very peripheral way with the magazine scene through its concern with good design. Founded in 1914, AIGA conducts an inter-related program of competitions, exhibitions, publications, educational activities, and projects in the public interest to promote the advancement of graphic design.

AIGA members work with magazines, books, and periodicals. The *AIGA Graphic Design USA* is published annually to record the best pieces selected in competition. The group also publishes its Membership Directory and Education Directory.

Postal Rate Commission was established in 1970 by the Postal Reorganization Act to be an independent regulatory agency. It is charged with the review and analysis of rates and classification proposals initiated by the Postal Service.

The PRC conducts research such as *At the Crossroads,* an inquiry into rural post offices and the communities they serve. The 1980 booklet studied problems associated with any proposed closing or consolidation and the effect upon such areas. This study showed a decline in the number of post offices from 70,064 in 1895 to 30,754 in 1975.

The commission's five members, appointed by the President and confirmed by the Senate, serve six-year terms. In addition to rate changes, the Commission reviews changes in postal service, investigates complaints concerning rates, fees, mail classifications, or services. It also publishes the *Consumer's Resource Handbook*.

Research and Engineering Council of the Graphic Arts Industry, Inc. is a group that deals indirectly with printers, publishers, equipment manufacturers, process engineers and systems designers, printing buyers, materials suppliers and management types. The Council transfers its knowledge through its functional committees: Printing, Technology and Environment, Prepress, Critical Trends/Needs, and Binding/Finishing/Distributing.

ELEVEN BASIC PRINCIPLES

With the ending of the 70s, *Folio* publisher J. J. Hanson believed it was a great time to be involved in magazine publishing in America. Speaking to the 22nd World Congress of the International Federation of the Periodical Press in mid-1979, Hanson offered 11 principal reasons to defend his optimistic statement. He based these comments on his own research as well as on conversations with leading magazine executives.

First, the relatively positive domestic economy and the growth of advertising budgets, despite forecasts of a recession.

Second, the high cost of television advertising as compared to magazine advertising.

Third, the growth of special interest and regional magazines, as well as demographic and regional advertising editions in national magazine, which has contributed strongly to advertising efficiency.

Fourth, magazine advertising rates have increased at a much slower rate than those for other media, especially television. Magazines thus have become more competitive.

Fifth, the clutter of broadcast advertising, which tends to diminish the effectiveness of many of these advertisements.

Sixth, a better editorial product. Magazines have become more responsive to readers.

Seventh, magazines have learned to use other media, like broadcasting, to promote themselves. They also are a direct beneficiary of more sophisticated direct mail efforts.

Eighth, improved management of magazines.

Ninth, the tapping of new revenue sources. Ancillary businesses have become profitable, thus permitting some magazines to improve their own products.

Tenth, tax laws are favorable to the magazine business, which help to provide investment capital for startups.

Eleventh, the public has accepted more and more magazines. Several reasons were cited for this last point: higher educational levels, more affluent population, and growth of special interests, due to more leisure time.

These factors will appear frequently in this book. Hanson's thought that "magazines are filling the 'need to know revolution' that has been sweeping the nation" is probably of paramount importance. As we study the publications in the following chapters we will see how some have succeeded and others have failed, depending in large part on their ability to satisfy this "need to know revolution."

2

The Big Three: TV Guide, Reader's Digest, National Geographic

CIRCULATION LEADERS among the American magazines include three publications with different audiences.

TV Guide has an audience that spends more and more time before television sets, an audience that seeks solace from the world's problems through a rapidly expanding medium.

Reader's Digest, for decades the nation's circulation leader before losing this position to *TV Guide,* continues to attract an audience usually recognized as being slightly above that favored 18-to-34-year-old bracket. Through a devoted following, this magazine has been in the 18-million-plus circulation category for years, stimulated regularly by sweepstakes and other promotions that often involve books especially designed to attract this more mature audience.

A recent newcomer to this over-10,000,000 bracket is the *National Geographic,* recognized the world over by its familiar yellow cover as well as its bright and beautiful pictures of numerous explorations, splendors of nature, expanding nations with their people and projects, and places to visit around the globe. Benefitting from the expanding travel boom and the growing interest in photography among the nation's millions, *National Geographic* has become an institution. Its headquarters is one of the major tour sites for visitors to Washington.

No other magazine currently threatens these three for the circulation leadership.

TV GUIDE: THE LEADER AND ITS COMPETITORS

Why do millions of Americans annually pay more than $345 million for a pint-size magazine that has television listings when their local newspapers pub-

The National Programming Department news room at TV Guide magazine's national headquarters, Radnor, PA. *Jules Schick photo*

lish these for no extra cost? This oft-asked question involves *TV Guide*, the nation's leader in circulation.

> The magazine covers—and criticizes—a communications medium that has become an important force in our lives . . . because television covers all the world we live in, and because *TV Guide* concerns itself with whatever television touches, the magazine has not only broad and interesting subject matter but also subject matter that is vital to its readers . . . If they also want intelligent, objective coverage of television as an entertainment medium and as what may be the most powerful force for change in our society, they do need *TV Guide*. [1]

Merrill Panitt, the magazine's editorial director since its inception, thus answers the question. He has been with the publication since Walter Annenberg, president of Triangle Publications, issued the first edition on April 3, 1953. In late 1952, Annenberg owned the Philadelphia *Inquirer;* Panitt was his administrative assistant who also wrote a television column for the newspaper.

The opposition paper, the *Bulletin,* carried a full-page advertisement on Nov. 19, 1952, for *TV Digest,* a 15-cent weekly serving Philadelphia with an audited circulation of 180,000. There were also television magazines in New York and Chicago, providing local listings as the *TV Digest* did in Philadelphia.

Panitt recalled the following conversation with Annenberg after the *TV Digest* advertisement appeared:

> How would it be, Annenberg said, if we were to print a color section with national articles in our Philadelphia rotogravure plant, ship that section around the country, and in each city we'd print the local listings and bind them inside the national color section?
>
> This time I (Panitt) paused. It was a wild idea, but television was booming and I knew from reader response to the *Inquirer* television column how much interest there was in the medium.
>
> Sounds possible, I said.
>
> He (Annenberg) developed the idea some more during that phone call. Staffs in each city. Emphasis on network shows. Complicated publishing logistics that would have to be worked out somehow. Advertising could be either national or local. We could sell magazine space the way radio and television sell time, with the advertiser buying as much coverage as he wanted. . . .

Some of Annenberg's friends who were publishers voiced the "it can't be done" philosophy, much as some of DeWitt Wallace's friends and potential publishers had several decades earlier when he had proposed *Reader's Digest.* Both Wallace and Annenberg have surpassed their own initial expectations.

On *TV Guide*'s 25th anniversary, the *Wall Street Journal* reviewed its operations, noting its giant profits and circulation.[2] This trend began almost from the start when *TV Guide* sold 1,560,000 copies of its initial issue, available in 10 areas: Chicago, Iowa-Nebraska, Minnesota, New England, New York Metropolitan, Northeast Pennsylvania, Philadelphia, Southern California, Southern Ohio, and Washington-Baltimore. Before the end of the next year, the magazine appeared in 27 regional editions.

During its first summer the firm lost money on *TV Guide,* a situation Annenberg and Panitt justified on the basis of lesser television viewing during the warmer months. Also, there had been an expensive initial expense, when Annenberg paid $2.3 million for the New York-based *TeleVision Guide,* over a million dollars for the Philadelphia *TV Digest,* and about a million for the Chicago *TV Forecast.* Annenberg selected the title for *TV Guide.*

This downward trend was reversed with the initial Fall Preview edition that year, which sold 1,746,327 copies. It continues to be the magazine's best seller each year. Today *TV Guide* is the only magazine in the world to sell a billion copies a year, accounting for one in every seven magazine copies sold in America. The *Wall Street Journal* claimed, "For all of its success, *TV Guide* has somehow never quite been accepted as a 'respectable' or a serious publication." At the same time, the newspaper admitted, "It isn't hard to see why the magazine hasn't endeared itself to network people. In recent years *TV Guide* has carped at the medium for a host of failings, ranging from mindless programming to tired summer reruns. Even so, the magazine's value to the industry is undeniable.'' Regardless of the *Journal*'s views, the magazine's treatment of the industry has instilled more reader faith in the weekly. They see *TV Guide* defending them, offering their views before the networks and thus serving as a go-between with the industry. In fact, Annenberg's early interest in such a publication was based in part on viewers' belief in the accuracy of such digests in the larger cities. Obviously, too, the listings with their brief explanations continue to attract today's readers.

TV Guide has grown with the industry. The 1950s were expanding years when millions of Americans acquired their first sets. Today it is estimated there are more than 75 million households with television sets and *TV Guide,* selling more than 18 million copies weekly, reaches a large segment of the available audience.

During the first year *TV Guide* collected $750,000 from advertising; $8,873 came from the first issue. This now exceeds $200 million annually. Fighting a negative attitude among some advertisers in the earlier years, the magazine has reported a steady gain, now carrying more in each issue than it carried that first year. For example, in 1979 the magazine carried 3,731 pages of advertising with revenues of $220,178,688. It regained its temporary loss to *Time* in ad revenues, although the newsweekly's worldwide revenues reached $295 million.[3]

TV Guide also boasts the largest advertising director in the industry, Eric Larson, who is 6 feet 8 inches, and weighs about 350 pounds. His leadership has become obvious as he directs the massive problems associated with handling the numerous national ads and working in the thousands of regional messages that appear in the more than 100 regional editions. Today *TV Guide* is considered a necessity by many firms, such as the CBS/Columbia record club which ran its first ad in the magazine in March, 1959. Advertisers are said to line up for months for the middle-of-the issue inserts. A full-page ad cost in excess of $65,000 in 1980.

When *TV Guide* began there were 244 television stations in America, including 169 VHF and 75 UHF, reaching some 30 million receivers. Annenberg's foresight was apparent—he realized that television eventually would become a dominant communication force in America.

Walter Annenberg acknowledged to the *Wall Street Journal* that the magazine's annual profits total ''more than $35 million but less than $50 million.'' Since Triangle Publications is solely owned by Annenberg and his sisters it need not inform the public about its financial operations. However, the ''Folio 400'' study in late 1980 placed *TV Guide* No. 1 in total operations, with revenues in excess of $566,889,000, including $220,184,000 from advertising, $131,877,000 from subscriptions, and $214,742,000 from newsstand sales. These figures are for 1979.

Annenberg stresses economy in his operations. "Annenberg is in charge, whether he is at his estate in California, spending five years as ambassador to the Court of St. James's, or occupying his beautiful offices at the *TV Guide* building in Radnor, near his Wynnewood, Pa., residence. He is referred to as 'Mr. Ambassador' in recognition of his role under the Nixon administration," according to Panitt.

Panitt confers with his staffers by telephone and telecopies. He makes weekly trips to New York to meet with the staffers of *Seventeen,* the Annenberg publication that Panitt serves as editorial director.

More than half of the 1,400 staff members work at Radnor with others scattered among the 34 offices in the nation. Operations began in Philadelphia before the move to Radnor in 1957. About half of the workers have been with the organization for more than six years. As the needs of the company increase, building facilities are expanded.

Annenberg's political views and *TV Guide*'s contents on occasions have upset critics. *More* magazine in 1976 and the *Wall Street Journal* feature in 1978 raised questions concerning "News Watch," a weekly column Annenberg inaugurated in early 1974. Five observers were selected, charged with critiquing the networks. They included Patrick Buchanan, a well-known conservative writer and a Nixon adviser who helped draft Spiro Agnew's attacks on the networks; Kevin Phillips, editor of *The Emerging Republican Majority;* John Lofton, former editor of *Monday,* organ of the Republican National Committee; John P. Roche, syndicated columnist and apparently the lone liberal in the group; and Edith Efron, a former *TV Guide* staff writer, and author of a controversial book about the networks.

According to Prof. David M. Rubin, Annenberg was "roasted by *The New Yorker* and *Time* for the obvious lack of balance among the contributors, and it was assumed by many that Annenberg was up to his usual tricks of manipulating content for personal ends."[4] Some of this stemmed, no doubt, from the first column by Buchanan, when he wrote: "Canvass the network news rooms and you will find as many Goldwater Republicans and Wallace Democrats as Father Abraham found 'just men' in the twin cities of Biblical times."[5]

Possibly the timing of "News Watch" served to create this adverse atmosphere. At the time of Watergate, some readers viewed the project as an attempt to provide Nixon much-needed support. Eric Sevareid called the column "Annenberg's revenge." After the publisher was blamed for some of the extreme comments in the column, the project was stopped with the explanation that television news coverage had improved.

Another criticism in the early years involved the shortage of hard-hitting articles. Panitt said he realized this narrowness by the mid-1960s, and since then not only has *TV Guide* carried more controversial articles but it has presented more recognized writers, such as Arnold Toynbee, Arthur Schlesinger Jr., Arthur Miller, and others, including many media leaders. Some have complained about the pay, although others consider it fair. Since articles generally are limited to 1,500 words, the $750 Edwin Newman received for his contribution appears fair. At least Newman thought so.

Some critics belie the magazine has an anti-television bias. If this is so apparent it remains what readers prefer. They don't want another Hollywood-type publication offering only a weekly mix of praise and goody-goody words about the industry it reports. Rubin believes that: "While the magazine can be counted on to keep abreast of regulatory and technological controversies (such as family hour, satellite communication and political debates), it ducks serious and lengthy reviews of television's major programming efforts." However, more and more program criticism has appeared since Rubin wrote this.

Gary Deeb, nationally syndicated television columnist, is another critic of *TV Guide*. He once termed the magazine "anything but a consummeristic publication," after charging Walter Annenberg with killing a story about the firing of NBC's Chicago consumer reporter, Roberta Baskin, because of some unflattering remarks about Standard Oil. Deeb added, *"TV Guide* plays kissy-face with the networks, even to the extent of printing editorials advising its millions of readers to be sure to 'sample' each of the 25 new prime-time programs that premiere each September."

Deeb admitted that *TV Guide* does blast network news coverage but believed this happened because Annenberg, like Nixon, thought "that the CBS, NBC, and ABC news divisions are being held captive by a bunch of radical-liberals and Communist sympathizers." (*Columbia Tribune,* July 23, 1980)

Unfortunately Annenberg left himself open to some of these charges when he endorsed Reagan for President in *TV Guide,* November 1–7, 1980. After more than one page of comments reviewing Carter's career, Annenberg wrote:

> *TV Guide* has never before taken a position in a Presidential election and as head of the company that publishes the magazine I intended that it remain silent in this one. I cannot, however, as a matter of conscience, refrain from speaking up when the result of this election is so critical to the future of the Nation. . . .
>
> An administration headed by Ronald Reagan . . . promises to offer—in place of more years of political expedients to bolster weak domestic and international positions—an end to disillusionment with Government and an end to the feeling that we no longer can control our own destiny . . .

The fact that some television performers attack *TV Guide* would appear to overcome those views about any "soft" approach. The *Wall Street Journal* reported that Jack Lord became so mad over an unflattering *TV Guide* article that he barred its writers from the "Hawaii Five-O" set. Howard Cosell once called a writer "a hatchet man for the bastards in Radnor who wouldn't run a nice story about him." Cosell's comment was printed in an article about him later.

Others feel any effort to maintain balance might hold back *TV Guide*. Rubin considers the magazine "too predictable," yet for this reason alone apparently millions of readers look forward to their weekly localized editions. Others believe the short articles may limit some potential in-depth accounts, but they do provide a convenient means for keeping up with television in reports that often can be read during two commercials and a station break. The thoroughness of its coverage of the industry cannot be denied and its station logs frequently are more accurate than those in some daily newspapers.

No one can debate the magazine's successful use of computers required to handle such a tremendous operation. In 1979 it created a new direct-line access system to handle subscriptions. This cut the necessary time to change an address from 4–6 weeks to 2–3 weeks. Some eight million *TV Guide* and 400,000 *Seventeen* subscribers are handled by these operations. Subscription processing has moved ahead from the old address plates to IBM tab cards to Univac III. Today the magazine reports the 32 Harris terminals used in Data Entry and the 16 in Customer Service are tied into the magazine's Sperry Univac 1180 computer.

A *TV Guide* representative attended IBM's first school in 1945, placing this magazine among the pioneers in the use of computers. Early in 1957 the accounting records for circulation, and later those for advertising, were shifted to punch card operations. More advanced computerized operations followed in 1963, and the next year the magazine converted to Univac III. The rapid growth of the magazine has required that it use the maximum capabilities of computers. Its first decade circulation reached more than 9 million and its coverage expanded from less than 100 to more than 500 stations. Regional editions grew to 70 and the weekly program pages reached 3,500 by 1963.

In the early years the story lines that describe plots of movies and television programs were written on 3 x 5 cards. These soon totaled 120,000, with 20,000 appearing weekly throughout the regional editions. Such data came from regional offices, where local programs are assembled. Advertisements, too, are sold through these offices.

When *TV Guide* reached its 25th birthday in 1978, the magazine was using between 8,000 and 10,000 program pages per week, computerized for the various regions. Printing such a complex magazine requires the most careful logistics. Four gravure plants produce the national editorial editions: in Philadelphia, Dallas, San Jose, and Gallatin, Tenn. This unit of the magazine requires some 1,100 tons of paper weekly, while 16 plants use 2,000 tons weekly to produce the inside units. It requires more than 162,000 tons annually to produce the 20 million copies printed weekly. More centralization of printing and a shift to perfect binding were planned for 1981.

What will *TV Guide* do with cable television? As Rubin points out, "The editors do not want to clutter up the listings with hundreds of programs unavailable to most of their subscribers, but they also don't want to lose cable viewers to other magazines that specifically serve their interests." Since *TV Guide* depends on commercial broadcasters to supply station listings, it becomes a touchy situation should the magazine also print cable logs that compete with them. There also are additional printing and processing costs for the numerous editions.

TV Guide tested its first Cable-Pay Edition in the New Mexico-El Paso area in early 1980. Subscribers were offered their choice of editions, and single copy purchasers had the same choice at the supermarket. A number of other editions have been carrying cable listings. Panitt noted in late 1980 that the solution to the eventual listing of 80 to 100 channels would be partially answered through the change to perfect binding which permits use of more inserts.

> Complete programming in such an event—150 channels—would merely confuse readers. So we'll handle it by listing the best and/or the most popular programs and then run for each channel, on the front page of the cable section, a general description of the kinds of programming it carries. We will be adding cable sections to various editions in the near future.

Panitt thus visualized the magazine in the future as "a TV *Guide*—we will *select* the best and most popular programs from all the channels offered, and run them."

Panorama Offers New Approach

Using the resources and know-how of *TV Guide,* the publishers inaugurated *Panorama,* a monthly review of television today and tomorrow, in February, 1980. The key editorial staff included Frank Wolf as publisher; Roger Youman moved from editorship of *TV Guide* to the new magazine, but later returned and was replaced by David Sendler; and Merrill Panitt became editorial director. Wolf also serves as *Seventeen* publisher and Panitt as *Seventeen* editorial director.

Panorama is another Annenberg creation. Panitt noted that "the ambassador has other ideas, but let's just wait on them." Annenberg returned to England for a visit in late 1978 and "came home very excited that there was a publication of this for us and told me (Panitt) to get on the Concorde to London not in a few weeks, but tomorrow."[6] There Panitt learned more about the technological developments, as well as ideas for a feature publication concerning television today. Before the newcomer had received its title, the public was informed it would cover television, cable, video recorders and other aspects of the industry's future. It was never conceived with the idea of becoming another mass publication. Rather, it was designed for those who watch less television than the national average. "It's dedicated to the new breed of television watchers, the sophisticated, intelligent viewer who demands a total perspective of the single most powerful force in our society," according to trade advertisements. It would be a select audience "that appreciates the best that television can afford."

One comprehends these objectives better by noting the major articles in the premier issue: How TV Will Cover the Olympics; Videocassette Recorders;

Complete Buyer's Guide; Alan Alda Talks About Life After M*A*S*H; Pictorial Preview of 1980's Big Movies and Miniseries; and Pay Cable: Waiting for Uncle Miltie. Regular departments included This Month, an around-the-world roundup of news; Perspective; Cable and Pay-TV; Q&A; Sports; Panoramic View; Surveys and Studies; Videocassettes and Discs; Yesterdays; and Rear View.

The magazine started with a circulation of 100,000, which has been growing gradually, reaching 125,000 by the end of 1980. Panitt noted that after a few issues they found it necessary "to cover all of television—present and future—rather than just philosophy, and we found that our readers were watching more, not less, television than the average." The reaction has been favorable and the staff feels they are on the right track with discs and cassettes coming into their own.

Annenberg is willing to invest $10 million in *Panorama* while seeking a circulation of 500,000 within two or three years. A dummy edition was distributed to potential advertisers.

Panorama ceased publication with the June 1981 issue, having reached a circulation of only 100,000 readers and with some reports indicating a loss of $5 million on the project.

Public Broadcasting As Competition

Such interest in television has prompted the development of home video equipment which has, in turn, brought about the growth of new magazines. With the advancement of programming by the Public Broadcasting System, another new publication arrived in late 1980, the *Dial*. Originally created to serve four major markets—New York, Los Angeles, Chicago, and Washington—*Dial* was sent to 650,000 contributors to PBS stations in those areas. It was designed to "deal with television programming developments and hopes to attract both national and local advertisers, including home video advertisers (and) home video equipment and programming marketers." As publisher Morton Bailey noted, "Public television has just begun its second quarter century. During this time a sizable chunk of the television audience has broken with the mass viewing habit and, instead, sought out a more selective form of communication." Expansion into other major markets is expected, with *Dial* going to those contributors to local public broadcasting stations. Each edition publishes local listenings and features local events. Opposition developed from other publishers, especially those with city and regional magazines, over the use of federal funds in a publication that competes for advertising dollars.[7]

Another newcomer was announced for early 1981. *Channels of Communications* claimed it would be "the first magazine to take television seriously . . . as a social, cultural and political force." It was a bimonthly.

Merrill Panitt, *TV Guide* editorial director, feels *Dial* is a good way for public television to raise money. *TV Guide* won't be affected by *Dial*, which is "an entirely different kettle of fish." Since *Dial*'s coverage is more limited it cannot compete with *TV Guide,* which covers the entire medium.

TV Guide owner Walter H. Annenberg early in 1981 announced a gift of $150 million to the Corporation for Public Broadcasting. This is to be given at a rate of $10 million annually for the next 15 years to finance the production of "high-quality, college-level" courses through telecommunications systems. It will involve radio, public television and cassettes. It is not expected to be ready until late 1982.

And Still Others

Some of the competition is short lived. *Watch: Television in the 80s* was launched in 1980 in Colorado "to reach consumer readers through video retail outlets" It didn't survive a year.

Video Trade News has appeared since 1975. Its publisher, Charles Tepher Publishing Co., started *Videoplay Magazine* for newsstand sales. It has been referred to as "the *Popular Mechanics* of video." United Business Publications added *Home Video* to its *Videography* to capture some of this new market.

Video, founded as a one-shot video hardware buyer's guide in 1977, became a monthly in 1980. Reese Publishing Company sees a home video boom that is concerned not only with hardware but with the programming.

Video Review arrived in April, 1980, the fifth such publication established in six months. It claimed a circulation of 50,000. There also are *Consumer Electronics* and *Audio Times.* *Cable Marketing* began in 1981 as a monthly tabloid.

Video Action began in December, 1980, calling itself "the *Esquire* of video magazines." *Advertising Age* devoted a special section to Consumer Electronics on January 12, 1981, and noted that *Video Action* had "positioned itself closest to the X-rated video market, drawing full page ads featuring Marilyn Chambers in 'Insatiable,' while turning off hardware marketers."

Cable TV magazine predicted a market of 35 million homes by 1985, up 63 per cent in five years. Its premiere national issue arrived in April, 1981, mailed to two million cable households. This followed an initial experiment in late 1980, for 200,000 subscribers in five cable systems.

Obviously all of these publications will not survive but so long as millions of Americans are involved in television in one way or another, other magazines will continue to hit the market, seeking a share of the audience.

READER'S DIGEST

In January, 1920, DeWitt Wallace printed his first copy of *Reader's Digest,* a 54-page dummy containing 31 articles condensed from leading magazines of his day. He peddled this around publishing houses and received only negative responses. After someone suggested he sell it himself by direct mail, today's *Reader's Digest* was born. In February, 1922, the magazine as we now know it arrived. Many of the articles of "enduring value and interest" came from publications no longer in business, such as *McClure's, Woman's Home Companion, Literary Digest, American, Outlook, Scribner's, Collier's, Vanity Fair, Munsey's* and others. But *Reader's Digest* continues.

Wallace, and his wife, Lila Bell, succeeded with "the Little Magazine," moving the 5,000 first issue circulation to 18,500,000 today. The 50th anniversary edition contained nearly 300 pages.[8]

Offices were moved from a basement room in New York City's Greenwich Village some 30 miles north to today's pseudo-Williamsburg-style headquarters in Chappaqua, near Pleasantville, New York. In an atmosphere resembling a university campus, staffers and visitors can walk past gardens, pools, statues and other pieces of fine art. Outstanding paintings hang from the walls in each office as well as along the hallways.

Reader's Digest has always had its devoted following, with its renewal rate in excess of 70 per cent, surpassed only by *National Geographic* among the major magazines. One of its most valuable assets is the subscription list and only three copies exist. This list is never sold, but it is extensively used for the company's sweepstakes, book sales, and other projects.

The magazine has been responsible for books, such as Theodore H. White's *Breach of Faith: The Fall of Richard Nixon,* and Cornelius Ryan's *The Longest Day.* It also assisted through financial backing with the research for *Roots* and it has produced some movies, including "Tom Sawyer." Since the early 50's, Reader's Digest Condensed Books have sold in the millions through its book club.

The Wallaces always have owned the firm, although they turned over the day-by-day activities to younger staffers in the early 70s. Nevertheless, there is a feeling that they are still there for major decision-making.

In their first issue, February 1922 "A Word of Thanks" was published, thanking the charter subscribers and making these observations about *Reader's Digest:*

1. Thirty-one articles each month—"one a day"—condensed from leading periodicals.
2. Each article of enduring value and interest—today, each month, or a year hence; such articles as one talks about and wishes to remember.
3. Compact form; easy to carry in the pocket and to keep for permanent reference.
4. A most convenient means of "keeping one's information account open"— of reading stimulating articles on a wide variety of subjects.[9]

Wallace was the son of a Presbyterian minister, Dr. James Wallace, who became president of Macalester College near St. Paul. Mrs. Wallace also comes from a family of Presbyterian clergymen. Thus one may note a religious streak

THE
READER'S
DIGEST

31 ARTICLES EACH
MONTH FROM LEAD
ING MAGAZINES.
EACH ARTICLE OF
ENDURING VALUE
AND INTEREST, IN
CONDENSED AND
PERMANENT FORM.

January, 1920

THE READER'S
DIGEST

THIRTY-ONE ARTICLES EACH MONTH
FROM LEADING MAGAZINES ~ EACH
ARTICLE OF ENDURING VALUE AND
INTEREST, IN CONDENSED AND
COMPACT FORM

FEBRUARY 1922

Facsimiles of the preliminary issue of *Reader's Digest* which DeWitt Wallace produced in 1920, and the actual first issue which appeared in February 1922, as a joint creation with his bride, Lila Acheson Wallace. The cover of the April 1982 edition.

DRAMA IN REAL LIFE

THE DOG
WHO WALKED THROUGH FIRE
PAGE 105

PAGE 70

CAR REPAIR
RIP-OFFS AND
HOW TO AVOID
THEM

DeWitt Wallace. *Photo by Fabian Bach-* Lila Acheson Wallace. *Photo by Bradford*
rach *Bachrach*

in the magazine, at least in the early years. DeWitt Wallace died on March 30, 1981, at the age of 91. Editor Edward T. Thompson said no major changes were expected in the magazine.

In the beginning *Reader's Digest* was sold only by subscription. Some reports indicate Wallace feared public exposure on newsstands would result in many imitators. As its circulation and profits grew, *Reader's Digest* began to pay authors for their condensed stories as well as to pay magazines for the right to reprint from their issues. *Reader's Digest* remains one of the better-paying publications, from the jokes and humorous items to the long-running feature, "The Most Unforgettable Character I've Met."

The Wallaces have been optimists, and many *Reader's Digest* articles reflect the Horatio Alger image that in turn reflects the success this couple has achieved in the magazine world.

Liquor Ads Accepted

A major decision was made in 1955—the acceptance of its first advertisements, following a $500,000 deficit in its magazine operations in 1954 and anticipated larger deficits in the years ahead. Before an official announcement could be made, the information reached advertising agencies and within two weeks the magazine had orders for 1,107 pages, three times the total planned for the first year.

Readers were surveyed, asking their preference—to retain the 35-cent per

55

copy cost and include advertisements, *or* increase the copy cost and retain the no-ad policy. Some 80 per cent preferred the use of advertisements. During the first decade of using ads, 1955–1964, the magazine received more than $351 million from this source.

At first no alcohol, tobacco or medical remedies were advertised. However, in 1979 the first liquor ad was accepted. Since 1924 the magazine has waged war on smoking, although *Time* reported Wallace "smokes steadily" and liked to drink and play poker.[10] Only a handful of subscribers cancelled because of the use of these ads.

Opponents have attacked *Reader's Digest* as they do most successful businesses. *Fact* magazine in early 1966 published a story titled, "The Pleasantville Monster," calling the magazine "dishonest, hypocritical, reactionary, irresponsible, ignorant, arrogant, money-grabbing swindle sheet." The story quoted from many *Reader's Digest* articles. At times governmental agencies have been critical of editorial-style advertisements, although they have always been marked "Advertisement." Apparently they are not so sufficiently identified or sufficiently different in layout and type choices from the editorial content to satisfy government agencies. Others have been critical of its conservative approach and some labor organizations have been critical of its pro-business feelings.[11] *Reader's Digest* staffers do not consider such attacks worthy of reply. As Editor Thompson said, *"Reader's Digest* is big and thus a target for others."

Its earlier practice of "planting" articles in other magazines and then reprinting them in *Reader's Digest* upset some, including the *New Yorker* which eventually denied *RD* such rights. Wallace realized the time would come when he could no longer depend entirely on sufficient consumer magazines to provide reprintable material. Thus today probably 75 per cent of the material is staff written, or at least staff inspired, while the magazine has few contracts with other publications for reprint rights. A sizable number of writers are kept on retainers. In addition, the magazine has available staffers around the world, many working on their international editions.

Nevertheless, *Reader's Digest* has more supporters than detractors, as its tremendous circulation indicates. Its readership increased during World War II, with circulation moving from 4 to 9 million. Today it sells some 18,500,000 copies in the U.S. and 12,500,000 internationally, appearing in 40 editions in 16 languages in 163 countries. No other publication comes close to this worldwide coverage. Recent editions have appeared in Arabic, Korean, and Hindi. African and Greek editions are forthcoming. Because of hard currency problems, a Chinese edition must be delayed.

What of the future? Apparently the magazine's circulation has reached a plateau, since it has varied only slightly from year to year. It remains a valuable monthly update of American life in many areas and it provides humor, plus opportunities for one to update his grammar, learn many new words, and become informed of a variety of topics. More than 50,000 items arrive monthly for the filler space; it has become an American tradition to think first of *Reader's Digest* when one sees, reads, or hears something he believes funny or at least out of the ordinary. Since only 100 to 175 of these items are printed each month, one can quickly compute the odds of being "published in *Reader's Digest.*"

In addition to the 50,000 offerings each month, the magazine also receives at least 30,000 first-person stories annually. The staffers scan more than 500 periodicals regularly, searching for potential stories to reprint. In addition, at least 1,500 book manuscripts are read for possible condensation. Obviously, no single reader is expected to find all the articles of interest to him each month. However, Editor-in-chief Edward T. Thompson believes every reader will have seven or eight articles with strong appeal in every issue.[12]

The magazine is used in many American schools, especially in English classes. In 1980, a double-spread ad by the International Paper Company featured comments by Thompson on "How to write clearly." Obviously drawing on his two decades as the magazine's editor, Thompson urged all writers to know their readers—"Don't write to a level higher than your readers' knowledge of it." Avoid jargon, but use familiar combinations of words. Thompson recommended the use of "first-degree words" such as "face" rather than "visage" or "countenance." Stick to the point, outline your topics, and be as brief as possible, since "condensing, as *Reader's Digest* does it, is in large part artistry." Common word wasters find no place in this magazine, which continues to stress the positive, not the negative.

The magazine may be more Republican than Democrat in its philosophy, yet such labels are not as valid in the 80s as they were in previous decades. *Reader's Digest* seeks to explain the role of the individual in solving his own problems, with emphasis on free enterprise. While the magazine tries hard to present both sides, it does not hesitate to come to its own conclusions. The magazine does keep abreast of the times. To obtain the best writers available, the magazine pays well. For original articles the minimum pay in 1980 was $2,600, while for reprints the publication paid the original writer a minimum of $450 a page and an equal amount to the magazine that published the article.

The symbol for *Reader's Digest* is Pegasus, identified by the ancient Greeks as the "beloved horse of the Muses—the nine children of Zeus who from their home on Mount Helicon provided inspiration and incentive for poets, musicians and other practitioners of the arts." The magazine notes today that "As the fountainhead of literary inspiration, Pegasus still watches over writers as their words cast new light where needed, often arousing a thunderous response upon the awakening of those who have slept too long. So it is that Pegasus most appropriately symbolizes the *Reader's Digest* today."[13]

New Member Joins Family

Reader's Digest presented *Families* in late 1980, a publication directed to those with children from "prenatal to college" age. Thompson said, "The magazine business has been moving toward specialization for some time now. I'd say we're the largest general interest magazine in the business, so we can't compete with ourselves. If we expand, it has to be into different subject areas."[14]

Thompson reported after the initial issue that the median age for *Families'* readers was 33, compared with 45 for *Reader's Digest.* The new concept appears accurate, since government statistics indicate there will be a growth in the number of families with parents 35 or younger in the years ahead, thus providing a market for *Families.*

The first issue was marked Fall 1980. It appeared in the more traditional-*Time* size format with six stories featured on the cover: Kids & Pot, What You Should Know; What Makes a Successful Stepparent?; Alex Haley: The Joy of Family Reunions; Teaching Kids the Value of the Dollar; The Best of Bombeck; and an extract from James Michener's *The Little Wanderers.*

Families is intended "to be more than an articulate and concerned adviser; it will also be informative and fun, and frequently provide a means for getting parents and kids together in an atmosphere of participatory warmth," according to the editors' welcome in this issue. In addition to the writers publicized on the cover, *Families* also had articles by Alvin Toffler and Tom Wolfe. The editors recognized the problems facing today's parents in "the dislocations of an increasingly mobile society, the erosions of inflation, the traumas of the sexual revolution."

Company blamed "unrealistic expectation for the magazine." Circulation reached only 430,000 at end.

NATIONAL GEOGRAPHIC

A unique publication that provides armchair journeys to the known and unknown centers of the world is the *National Geographic,* the voice of the National Geographic Society. This group was founded in 1888 after 33 eminent men responded to an invitation to meet in Washington "for the purpose of considering the advisability of organizing a society for the increase and diffusion of geographical knowledge." Geography may not have been one of the most popular topics of that day, but today, thanks in part to the *National Geographic,* millions of Americans have developed a greater interest in the subject. No doubt the increased interest in travel and in photography has contributed to this situation.

Gardiner Greene Hubbard, a Boston lawyer and philanthropist, was the guiding force behind the National Geographic Society. Hubbard, the group's initial president, helped to organize the first telephone company for his son-in-law, Alexander Graham Bell, who followed as the Society's leader in 1889. Among the outstanding individuals involved in the Society's founding were General A. W. Greely, noted polar explorer; Major John Wesley Powell, ex-

plorer of the Colorado River; George Kennan, traveler to Siberia; Henry Gannett, distinguished cartographer; George Brown Goode, naturalist, and others, including topographers, meteorologists, geologists, geographers, and military officers.

During its first seven years, the *National Geographic* appeared irregularly, published only when sufficient editorial material had accumulated. From its start, the publication has provided maps and charts. Today it distributes more than 30 million maps annually. Early articles were technical and scientific, with limited appeal. Bell, however, desired to improve the magazine and after he became president he hired his daughter's prospective suitor, Gilbert Hovey Grosvenor, to provide editorial guidance. Bell urged Grosvenor to popularize the science of geography, to transform the magazine from "one of cold geographic fact . . . into a vehicle for carrying the living, breathing human-interest truth about this great world of ours to the people." By 1901, he was the managing editor, having pushed the *National Geographic* circulation past its first thousand. It reached its first million in 1935. Two years later he was the editor-in-chief, a position he held until 1954. During his tenure, Grosvenor brought the printing of the magazine from New York to Washington and, eventually, the Society produced its own maps. Grosvenor's Seven Guiding Principles included the following:

1. Absolute accuracy.
2. Abundance of instructive and beautiful illustrations.
3. Everything must have permanent value.
4. Avoid trivialities and material of a purely personal nature.
5. Nothing partisan or controversial.
6. Only what is of a kindly nature; nothing unduly critical.
7. Plan each number for maximum timeliness.[15]

Frederick G. Vosburgh, who became editor in 1967, said when he took office, "Our aim is to present articles of permanent value that avoid controversy or partisanship . . . Our readers like to learn—as long as they don't have to work too hard."[16] Magazine historian Frank Luther Mott recorded, "for more than half a century the *National Geographic* magazine has not published a single monthly number that has not been interesting and informative, with some measure of permanent value."[17] He could have added, were he still around, that this philosophy continues today.

Although termed a picture book by some, the *National Geographic* is for millions of readers one of the best examples of today's photojournalism, portraying the big stories through the use of editorial comments and excellent photography. The breakthrough in the use of pictures came in 1905 when 11 pages were devoted to pictures of the mysterious city of Lhasa in Tibet. By 1908, pictures occupied more than half of the available space.

First color photography appeared in 1910, showing scenes and people of China and Korea, using the Autochrome process. Mott added that "it was the advent of color in the next decade that really transformed the *Geographic* into a kind of periodical never before known.'' It remains known for publishing many firsts, including the first picture to show curvature of the earth, the first successful natural color undersea pictures and the first successful color photos taken from the air.

Since the early years the Society has sponsored expeditions and research projects, having helped Robert E. Peary to reach the North Pole and Richard E. Byrd to fly over the South Pole. Since the 1950s it has encouraged an expansion of space exploration, translating scientific data into stories all readers can understand. This ability to remove much of the technical and complicated terminology has increased its appeal to millions. By the mid-1980s, the Society had supported more than 1,800 explorations and research projects, "adding immeasurably to man's knowledge of earth, sea and sky.'' During World War II the Society's files of 350,000 pictures were made available to the government. Many were used to plot bombing missions.

Since the organization of its book service in 1957, the Society has published dozens of volumes with many reaching best-seller status. In 1965, the Special Publications division was organized. *Our Country's Presidents,* the first production, was selected as one of the 100 best reference books by the American Library Association.

Public Service books also have been published, with *The White House: An Historic Guide* the pioneer volume. This book was suggested by Mrs. John F. Kennedy and the Society produced it as a public service. Several million copies have been sold, including 250,000 during its first three months.

Profits from this project have benefitted the White House Historical Association, the United States Capitol Historical Society, the Foundation of the Federal Bar Association, and the Washington Monument Association. These books have informed the nation about the Capitol, Supreme Court, Washington Monument, and our presidents.

Since the 1965–66 season, the Society has produced programs for television. The first, "Americans on Everett,'' won eight significant awards. Others that followed also have been cited for outstanding contributions to a better knowledge of the world. Subjects have varied from the Amazon to Siberia, from Reptiles and Amphibians to Wild Chimpanzees.

To further promote the interest of geography, the magazine has produced atlases, globes, and related items. For the younger audience, the *School Bulletin* appeared from 1947 to 1975, 30 weeks each year during the school months. The *Bulletin* likewise won numerous citations for its work. The *World* was started in 1975, designed for those readers in the 8 and older age group, and to replace *School Bulletin.* Gilbert Grosvenor said, "I want to get kids to read in spite of television.'' Within three months, the *World*'s circulation reached a million. Its chief competitors are *Highlights for Children* and *Ranger Rick's Nature Magazine.*

Each week more than 2,000 newspapers, wire services, and radio and television stations receive news bulletins from the Society. Filmstrips began in 1968, with more than 60,000 now available. In late 1969, the Society presented its first recording of folk songs of various countries. In other words, it was "geography put to music," as the Society observed. Today more than 10,700,000 subscribers receive the *National Geographic* each month, quickly recognizing its famous yellow cover. Originally this appeared in a reddish brown cover, in 1888, and by 1910 it had acquired a buff border. Later, the cover became yellow; oak leaves, acorns and hemispheres were added around the name and table of contents. By the 1960s more photographs were appearing and the border was narrowed. In 1979, the border was abolished.

It is a fallacy for anyone to call the *National Geographic* strictly a travel magazine. It is much more than that. It continues to follow the original goals of the Society, to provide information of interest to readers of all ages. Famous art works have been reproduced for the benefit of those unable to witness the classics of the ages. It continues to enjoy a renewal rate in excess of 90 per cent.

In 1964 the present headquarters in the heart of Washington were dedicated and four years later its Membership Center Building in nearby Gaithersburg, Md., was opened for records and correspondence. The *National Geographic* is the voice of a non-profit society, but under the 1968 Tax Reform Act is required to pay taxes on its advertising revenue.

In 1979 the total revenue of the Society reached $193 million, with $105 million from the magazine, $25 million from advertising, $10 million from *World* magazine, $52 million from books and other publications, and a million from miscellaneous sources.

Production costs for paper, printing, and postage reached $106 million in 1979, salaries and benefits totaled $41 million, promotion $19 million, utilities and other operating costs accounted for $15–16 million, research grants $2.2 million, and miscellaneous $9.4 million, for a total of $192.6 million. In addition, the Society gained $8.2 million from investments.

Guidelines for Writers, Photographers

National Geographic averages 140 editorial pages per issue printed on gravure presses. Currently the advertising copy is offset. All of the printing is done in Corinth, Mississippi.

The magazine offers guidelines for writers and photographers, since contributions come from many fields. Presidents, statesmen, scientists, and specialists have been involved in articles. Stories may "deal with any part of the earth—or universe—from the teeming pavements of New York or London to equatorial jungle or the craters of the moon." The emphasis appears to be on photographs. Writers are told to relate their stories in straight-forward sentences and paragraphs; long descriptions of illustrations are not necessary. Photographers are urged to include people whenever possible but "not stiffly posed or looking at the camera." Other suggestions for presentation of "humanized geography'' involve physical aspects or features of a locality; people at work as well as enjoying amusements; typical dress, festivals, customs, and way of life; industries, handicrafts, commerce, and transportation; art and architecture of unusual or traditional design; important public institutions and public works; scenes of historical significance; natural history—animals, birds, plants, insects, fish; and the strange and curious.

National Geographic photographers have won major awards for their contributions to a better comprehension of our world. Since readers find such photos valuable for years, it is no wonder that some persons fear the country eventually will sink under the weight of millions of copies of ''that magazine with the yellow cover.'' Americans religiously avoid discarding the Bible and the *National Geographic*. Copies of the magazine appear at church bazaars, used books/magazine fairs, garage sales, and other places. But seldom do they appear in garbage pails. One just doesn't throw out the *National Geographic*. Such weight represented by these millions of saved copies has led some to consider the *National Geographic* a ''doomsday machine.'' Thousands of families retain the magazine for years.

In 1980, Wilbur E. (Bill) Garrett became editor, replacing Gilbert M. Grosvenor, who became the Society's president. Garrett, who joined the magazine in 1954 as a picture editor, has won numerous awards for his many articles in the magazine and his work with the Society's television specials. He carries on the magazine's goals, being a stickler for accuracy.

A former long-time employe of *National Geographic,* in commenting upon Garrett's appointment, recalled: ''There are probably still many who go into the *Geographic*'s never-never land and have a hard struggle with the mad hatter. I have often wondered and stood in awe at the likes of Mr. Garrett who apparently knew where he was going from the beginning. *NGM* made a good choice—he is a shrewd and crafty politician but a hell of a hard worker who really gets things done.''

Two Gain, One Loses

With the end of 1980 two of the big three recorded slight circulation gains. *Reader's Digest* inched closer to its former position as the leader in America, increasing its total circulation to 17,898,681, a gain of 0.1 percent over the 1979 year-end figure. This was, of course, mostly from subscriptions, which totaled 16,764,806.

National Geographic recorded a gain of 2.9 per cent over 1979, bringing its circulation to 10,711,886. Only a handful of these, 5,483, were reported as newsstand, or single-copy sales.

The big loser was *TV Guide,* no doubt feeling the effects of more competition and feeling some side effects from one of the worst television seasons in the nation's history. Its circulation dropped 5.6 per cent, reaching 17,981,657. A drop of 9 per cent was reported in subscriptions.

Time's 1981 advertising income of $253,440,762 returned it to top position, ahead of *TV Guide*'s $239,251,016. At the end of 1981 *Reader's Digest* regained the circulation lead with 17,927,542 compared to *TV Guide*'s 17,670,543.

These three remained the leaders, with no other magazine threatening their standings. Should these figures continue along this path, *Reader's Digest* may take over in 1982. These figures are compiled regularly by the Audit Bureau of Circulation and released through such sources as the Magazine Publishers Association, *The Gallagher Report* (which provides excellent statistics throughout the year), and the trade periodicals, such as *Advertising Age, FOLIO, Magazine Age,* and others.

3

News, Opinions and Ideas:
Newsweeklies and
Persuasive Publications

EACH WEEK nearly 10 million Americans buy copies of the three top-selling news weeklies, anticipating well-rounded accounts of activities throughout the world for the previous seven days. Some 50 million read these magazines before each week ends.

In addition, several hundred thousand read opinion magazines, such as the *Nation, New Republic, Progressive, Commonweal*, and other lesser-known periodicals. Allan Nevins believed historians should read magazines from the left to the right to obtain a true picture of the thinking patterns of Americans.

And there are others that have been around for more than a century, such as *Harper's* and the *Atlantic*. These, together with the younger *Saturday Review*, also have their devoted followings.

News magazines have existed for nearly two centuries; modern day news weeklies, however, began in 1923 with *Time*. Among the forerunners was the *New-Haven Gazette and the Connecticut Magazine* in 1786. From 1811 to 1849, *Niles Weekly Register* provided accounts of Congress, economic highlights, foreign dispatches, and other valuable information still useful to today's historians. For many years the *Saturday Evening Post*, founded in 1826, was a news-oriented magazine.[1] Horace Greeley's *New Yorker*, termed a miscellany because of its varied contents, in 1830 had departments with some attention to news coverage. *Frank Leslie's Illustrated Newspaper*, which later became *Leslie's Weekly*, began in 1855 and ended in 1922. In some ways it resembled today's *National Enquirer, Star*, and *Globe*, with its more sensational coverage of crime and scandals. *Leslie's* was the first magazine to conduct a presidential survey of its readers. In 1916 and 1920 it conducted a small poll of its readership. The latter one asked persons to indicate how they voted in 1916 and how

65

they planned to vote in 1920. Readers had to clip the coupons from the magazine and return them. It wasn't too successful, with 7,462 returns. The poll winner was General Leonard Wood, with Senator Hiram Johnson of California the runnerup. The magazine's circulation at the time was 500,000.[2]

Harper's Weekly, another valuable forerunner to our news weeklies, reported the nation's highlights from 1857 to 1916. Famous for printing Thomas Nast's editorial cartoons, *Harper's Weekly* offered readers and researchers valuable data about Americans and their interests for nearly six decades. It stressed political issues, with a heavy offering from the leading authors of the times. Mott credited its success to being "a vigorous political journal of conservative tendencies."[3]

Literary Digest

Better remembered by older Americans is the *Literary Digest,* started in 1890 by Isaac Funk and Adam Wagnalls. In some ways similar to contemporary weeklies, *Literary Digest* offered condensations of articles, mostly collected from newspapers. Mott said the magazine was the "impartial recorder of public opinion as expressed in the press, as well as a repository of digests of, and extracts from, current informational literature."[4] There were the traditional departments, including politics, art, literature, education, science, philosophy, religion, sociology, and, of course, miscellany as well as sections about the press and books. "Topics of the Day" came entirely from newspapers as did the "Slips that Pass in the Type," a collection of typographical errors. For years it circulation was second only to the *Saturday Evening Post.* And, like the *SEP,* the *Literary Digest* was sold door-to-door by thousands of youngsters across America. Although it was not a news magazine in the meaning of that term today, it was the best in its early days.

Literary Digest was impartial, neither editorializing nor promoting causes. The magazine conducted the most massive polls in publishing history, mailing millions of postal cards to subscribers, telephone owners and automobile owners. Unfortunately, this represented a minority group in the 20s and 30s and the result reflected the situation. Eleven million cards were mailed in 1920; 16,500,000 in 1924, and 18,000,000 in 1928. In 1932 more than 3,500,000 cards were returned for a record response. In 1936 the card voters gave the presidential nod to Alf Landon over Franklin D. Roosevelt, seeking a second term. Although some historians blame the demise of *Literary Digest* on this massive error, the magazine already had been affected by the Depression and by the arrival of *Time* and *Newsweek* with their better and more informal coverage.

A publication directed to boys and girls was started in Washington in 1894. *Pathfinder,* which sold for a nickel, passed a million circulation before it disappeared in the 40s. It was the "historian of the present" that sought to show "the way through the jungle of events." And a few years later, a tiny weekly, *Quick,* offered a "wholly fresh adventure in journalism. Brisk, terse, and packed with facts, it is the timely answer to the need of busy people to be kept informed at a minimum cost in money and in reading time,'' it claimed. It was a product of the *Look* organization.

Time

Briton Hadden and Henry R. Luce brought *Time* to the world on March 3, 1923, with a 32-page weekly that attracted some 9,000 subscribers plus a few thousand newsstand customers. The weekly news-magazine had 22 departments, opening with National Affairs and closing with View With Alarm, a collection of brief paragraphs telling about stories on earlier pages. There were about seven pages of advertisements, including a house message urging readers to remit $5 for a year's subscription.

Time became the nation's No. 1 news magazine in circulation and in advertising revenue. It has changed since the early leadership of Luce, who took over entirely following Hadden's early death in 1929. Many readers forget that *Time* was published in Cleveland in 1925–27, and that in 1924 Hadden and Luce started *Saturday Review of Literature,* which they operated for two years.[5]

Although competition from *Newsweek* continues to be intensive, *Time* has dominated this select market for forty years. A well-researched series of newspaper articles about these two weeklies by *Los Angeles Times'* writer David Shaw in 1980 observed that *''Time* is now—once again—the better newsmagazine.''[6]

''Time does the better job covering foreign news, science, religion and music, as well as in its overall design, appearance, use of color photography and, generally, in its overall writing and editing,'' Shaw noted, after interviews with more than 60 past and present staffers of the two publications.

From the start, Luce conceded *Time* would have some prejudices. He acknowledged he was a Protestant, a Republican, and a free enterpriser. He made no effort to hide his support of Eisenhower and other Republicans.

The magazine's early style was parodied as ''Backward ran the sentences until reeled the mind.'' Another writer noted, ''Still never has stood *Time* since it invented backward sentences.''[7] Among complaints heard from time to time is an overstress on Eastern United States stories, when equally interesting stories appear some distance from New York. One *Time* editor told Shaw, ''You can get non–New York stories into the magazine more easily if they conform to the editors' stereotypes. Do an academic story out of Boston, a farm story out of the Midwest or a kook-weirds story out of L. A. and you can get it in.''

Old Style Gone; Still a Trendsetter

Time's oft-quoted ''awkward sentence style'' has been abolished. In its earlier day, *Time* coined many words, now accepted in our language, such as socialite, guesstimate, tycoon, pundit, kudos, and moppet. It merged words with ''&'' that were usually accepted in the singular sense, such as ham&eggs, husband&wife, and safe&sane. It used exciting adjectives and adverbs to replace dull words such as "say" or "walk." Editors said they were forced "to use a string of adjectives to give a thumbnail sketch" but admitted they preferred nouns that made adjectives unnecessary. On its 40th birthday, *Time* claimed "there is now no conscious infusion of a precise style of writing, but there is an abiding interest in style as an important part of our job."[8]

Time has its critics. *Nation* in 1959 called it "the weekly fiction magazine," with stories written in the same manner as fiction, containing a protagonist, an antagonist, and a complication.[9] The *New Yorker* headed a story about the magazine's use of words, *"Time* Lumbers On,"[10] while a *Harper's* story, "There are oo Trees in Russia" by Otto Friedrich, considered *Time*'s fetishism for the facts. Friedrich asked "whether these facts, researched and verified at such enormous trouble and expense, really matter." He also wrote, "the theory that the knowledge of lesser facts implies knowledge of major facts . . . that *Time* knows everything there is to know."[11] Friedrich, by the way, was in charge of *Time*'s Special 1776–1976 issue published July 4, 1976. This issue, which required nearly two years to put together, was the first special ever published under the *Time* logo. A press run of 5.5 million was *Time*'s largest.

Critics have charged that *Time* favors Republican presidents over Democrats. David Halberstam, in *The Powers That Be,* termed Henry Luce a "national propagandist . . . the most important influential conservative-centrist force in the country."

Time remains a trendsetter. For example, in 1979 the magazine published the 64-page annual report of Gulf & Western as an advertisement. This represented more than $3 million in advertising revenue, plus media recognition for the unusual project.[12] *Time*'s Man of the Year is another trendsetter. It aroused criticism from many quarters in 1980 when it named Iran's Ayatollah Ruhollah Khomeini Man of the Year. Unfortunately, many readers failed to note *Time*'s disclaimer that this choice did not represent any endorsement of the Ayatollah. After all, *Time* had selected Hitler in 1938 and Stalin in 1939 and 1942 for the same citation, both without any endorsement of their activities.

Difficult as it may be to determine influence, one must credit *Time* and the other newsmagazines for bringing about changes in newspapers. David Shaw noted that newspapers have "become more like news magazines in their style and content, with more analytical, behind-the-scene stories, more impressionistic writing and more social trends stories; simultaneously, newsmagazines have become more like daily newspapers in their present practice of breaking news stories." Time Essays, in some ways similar to editorials in newspapers, were inaugurated in 1965 with the first on the United Nations.

Newsweek

Ten years after *Time* appeared, its first serious competition arrived. *Newsweek,* as it was first spelled, was the product of Thomas John Cardell Martyn, one-time foreign news editor of *Time.* He became the business manager and Samuel T. Williamson became the first editor. The initial issue, on Feb. 17,

1933, carried seven photographs on its cover. Each was to depict the top news story for each day of the previous week. Nazi troops in action occupied the largest photo. Raymond Moley appeared, sunning himself in Florida while waiting for President-elect Franklin D. Roosevelt to call for his advice.

The 32-page weekly was departmentalized, with numerous photos spread throughout. In its third issue the editor noted that *News-week* "does not take the place of a newspaper, though it is organized like one; it is an indispensable complement to newspapers, because it explains, expounds, clarifies." Obviously attempting to attract readers who disliked *Time,* the newcomer tried to be less biased, with its writing closer to newspaper style, using inverted-pyramid leads. Since this was the antithesis of *Time*'s style, it pleased some readers. Full-page photos appeared on the cover in the second year, with a picture of Hitler and Mussolini walking together, plotting the downfall of the western world. The next week Mae West provided a lighter news subject for the cover.

"The Magazine of News Significance" became *Newsweek*'s slogan after it merged with *Today* in 1935. Some readers believe that after this merger *Newsweek* began to editorialize news stories in a more interpretive manner.

Some writers date *Newsweek*'s move to overtake *Time* with its acquisition by Philip Graham, Washington *Post* owner, in 1961. Shaw observed that *"Newsweek* was so undistinguished in those days that *Time* virtually ignored it." In such a position *Newsweek* could gamble on stories. *Time* is said to have ignored a proposal to do a cover story on the Beatles, dismissing them as "a bunch of long-hairs who didn't mean a thing." On the other hand, *Newsweek* covered stories such as the Beatles and social and political issues, including the civil rights movement, the ultra-right, gay rights, physical culture, evangelicals, senior citizens, and unwed couples living together.

Newsweek was the first to provide bylines for writers, long a problem for both weeklies. For years the writers suffered from anonymity. Stories are put together by the committee process. Reporters submit thousands of words for a file on a given subject; some have submitted 20-page reports only to read a line or two of their own work in the final story. While the critics were the first to be publicly credited for their work, others were added, including researchers. *Newsweek* also inaugurated a practice of permitting reporters to read stories before they appeared in the magazine. To many, *Newsweek* has been more personal in its writing than *Time* in recent years.

For a time *Newsweek* became excited over entertainment subjects, some rather trivialized according to some critics. After *People* magazine reached several million readers, *Newsweek* editors began to focus more on similar subjects, such as gossip, disco, movie and television stars, and similar light topics. This resulted in a decline of newsstand sales; obviously, *Newsweek* readers wanted news; *People* readers preferred entertainment.

As the 80s opened, *Newsweek* changed with fewer cover stories on pop culture or the arts. *Newsweek* has reacted faster on some major stories in the past, such as the Johnstown massacre. It was able to substitute a one-page story and two pictures on the initial report, and carried 26 pages the following week, compared to eight for *Time*.

Using the latest of video terminal equipment, *Newsweek* is put together in New York. Then the copy is sent to its pre-press center in Carlstadt, N.J., with each page moving in less than two minutes on private data-transmission wire. There the film is made and copies sent to printing plants in Lancaster, Pa., Chicago, London, Hong Kong, Los Angeles, Jonesboro, Ark., and Pewaukee, Wis.

Both magazines have research organizations. *Newsweek*, for example, upset some television executives in 1978 when it sponsored its "Eyes On" study, which claimed that readers of newsweeklies looked at 85% of the magazine's ad pages. Meanwhile, only 70% of a television audience stayed with their sets during commercials.[13]

How Alike: How Differ

Shaw's research prompted him to note that *"Newsweek* is thought to be superior in domestic reportage, columns, sports coverage, book reviews and most entertainment cover stories. Despite some lapses, *Newsweek* has also long been quicker than *Time* to react to most major news events and social trends."

Another compared them to CBS and NBC nightly news shows: "They're both damn good at what they do. One week, one is a little better; the next week, the other is a little better. But over the last few years, I think *Time*, like CBS, has usually been just a little bit better more often." Both *Time* and *Newsweek* tend to ignore the No. 3 weekly, *U. S. News & World Report*, which is different in its organization of news, its style and its appeal. All, obviously, have their faithful followers.

In many ways *Newsweek* battles *Time* for the same readers, those persons in their late thirties with some college education. They usually live in metropolitan areas with incomes exceeding $20,000. Males account for 60% of the readers. Shaw noted that fewer than 10% of the readers of *Time* will read *Newsweek* and vice versa. Both groups tend to defend their choice with enthusiasm; both magazines consider newspapers and television as serious competitors.

Newsweek, like *Time*, has been accused of too much Eastern orientation, too much influence by the *New York Times*. Some of their editors have suggested that staffers read such newspapers as the *Chicago Tribune*, the *Los Angeles Times*, and others west of the Hudson River. For example, new plays on Broadway are often reviewed; new plays in Chicago, St. Louis, or the West Coast seldom are. *Newsweek* has done more in the 80s with coverage of Phil Donahue, who uses Chicago for his home base. Both focus attention on Hollywood with its movies and television productions.

Both magazines are printed on the week-end and often have to break into the Sunday morning press run to provide for late-breaking stories. Sophisticated computer technology now enables both magazines to make such changes with little cost compared to the $250,000 it cost *Time* to cover the Three Mile Island incident at the last moment. Also, these two weeklies often have alternate covers ready, for presidential campaigns, important athletic events, and trials of such well-known personalities as Patty Hearst.

Reporters for both are called upon to supply facts, specific details, and statistics often overlooked by daily newspapers and wire services. Researchers often pressure reporters to obtain minor details and *Time* staffers are provided an "errors summary report" that records the mistakes in each issue. They can identify each error, whether it be by a correspondent, a researcher, or a writer.

Newsweek, planning for the years ahead, is spending millions in public advertising to promote itself. *Newsweek* seeks to sell advertisers and potential readers on the concept that it is livelier, more fun and more breezy than its competition. It prefers the term "news-weekly" rather than *Time*'s use of "newsmagazine." Since some 60% of all advertising business originates in New York, *Newsweek* uses the *New York Times* as well as trade publications for these messages. The magazine mapped its future on a two-point campaign: get good eyewitness reporting and stay on top of the news. In these ads such terms as newspirited, newslively, and newswinning were used to promote the weekly.

Time and *Newsweek* continue to compress thousands of words into hundreds of words each week, hoping to remove some of the confusion of complex stories. There is little doubt that *Time* has shifted some of its long-time love affair with the Republicans. Other changes have been influenced by the growth of *Newsweek* under the Graham family ownership since 1961.

Time's final circulation report for 1980 placed its paid circulation at 4.3 million, while *Newsweek*'s was 2.9 million.

U. S. News & World Report

For years the names *U. S. News & World Report* and David Lawrence were synonymous. Justifiably so. In 1926, Lawrence established a national newspaper, the *United States Daily.* In mid-1933 this was succeeded by the *United States News* that became a weekly instead of a daily. This was designed for readers who preferred more in-depth data about the government. In 1940, *United States News* adopted a magazine format, with a red-white-and-blue cover, more color printing, photographs, charts, and illustrations. In mid-1940 Lawrence launched *World Report* to deal with international affairs. By January, 1948, these periodicals had merged.

Lawrence, born on Christmas day in 1888, scored a beat with his report on the death of Grover Cleveland. While attending Princeton, Lawrence was a close acquaintance of the Clevelands, and Mrs. Cleveland gave him the story of her husband's death for the Associated Press. Lawrence was a lifelong friend of Woodrow Wilson, who moved from the presidency of Princeton to the presidency of the nation. Lawrence worked for the AP, served as Washington correspondent for the *New York Post,* and in 1919 established his own news service, the Consolidated Press. In 1968, after publishing his own periodicals since 1926, Lawrence offered these comments about his career, explaining his goals for *U. S. News & World Report:*

> It (*U. S. News*) is basically a two-way system of communication between the people of the United States and their government. It has become an important means of communication also between the people of America and the peoples of the rest of the world.

> It is truly dedicated to a single purpose—to give the information that intelligent people need and want in order that they may make up their minds and exercise in their own way a proper influence upon national and international policy.

> . . . until 35 years ago there was no magazine with an adequate explanation and correlation of what the day-to-day actions of Government really mean to the economic life of the individual and his enterprises.

> For 35 years all members of Congress, all important officials in the executive agencies, and all members of the federal judiciary have been receiving, without fee, *U. S. News & World Report* every week. In the same way, all the governments of the world receive it regularly for their prime minister and presidents, their foreign secretaries, and their legislative leaders.[14]

U. S. News differs from *Time* and *Newsweek.* It is devoted entirely to news of national and international affairs, unlike the other two that cover a broad spectrum of topics. *U. S. News* is not departmentalized. It is employe-owned, an arrangement Lawrence made in 1962 before his death in 1973. The publication is edited in Washington rather than in New York, where the other two originate.

Lawrence's editorial comments appeared on the last page. He is remembered at Princeton through scholarships established in his name by the magazine's staffers.

"America's Third Century—A Look Ahead" was the theme for its 32-page bicentennial supplement in 1976. The magazine has featured noted personalities in a series of promotional ads, paying each individual a token $1. Reggie Jackson, Dick Cavett, Cheryl Tiegs, Lee Iacocca, Andy Warhol and others have appeared in these messages, proclaiming their long-time devotion to the publication. The magazine also attempts to inform its readers of changes, especially in upgrading its production. In mid-1974 it began its transformation to computer operations, and more advanced electronic publishing. Also in 1977 the magazine underwent a typographic facelift, described as "simply a new dress on the same old body."

Looking into the future, current publisher John H. Sweet predicted: "If we're going to smoke a pipe of dreams by the end of the century, a subscriber to this magazine may be able to punch a button on a home TV screen and call up the latest reports—on a daily instead of a weekly basis. Somebody may come up with a way that will eliminate the printing press."[15]

In 1980 the magazine followed the trend to offset printing, with more four-color editorial pages and last-minute national four-color advertisements. Marketing and readership research projects continue to be conducted regularly. Staffers learn that readers gain a fuller understanding of the news in the publication, which they view as accurate and reliable, offering all sides of controversial issues.[16]

Noted for its lengthy reports, such as the 86 pages devoted to the full text of the Pearl Harbor report printed Sept. 1, 1945, *U. S. News & World Report* continues to offer in-depth interviews and studies of major news subjects.

PERSUASIVE PUBLICATIONS: MAGAZINES OF OPINION

Since the development of magazines in America, those classified as intellectual journals have been significant, less by their numbers than by their readership. Such influential "intellectual journals transcend the limitations of geographic distance, large numbers of people and narrow specialization. They provide for both communication and feedback," according to *Change* magazine.[17] Such periodicals are classified under several titles, including "Political and Social Topics," the heading used by Standard Rate and Data Service *Consumer and Farm Magazine* listings. They are also known as magazines of dissent and magazines for minority interests.

The variety of these publications can be seen from the group in SRDA: *Columbia Journalism Review, Commonweal, Conservative Digest, Crisis, Foreign Affairs, Foreign Service Journal, Human Events, Nation, National Review, New Republic, New Spirit, Political Science Quarterly, Progressive, Reason, Spotlight, Washington Monthly* and *World Press Review*. Some of these are well known, others not so readily recognized by the general public.

Since the combined circulation of these magazines would be less than half of *People*'s and only a fraction of *National Enquirer*'s, their influence is determined by the impact they have on opinion leaders, those individuals who are most quoted in the media or who have some decision-making responsibilities on a broad basis.

Despite their low circulations, these periodicals long have maintained devoted readership following. Dr. Theodore Peterson pointed out that they have "walked a lonely and precarious road in the 20th Century—lonely because their views were invariably the unpopular views of the minority, precarious because they were chronically in financial distress."[18] They cover a broad spectrum, including politics, social and political issues, economics, educational, racial, and others. They have on occasions represented movements in America, such as the muckrakers at the turn of the century as well as the Progressive trend. Today's periodicals had their forerunners in such magazines as *American Mercury, Forum, North American Review, Nineteenth Century, Contemporary Masses, Liberator, New Masses, Common Sense, Politics, Freeman, Arena, Independent, Outlook, Reporter,* and others. Many of these disappeared in mergers with other magazines. A few survived for a considerable time, including *North American Review,* which appeared for 115 years before it died in 1940. It never reached more than 76,000 circulation. A few were established by church groups, such as the Congregationalist-supported *Independent.* [19]

These are tenacious publications that survive to continue presenting their messages to limited segments of our culture. They are often moralistic and idealistic; they seek to bring changes in our relationship with each other and with other nations. In order to survive they have persuaded benefactors to donate to the "causes" and they have united in their production efforts. For example, the *New Republic* and the *National Review* joined in selling advertisements in 1969 although editorially they remain far apart.

Another group joined in seeking national ads, calling themselves "The Leadership Network." In 1980 this included the *World Press Review, New Republic, Commentary, Foreign Affairs, National Review, New York Review of Books, Columbia Journalism Review,* and *Technology Review.* A pot-pourri of varied interests, they are together only in their desire to survive in the competitive magazine marketplace.

These magazines provide material for discussion of the complexities of our present-day society. Since these themes are broad the readership varies from the extreme left to the extreme right. All readers have concern over the issues, but they differ on the means for solution. Topics cover taxation, social reform, immigration, civil rights, relations with other nations and especially with Russia, and special news events. Some of the magazines have developed strong departments covering fine arts, popular arts, literature and areas not fully analyzed in the more popular magazines. And, of course, presidential campaigns occupy considerable space, Often these publications offer readers more than *Time* or *Newsweek.* In 1925, for example, *Nation* printed the entire bill creating Great Britain's social insurance plan for Americans to study.

Nation

Founded in 1865, *Nation* today "sells on the basis of its writing, and the writing is super." [20] When it began, *Nation* devoted seven pages to the Negro enfranchisement question. Famous editors have included Edwin L. Godkin, William Phillips Garrison, Oswald Garrison Villard, and others. When this magazine of dissent and protest reached its 75th birthday, President Franklin D. Roosevelt wrote: "No one would ever accuse the *Nation* of seeking to become a popular organ." Losses for a 12-year period covering the 60s and 70s were reported at $1,500,000 by the *Wall Street Journal* on Dec. 27, 1977. At that time the magazine was acquired by a group of 20 investors, led by Hamilton Fish, a 26-year-old Harvard graduate. They paid $150,000 for the publication which had a circulation of 25,000. It had peaked at 40,000 in the early 40s. Writers for the *Nation* are devoted to their causes, since their pay remains quite low. The *Nation* has survived because benevolent philanthropists have backed it from the start. In 1980 the *Nation* assumed the 18,000 subscriptions of *Seven Days,* which folded after an erratic career.

New Republic

Herbert Croly for years edited the *New Republic,* a journal of opinion started in 1914 with a circulation of 875 and aided by millionaire Willard D. Straight and his family. H. L. Mencken called the early staffers ''kept idealists.'' Walter Lippmann was one of the pioneer editors and on the occasion of the magazine's 50th anniversary, noted that the *New Republic* was to become ''some kind of school, perhaps a university to be located in Washington and to be devoted to education for the public service . . . Our purpose was not partisan, factional, personal, or ideological; it was educational. And the attitude of this journal towards affairs was to be that of the scholar seeking the truth no matter whom it hurts or whom it helps.''[21]

The Washington column always has been signed TRB, representing the *B*rooklyn *R*apid *T*ransit spelled backward. It seems that when the staffers were taking the material to the printer they decided on the spur of the moment a ''signer'' was needed for this column and someone noted they were riding the BRT. Frank R. Kent and later Ken Crawford wrote TRB until 1943 when Richard Lee Strout took over. Briefly in the 40s Henry A. Wallace was editor of this liberal periodical.

New Republic has had several owners, including Gilbert A. Harrison in 1953. He later sold to Martin Peretz, a Harvard lecturer, who took over for $380,000. Peretz and Harrison were quoted in 1974 as saying, ''In a day when politics and culture have been debased and when 'news' is largely what the mass media say it is, we believe there is a special role for a journal which strives to be scrupulous with fact, independent of fashion, and attentive to the lessons of history.''[22]

National Review

To the far right of the *Nation* and the *New Republic* is the *National Review,* established in 1955 by William F. Buckley Jr. and his sister, Priscilla. Today one can hardly separate the magazine from Buckley, a millionaire Ivy Leaguer, columnist, commentator, and author of many books. While some individuals believe Buckley has failed to develop a genuine conservative philosophy no one disagrees that he has waged a continuous attack on the liberal line. On occasions Buckley may appear irreverent and he may not be fully comprehended, yet his sense of humor often is evident. When President Jack Kennedy waged his battle against poverty, Buckley suggested that the nation's leader declare the *National Review* a disaster area and appropriate anti-poverty funds for its survival. Buckley once remarked that ''the Catholic Church doesn't break even; neither does Harvard, or the Democratic Party. All of these eminently successful enterprises flourish despite huge annual deficits, which are made up only by the constant generosity of their supporters; yet no one expects any of them to vanish very soon."[23]

From a circulation of 100,000 for its 10th anniversary, *National Review* now has about 90,000. The magazine has been described as "always a balance of nicely aimed journalistic needling" by *Time* as it reflected on Buckley's "radical conservatism."[24]

The *National Review* celebrated its 25th anniversary with an enlarged edition on December 31, 1980, and a dinner for 600 persons at the Plaza Hotel in New York. Now "an Establishment organ," the *National Review* finds the political center of the country has merged with the magazine's philosophy.

Richard Nixon said "It is most appropriate and significant that *National Review* celebrate its 25th anniversary in the Reagan landslide year. You have my best wishes as you continue to be the voice of responsible conservatives in America."

Ronald Reagan was a speaker at *National Review*'s 20th anniversary banquet and told how he would "settle into my favorite chair, *National Review* in one hand, the dictionary in another" when each issue arrived. He also told that 1975 audience that by *National Review*'s 25th anniversary, he would be in the White House.

And Others Have Their Followings

Africa Reports provides Americans with stories of Africa, especially the lesser-known countries. Every two months it appeals to business leaders and academic leaders with its circulation of 10,500. This magazine has been published since 1956.

American, a pioneer with a 1909 start, probably belongs with religion publications. This Jesuit Catholic weekly is designed for conservatives and anti-Communists. Its articles are well researched.

The Columbia Journalism Review began at Columbia University in New York in 1961, with support from education foundations. It seeks to be a national monitor of media, although some educators feel it is too Eastern-oriented. As expected, many of the 35,000 subscribers are from the academic world. The magazine also publishes the regular reports of the National News Council.

Commentary is a monthly that provides a wide range of topics, with many departments. It began in 1945 and has a circulation of 50,000. From its surveys, *Commentary* notes that nearly 74 per cent of its readers have written elected officials about public business, indicating a concerned following. Articles seek to clarify major issues.

Commonweal, by Catholic laymen, began in 1924 and reaches some 20,000 readers bi-weekly. Obviously related to religion, *Commonweal* covers public affairs topics, such as political, social, and cultural. There are basic departments as well. Along with *America* it also can be classified among religion periodicals.

Conservative Digest clearly reveals itself through its title. Published since 1975 in Falls Church, Va., it exposes government actions that it often mentions in such departments as "Bureaucratic Blunders." Its 100,000 circulation in part reflects the nation's current conservative element. News personalities are interviewed to supplement coverage of major events.

Crisis is the official publication of the National Association for the Advancement of Colored People. Its circulation of nearly 120,000 reports on the problems, concerns, and achievements of the Black people. The monthly was 70 years old in 1980.

Foreign Affairs covers international affairs in many areas, such as social sciences, political and cultural. It began in 1922 and traditionally has maintained a high readership among the leaders in the governmental and academic worlds with its 77,000 circulation.

Human Events is a conservative weekly that focuses on both foreign and domestic topics. Since 1944 it has reported on governmental activities, with interest on Congress and the major Washington departments. Its circulation of 55,000 was down from the 1978 circulation of 67,000.

Progressive is a pioneer in this group, dating from 1909 in Madison, Wis. As the title indicates, it approaches domestic and foreign affairs from the progressive viewpoint. Its circulation of some 45,000 seems extremely small, yet for at least a brief moment it received national coverage over its proposal to print an article with instructions for making the H Bomb.

Washington Monthly may be included here as well as with the city and regional magazines. Founded in late 1979, the magazine has passed 39,000 circulation. It is designed for "well-educated people interested in politics and government" who are well read. Its circulation extends well beyond Washington. It offers readers an opportunity to learn more about who's who in the federal government and what they are doing, good or bad.

World Press Review, a monthly since 1974 and formerly called *Atlas,* regularly reviews more than a thousand foreign publications. It is a nonprofit educational and informational product of the Stanley Foundation. It covers all shades of opinions without bias.

MAGAZINES OF IDEAS

Harper's, Atlantic, and *Saturday Review* have been termed magazines of ideas, possessing a strong literary focus and air of urbanity. They have long histories of survival, outlasting many publications with much more circulation and greater advertising revenues.[25]

They have been credited with brilliant reportage, along with their advocacy of significant causes in American culture.

Harper's

In June 1850, *Harper's* magazine began, "as a tender to the business of Harper & Brothers and as an eclectic journal; let us say as a sort of *Reader's Digest* of its day." The four Harper brothers owned a major printing plant which produced some of the nation's most widely read books. They planned to include the works of many of the Victorian novelists in their new magazine, designed for literate American readers.

Harper's became an immediate success and within six months it reached a circulation of 50,000. Only Harper & Brothers ads were included in the early issues. Henry J. Raymond, founder of the *New York Times*, was an editor at the start; later Henry Mills Alden served for half a century, 1869–1919.

Many new magazines arrived to compete with *Harper's*, but few survived to the present. *Munsey's* and *McClure's* were better known to the masses, as were the more popular *Ladies' Home Journal* and *Saturday Evening Post*. There were also others, usually more sensational in their efforts to attract a larger viewing audience.

Harper's never sought the mass audience; it always sought the literate audience. It has remained a cultural and intellectual leader. The publication did change some under the editorship of Thomas B. Wells, who directed its focus "to thoughtful and discriminating people, of whatever income bracket, who appreciated fine quality, felt a deep sense of responsibility for the general national well-being, and possessed genuine intellectual curiosity."[26]

In 1941, Frederick Lewis Allen became its editor. Famous today for such books as *Only Yesterday* and *The Big Change*, Allen once told University of Missouri journalism students about his aims for *Harper's*. These were reprinted in the magazine's centennial number in June 1950 and they remain as appropriate for *Harper's* as they did when first discussed.

1. The magazine must be interesting—interesting enough, at least, to hold its subscribers and newsstand buyers and find new ones.
2. A monthly magazine should provide news, in the widest sense—more selective, more considered, and more concentratedly illuminating than the newspaper or even the news weekly can ordinarily provide.
3. It should provide interpretation and discussion of the important issues before the public.
4. The magazine should provide a platform for original and inventive thinkers, for voices crying in the wilderness, for really creative ideas wherever they may be found.
5. The magazine should provide a vehicle for the artist in literature—in fiction, in poetry, in the essay, in whatever form he may invent, within the limits of space available.

Such aims are difficult to achieve. The times can create difficulties, such as the Civil War. The Harper men were Democrats who wanted their magazine to remain nonpartisan. Yet they lost many readers in the South during the war. After this war, they were able to print the works of more American writers, such as Carl Schurz, James Thurber, Walt Whitman, Katherine Anne Porter, and others, indicating the variety of their readers' interests.

John Fischer succeeded Allen in 1953 and in 1967 Willie Morris took over, with an expressed desire "to see *Harper's* create a broader appeal, especially to youth. The idea is to be relevant, and we fully intend to be that."[27] Morris lasted for less than four years, his departure precipitated in part by his conflict with the owners, The Star and Tribune Co. led by John Cowles, Jr., and in part by his printing of a lengthy article by Norman Mailer, "The Prisoner of Sex," which took all of the March, 1971, issue. Mailer peppered his article with obscenities, in offering his sweeping counter-argument to women's liberation movements and to Kate Millett in particular.

Morris also printed articles by William Styron, Arthur Miller, J. Kenneth Galbraith, and others. David Halberstam said Morris "took a musty, dying magazine and made it brilliant and unpredictable."[28]

In mid-1980, the media world was saying "Farewell to *Harper's*", then in its 130th year. Its expected death was blamed on low subscription income as well as the usual increase in operating costs. In addition, the magazine's revolving readership failed to provide the sturdy base it had maintained in earlier decades. Two editors, with different goals, had followed Morris: Robert Shnayerson, a former *Time* editor, and Lewis H. Lapham, a former newspaperman from California.[29]

But just as the death bells were tolling, *Harper's* received a new lease on life, saved by support from the MacArthur and the Atlantic Richfield Foundations. What's ahead remains to be seen, of course, but if it can retain at least 200,000 literate readers, its long and exciting career can move ahead to its second century of service. Robert Taylor, writing for the Field News Service, thought *Harper's* projected death was due to "the galloping illiteracy of the American public. The magazine perished most grievously because people don't like to make the minimal effort required to read a magazine."[30] If Robert Taylor is correct in this analysis, *Harper's* has a challenging time ahead.

Atlantic

Seven years after the birth of *Harper's*, the *Atlantic* monthly arrived in Boston to help the anti-slavery cause and eventually to carry the literary works of such writers as Longfellow, Holmes, Hawthorne, Thoreau, Lowell, Whittier, Stowe, and many others among the greats in American literature. For $4 Julia Ward Howe sold her poem, the "Battle Hymn of the Republic," to *Atlantic*, where it first appeared in February, 1862. Others also arrived during the magazine's pioneer days, including "Paul Revere's Ride" and "The Man Without a Country."

James Russell Lowell started the *Atlantic* in 1857, a publication devoted to literature, art and politics. Among the other editors have been William Dean Howells, Bliss Perry, Ellery Sedgwick, Edward A. Weeks, Jr., who served 28 years before being succeeded by Robert Manning in 1966.

Manning made the *Atlantic* "more aggressive, topical and visually pleasing," while broadening its political coverage. And "it remains the foremost showcase for serious fiction and poetry in the U.S." Under Manning the magazine has become "less genteel and more aggressive" as the editor "moved *Atlantic* right out of Oliver Wendell Holmes into the 20th Century," according to *Time*.[31]

A Boston real estate tycoon, Mortimer Zuckerman, acquired the magazine in early 1980, after it had been in the Marion Danielsen Campbell family since 1938.[32] For some time *Harper's* and *Atlantic* have shared the same business offices, seeking advertisements for both at reduced rates. Whether the editorial operations of these oldtimers on the American scene will ever be combined depends at least in part how well they will be able to find sufficient literate readers and at the same time sufficient backing from those interested enough to cover any debts.

Saturday Review

The *Saturday Review* and Norman Cousins have been one and the same for so long it is impossible to discuss the magazine without equal attention to its longtime editor. Cousins joined the magazine in 1940, after earlier work on *Current History* and the *New York Evening Post*. The magazine had a circulation of 20,000 when he started, some 600,000 three decades later.

When the magazine first appeared in 1924 it included "of Literature" in its title to distinguish it from a famous English periodical. In 1952 the two words were dropped. Originally the magazine was a supplement, called *The Literary Review*, in the *New York Evening Post* from 1920 to 1924. When the *Post* was sold the supplement was stopped. Henry Canby, a Yale professor, and others acquired it and started the *Saturday Review*. Canby shaped the polcies until Bernard DeVoto took over 12 years later. In these early years, the magazine was noted for its book reviews and discussions about the literary scene. During its first two decades it was estimated that the *Saturday Review* lost a million dollars, made up by such men as Thomas Lamont; Harry Scherman, founder of the Book-of-the-Month Club; and Everette Lee De Golyer, a Texas oil man who turned over his ownership to Cousins shortly before his death in 1956.[33]

Cousins joined *Saturday Review* in 1940 at a time when America was changing from its role of isolationism to one of world leadership. His initial editorial was a plea for more ice storms, noting that it was "too bad there can't be one great big ice storm all over—over those battlefields in Europe especially. Because when men have to fight to keep alive against the cold, they stop thinking about fighting other men . . . we lose electricity, we can't listen to the radio . . . go to movies . . . so we have to sit around a fire and swap ideas.''[34]

Contributors have come from a varied lot, from Fulton Sheen to Goodman Ace, from Leon Trotsky to John Ciardi, from H. L. Mencken to William Rose Benet, who wrote ''The Phoenix Nest'' for years.

In 1961 the McCall Corporation acquired *Saturday Review*. This firm was later bought by Norton Simon, Inc. For a brief time, Cousins shifted to *McCall's* magazine but returned to *Saturday Review* in 1968. Later he attempted to buy the magazine but lost in the bidding to two young entrepreneurs, Nicholas H. Charney and John J. Veronis, who had founded the successful *Psychology Today*. These two changed the magazine drastically; in fact, some persons feel they wrecked it, because longtime readers weren't prepared for such sudden changes.

Charney and Veronis took the major *Saturday Review* units and made them into weekly editions in 1972. Rather than subscribe to the weekly *Saturday Review,* one could subscribe to any or all of four new monthlies—Education, Science, Arts, and Society. Not only were readers confused, but potential advertisers were as well. Shortly after these changes, Cousins was out and Charney became the editor. Later Cousins established his own magazine, the *World*. By 1973 the *SR* experiment had failed and *Saturday Review/World* appeared. *Saturday Review* had filed for bankruptcy. The young publishers failed to convince readers or advertisers that their experiment was practical.[35]

Saturday Review acquired a new owner, Robert I. Weingarten. He, along with Al Kingon as editor-in-chief and Carll Tucker as editor, have redirected this famous publication, with improved graphics and a broader coverage. Meanwhile, in 1978 Norman Cousins moved to Los Angeles to start a teaching career at the University of California in Los Angeles in the humanities. His courses are directed to medical students.

Meanwhile, Weingarten reported that *Saturday Review* had become profitable in late 1980, while maintaining a circulation in excess of 500,000.

New Times

Another fascinating publication which disappeared after about six years is the *New Times*. Started in October, 1973, *New Times* featured a story by Joe McGinniss, author of *The Selling of the President 1968,* about Watergate. The author wrote, ''There are a lot more things we have to look into.'' George A. Hirsch, publisher, ran satire and features for a 60 per cent-male dominated, age 30 audience. The bi-weekly often stirred up debates, such as an article in the Feb. 6, 1978 issue that claimed some magazines gave celebrities editorial control over articles about them.[36]

Less than a year before its death, *New Times* was sold to MCA Inc. However, the magazine lost readers to *People,* with its emphasis on celebrities, and to *Time* and *Newsweek,* which began to cover more of the stars formerly featured in *New Times*.

Hirsch's "End of a Dream" came with the Jan. 8, 1978, issue, and his comments remain appropriate for the magazine industry:

> The name of the publishing game is the economics of circulation. To meet the skyrocking costs of putting out a magazine, all publishers recently (1978) have been forced to raise subscription prices . . .

Editor Jonathan Z. Larsen added:

> From the beginning it was our hope that there was a place out there for a medium-sized magazine that did not have to be sold on the basis of celebrities, sex, or "service journalism," but rather on the strength of solid reporting by the best writers we could find . . .

William Safire once wrote that *New Times* had "an adversary relationship to the world" as it published issue-oriented, hard-news orientated articles, the result of investigative reporting.

Apparently Bob Greene summed up the problem well, in a comment that still is appropriate for some magazines that have similar experiences. "It just had the misfortune of coming along during the wrong decade . . . Unfortunately, the magazine-reading public was growing tired of long stories about subjects that were sometimes complicated."

New Times had a circulation of 356,000 at the time of its demise, after publishing 138 issues. It broke a number of major stories, including interviews with Bill and Emily Harris during the Patty Hearst trial, and the racial slurs voiced by then Secretary of Agriculture Earl Butz, which brought about the end of his government service.[37]

Mother Jones

Named for a self-proclaimed "hell raiser," *Mother Jones* magazine was founded in 1976. Today its circulation exceeds 220,000. Mary Harris "Mother" Jones (1830–1930) was a socialist, an individualist, a pioneer union organizer who sought prison reform and improved working conditions even if strikes were necessary.

Mother Jones follows such magazines as *Ramparts, Rolling Stone, New Times, Politicks,* and *Seven Days*—periodicals that covered the business, political and economic scene in what some observers labeled a "radical matter." Three former editors of *Ramparts* were responsible for the founding of *Mother Jones,* which today is published by the Foundation for National Progress, a non-profit group in San Francisco.

In raising the question, "Would Mother Jones buy '*Mother Jones*'?" Michael Scully observed:

> The real success of *Mother Jones* is that it has managed within its pages a tentative reunion of most of these divergent sects, which in fact have little more in common than the dissatisfaction of their members—some with technology, some with mixed-capitalism, some with the tedium of representative government, some with their parents or themselves . . .

Mother Jones magazine . . . is unmistakably antimodern, although, as does so much of what was once called the counterculture, it divides on the manner of its opposition to modernity. That is part of its appeal. And it is community, the longing for which shapes the counterculture's complaint against modernity, which illustrates the radical left's split personality.[38]

Mother Jones calls on readers to "meet the magazine that's won a dozen major journalism awards in three years—and pick up some bright, bold ideas on how to live the Eighties." Onetime publisher Mark Dowie claims *Mother Jones* "is to stalk stories likely to boil the blood of the corporate world, which it considers the hidden government of the country." It also has been labeled the "reverse *Fortune.*" It claims to be "creating a blurred vision of a better world." But the magazine has eye-opening covers, excellent graphics, and spirited writing. The staff operates in a semi-collective fashion, although it has changed from its original concept of equal pay for all workers. Operating on revenues of $2.5 million, *Mother Jones* often has been in the red. The magazine has attacked the Pinto car, corporate malpractice, smoking, and other topics. The average reader is 32 with a household income of $23,300, who apparently finds the wide range of subjects to his liking.[39]

4

Business Press:
General and Specialized

SINCE THE FOUNDING of America interest in business has been a fascinating topic for many individuals. Early cities, established along the coasts and near rivers to utilize the maximum benefits for commerce, utilized "prices current" publications to satisfy the need for information. Many early newspapers also carried news about the arrival of ships with their goods for sale as well as other items concerning business opportunities.

Under this title of general business such publications as *Barron's, Dun's Review, Forbes, Fortune, Business Week, Nation's Business, Money, Changing Times, Inc.* and others will be reviewed. Primarily these are designed for the general commercial interests, as well as some consumer audiences, in contrast to the more specialized publications prepared for limited groups with narrow interests.

Among the least understood medium in the magazine market is that "other" business press. There is, in fact, some disagreement as to its most appropriate title: industrial, technical, trade or scientific information industry. Most agree that these magazines, and in many instances allied newspapers, directories and catalogs, are designed more for professionals to provide and interpret essential business information. Entertainment is not their major objective as it is with newspapers and many consumer periodicals.

Walter E. Botthof, at one time publisher of Standard Rate & Data Service, Inc., defined the characteristics and function of the business press by dividing the publications into these major categories:

> Technical, industrial, professional, business news, institutional, and merchandising. The technical or industrial publications were edited for people in

business, industry, the sciences and the professions. The professional publications were for physicians, surgeons, lawyers, architects, scientists, sales and advertising people and others. Institutional publications were for those employed in hotels, hospitals, schools, colleges, clubs, restaurants, prisons, and others. Business news publications were designed to give news and its interpretation to administrative and managerial executives. Merchandising, or so-called trade papers, were for dealers, jobbers, wholesalers and their supervisory staffs and others.[1]

An additional explanation of this area of the business press was provided by The American Business Press, Inc., in a special *New York Times* supplement of March 19, 1967, in which the group noted:

> The major difference between these publications and the ones you read is that our advertising and editorial pages are concerned not only with an end product but with the myriad of industrial and business activities that make the end product possible. And make it possible for you to buy it whatever it might be—house, automobile, soup, refrigerator, furniture, clothing, a quart of ice cream, a set of golf clubs . . .

While there are only a limited number of general business publications, there are ABP estimates of 2,500 of the latter periodicals, with other estimates as high as 3,500. Some obviously are excellent publications while others may not be worth the paper they are printed on.

"Business publishing today is the strongest it's been in our hundred years in the business and it is getting stronger," according to Chilton president, William A. Barbour. This comes in part from the information explosion, highlighted by tremendous advances in technology. Barbour noted that every single month 100,000 new technical papers are published. No wonder these publishers are bullish about their future. Whether "the business magazine of the future will be an electronic medium, it will be business information the businessman *must* have to do his job," according to Chilton vice-president Donald W. Altmaier.[2]

When James L. C. Ford wrote his book, *Magazines for the Millions,* he too observed the problems of identification. He thought industrial publications covered manufacture and marketing and the intricate complex of technological activity. They include the journals of news and comment and opinion which represent the industrial community. Also called trade and business publications, the industrials are of three main types—manufacturing, merchandising, and trade association.[3]

In today's society there is a continuous need for business communication which places a heavy burden on these publishers. The potential market for the consumer-type business magazines, such as *Changing Times* and *Money,* continues to expand. And obviously the complex business world would encounter difficulties operating without the information supplied by the more specialized magazines. Businessmen must know what is happening in the markets, what their competitors are doing, and what the government requires of them. Individuals, too, are wondering what the government requires of them, what changes are occurring in the financial world, and where best to place any extra funds. This expanding interest in the business world has been demonstrated by the rapid growth of the *Wall Street Journal,* with its nationwide circulation nearing 2,000,000. Many of these readers turn to business magazines for additional information.

This, of course, is not a new trend in America. Since the 1750s, American merchants have depended on such publications. There were some 15 "prices current" publications in New York, Philadelphia, Boston, and Baltimore. After the turn of that century more specialized magazines appeared, such as the *Butchers' and Packers' Gazette* in 1808, *American Journal of Pharmacy* in 1825, and *American Railroad Journal* in 1832.[4]

Iron Age Excellent Example

No single publisher can dominate today's business press because of its variety and magnitude. It has become specialized to the point that there is specialization within specialization. Many of the magazines are family owned; many are closed corporations that specialize in a limited area; and a few are more than a century old. Most, however, have been founded since the end of World War II.

Another approach to the study of the business press is to recall that "most publishers are intimately connected with the industry they serve and it is their special talents in and knowledge of these industries that make their communication forms marketable," according to G. Renfrew Brighton, chairman of Business Journals, Inc.[5]

A good example of Brighton's views is the *Iron Age.* John Williams came to the United States from Ireland in the mid-1850s. He was a hardware man, yet when he reached Middletown, N. Y., he could learn little about the hardware business there. So in 1855 he founded *The Hardwareman's Newspaper.* Renamed the *Iron Age* in 1859, this magazine has become the "unifying force for this vast and diverse industry that is nonetheless linked by a common bond of materials, processes, equipment and technology," according to Chilton executive William A. Barbour. Chilton now publishes *Iron Age,* which has through the years become more and more valuable to the industry, with more editorial research directed to managers with influence. A winner of numerous awards, *Iron Age* "has demonstrated that great institutions can endure and prosper if they continue to fulfill the changing needs of the public they serve," Barbour added.

What *Folio* magazine did for consumer magazines, *ADWEEK* magazine performed in part for the business press in a special report in late 1979. Discussing "The Survival Medium," *ADWEEK* editor Lawrence Bernard wrote:

> Perhaps the most remarkable fact about the business press is that there is so much of it. There's virtually no legitimate business or profession that does

Business Publications, Ad Pages, Dollars, Circulation

Year	Number of Publications	Ad Pages	Ad Dollars	Distribution
1962	2435	1,125,000	$ 535,600,000	51,720,838
1963	2496	1,160,000	593,700,000	55,035,278
1964	2559	1,165,000	634,200,000	56,230,113
1965	2548	1,205,000	682,400,000	60,000,640
1966	2395	1,254,000	735,300,000	61,306,151
1967	2316	1,219,000	760,000,000	56,900,000
1968	2335	1,201,000	781,300,000	57,003,530
1969	2402	1,231,794	849,900,000	63,603,915
1970	2376	1,093,311	836,100,000	62,334,708
1971	2335	1,023,563	813,800,000	62,464,266
1972	2381	1,083,080	882,100,000	63,181,894
1973	2380	1,133,742	978,900,000	64,927,312
1974	2356	1,175,740	1,024,400,000	64,451,369
1975	3163	1,150,000	1,075,000,000	65,500,000
1976	3246	1,261,550	1,300,000,000	65,700,000
1977	3252	1,371,300	1,400,000,000	66,000,000
1978	3359	1,500,000	1,500,000,000	68,000,000
1979	3474	(not available)	(not available)	(not available)
1980	(not available)	1,950,000	1,975,000,000	71,000,000

Source: American Business Press. No. of publications in 1975–79 from SRDS.

not have its business paper. From airlines, air conditioning installers, and anaesthesiologists, to wood workers, wire buyers, and zip code users, there is at least one publication serving those interests.

Bernard's survey noted the growth in business publications since 1962, based on the chart published above. He also noted the "information and technical explosions (that) make business magazines more vital than ever" but warned about the conflict between "class vs. trash" periodicals. This study, more concerned with the advertisements, noted that "specialized trade publications are efficient in reaching what they term 'vertical' markets—clearly defined industrial sectors that have been targets for campaigns aimed at generating sales." However, these magazines must also compete with consumer magazines "when top management becomes the target."[6]

ADWEEK's roundtable discussion about the business press in the 1980s involved John K. Abely, president, Technical Publishing Co.; William A. Barbour, president, Chilton Co.; Charles P. Daly, group executive, Litton Publishing Inc.; Sal F. Marino, president, Penton/IPC Inc.; Paul F. McPherson, president, McGraw-Hill Business Press, Inc. Bernard, the moderator, covered the comments in his magazine's special section. Among the predictions and warnings by the panelists:

A future continuation of a scientific approach is expected to evaluate what the market needs and what the business press is giving in terms of content and how well it's being delivered.

The business press has come of age, because people find a continuing need to upgrade their know-how and skills. Thus readership studies must be continuous.

More than two-thirds of the ads in the 1,500,000 pages per year are in color. With a more critical audience, advertising agencies must produce a better product for these publications.

Is a reader looking for a magazine, or is a magazine looking for a reader? That guideline will direct many publishers as they turn to new magazines. Yet ABP president Mill calls for the elimination of 50 per cent of the business papers "because we wouldn't miss them."

Tax laws will continue to move some smaller companies, especially those still family-owned, into the larger public-owned corporations. However, an independent publisher will have a better chance to succeed in the magazine world than in the newspaper world because of less start-up expense.

With more limited circulation than many consumer magazines, the business press must remain dependent upon the Postal Service. Thus higher mailing costs will continue as a major factor as will paper, printing, and other expenses.

Business magazine publishers will continue to be involved in related business, such as book publishing, seminars, conferences, direct mail, and related areas.

"We have an orderly business. We know what our product is. We know what an advertising page is worth. We set the price for that page and we charge that price to all comers," concluded Paul McPherson of McGraw-Hill.

It comes as no surprise to learn that as the 80s opened the business press reported that both readership and profits were up and "a mood of acquisition and diversification prevailed among the publishing bastions."[7]

THE GENERAL PUBLICATIONS

There are a few weekly and monthly periodicals addressed to a wider audience than the specialized trade magazines. They have gained in circulation and advertising revenues from their leadership in broader areas. Three have observed their 50th anniversaries in recent years, attesting to their popularity and continued success.

Forbes

A pioneer magazine is *Forbes,* started on September 15, 1917, by Bertie Charles Forbes. Born in Scotland in 1880, Forbes left school when he was 14 to become a printer's devil for 75¢ a week. Two years later he became a reporter in Aberdeen and later an understudy to Edgar Wallace, mystery writer. Forbes came to America and eventually was Hearst's business and financial editor on the *New York American,* where he established his name in the business world through a daily column which eventually was syndicated.

On its 50th anniversary, the magazine recalled how Forbes capitalized on his reputation, preferring the title *Forbes* rather than his initial choice, *Doers and Doings.* To reach business leaders, Forbes rented a room at the old Waldorf Hotel, which provided an opportunity to mingle with the "great men" in their own surroundings. He interviewed many of the nation's leaders, including John D. Rockefeller and Frank Woolworth; J. P Morgan, however, had Forbes thrown out of his office. Then it was not uncommon for business leaders to seek anonymity.

Early issues of *Forbes* would be termed "corny" by today's standards, yet Forbes was critical of a businessman who would "grind employees and then donate a million dollars to perpetuate his name." He urged business leaders to provide more employee benefits, such as group insurance, at a time when this was not considered necessary.

Before he died in 1954, Forbes had acquired competition from *Dun's Review,* which had grown stronger since its start in 1893; *Barron's,* 1921; *Business Week,* 1929; and *Fortune,* 1930. It was difficult for these to maintain publication during the Depression, when ad pages and circulation declined.

Bruce Charles Forbes, the founder's oldest son, took over in 1954, with B.C.'s second son, Malcolm Stevenson, editor-in-chief and publisher. Bruce died in 1964 when only 48.

"While *Forbes* has always believed in business, it has never believed that business was perfect," the magazine noted. The family control continues, with estimates of profits in excess of $10 million annually. The founder's belief that "Business was originated to produce happiness, not pile up millions" has been continued by Malcolm Forbes, termed "The Happiest Millionaire." Interviewed by *Playboy,* he was described as having a versatile personality, a man with great interests in such diverse areas as ballooning and motorcycling. He spent in excess of a million dollars planning a balloon flight across the Atlantic, which was aborted by a last-minute failure in ground equipment.

For its 60th anniversary edition, September 15, 1977, *Forbes* recalled American business highlights in words and pictures. It maintains its place in the competitive race with *Fortune, Business Week,* and the others and continues to publish inspirational stories, short and to-the-point articles about company trends and actions, items of interest to investors, and "Thoughts." In late 1979, *Forbes* published its 5th annual Arabic issue, entirely in Arabic to inform the Arab world about American business activities.[8]

As the 80s got underway, *Forbes* and *Fortune* were head-to-head in their circulation battle, with *Forbes* claiming 680,000 and *Fortune* 670,000. For the five-year period, 1975–1979, *Forbes* led in total advertising pages.

Fortune

Another successful business/finance magazine is *Fortune,* founded during the most unlikely period, the Depression. Its $1 price was also entirely unreasonable while Americans were unemployed and were wondering about their next meal. *Fortune*'s large size, 11¼ x 14 or the dimension of a briefcase, and its luxury format appeared irrational for 1930. It was so big, with its 110 pages of ads and two pounds of quality paper, that it had to be gathered and sewn by hand. The *New York Times* called it "sumptuous to the point of rivaling the pearly gates." Others too were overwhelmed with this unusual magazine.

Henry Luce created *Fortune* after recognizing the interest displayed in *Time*'s business news. As John Tebbel wrote, "Luce saw clearly that business was the preoccupation of a great many people, but cannily he chose the upper managerial level as the one audience that had not yet been exploited by publishers."[9] Upon this premise, "*Fortune* became one of the miracles of publishing history," a valuable source of information. In reviewing the 50th anniversary issue, *Advertising Age* columnist James Brady referred to "a glossy magazine, devoted exclusively to that dreariest of subjects, Business . . ." Brady believes, as do others, that Luce's selection of this title aided tremendously in the magazine's initial success.[10] Robert T. Elson's history of Time Inc. notes the venture was carefully researched, both editorially and business-wise. A dummy issue was produced in August 1929 just before the Big Crash.

Staying with Luce's apparent design for brief titles not only for his magazine but for the articles and departments, the first issue offered stories on Hogs, Freezing, Banks, Islands, Glass, James, Biltmore, Portfolio, R.C.S., Color, Orchids, Orient, and Rothschilds, and Off the Record, Statistics, Transactions, Markets, and Face. Artist Thomas M. Cleland designed this cover, showing the wheel of fortune in an elaborate setting. The cover required partial printing in one Brooklyn plant, while the gravure forms were printed in New Jersey. It was not until 1932 that the magazine was produced in a single plant.

Margaret Bourke-White, then an unknown photographer but destined to become one of the nation's best, presented a portfolio of pictures about iron, steel, coal and ships in her account of trade routes across the Great Lakes. She made "art out of industry." She related in her autobiography, *Portrait of Myself,* that Luce told her "The camera should explore every corner of industry, showing everything, from the steam shovel to the board of directors. The camera would act as interpreter, recording what modern industrial civilization is, how it looks, how it meshes . . ."[11]

The magazine's purpose was "to reflect industrial life in ink and paper and word and picture as the finest skyscraper reflects it in stone and steel and architecture." *Fortune* would "peer into dazzling furnaces, and into the faces of bankers" and would follow "the chemist to the brink of worlds newer than Columbus found." It would "inquire with unbridled curiosity" and would "make its discoveries clear, coherent, vivid, so that the reading of it may be one of the keenest pleasures in the life of every subscriber."

In-depth reporting has characterized *Fortune* from its start. For example, some 15 pages in the third issue were devoted to the Cornelius Vanderbilt family. Upper-class personal habits were covered so readers could reflect upon the good times before the Depression. Among the early writers were Archibald

MacLeish, Russell Davenport, Dwight Macdonald, Edward E. Kennedy, and others. The advertisements, too, reflected only the best, "the afterglow of a great age of prosperity." For more than a decade a Packard ad appeared opposite the table of contents.

Changes have occurred as the magazine keeps in harmony with the changing world. An economic forecast business roundup appeared in 1948. The famous 500 list of the largest corporations first appeared in 1955 and a decade later a similar list of the largest firms outside the United States was presented. Industrial surveys began in 1967, and in 1972 the size was cut and a graphic face lift undertaken.

In January, 1978, *Fortune* changed from a monthly to a fortnightly. "There's more than this new about the new *Fortune* than its frequency. Fewer and larger photos, the absence of ad bank, a new body type and a sprinkling of shorter stories 'open the book,' thus quickening the pace for editorial scoop possibilities and allowing for advertising flexibility and ad concentration in peak periods," said ad director Jim Hoefer.[12]

Luce's "improbable dream" celebrated its 50th year with an anniversary edition Feb. 11, 1980. A phenomenal half century was recalled with articles from earlier issues. Managing editor Robert Lubar reflected on this era, which "contained the worst depression, a war bloodier and more far reaching in its consequences than any previously fought, man's first voyages to the moon, the dawning of the nuclear age and the computer age, and the evolution of the modern corporation." *Advertising Age* columnist Brady concluded that "there is a heft and a feel and a sleek comfort to the contemporary *Fortune* which seems to be saying that however chaotic the world seems, from that wretched bridge at Chappaquiddick to these self-flagellating vagabonds squatting in our embassy, there remains at least here, in its glossy pages, a solidity and a focus."[13]

Today *Fortune* claims to be the pioneer it has always been with its interest in the *literature* of business and it remains "the world's standard of what a business magazine should be." It continues to reflect Luce's early concern for the complete story. For example, in a 1978 story about Boeing, the photographer shot 1,116 pictures—the magazine used five. And 600 staff hours were required by the reporters and researchers to put the story together. Luce would be pleased with today's *Fortune* and such accounts as the 50 "private rich" Americans who have made their fortunes in private corporations.

Business Week

McGraw-Hill Publications' flagship, *Business Week,* noted in its 50th anniversary edition Sept. 3, 1979, that it was "aging beautifully."[14] This 200-page edition offered information about the past, present, and future of the business world. Started a month before the big stock market crash, *Business Week* warned in 1929 that "Stock prices are generally out of line with safe earnings expectations, and the market is now almost wholly psychological—irregular, unsteady and properly apprehensive of the inevitable adjustment that draws near.''

Business Week has never been ''content to be a mere chronicle of events. It aims always to interpret their significance.'' Editor-in-chief Lewis H. Young claimed it was ''not our function to review the business news'' but ''to anticipate what's going to happen.'' The company wants stories that anticipate the news, provide insight, and analyze trends. Designed to reach readers on Friday, the circulation goes primarily to management personnel.

Looking ahead into the 80s, Publisher Rowland Bernard Alexander said, ''I think, in general, the business publication field is healthy. We want to continue to share in the growth of the category, and get in on our fair share. Well, maybe a little more than our share.''[15] He looked forward to ad revenues of $150 million in 1982.

In reflecting on its first half-century, the magazine noted that: ''Just as 1929 was a watershed year, 1979 is one of transition. By 2029 people will have recognized that today marks the end of the industrial society as we have defined it.'' The challenge for the next half century would be to ''devise a way for government to fight inflation while creating a stable environment in which individuals can express themselves, achieve their aspirations and enjoy the fruits of new technology.'' In the future, communications and information processing technology will become a ''super-industry.''

Nation's Business

''Edited for those in business, industry, and national affairs, *Nation's Business* covers economic trends, government actions, international developments and legislative issues.'' As the spokesman for the United States Chamber of Commerce, *Nation's Business* appropriately is edited in Washington. It is designed for top management—the presidents, board chairmen, and the chief operating officers of the nation's business corporations.

Established in 1912 as a newspaper, *Nation's Business* adopted its magazine format four years later. Some individuals believe that the success of this magazine helped to inspire the founding of *Fortune*. Analytical, with in-depth, substantive articles, the magazine extends the reach of the Chamber of Commerce's goals and objectives. The organization also uses newsletters, speakers, and research to supplement these goals. *Nation's Business* does not appear on newsstands. Subscriptions are tied in with a complicated dues system operated by the Chamber. Today, its circulation base is 1,265,000, an all-time high, and climbing, reflecting the nation's concern about the business arena.

In mid-1979, the Chamber established a weekly tabloid, *Washington Report*. It is an advocate newspaper exclusively reporting and analyzing governmental activities and their impact on business. Speaking out for business, *Washington Report* appears on Monday. Its initial 350,000 circulation doubled by the end of its first year.

Dun's Review

Established in 1893 and owned by Dun & Bradstreet, *Dun's Review* is a controlled circulation magazine, termed the "Patriarch of the general business magazines."

In its own advertisements, *Dun's Review* explained its limited appeal, calling itself "The magazine for corporate Top Honchos," those persons who are chairmen, presidents or senior executives of the 50,743 United States companies with a net worth of a million dollars or more. This limits its appeal to the top one per cent of the nation's companies. Thus the readership of *Dun's Review* will include many millionaires.

Dun's Review appears to be more akin to *Nation's Business* than to others in this group. In its publisher's statement it claims to present the trends and studies of "corporate performance; government vs. business; stockholder relations; foreign markets; tax matters; economic forecasting; executive compensation; corporate takeovers; finance and investments; marketing; the nation's economy; corporate ethics; executive development and corporate communications."

Barron's

The weekly Dow Jones publication, *Barron's,* also is called the national business and financial weekly in its subtitle. According to one report it was established in 1909, yet another says 1921. Ayer Directory and SRDA agree on the 1921 date. This weekly tabloid has more of a limited audience than *Dun's Review.*

According to its publisher's goals, *Barron's* contains industry-wide studies and individual company analyses, edited for private investors, professional money managers and corporate executives. Commodities and options are discussed along with performance records of securities. Economic indicators are provided but "no personal writeups or investment advice is given."

Money

Money, devoted to enlarging the readers' share of responsibility and enjoyment, made its debut in October, 1972, at $1.50 per copy. Coming from Time Inc., *Money* was designed to report about "the kind of people whose lives and activities elude conventional definitions of news."

Each month *Money* reviews finances of one family, or an individual, noting income and expense items, and then summarizing through a review of the overall picture by a panel of investment experts. As *Money* claims, "unlike other financial magazines that advise a young executive what to do with his company's money, we tell him what to do with *his* money."

The initial issue, for example, discussed prescription drugs and price variations, property syndicates, working wives, borrowing techniques, car insurance, travel, and other topics designed for its younger audience. The majority of the readers are college educated, working in professional and managerial areas. With the nation's readers so concerned over today's economic picture, it is logical to expect continued growth for *Money*.

Inc.

The nation's smaller companies now have their own business publication. *Inc.* was started in April, 1979, with a non-paid circulation of more than 400,000, making it the fourth largest business magazine in America. Later it switched to paid and non-paid circulation, with 220,000 paid and 180,000 non-paid on a controlled basis. It "doesn't talk to the top executives of America's biggest businesses" but to those in smaller firms.[16]

Publisher Bernard A. Goldhirsh wrote in *Inc.'s* second issue that "smaller companies account for half of all innovation in this country. And they are much more efficient at it than big companies, generating 24 times as many innovations per R&D dollar spent." He added: "It is becoming clear to the nation that when smaller companies are allowed to function at their best, innovation will increase and society as a whole will benefit."

Among the magazine's goals are profiles about smaller firms on their way up, how they overcame growing pains and weaknesses in management, as well as problems in developing adequate capital. Stories concern management theory, with case histories. Its audience obviously will be similar to those of *Forbes, Fortune, Nation's Business* and others except for the financial base of their businesses. They include the "risk-takers, the innovaters, the builders, the independent-minded who enthusiastically accept the challenges that most prefer to let pass by." A comprehensive and lively journalistic approach is another goal for *Inc.* Early research revealed there were slightly more than 100,000 companies in the potential audience, firms with sales volumes between $1 million and $25 million. Other estimates place the total at 250,000 companies, representing about 32 per cent of the Gross National Product.

More traditional topics are covered in departments such as Financial Management, Personnel Management, Marketing, Sales, Administration, and Operations. It is published by the United Marine Publishing, Inc., in Boston, a firm that also issues *Sail, Motorboat, Marine Business* and related directories. United invested $2 million for pre-publication expenses. *Inc.* acquired *Successful Business* from the 13-30 Corporation.

Changing Times

"*Changing Times* Changes Look" informed the magazine world in 1980 that this 33-year-old publication would for the first time accept advertisements. Publisher Austin Kiplinger said the "unavoidable conclusion was that costs were going to rise faster than our revenues. The choice was running out of steam, turning it over to someone else, or investigating the possibility of accepting advertising." After advertisements began appearing only 129 angry subscribers cancelled their subscriptions. Looking ahead to a more demanding public in the 1980s, *Changing Times* will seek to better educate its readers.

Founded in 1947 to "supply a panorama of business-oriented articles for businessmen," *Changing Times* has in recent years sought to "provide practical information on how to live better. Subject matter covers investments, insurance, education, home ownership, recreation, taxes, social security, automobiles, health, and planning a career. Regular editorial departments include features about jobs, recreation, books, home maintainence, things to live for and answers to readers' questions." [17] Circulation of *Changing Times* passed 1,350,000 copies in mid-1981.

In commenting on the changeover from an adless publication, editor Sidney Sulkin said ads would permit as much as 40 per cent more editorial content. To carry on the varied content of *Changing Times,* Sulkin noted that future articles would include such as "How exercise can do you wrong. New kinds of mutual funds. A careful look at what's ahead for the housing market. Life insurance for the first-time buyer. Dreamy vacations you can afford. Oh yes, more tax tips." In other words, the magazine will continue to help the businessmen and individuals to manage their own affairs better.

Advertising Age columnist James Brady wrote that "it is generally accepted that with *Fortune* magazine Henry Luce brought sophistication and considerable style to what had been, until then, a relatively-undistinguished sort of Journalism."

> *Fortune* seemed to be saying that business news stories or profiles of business companies or leaders did not have to be dull or dreary in order to be considered responsible. They could, in fact, afford to be readable.
>
> In the years since, *Business Week* under Lew Young, the *Wall Street Journal* of Barney Kilgore, *Women's Wear Daily* under John Fairchild, and a handful of other publications have taken on a sophistication of their own, which the old-fashioned Nuts & Bolts Quarterly-type paper would have sniffed at as "consumer journalism."
>
> Of course, there are still trade papers and business sections of general interest papers that remain dull, placid, tame. And there are incentives for them to stay that way. A newspaper rarely loses advertising for writing critically of a criminal, an outfielder or a politician. Papers do lose advertising when they run critical pieces about companies and businessmen. [18]

NOW THE SPECIALIZED PUBLISHERS

Specialization of a high order is the keynote practice among business publishers even more than among other publishers. J. B. Lippincott Co., for example, has magazines in the health field. The firm estimates there are more than 2,500 healthcare publications in America and probably more than 6,000 in the world. Lippincott's publications include *American Journal of Clinical Pathology, American Surgeon, Anesthesiology, Annals of Surgery, Cancer,*

Clinical Nuclear Medicine, Clinical Pediatrics, Clinical Preventive Dentistry, Diseases of the Colon and Rectum, Hospital Pharmacy, Investigative Radiology, Laboratory Medicine, NITA, Review of Surgery, and *Transfusion.* [19]

And there are others in the medical field, such as Charles B. Slack, Inc., a New Jersey publisher with these specialized magazines: *American Journal of Medical Sciences, Journal of Allied Health, Journal of Continuing Education in Nursing, Journal of Gerontological Nursing, Journal of Nursing Education, Journal Pediatric Ophthalmology Strabismus, Journal of Psychiatric Nursing & Medical Services, Nursing, Occupational Health Nursing, Ophthalmic Surgery, Orthopedics,* and *Today's OR Nurse.*

Another publisher with quite a variety of periodicals is Chilton. These indicate what many of the major operators are doing, providing a variety of topics to tap a variety of markets. Chilton's include *Accent, Automobile Industries, Automotive Marketing, Commercial Car Journal, Control Equipment Master, Distribution Worldwide, Electronic Component News, Fleet Specialist, Food Engineering, Food Engineering Master, Hardware Age, Instrument & Apparatus News, Instruments & Control Systems, Iron Age, Jewelers' Circular-Keystone, Motor Age, Product Design & Development, Review of Optometry,* and three international publications: *Automotive Industries International, Food Engineering International,* and *Iron Age Metalworking International.*

In addition, Chilton operates Ad-Chart Services, a book firm, directing marketing, printing and research facilities, Information Services, Management Information Services, Marketing & Advertising Information Center, National Price Services and Naughton Studios. In 1979, the firm was acquired by the American Broadcasting Company, which paid $23 million for 44.6 per cent of the outstanding stock. [20]

Another interesting firm is the Watt Publishing Co. of Mount Morris, Ill. Established by J. W. Watt, a Scotsman who came here as a lad with nothing except ambition and talent, the firm dates from the *Poultry Tribune,* established in 1885. The firm still concentrates in this area, with these other magazines: *American Dairy Review, Farm Supplies, Feed Management, Industria Avicola, Petfood Industry, Pig International, Poultry International, Turkey World,* and *Who's Who in the Egg and Poultry Industries* with its international editions as well. Orvel H. Cockrel, vice-president and publisher, feels "almost anyone can still launch a publication, if they have an idea and the courage to do so. The investment requirements are very minimal." [21]

Now more than 80 years old, the Hitchcock Publishing Co. has seven monthly magazines and two annual directories. Founded in 1898, the firm has grown to include direct mail marketing, executive books, computer services and market research. More than 200 employes handle the firm's $15 million-plus annual income. Among the firm's publications is *Quality,* designed "for better product assurance and reliability." [22] Its market covers manufacturing and service industries, research and development, government and the military. It serves as "both spokesman and discussion vehicle for the inter-disciplinary activities required to assure product quality.'' Other Hitchcock publications include *Industrial Finishing, Assembly Engineering, Infosystems, Office Products, Assembly Engineering Master Catalog,* and *Machine and Tool Directory.* The American Broadcasting Co. bought the firm in 1978. Hitchcock published ''The Information Revolution in Manufacturing'' in all of its magazines in May, 1980, a report that covered information processing data as related to manufacturing.

And The Years Ahead?

What's ahead in the 1980s for the business press?
Chilton President William A. Barbour predicted:

1. There will be more specialization in the markets.
2. There will be more definition and refinement of special reader interest.
3. There will be more audience segmentation.
4. There will be more exploration of new compatible delivery systems for information distribution.
5. There will be more use of electronic delivery systems—tapes, discs, audiovisuals, films, books and microforms to complement conventional print editions of publications.

The business magazines ''will remain the most effective and cost efficient way for you to get your message into the minds of the most important buying influences for your product or service,'' he added. However, as the 80s opened,

Business Press Advertising Pages (1930-1980)

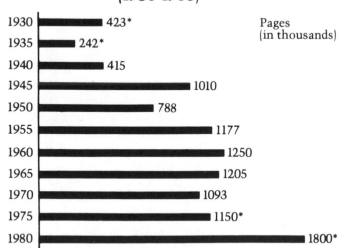

Year	Pages (in thousands)
1930	423*
1935	242*
1940	415
1945	1010
1950	788
1955	1177
1960	1250
1965	1205
1970	1093
1975	1150*
1980	1800*

*estimated
Source: American Business Press, Inc.
From *Advertising Age* (June 16, 1980) S-42.

Barbour and others were a bit pessimistic as advertisers waited for a clearer view of the business world, the influence of inflation, and plans of the federal government, especially as it changed from Democratic leadership to Republican leadership in 1981.

Some publishers were reluctant to forecast a continuation of the remarkable gains of the 1970s. McGraw-Hill President Paul McPherson predicted continued gains but less than in recent years, with hikes in ad pages from 3 to 5 per cent. Technical Publishing Co. chairman Jim Tafel predicted 2 to 3 per cent page growth, with revenue hike of 12 per cent at the best, both below his 1979 figures. A slightly smaller growth was seen by Penton/IPC Chairman Tom Dempsey, Better page and revenue growth was expected by David Wexler, publisher of Cahners' biggest magazine, *Institutions*.[23]

5

Magazines for Women: "Seven Sisters" to Ms.

OF THE MAJOR AREAS in magazine publishing, more changes have occurred within the women's field than in all others. This, obviously, reflects the changing role of women in today's society, with considerable reaction to the ERA and Ms. movements, as well as the entry into the nation's work force of millions of women who formerly considered their roles to be home-bound.

Women's magazines long have exercised considerable influence over their readers, as Roland Wolseley wrote in 1973:

> For years leading magazines aimed at women have had long-range effects in creating stereotypes in their readers' minds. The American female from girlhood on has been encouraged by these periodicals to believe in certain circumstances as normal and to be taken for granted—for example, that the primary goal is to be taken care of by a man, preferably through marriage. In any case, to achieve the goal in one manner or the other it is necessary to be physically as attractive as possible.
>
> For the most part, women have been portrayed by magazines as not really interested in public affairs, certainly not to the exclusion of what touched their lives more personally . . . there was little discussion of political and economic problems. Racial injustice was scarcely mentioned.[1]

Changes are readily evident today among the magazines found on thousands of newsstands. No longer are they dominated by the "Seven Sisters": *Ladies' Home Journal, McCall's, Good Housekeeping, Redbook, Cosmopolitan, Woman's Day* and *Family Circle*. Some sources consider *Better Homes & Gardens* here rather than *Cosmopolitan*. However, *Cosmo* will be placed in this category while *BH&G* will be with the shelter magazines.

These magazines through the decades have dispensed information considered appropriate for the times, advising readers how best to handle problems associated with the home, with raising children and with growing a garden. Today, however, millions of women are neither confined to the kitchen nor to the home.

With changing interests of readers, magazines have been forced to redirect their contents to maintain their circulation. Some have succeeded, others have failed. Many middle-aged women today have been raised with the "Seven Sisters." Some of these periodicals have redesigned their appeals, with more columns and features on job openings for women, with help in handling their financial affairs, and with assistance in handling other problems encountered with their changing lifestyles. Some feel, however, that these periodicals have "a stodgy image with younger women. Few magazines have successfully repositioned themselves." Nancy Yoshihara, writing in the *Los Angeles Times,* adds: "Old housewife tales clichés have become outmoded. No longer is the woman confined to her kitchen, scrubbing dishes until she can see her face in them."[2] Today's woman seeks more information about the working world, about making and handling money, and coping with both her job and her home, and, at times, raising a family as well.

According to the Women's Bureau, U.S. Department of Labor, in 1890 only 18 per cent of all working-age women had jobs or wanted them. Today's figures are greatly changed. By 1978, about 42 million women were in the labor force, constituting more than 40 per cent of all workers. That same year, nearly 60 per cent of all women between 18 and 64 were workers, with the higher participation among women 20 to 24. And among those with four or more years of college, 60 per cent were working. Since World War II, the number of working mothers has increased more than tenfold. One in seven families was headed by a woman in 1978.

On the negative side many women remain concentrated in low paying, dead-end jobs, earning on the average three-fifths of what a man does. And this is especially bad among minority-race women.[3]

Apparently the traditional family discussed decades ago in women's publications, the family with the husband working while the wife remained home raising the children, is disappearing. This recent change has created a significant explosion in the labor force and has been labeled "the most outstanding phenomenon of our century" by Eli Ginzberg, chairman of the Commission for Manpower Policy.[4]

Women received their first American magazine in 1828 when Mrs. Sarah Josepha Hale published *Ladies' Magazine.* Before the year ended this became *Godey's Lady's Book,* one of the most famous of all times. It faithfully served the women until 1898.

Meanwhile, in 1883, the *Ladies' Home Journal* appeared as a spinoff from Cyrus H. K. Curtis' *Tribune and Farmer.* It was edited by his wife, writing under her maiden name, Louisa Knapp. In 1889, Edward W. Bok became the editor and in 1903 the *Ladies' Home Journal* became the first real magazine to reach a million circulation. Bok's philosophy apparently was appropriate for his time; he thought men belonged in the business world, women in the home. He expressed these fears about any change in this arrangement in 1900:

> The tendency for women to go into business occupations other than dressmakers, teachers, and domestic helpers began about 1870 . . . and by 1890, over four million women were employed. But women are being dismissed now—they have not shown themselves competent to fill positions. They have never trained for business and do not and cannot understand its essential requirements. They can't stand the physical strain of the keen pace. The twentieth century will in no other aspect be so marked as in the natural and divine division of the world's labor which America is destined to present to the world, men for business and women for the home.[5]

Bok's views would upset many readers today, men and women alike. In early 1900, however, he probably expressed the opinions held by many, especially those reading the nation's magazines.

Changes have occurred. Frank Luther Mott wrote in the mid-1950s that the magazine's "effect today may be a little more on women's thinking and a little less on their fancywork and rules of etiquette, but in kind it is the same authority and control."[6] During the 1960s the *Ladies' Home Journal* ran relatively few articles on careers for women and even by February, 1975 it viewed women as still uneasy about "the commitment to a career-oriented life."

In early 1970, *Ladies' Home Journal* editor John Mack Carter's office was invaded by more than one hundred women's liberation advocates, demanding his resignation and calling for magazine space to convey their views to the public. In addition to gaining nationwide publicity from the incident, Carter admitted he learned what they were talking about. The women demanded "an immediate stop to the publication of articles that are irrelevant, unstimulating and demeaning to the women of America."[7] As a result of the confrontation Carter granted permission for the women to use eight pages in the following August edition to express the views of the feminist movement. Three years later Carter became president of Downe Communications, Inc. and Mrs. Lenore G. Hershey took over as the *Ladies' Home Journal* editor, the first woman in that position since Louisa Knapp Curtis started the publication. Hershey's initial message to readers in January 1974 said:

> We will continue to produce the kind of magazine that will amplify, enlarge, and illuminate the life of its readers . . . we will continue to provide you with help and guidance in almost every aspect of your life . . . from the world of the home to the world of business to the wider world of ideas and values . . .

Betty Friedan, a decade ago, charged that the women's magazines of the early 70s were "irrelevant to today's younger and concerned woman." As that decade ended, the *Ladies' Home Journal* was skipping its former homemaking department and focusing more on the working woman in such areas as fashion and beauty topics. More *People*-type personality sketches appear, often featuring movie and television stars. And sex is there, too. When the magazine, in 1975, cut its circulation base from 7 to 6 million it astonished the publishing world by bringing in 56 per cent of its revenues from its readers.[8] Its 1981 rate base was 5,500,000.

No doubt its long-used slogan—"Never underestimate the power of a woman"—finally has found a home, the *Ladies' Home Journal*.

McCall's

Other women's publications that began in the 19th Century still occupy leading places in our society. *McCall's*, which began as *The Queen* in 1873, acquired its present name in 1897. As it evolved through the years it reached its first million circulation in 1908. For a time, *McCall's* was divided into three units: Fiction and News, Home Making, and Style and Beauty. In 1949 Eleanor Roosevelt became a regular contributor, answering readers' questions.

When *McCall's* circulation dropped in the 1950s, a "togetherness" campaign was inaugurated to sell the magazine as a publication for the entire family, not just the woman in the home. This concept failed to halt the decline and by 1958 *McCall's* became the "First magazine for women."[9] Circulation climbed as the magazine began to use more "brisk writing, flashy color and splashy layouts."

In the "Battle of the Amazons" *McCall's* overcame the *Ladies' Home Journal* in 1960, a decade of confusion when the magazine changed editors and owners. With the opening of the 70s, the Magazine Industry Newsletter noted a new editorial and graphic direction for *McCall's*, "an editorial philosophy oriented more towards the intellect rather than the pragmatic." *MIN* also believed that "Much of the material would make a better-than-average issue of *Life* . . ." Still, "the magazine readers' feminine eye generally leads more to home and heart than to mind and social issues."[10]

Shana Alexander, formerly with *Life,* served briefly as editor in 1970. When she cut back on service features she claimed *McCall's* was in tune with the women's revolution.[11] The next year *McCall's* cut its large format to the standard *Redbook* size. Its circulation base also was cut, from 8.5 to 7.5 million. Although cooking, fashions, food and beauty topics continued in the 70s, an early 1971 cover featured articles on "Your Legal Rights as a Woman" and "Sexual Problems of Single Women." Its 1981 rate base was 6,200,000.

In its largest issue ever, April 1976, *McCall's* celebrated its 100th anniversary, although some historians would challenge that date. The past was recalled, merged with well-known writers of the times.

Good Housekeeping

Good Housekeeping followed *Ladies' Home Journal* by two years. Its initial issue in 1885 in Massachusetts offered prizes for articles on housekeeping problems such as "How to Eat, Drink and Sleep as a Christian Should." More emphasis was placed on food and cooking, less on fashion and beauty. Eventually, the Good Housekeeping Institute and its Seal of Approval became a successful advertising gimmick, although its use has declined in recent years. The Institute has never lost a legal case, although it has been sued nearly 20 times. Some potential advertisers have withheld their messages in protest to the testing program, which started in 1902.

Good Housekeeping came under the Hearst ownership in 1911. From its beginning it invited contributions from readers. Its first serial appeared in 1886 and illustrations began in the mid-1890s. By 1908 its circulation had reached 200,000. *Good Housekeeping* long has been respected for its fiction, with many name authors contributing regularly. In the Depression, *Good Housekeeping* was one of the few profitable magazines.

Good Housekeeping remains Hearst's stellar publication. John Mack Carter is the only individual to have been editor-in-chief of three major women's magazines, the *Ladies' Home Journal, McCall's,* and currently *Good Housekeeping.*

However, this publication faces problems similar to the others of the "Seven Sisters." A recent comment by a middle-aged female executive told the story: "I bought *Good Housekeeping* and *Ladies' Home Journal* to learn how to keep house. Now, I'm trying to forget how to."[12]

With the opening of the 80s, *Good Housekeeping* advertised on its cover that it had 20 million readers. Carter's desire to serve his readers is apparent in the Editor's Notebook. For example, he calls for more information about cancer; he is a board member of the American Cancer Society. He uses his publication to bring "information about prevention and treatment to its readers," a noble goal.

A varied menu is still placed before the readers, with articles from diets to profiles of prominent Americans to helpful household advice. Its fiction continues, with monthly novels and shorter pieces. An eight-page monthly section, The Better Way, provides valuable hints for all readers, men and women, about day-by-day situations. Its annual Most Admired Women Poll continues to attract considerable interest.

Redbook

Another "sister" with her target women between 18 and 34 is *Redbook.* Originally published in Chicago where it began in 1903, *Redbook* was acquired by the McCall Corporation in 1929. At first this monthly publication specialized in short stories, offering such famed writers as H. G. Wells, Sinclair Lewis, Jack London, and others. It was the first to print portions of Carl Sandburg's *Lincoln: The War Years.* In the post-World War II years the magazine turned to the young adult audience, printing more articles concerning social and moral issues. In 1952 it adopted "The Magazine for Young Adults" for a subtitle; in 1970 this became "The Magazine for Young Women."

Controversial and significant issues dominate the magazine. Sey Chassler, the seventh editor of *Redbook,* wants to expose these issues to "today's vital, intelligent and sophisticated young woman, who is seeking new ways to shape her role in this ever-changing world."[13]

Redbook has pegged its circulation in the 4,500,000 neighborhood. Its success in reaching its goal is evident by its continual increase in advertising income and its special interest publications such as *Redbook's Young Mother* and *Redbook's Be Beautiful.* To attract more advertisers, it established the *Redbook Gold* edition in 1979, designed for 500,000 subscribers in high-consumption zip code areas plus a million bought on the newsstands. The median age for *Gold* is 32, with 1979 median income per household in excess of $21,000, obviously a top quality group.

Chassler redesigned the magazine in 1979 to overcome "the ad clutter in the front of the book and the gray ghetto in the back." Early pages were to be devoted to editorial service pieces, lead articles and fiction, plus regular columns and features. Chassler promised advertisers more four-color editorial adjacencies, and predicted these changes would bring a "small revolution in the magazine field."[14]

Redbook appears ready for the 80s, prepared to offer women more information that will redefine "their roles as wives, as mothers, as wage earners, as social beings." It was sold to Hearst in 1982.

Cosmopolitan

Few magazines today have changed as drastically as *Cosmopolitan,* founded in 1886 in Rochester, N.Y., as a first-class family publication, and combined with *Hearst's International* in 1925. Since 1952 it has been known simply as *Cosmopolitan,* and in recent years by a shorter title, *Cosmo.*

Although originally planned to have departments for women and younger members of the family, it became a general literary monthly, according to Frank Luther Mott.[15] By the late 1890s, *Cosmopolitan* had joined the leaders among the ten-cent illustrated monthlies and had become one of the famed muckrakers. It started Cosmopolitan University, a correspondence school that offered free education to readers.

Stories dealt with major topics and for some time fiction dominated the magazine's contents. *Cosmopolitan*'s novels and short stories were widely read. When Hearst took over his first magazine after a spectacular career in the newspaper world, *Cosmopolitan* became more sensational. Mott concluded in the mid-50s that *Cosmopolitan* "was a part of the magazine revolution of the nineties, strong in ideas, individualistic, functioning in many fields. Under the Hearst ownership it has been a striking and entertaining magazine, various and plentiful in its content."

In 1962 Helen Gurley Brown's book, *Sex and the Single Girl,* offered millions of readers her version of a new morality. This helped to break a barrier that permitted many other sex-oriented books to follow. In 1965 she became editor of *Cosmopolitan,* although she lacked any previous magazine experience. Soon she became known as "The Iron Butterfly." She admitted her name "got to be synonymous with the new morality. A lot of people were shocked by that morality."[16] At the time she took over, *Cosmo*'s circulation was less than 800,000 and the owners were considering its death. Apparently the publishers knew about Brown, since this magazine had published an unfavorable review of her book only a month earlier.

Within a few years Brown turned *Cosmo* into a "sort of a female *Playboy*." In recognizing the needs of the young women, married or single, she directed *Cosmo* to them. The magazine continues to sell 96 per cent of its copies on newsstands, a situation strengthened by a subscription rate that is $3 more per year than the single-copy costs. This situation pleases both management and advertisers, since such direct sales are more profitable than subscriptions and since persons tend to read magazines more when they purchase them directly than by mail.

Simmons readership studies near the end of the 70s indicated Brown's audience was what she desired. Some 68 per cent of the readers were in the 18 to 34 age bracket, well educated, with 65 per cent employed. More than 81 per cent lived in metropolitan areas. Readers were about equally divided between single and married, with a median age of 28. *Cosmo* claimed that 85 per cent of its readers don't take *Mademoiselle*, 71 per cent avoid *Glamour*, and at least half don't become involved with *Reader's Digest, Ladies' Home Journal, McCall's, Woman's Day,* and *Family Circle.* Obviously, Brown has carved out the "Cosmo Girl" into a devoted client group for her messages, recommendations, and suggestons concerning daily living. And with a circulation approaching three million, death is no longer a threat around *Cosmo*'s New York headquarters. Such success has prompted a spin-off, *Cosmo Living,* which reached newsstands in early 1980. With a press run of 300,000, and 95 pages of ads, the magazine looked ahead to a fall edition with higher circulation. Also in 1980, *Cosmo* appeared in a German edition, the 15th offshoot on four continents.

Family Circle and Woman's Day

The two newsstand leaders, *Family Circle* and *Woman's Day,* continue their fight for leadership in supermarket sales. Competition, however, has increased from the national tabloids, from the increase in the cost of living, and the higher gas prices that limit trips to the market places.

Family Circle began as a free weekly for customers in New York and Washington grocery chains in 1932. The 24-page publication featured Bing Crosby, Joan Crawford and Douglas Fairbanks Jr. on the covers, while the contents included items about radio programs, movies, humor, recipes, and styles.

Fourteen years later *Family Circle* ended its giveaway status and was sold for 5¢ a copy. The 96-page publication was distributed in more major chains. In 1932 it introduced sectional advertising along with new editions in England

and Germany. In recent years editions have been started in Australia and Japan. *Family Circle* continues its innovative ways, becoming the first tri-weekly after moving to 13 issues in 1977 and 14 in 1978. This was termed "a whole new kind of marketing tool." The magazine was the first to adopt the Universal Produce Code to speed market checkout.

Robert Young, publisher, said in 1979 that "old rules won't hold in this newly splintered marketplace, and no organization stands a better chance of chalking up a winning entry than one blessed with a solidly entrenched business/distribution edge balanced by the editorial acumen to write a new rulebook." He considered *Family Circle* "in the forefront of the women's movement concerns before Betty Friedan ever discovered it."[17]

In 1981, *Family Circle* offered advertisers seasonal circulation guarantees, with possible cash rebates for failures to reach goals. *Woman's Day* claimed, "We've been doing that since last year (1979)."

Family Circle is edited for the contemporary woman, with material on health, beauty, self-improvement, fashion, crafts, home management and improvement, and family care.

Its competitor, *Woman's Day,* arrived in 1937, a monthly distributed by the Great Atlantic and Pacific Tea Co. It, too, developed from a giveaway, A&P Menu Sheet, before it became a 3¢-a-copy magazine. It was involved in antitrust litigation and was sold to Fawcett in 1958. Currently it is owned by CBS Publications.

Woman's Day added a 13th edition in 1976, starting its race with *Family Circle* to claim more advertising pages. It added its 14th issue in 1978, 15th in 1979, and predicted its 16th in 1981, depending on paper supply and the economy. It, too, is edited for the contemporary woman, with coverage of food, housing, building, home furnishings, apparel, appliances and cosmetics, toiletries, etc. Columns cover travel, medicine, automobiles, money management, and pet care. Family life, child care and self-fulfillment are other topics.

Family Circle and *Woman's Day* both offer numerous geographic and demographic editions. In 1980, *Family Circle* had a rate base of 8.35 million, while *Woman's Day* had 8 million. Sales vary for both with individual editions often exceeding 9 million.

Headlines over newspaper and magazine articles tell the story of the changes the "Seven Sisters" are experiencing as they seek to keep up with their ever-moving audience. "Women's Magazines Drive Me Crazy" reported one writer, while a newspaper story told of "Selling Sex, Sin and Suffering." Another told of the "High-stakes Guessing Game" in the fight to woo readers. Still another claimed "Women Getting a Bum Steer in Glossing Working Girl Articles."

"Women's Magazine Dilemma: Who Are They For?" may be answered at least in part by a look at the "other side," those newcomers with their specialized appeals and their growing circulations.

NEW MORALITY, NEW INTERESTS

During the 60s and 70s, new publications reflected the rapidly changing viewpoints of younger Americans, especially those in the oft-surveyed 18 to 34 age bracket. This was more true with women readers.[18]

The "Seven Sisters" encountered competition from this new feminist press. Reflecting the specialization impact then evident in the publishing world, these magazines attempted to better pinpoint their audience. Some were designed for working women in general, others for those who had climbed higher in the executive world. Others were for Black women or for working mothers who combined their new careers with their more traditional homemaking duties. Some of these publications survived while others encountered too much competition and folded.

Some of the newcomers imitated those in the masculine market, not only in their titles but in their contents, such as *Playgirl* vs. *Playboy*. Male nudity found a big play in some publications until circulation declines indicated that market was not so well established as that for female nudity.

Women's associations also expanded their communications with their members, improving their publications to attract more readers and advertisers. Another specialized appeal became evident with the appearance of *Big Beautiful Woman*.

There is no reason to anticipate an end to this flood of feminine-oriented publications. The number of working women continues to grow. Newsstands, however, can accommodate only so many publications; when new ones arrive, others may be forced to reduce or halt their printings.

Ms. Sets the Pace

To understand the success of *Ms.* magazine it is necessary to recall the cultural revolution of the 1960s, the civil rights movement, and the activities of organizations devoted to achieving greater equality for women. The title *Ms.* became their symbol. When the established media remain unresponsive to such changes in our social climate, new means of communication will develop, as seen in the hundreds of underground campus and community newspapers that appeared.

Thus a feminist press arrived to fill this gap that women claimed existed within the nation's newspapers and magazines. In 1970, for example, *Essence* arrived to offer self-awareness to urban Black women. The next year others were published, such as *New Woman,* a form of *Playboy* for women; *Progressive Woman,* for mature, intelligent working women; *You,* for middle-class white women, and others. Some were directed to men as well, at least indirectly.

Gloria Steinem changed the women's magazine business, probably more than any individual in this area. As a contributing editor to *New York* magazine in 1970, she developed her concept for a national feminist publication, with a staff retaining editorial control, with advertisements carefully scrutinized to eliminate any demeaning inferences about women, and with some of the profits utilized to assist the women's movement. Her magazine would contain two-thirds editorial content, exceptionally high among magazines. At that time the "Seven Sisters" carried considerable advertising, some so much that it was often difficult for readers to locate the editorial units.

Steinem was assisted by a *New York* editor, Clay Felker, who permitted her to produce a 44-page insert for his 1971 year-end edition, an unusual method to introduce a new publication to the public. With 300,000 sold, the newsstand sales broke all records for the *New York*. In January, 1972, this same magazine assisted with financing the first nationwide edition of *Ms.*—that also was sold out. The 300,000 copies were expected to remain on the newsstands for two months; they remained only eight days. *New York* paid the production costs for this spring edition and shared in the profits. From this premier edition came 36,000 subscriptions.

Although the majority of the purchasers of *Ms.* were women, only a few were memebers of the liberation movement. In "A Personal Report" in the January, 1973 issue of *Ms.,* the editor revealed the tremendous response from American women. Not only did subscriptions come in by the thousands, but letters and manuscripts flooded the two-room office used by the staff. Newsstand sales continued high after the magazine went on its own in mid-1972 and subscriptions totaled 45,000 within six months. Realizing there would be a shortage of advertisements at the start, *Ms.* initially charged $1 a copy. In addition to the sold copies free copies were provided for women's prisons, for some women on welfare, and for others just unable to pay. Funds for this came from extra contributions by women subscribers.

Ms. has been directed to those in the women's movement as well as for those not yet involved. Events moved so rapidly the first few months that the editors later admitted they could not do as much as they desired in such areas as providing more history of the women's movement. More humor was projected since "existing forms of humor are often put-downs on (women) as a group."

Early in its existence, the publishers created the Ms. Foundation for Women, Inc., mostly as a method for sharing income with the movement. Grants for deserving women's projects will be available from these funds, according to Patricia Carbine, publisher and editor-in-chief. On the basis of this plan, *Ms.* gained a nonprofit tax status which meant:

> Salvation for *Ms.* as an independent or non-affiliated magazine; a minor change in editorial direction; and a new economic structure that gives the magazine privileged postal rates and allows for the infusion of tax-deductible grant money from outsiders.[19]

On the other hand, *Ms.* must not become involved in political campaigns unless candidates are treated equally. The 50 per cent cut in postage should

offset this handicap. Advertising will continue to be taxed as it is for all publications. Now a subsidiary of the original Foundation, called The Ms. Foundation for Education and Communication, has been chartered to operate the
publication. Early foundation support also came from Marlo Thomas, who
helped with a "Free to Be . . ." best-selling record, book, television special,
and educational films.

Ms. opened a new area for many women. It sponsored the *Ms.* Mile to
recognize women athletes, with Wilma Rudolph, winner of three Olympic
medals in 1960, presenting the awards. Articles soon won national recognition,
along with awards for content, graphics, and service. More than 450 writers
contributed to its content during the first two years, not all of them women.
This apparently was a wise decision, since some reports indicate readership
among men may reach 40 per cent. The magazine has published books, such
as *Wonder Woman, Ms. Reader, Ms. Guide to a Woman's Health,* and others,
as well as records and numerous reprints of *Ms.* articles.

Along the way Warner Communications invested a million dollars in *Ms.*
for 25 per cent of the ownership. Within seven months of its founding, *Ms.*
reported a profit. Publisher Pat Carbine credited this to minimized overhead,
inexpensive offices, a dedicated staff and circulation success. A 70 per cent
renewal rate also helped the money flow. Carbine's goal is to make *Ms.* a
necessity for readers rather than a luxury.[20]

Staff members can laugh today when they recall Harry Reasoner's prediction after seeing the Preview Issue: "I give *Ms.* five months." Five years later
the magazine reported advertising growth from $517,627 the first year to
$2,158,550 the fifth year. Its circulation remains in the 500,000 neighborhood.

Meanwhile, founder Gloria Steinem became a Washington researcher,
looking for material for a book on feminist philosophy. As the 80s opened, she
said changes in the magazine were necessary "because change is what *Ms.*
magazine is all about." The magazine has become easier to read, more innovative and colorful, with more visibility for advertisers. For the 1980s, *Ms.*
promised new departments such as Parenting, Organizing, and Personal Style.
No doubt this supports Steinem's fifth anniversary statement that "the bottom
line was that women are indeed full human beings, that the sexual caste system
is unjust and unjustifiable."

New Woman

A preview copy of *New Woman* appeared from Fort Lauderdale, Fla., in
October, 1970. Known more for its attraction to university students on spring
breaks and for retirees the year around, Fort Lauderdale appeared an unusual
setting for such a publication as *New Woman*. Editor-publisher Margaret Harold
said her magazine would be: "Anti-subordination, yes; anti-men, no. We have
nothing against the furry little bastards except that making them No. 1 has
made us No. 2 . . ." *New Woman* would serve those who are achievers, those

who "change the atmosphere" and are excited and exciting. The female self, not selflessness and subservience, would be a goal, too.

When the first public issue appeared in mid-1971, Harold reaffirmed her concepts: "It's time to examine and discard the outdated ideas, stultifying traditions, stifling influences and unfair laws that have stifled, stultified, outdated and been unfair to both men and women. This is the Renaissance."

Now a bi-monthly, *New Woman* offers advertisers a guaranteed million sales, with a large, 71 per cent, newsstand sale. It claims to be for the "thinking woman . . . to give guidance, information, a new image and a new way of life to female doers." It enters the 80s with its basic objectives intact.

Viva

Sometimes it is wise to study not only the rise of a magazine but its fall as well to obtain a better view of the market. *Viva,* an international magazine for women, arrived in October, 1973, published by *Penthouse* owner, Bob Guccione. He called *Viva* his own newborn child, "An infant . . . fragile, undisciplined, painfully vulnerable. It was conceived out of a lifelong love-relationship with women." He predicted *Viva* would "become an integral part of the mad, mad world into which she was born."[21]

Obviously calling upon his experience with *Penthouse,* Guccione said *Viva* would be his kind of woman, "a lusty, real, indefatigable, down-to-earth, fetching, bright, sexy, uncompromising woman." He also said he was "simply taking the *Cosmopolitan* format one emotional step forward."

By 1976 *Viva* had dropped total male nudity from its pages to help improve supermarket sales. However, by late 1978 *Viva* was gone. *Newsweek* suggested a reason for its demise: "When it began, the monthly was full of breathless advice about sex and lucious photographs of nude men. Not surprisingly, *Viva* appealed more to men—gay and otherwise—than to women, and not at all to magazine distributors."[22] Editor Kathy Keeton, a close friend of the publisher, blamed "the prejudices of the bloody distributors . . . (who) thought it was a dirty magazine for women."

Self

"Your guide to shaping up body and mind fast" was *Self*'s appeal to potential readers when it reached newsstands in January, 1979. For its publisher, Condé Nast, this was the company's first new magazine in 40 years. Obviously attempting to profit from the craze for physical fitness, *Self* also concerned itself with emotional fitness. Publisher Peter Diamandis said the magazine is for "the woman who wants to be good at everything, and has to keep physically and emotionally fit to do her best."[23]

For 14 months, staffers mapped plans for *Self,* seeking to determine its objectives. S. I. Newhouse Jr. proposed a health-oriented magazine in 1977 that would cover not only the 18–34 group, but women in their 50s. Editor Phyllis Wilson still believes women of all ages eventually will find material of interest in *Self*. The initial issue sold 350,000 copies on newsstands, and by the third issue, *Self* claimed that same number of subscribers.[24] By mid-1981 circulation had topped a million.

Playgirl

An "entertainment magazine for women" arrived in June, 1973, named *Playgirl*. Its Los Angeles publisher placed 600,000 copies on the market. With *Playboy* no doubt on his mind, he informed readers about the newcomer:

> Potentially she is that ageless, magnetic, charismatic woman you look at every time *you* glance at *your* reflection in the glass . . . to be a PLAYGIRL simply requires that you open your heart and your mind to the secrets of life's meaning—and take advantage of all of its magnificent potentials.

Playgirl also is a romantic, intelligent, capable of living life to its fullest, and totally honest with herself in a variety of areas.

A four-page foldout showed a nearly-nude Lyle Waggoner as "Mr. Super Cool," *Playgirl*'s Man for June. The magazine was an immediate success when its circulation went from 600,000 to more than 2 million for the seventh issue. The owners thought *Playgirl* was unconventional, unprecedented, unparalleled. This circulation, however, failed to continue through the 70s and as the 80s opened, *Playgirl* was advertising a "circulation growth" of 10.4 per cent between 1978 and 1979, a jump from 661,000 to 730,000. Attempts to sell male nudity to women had failed and when the circulation began its decline, editor Barbara Cady said *Playgirl* would use investigative pieces on more serious topics, such as kidnapping of children in custody suits, incest, growing use of Valium, and similar topics. She said male nudity would continue with improved photography. Couples continue to dominate the covers, selected to attract an audience slightly younger than some other women's books, 26.5 years. More than 60 per cent of the readers work and nearly that many are married.

For the 80s, *Playgirl* expected its circulation to reach a million, with gains in advertising revenues as well. Still, some companies refuse to advertise in *Playgirl,* as some avoid *Playboy,* believing such publications might be a threat to their business. Some feel *Playgirl* carried too many sex-oriented ads. Both French and German language editions are projected for the 80s, with a possibility of a Spanish-language version and an Australian edition.

Playgirl in 1980 turned the tide established by *Playboy* by presenting centerfolds of nude male military personnel. Top Pentagon officials had mixed reactions. Some high-ranking officers shifted the decision-making duties to individual commanding officers. *Playgirl* also sought policemen for such photos, although one Los Angeles officer said he hoped such males "would at least have a traffic ticket book covering his vulnerable parts."[25]

Working Woman

From its start in 1976, *Working Woman* has aimed its contents toward the "women who want to get ahead in their careers." So readers will find more articles economically-oriented than physically or emotionally slanted. For example, its November, 1978, edition contained such topics as If You Had $50,000; Will Bitter Medicine Make the Economy Healthier? Gifts That Make Business a Pleasure; and Easy Little Dinners for November.

This particular issue was labeled "Big Money Issue" with such stories as these: Do You Work for Fun or High Income or Both? When It Comes to Spending Why Are So Many Women Cheap? When It Comes to Expense Accounts, Why Do Men Get the Gravy? In addition, regular departments tell about women at work, offer consumer advice, provide legal help, and the like. Women who have gained success in the business world are featured in inspirational articles.

For a brief time, in 1977, the magazine had difficulty, going into bankruptcy. But it has returned under new owner Hal Publications. Kate Rand Lloyd, of *Working Woman,* believes the magazine's editors feel "it is impossible to chop the reader's needs off at the office door. To be her most productive, confident, and healthy best, she must be satisfied that the thousands of decisions she makes, minute-to-minute or year-to-year, are generally sound ones. It's the work of *Working Woman* to help the reader make this happen."[26]

Working Mother

McCall's *Working Mother* appeared in 1978 shortly before Working Mother's Day was to be observed in at least 40 states, an event sponsored by the publishers. This was McCall's second attempt in 102 years with a new publication, the other being *Your Place,* aimed for the youthful apartment/home owner seeking information on decorations and other such needs.

McCall's officials believed there were 15,000,000 working mothers with children under 18, potential subscribers and readers for their new magazine. Both of these publications were to be bi-monthlies.

Working Mother, with a circulation of over 300,000, shifted to a monthly publication base in late 1981.

Big Beautiful Woman

In mid-1979, a newcomer arrived from Century City, Cal., titled *Big Beautiful Woman.* Designed as a bi-monthly, it featured fashions and tips for large-size women. In seeking attention from an audience estimated at 25 per cent of the population, *Big Beautiful Woman* sought to "bring respect from the smaller world around us."

Editor Carole Shaw, herself 5-feet-7, 200 pounds, told her readers that "you are who and what you are and your dress size has nothing to do with your success or failure as a person. You are neither smarter, better educated nor, for that matter, jollier than a person of smaller physical dimensions." The magazine's goal was to show "beautiful fashions modeled by women who can actually wear these styles." Shaw invested $250,000 of her own money "out of deep personal pain and frustration." *It's Me,* "not for little women," began in 1981, backed by Lane Bryant, women's retailer for larger sizes.

OTHER WOMEN'S PUBLICATIONS

Be Alive, termed a magazine for today's woman, appeared in mid-1977. "Devoted to modern thinking and progressive women in all walks of life," its cover featured a pot-pourri of topics.

The Executive Female Digest appeared in January 1978, a spinoff from a newsletter published by The National Association of Female Executives, for its 18,000 members. Director Wendy Rue said the *Digest* was not similar to other women's publications. "We've the only magazine isolated to work situations, career advancement and financial independence."

Early in 1981, *Woman's World* was launched as the first weekly for women. No subscriptions were taken nor any advertising at the start. Its publisher, Heinrich Bauer North America Inc., expected to spend $10 million to promote this in the biggest, possibly riskiest, start of the year.

Another magazine for executives, *Savvy,* had its premier edition in late 1979 after several years on the planning board. This, too, was for "women who enjoy their career as the focal point of their lives," especially the executive. Editor Judith Daniels aimed *Savvy* to the two million women who earn $15,000 or more. "We don't want *Savvy* just to be an office manual. We want to include other areas—the reader's relationship with the men in her life—boyfriends, husbands, bosses; political and social issues; service information."

In early 1980 *Savvy* noted "the man shortage," and the problem the women face: "Where are the Men for the Women at the Top."[27]

Woman was the title of a prototype issued by Time Inc. in 1977. The first issue was for in-house use, while the second was tested on newsstands and in supermarkets in 12 cities. Time Inc. apparently put an hold on this while it turned attention to the science market.

Lady's Circle is a Lopez Publication, aimed for homemakers and working women. Founded in 1964, before the big rush for the woman's market began, *Lady's Circle* has a circulation of 156,000.

Women in Business is published nine times annually by the American Business Women's Association in Kansas City. The *Homemaker* is also for an organization, the National Extension Homemakers Council. It began in 1977 with the rural women the primary target.

In late 1980 *Playgirl* came out with *Slimmer,* designed for the health and beauty goals of today's woman.

Biarritz, for "the world woman who knows who she is and where she is," appeared in mid-1980. The initial rate base was 200,000.

OLDTIMERS/NEWSCOMERS AMONG LEADERS

Some publications don't fit exactly into a convenient slot, although they are so well known among American women that their names are readily recognized.

These include *Harper's Bazaar, Vogue, Mademoiselle,* and *Glamour.* Each has its distinct appeal and its distinct following. Each has been around long enough to be aware of the necessity to be on the alert for any shift in the likes or dislikes of its following. *Town & Country,* too, is different.

Town & Country

One of the nation's oldest magazines, dating to 1846, *Town & Country* continues its appeal to the affluent audience. Its cosmopolitan flavor is present in stories on fashions, beauty, gourmet meals, and social affairs around the world.

Nathaniel Parker Willis and George Pope Morris founded the *National Press: A Home Journal* in New York. Later they shortened the title to *Home Journal* and in 1901 it became *Town & Country.* Willis was a poet and essayist; Morris was a popular song writer, known best for his "Woodman, Spare That Tree."

One of today's most beautifully printed periodicals, *Town & Country* has a circulation approaching, 270,000. Its 9 by 11 inch format is unusual. Hearst acquired the magazine in 1925.

Harper's Bazaar

The name "Harper" has played a significant role in the history of American magazines, with *Harper's Monthly* and *Harper's Weekly* quite famous. In 1867, the book publishing firm established *Harper's Bazar,* "a repository of fashion, pleasure and instruction." The name acquired its present spelling, *Harper's Bazaar,* in 1929.

In 1913 the magazine was bought up by the Hearst Corporation. Although it had had a good start, it began to lose money. Hearst changed its approach from a family journal to a magazine for an upper-income audience, interested in arts, communities, travel, beauty, health, and the professions.

Margaret Sangster edited *Harper's Bazaar* for a decade near the end of the last century. Carmel Snow was editor from 1934 to 1957, and in 1971, James Brady moved from the editorship of *Women's Wear Daily* to the *Bazaar* with instructions to make the magazine "hot." [28]

Others followed Brady, who went to *New York,* in the musical-chair-game, "Who is publisher now?" Reportedly, *Harper's Bazaar* lost more than $6 million in five years. In 1977, Martin Schrader became publisher and Anthony T. Mazzola editor, both moving from another Hearst magazine, *Town & Country.* The magazine has since turned the corner profit-wise.

Harper's Bazaar en Espanol was started in Latin America in late 1980, with a 200,000 circulation. Its American circulation exceeds 600,000.

Vogue

Another long-established magazine, started in 1892 as a weekly, *Vogue* was designed for the socialy-prominent people along the Eastern seaboard and in Europe. When founded, its competition included *Godey's Lady's Book, Peterson's,* and *Delineator. Vogue* was to be "a dignified, authentic journal of society, fashion, and the ceremonial side of life."

It was acquired in 1909 by Condé Nast, and by 1954 it was called "The world's No. 1 fashion magazine" by *Time. Vogue* and *Harper's Bazaar* helped to develop the "fashion press" after World War I. In 1936, *Vogue* merged with *Vanity Fair,* then edited by Frank Crowninshield, who joined *Vogue* as arts editor.[29]

Under the editorship of Diana Vreeland, *Vogue* turned its spotlight in the 1960s on the "jet set" and the "beautiful people." Before his death in 1942, Condé Nast had limited the circulation to 150,000, a trend followed by some magazines in the 1960s and 1970s.

Labeled today "the book women live by," *Vogue's* trade messages claim the magazine "gives her diets that work. Regimes that make her healthy. Beauty that makes her beautiful. *Vogue* makes her better traveled and a better traveler. No wonder *Vogue* is the book women live by. The gospel."

With a circulation over a million, *Vogue* covers fashion, beauty, health, fitness, travel, arts, money, food, entertaining and home furnishings.

Mademoiselle

In 1935 a well-known publisher, Street and Smith, founded *Mademoiselle.* Twenty-four years later the magazine was sold to Condé Nast and today it has a circulation well over 1,085,000.

Mademoiselle claims many "firsts" in its history, including the introduction to the fashion world of the trench coat (1935), Bermudas (1939), strapless dress (1948), car coat (1952), and bikini (1959).[30]

Truman Capote was supposedly introduced by the magazine and other prominent American authors appeared in its pages, including Tennessee Williams, William Faulkner, Edward Albee, Jessamyn West, and many others.

Since the publication appeals basically to young women, 18 to 34, *Mademoiselle* has a College Board and selects 20 college students annually to spend a summer in New York on its staff. It also sponsors college writers interested in writing fiction.

Calling itself "The magazine for smart young women," it stresses fashion, beauty, careers, education, art, travel, college, and political topics. In some areas it has been ahead of the times, such as a series on the "new morality" in the 1960s when such topics were not too generally discussed in the open.

Mademoiselle's 1980 was a record year, with ad page volume its highest in a decade. Newsstand sales now account for 70 per cent of its circulation. Its use of the all-gravure process and saddlestitch binding went into operation in mid-1981.

Glamour

Started in 1939 by Condé Nast, *Glamour* assists the young working women, with information on fashion, careers, travels and other topics of concern for those between 18 and 35.

In contrast to some of the other women's magazines, *Glamour* readers were expected to sew their own dresses rather than shop for them in the exclusive stores around the world.

The Street & Smith firm was sold to Nast Publications in 1959 and *Glamour* was combined with *Charm*. Today's "how-to-do" articles tell about many areas. Its success under the editorship of Ruth Whitney is evidenced by its circulation of nearly 1,900,000.

Women's magazines have changed enormously during the past five to ten years, according to editor Whitney, because women have changed so. With monthly research on readership, *Glamour* is able to publish a mature magazine reaching the needs of its audience. Letters to the editors also determine future articles and projects, since any successful magazine must think in terms of the readers and their cares and needs.

Whitney noted how magazines must change by referring to articles on the then potential depression. The August edition, traditionally the college issue which usually sells some 150,000 extra copies, discussed penny-pinchers' needs in 1979.[31]

There are few women in the marketplace today who aren't served by some magazines. *Glamour,* similar to its many competitors, has its own market. For example, some 80 per cent of its readers are women who work. Various studies indicate the median age is between 23 and 28.

Parents

In October, 1926, *Parents* magazine was established by the Parents' Magazine Enterprises, Inc., a company owned for more than a half-century by George Joseph Hecht and his family. This magazine has always been concerned with the raising of children from crib to college and with offering valuable suggestions for the parents to achieve their goals.

Hecht was honored at the age of 80 in 1976 for his work with *Parents*. Two years later the magazine acquired new owners, the West German publishing house of Gruner + Jahr. They began a revitalization program, with a new emphasis on single-copy sales. At that time more than 99 per cent of *Parents'* circulation went directly to subscribers. Circulation had declined from 2 million to 1.5 million and the new owners set about to reverse this trend. With a new logo and with other changes, the publishers succeeded.

Nevertheless, *Parents* remains unique in its field, covering both parents and children. It is probably the only such magazine today, "reaching women at a special time of their lives, not at a special age, a time when they graduate from school, set up their own households, go to work, get married, have children.'' This description of *Parents* was presented by the publishers in a special "Sales Call" reported in *Madison Avenue* magazine in March, 1980.

Parents copies are sent to 5,000 obstetricians' offices each month and 500 subscription stubs are returned each month. It remains a woman's periodical, reaching the 18 to 34 group.

6

Esquire *to the Skin Book Boom:* Playboy, Penthouse, *Others*

Esquire revolutionized the masculine magazine field when it arrived in the autumn of 1933, a class publication that was oversized, and, at 50 cents a copy, considered over-priced by many. In 1980, a "new" *Esquire* was making waves in the magazine world, the work of two young Southern publishers. It represented another in a series of transformations *Esquire* has experienced since the 30s.

Founded by Arnold Gingrich as editor and David A. Smart and W. H. Weintraub as publishers, the initial issue contained articles, many in the public domain, by such men as Ernest Hemingway, John Dos Passos, Erskine Caldwell, Dashiell Hammett, Gilbert Seldes, Joseph Auslander, James T. Farrell, Gene Tunney, Douglas Fairbanks, Jr., Bobby Jones, and the first of more than 30 years of cartoons by E. Simms Campbell, who also created "Esky" as the little guy with ogling eyes and an upswept mustache. George Petty's cartoons were there too. And later would come the Vargas girls, who eventually made the transition to *Playboy*.[1]

The fashion-oriented magazine paid its writers $100 for a story, quite good for the Depression era. The next year it became a monthly and within three years had a circulation of 625,000. Famous writers continue to display their works through *Esquire*. However, during World War II the monthly "became a sort of uptown *Argosy*" and Gingrich left. It also became involved in a hassle with the Postmaster General, who removed its second-class mailing privileges, saying "it was not devoted to information of a public character or to literature." *Esquire* won when the Supreme Court said the Postmaster General had "no power to prescribe standards for the literature, or the art which a mailable periodical disseminates."[2]

Gingrich returned in 1952. Clay Felker, long associated with the magazine, was on the staff before taking over as editor of *New York* in 1962. In the 1960s the magazine was cited "for its editorial creativity and diversity, its original typographical and pictorial presentation, and its penetrating reporting of character and social trends." Gingrich urged his staff to keep its dissent; keep the essay, too, since: "It's the last haven in print for the meandering and browsing of those who look for the shunpikes to avoid the somnolent hyposis of the turnpike's forced sprint."[3] Gingrich died in 1976, shortly after involving *Esquire* in its most controversial situation, the sponsorship by the Xerox Corp. of a 23-page article by Harrison Salisbury which ran as "sponsored reporting" according to some critics. Xerox, however, did not exercise any editorial control over the article and *Esquire* compared the incident to corporate underwriting of prestige television programs. E. B. White, of *The New Yorker,* feared the erosion of the free press, while Norman Cousins of the *Saturday Review* said he was "jealous they didn't come to us."[4]

Another Gingrich innovation was the use of seven different covers for the June, 1968, edition. In addition to the basic design, *Esquire* featured different covers for Washington, Omaha, Los Angeles, Dallas, New Orleans, and Chicago. The magazine claimed it had something special to say to each of these communities.

Esquire opened its pages in the 1960s to many of the "New Journalists," including Gay Talese, Tom Wolfe, and others. Its 40th anniversary edition in 1973 included 564 pages, with material from 41 Pulitzer Prize winners and 15 Nobel Prize winners. The next year a Super Sports issue required nearly 400 pages.

Felker returned to *Esquire* in 1977, with financial assistance from London publisher, Vere Harmsworth, making his initial financial contact with an American publication.[5] Felker and his art director, Milton Glaser, were ready to mix "fresh ideas with the solid foundations of what was successful in the past," when Arnold Gingrich was its editor.[6]

These two men issued a dummy for the new edition that was to become a fortnightly. Felker said in this dummy edition:

> In creating a new *Esquire* we are lucky to have a rich heritage of almost forty-five years of the old *Esquire* to draw on. Looking back over the old issues, we were particularly struck by the freshness and the quality and, above all, the strength of the editorial formula of the very first *Esquire.*

Another change occurred in mid-1979, when two young men operating a company called 13-30 Corp. in Knoxville, took over the publication. Chris Whittle and Phil Moffitt had created several controlled-circulation magazines aimed for young persons, including *Nutshell, Graduate, 18 Almanac,* and *New Marriage.* These men had been classmates at the University of Tennessee. In 1970 they incorporated, using the title to represent their target market, persons between 13 and 30 years old. Their 13-30 Corp. had revenues of about $10 million and *Esquire* added some $12 million. They expected to more than double both by 1982. Financial assistance was provided in 1979 by The Bonnier Magazine Group in Sweden. *Esquire* returned to monthly status in March, 1980, with a new logo and new internal design.[7] The firm published its first trade magazine, *Floor Sales Quarterly,* in 1980.

PLAYBOY, PENTHOUSE AND OTHERS

Once referred to as the "merchants of raunchiness" by *Time,* the current men's magazines can be dated from the arrival of *Playboy* in 1953. However, publications often labeled "dirty" have existed in America for decades, but seldom did they occupy such a large space on the nation's newsstands nor did they clutter the mails so.

Hugh Hefner "made skin magazines successful and quasi-respectable by photographing not tarts but the wholesome-looking girl next door," according to his major competitor, Bob Guccione, of *Penthouse.*[8] Hefner has also been called "Father Rabbit" and has been the subject of many interviews, radio and television programs, books, and articles. Gay Talese's 1980 book, *Thy Neighbor's Wife,* devoted considerable space to Hefner's activities.

How important are these publications? In 1977, for example, the *Magazine Industry Newsletter* reported that the men's books were collecting some $300 million annually from newsstand sales. Two years later, for 1979 newsstand sales, *Folio* reported that *Playboy, Penthouse,* and *Hustler*—the three leaders—earned $258 million of their income from this source.[9] No wonder news dealers prefer to stock these magazines; regardless of their contents, they do bring in considerable income. And there are also dozens of other lesser-known titles on the newsstands.

Playboy's first issue arrived undated in December, 1953. Hefner, unsure about his future in publishing, had invested $600 of his money and had borrowed $6,000 to launch *Playboy,* more or less from his own kitchen where the layouts and copy were prepared. On this foundation he has built an empire with revenues in excess of $200 million annually, including non-publishing income. His daughter, Christie, is being prepared to take over the operation of Playboy Enterprises. The magazine, which reached its first million circulation in 1958, is the major element in the business.

Hefner believes he is "more creatively oriented than business oriented." Some of his ill-fated business venture proved this to be true, including his moves into the hotel area and into making movies. He also feels that today "we (our nation) are becoming openly interested in sex."[10] This change has occurred since *Playboy* began. He may be right about this public reaction; one can conclude this after visiting many newsstands and witnessing the growth of sex-oriented publications.

Playboy once operated casinos in England. In Atlantic City its hotel/casino opened in 1981. For years casinos in England accounted for much of the firm's profits. Hefner has clubs in both nations, the first United States unit having been started in Chicago in 1960. In the future, Hefner sees more in print, film and electronic media coming from his empire, no doubt under the leadership of Christie. In 1980 the firm produced specials for pay cable use. The firm earned more than $13 million in income of $363 million for 1980.

The financial success of *Playboy, Penthouse,* and the others has not been achieved without problems. Some supermarkets and newsstands require these magazines to provide wrappers for their nude covers. Others have placed them where younger readers may not reach them. Some keep copies under the counter, selling only to adults who request them. And on occasions community leaders have gone to court to have them banned. Most store owners answer with the traditional reply: "People want to buy these magazines and someone is going to sell them. Why not me?" Nevertheless, many dealers do separate the "skin books" from other consumer publications. *Playboy,* and especially *Penthouse,* return so much profit that they are reluctant to hinder sales by any fashion. In the opposition to the magazines as a group, some of the lesser known publications may lose sales, especially the "King Raunch," as *Time* described Larry Flynt, founder of *Hustler,* who claims, "Neither Hefner nor Guccione wants to admit that people are buying skin mags for a turn-on first and for editorial quality second."[11]

Playboy

Many individuals and firms have profited from Marilyn Monroe and her legend. The same can be said of Hugh Hefner, who used her nude photo in his initial edition of *Playboy,* a forerunner to today's Playmate. This issue, which appeared in late 1953, sold for 50¢ and of the 70,000 printed, 51,000 were sold. Those have since become collector's items.

Born in 1926, in Chicago, Hefner came from a Protestant fundamentalist background; however, his parents practiced intellectual freedom and urged their son to ask questions when puzzled. Hefner terms himself a liberator. He defends his actions by saying, "What the world calls morality is not necessarily moral." In answering charges that *Playboy* exploits women, Hefner said: "I buy a model's services at a fair rate of pay. It's utter foolishness to think that the only sexual objects are the homemakers."[12]

After Army service, Hefner attended the University of Illinois where he drew cartoons for the campus humor magazine. Early in his teens he adopted *Esquire* with its famous Petty Girls' drawings as his idol and after his university years he joined this magazine as a promotion copywriter in Chicago. He turned down a promotion which would have required his moving to New York, demanding $5 a week more than *Esquire* was willing to pay. The rest is history.

When one studies the development of *Playboy* one becomes aware of Hefner's indebtedness to *Esquire.* He used material in the public domain in early issues. Since *Esquire* had its Esky, Hefner needed his symbol too. "The rabbit had a kind of connotation and putting him in a tuxedo at the same time gave him a touch of sophistication. I thought it would be humorous and a charming symbol,'' he recalled. Yet all of this would have been hopeless without Marilyn's picture.

Hefner early sought a wide audience, between 18 and 80, although today the median age of his readers is about 30. He quickly proclaimed *Playboy* would not be a family magazine, but rather would be a "pleasure-primer styled to the masculine taste.'' His photographs set *Playboy* apart from other skin magazines since his Playmates "were healthy and attractive and if you could talk to a magazine—no doubt some did—you would have been tempted to ask, 'What's a nice girl like you doing in a place like this?' ''[13]

What keeps *Playboy* at the top? Hefner says it "remains a contemporary magazine by both reflecting and affecting the changes that have taken place.'' He considers television his major competitor rather than *Penthouse,* a magazine he feels "isn't related to anything . . . It's the modern equivalent of Victorian pornography.''[14] In the mid-1970s, *Playboy*'s circulation declined, from its peak of 7,200,000 to under 5 million, which prompted Hefner to re-establish its goal, "a life style book and an entertainment magazine in which sex would be one important element within a total package.''

Per-copy costs continue to climb, usually followed by a temporary slight decline in circulation. However, when it went to $2 it lost few readers. Special year-end and anniversary editions cost more.

Playboy remains "a response to the Puritan part of our culture which isn't anti-sexual.'' No doubt many agree with Hefner, who claims *Playboy* continues to exercise considerable influence in today's society. Many of its imitators are more sexually explicit, a situation that could not have existed on such a wide scale prior to *Playboy*'s arrival. It also has affected art, moving interest from the Norman Rockwell type of painting to more pop-art styles. And it also has affected women's periodicals.

Hefner has become a national symbol and, to some, an idol. His lifestyle has become as well known as that of some presidents, or at least, some of their brothers. Most followers know about his heavy consumption of Pepsis, his mansion in Chicago, and his West Coast playgrounds. Many airport visitors have been astonished to see the Bunny plane he formerly owned, painted in black except for the white rabbit on its tail. Gay Talese believed the nation desired more information about this unique personality so he devoted considerable space to his interests in *Thy Neighbor's Wife.* Two parts were reprinted in *Esquire.*[15]

Daughter Christie Next in Line

Hugh's daughter, Christie, is a vice president and a corporate office of Playboy Enterprises. She began her duties in 1975 and assisted in the magazine's 25th jubilee, which resulted in a 400-page issue, television and radio specials, Art of Playboy exhibit, a Playmate reunion, and numerous tributes and social events.

Christie believes the forthcoming emphasis will be on the second generation of *Playboy*. "The 'me decade' means young-thinking people who are placing a premium on enjoyment of life." She also notes that club keys now are being merchandized to women.[16] Christie, no doubt, reflects her father's philosophy that the public is catching up with the magazine. *"Playboy* remains a very contemporary magazine by both reflecting and affecting the changes that have taken place . . . It will change to the extent that society and its perspective changes."[17]

Christie Hefner has been described as "the apple of her father's eye, smart, cool and quick, an ardent feminist, an avowed Ms." A Phi Beta Kappa from Brandeis University, Christie became involved with the company's casino-hotel operation in Atlantic City in 1981, where *Playboy* Enterprises has from $35 to $50 million at stake. She will continue to promote feminist causes and possibly launch a new magazine or two. Since "modeling" doesn't appeal to her, she has no intention of posing for the centerfold.[18] *Vogue* magazine has approached her for fashion photographs but she professes a dislike for cameras.

The magazine has experimented with some one-shot periodicals and has others on the drawing board. The first was *Playboy's Guide to Electronic Entertainment*. To follow will be *Playboy's Guide to Fashion* and guides to photography, automotive, travel, food and drink.[19]

Hefner believes "that sex, far more than religion, is the major civilizing force on our planet" so it is easier to understand his hope that he "be remembered as someone who had a significant impact on society in a way (he) feels is important."[20] His Playboy Philosophy series ran for 25 issues, with excerpts appearing in the 25th anniversary number.

The magazine has on occasion been sued, but to date has not lost in court. Carol Baker claimed "great mental suffering, anguish, and distress" over her nude shots which she had approved earlier. Many of the important movie and television stars have appeared in *Playboy* with or without their clothes, especially in recent years when the magazine has reproduced many scenes from X- and R-rated movies. Suzanne Somers' nude shots appeared a decade after they were posed and that dispute helped newsstand sales. It increased her exposure beyond her television audience and for a brief time it cost her some television commercials.

Some advertisements are rejected, the "how to improve yourself type," yet among those accepted some questions arise. Several major automobile makers have stayed away, although the magazine continues to be so large that its size might eventually endanger "the girl in the middle." What if the magazine no longer can be stapled? What if it must be put together by the perfect-binding method?

"The Great *Playboy* Furor," as *Newsweek* labeled it, occurred in 1976 when the publication featured an interview with Presidential-candidate Jimmy Carter. In this article Carter admitted, "I've looked on a lot of women with lust. I've committed adultery in my heart many times.'' Newspapers had a field day, headlining the story with such titles as ''Sex, Sin, Temptation—Carter's Candid Views,'' ''Carter on Sin and Lust: I'm Human . . . I'm Tempted'' and ''Truth is Out.'' It had no visable effect on his campaign.

Playboy appears in many foreign editions, including German, Italian, Spanish, Japanese, Brazilian, Mexican, Australian, and French. These international editions add more than 2,100,000 to the 5,500,000 U.S. circulation. The foreign editions generally are smaller, from 135 to 200 pages compared to the 250 to 300 pages for the American edition.

Not all of Hefner's magazines have been so successful. In the 1960s he lost money on *Show Business Illustration* and *Trump,* a *Mad*-like humor magazine. *Oui,* however, has been more successful. Founded in October, 1972, this monthly apparently has an audience similar to *Playboy*'s—young men seeking better relationships between men and women. The initial issue said, ''The magazine publishes pictures of naked people, mostly women. Twenty years ago that was an unpopular thing to do because people thought of the unclothed body as a dirty, ungodly thing. Now it is an unpopular thing to do because people feel that women are treated far too much as objects by our culture, and publishing glossy photographs of them laid out like new watches or automobiles tends to reinforce this vicious stereotyping . . .''[21] Noting how complex this issue appeared, the editors invited readers to comment.

Oui's slogan has been ''For the Man of the World.'' This magazine, published by *Playboy* under a licensing agreement with French publisher Daniel Filipacchi, reached a circulation peak of 1,600,000 six months after its debut, but its 1980 figure had dropped to about 900,000.

For the 80s Hefner sees a need for *Oui* to be ''more service-oriented and more useful.'' He wasn't happy with the redesigned version in early 1980. Meanwhile, his intention appears to be to make *Oui* a *Cosmopolitan*-type magazine for the young men.[22] The company also publishes *Games,* ''America's favorite indoor sport.'' Its 1981 circulation had passed 600,000.

Penthouse

Only *Penthouse* has been a serious threat to *Playboy*. Bob Guccione established this magazine in America in 1969, after publishing it for four years in England. In the mid-1970s *Time* provided the following picture of the skin struggle for readership:

> (Since 1969) the two antagonists, as well as such panting competitors as *Gallery, Genesis, Dude, Club, Game, Cavalier, Adam,* and *Hustler* have been leaving less and less to the imagination. *Playboy* has expanded its Playmate of the Month spread from two or three pages to as many as nine. *Penthouse* routinely features male–female and female–female couples. Hefner's *Oui,* which set out three years ago to out-raunch *Penthouse,* is a virtual consumer guide to self-abuse, sadomasochism, bondage and other subjects that were once the province of hard-core pornography.[23]

Like Hefner, Guccione put together the first issue of his magazine mostly alone. Within 18 months he had repaid his obligations and within two years had started another magazine, *Forum,* primarily a collection of confessionals about sex exploits and fantasies. Five years after his arrival in America, his *Penthouse* had threatened *Playboy*'s circulation lead. Its 4 million circulation, however, never caught *Playboy*'s lead. He does better on the newsstands, since some 96 per cent of *Penthouse*'s circulation is sold there, while *Playboy* has only 40 per cent of such sales.

Today Guccione also publishes *Omni* and *Variations.* He works a heavy schedule yet lives a monklike style. *Money* magazine wrote about "The Wages of Skin," noting that Guccione planned to move into a "seven-story house on Manhattan's Upper East Side," after spending $4 million to remodel it. He is the sole owner of his publishing empire, valued between $150 and $300 million.[24] Both Hefner and Guccione love the informal, open-shirt style, apparently an attempt to emphasize their masculinity. All of Guccione's efforts have not proved successful. He lost a million dollars on *Lords,* a man's fashion magazine in the 1960s, and another million on *Photo World* in 1970. Even *Viva* cost him more than $14 million before it died. His latest, *Omni,* appears destined to a better fate, having recovered most of its start-up cost within two years.

Like Hefner, Guccione also has poured money into movie making and into the Atlantic City casino business, although he has encountered some financial delay there. Both men operate social clubs in England.

Guccione and the No. 3 publisher in this category, Larry Flynt, have engaged in an expensive libel suit. An Ohio jury in early 1980 awarded Guccione $39 million on a libel and invasion of privacy suit against *Hustler.* The issue involved a photograph of Guccione's head "that a retoucher put on a nude person taking part in a homosexual act." This might taper Flynt down a degree or so from his earlier statement that "Bob Guccione is just selling the same thing, but we are proud of it."[25] Guccione once said that Flynt's *"Hustler* has all the allure of a six-car accident. Morbid curiosity."[26]

Guccione has other magazines on the drawing board as well as special editions of his current holdings. *Viva* might even be renewed and an *Omni* fiction special is underway.

Penthouse received nationwide publicity such that money couldn't buy in early 1981 when it published an interview with Rev. Jerry Falwell, founder of the Moral Majority. It wasn't the interview that upset the television minister as much as it was its use in *Penthouse,* which the Virginia minister termed "a salacious, vulgar magazine." Falwell granted the interview to two freelance writers but denied he knew the material would appear in *Penthouse.* Falwell was, as usual, critical of American morals and when his article appeared "sandwiched between photo layouts of naked women, sex ads, bawdy jokes and risqué cartoons," as the United Press International reported, the minister sought a halt to *Penthouse* circulation. He lost in the courts.

Falwell also said he never objected to Jimmy Carter admitting he had lusted after women in his heart, but he said, "Giving an interview to *Playboy* magazine was lending the credence and the dignity of the highest office in the land to a salacious, vulgar magazine that did not even deserve the time of his day."

Penthouse, delighted at this extra, free, publicity, predicted it would sell at least 500,000 extra copies of the "Falwell edition."

Hustler

Just a farm boy from Kentucky is the way *Hustler* publisher Larry Flynt describes himself. With the opening of the 80s, *Hustler* had a guaranteed circulation of 1,800,000 with all but 35,000 sold on newsstands, a more profitable operation. However, the magazine peaked at 1,960,000 in 1976 and then dropped.

Hustler, which once published 30 nude photographs of Jackie Kennedy Onaissis swimming, no doubt has pushed *Playboy* and *Penthouse* nearer to hard-core pornography. *Hustler* was founded in Columbus, Ohio, in 1974, by Flynt, then a restaurateur. It is difficult to describe the extreme to which *Hustler* has gone to attract its jaded audience. "The Magazine Nobody Quotes" has been used as one of its slogans, yet the magazine returns a good profit, once estimated at $20 million a year.

Hustler publisher Flynt was recruited by President Carter's sister, evangelist Ruth Carter Stapleton, in late 1977 and *Newsweek* labeled the story, "Hustling for the Lord." Newspapers and magazines across the country carried an account of Flynt's confession before a Houston congregation. He said he would turn over the publication's control to his wife.

Two years later *Hustler* celebrated its fifth birthday and Flynt, listed as publisher and chairman of the board, wrote about his recent conviction in Georgia on counts of obscenity for selling *Hustler.* Flynt observed that "freedom of choice can no longer be taken for granted" as he called for obscenity prosecutions across the nation so all Americans would know first-hand how their rights were being threatened.[27]

Hustler offered a million dollars in prizes in a sweepstakes to build circulation in 1978, but postponed the drawing after Flynt was paralyzed in a Georgia shooting on March 6. This incident followed his arrest in Atlanta for obscenity charges. But this didn't upset the contestants, who sued. Flynt won, at least partially, an Ohio suit, although the decision still left the possibility that *Hustler* would be judged guilty of overt nudity and vulgarity.

Flynt also offered a million dollar reward in 1977 through full-page advertisements in 15 major newspapers for "information leading to the arrest and conviction of anyone involved in the planning or execution of President Kennedy's murder."

Flynt has been interested in expanding his publishing activities. Once he planned five magazines but these never materialized when both his health and his funds declined. He did acquire the Atlanta *Gazette,* a youth-oriented weekly, and the *Los Angeles Free Press.* The latter was suspended following the assassination attempt after he had said he planned to turn the *Free Press* into a "hard-hitting national news weekly." Althea Flynt, his wife and a former go-go dancer, has led a no-nonsense approach in managing his company since the shooting. She has curtailed activities and has cut back on staffs. In 1976, however, the firm started *Chic,* which reported a circulation of 267,000 in 1979. Briefly, the Flynts were publishing the *Plains Georgia Monitor,* but criticism of Billy Carter cost the pair advertising as well as a sales outlet at Billy's garage.

Hustler and *Chic* newsstand sales declined in 1980, although both reported slight gains in subscriptions.

There Are Others

Gallery, one of the "others," appeared in November, 1972, with F. Lee Bailey listed as publisher. He informed readers they could "expect a hefty supply of dressed and undressed ladies in our pages." It also contained eight pages of photographs of "Linda" by John Derek, better known today as the husband of "10." The magazine copied many of *Playboy*'s techniques, type faces, designs, departments, and the like. It even had the same subject for that month's interview—Jack Anderson.

Genesis arrived the same year and now has passed the 400,000 mark.

New Man began in 1981 as a monthly "for the young exec in his second or third career advancement who was not taught domestic survival." The debut copy noted it was the "national magazine for single men."

There Are Others, Too

Any trip to the newsstand will quickly reveal that the men's magazines, or girlie periodicals, occupy considerable space. Since they are usually high price, they bring the dealers considerable profits. And so they will continue to be available in the open market.

"Folio 400" listed the following men's publications in this category: *Playboy, Penthouse, Hustler, Oui, Gallery, National Lampoon, X Club, High Society, Velvet, Genesis, Cheri, Chic, Swank, Players, Club International, Eros, Adam,* and *Stag.* And there are dozens of others with irregular publication dates and lower circulations. Since their production costs are well below those of the better quality magazines such as *Playboy,* they need not sell many copies to return a profit.

7

The Young, the Romantic, and the Prime Timers

CHILDREN BECOME aware of magazines as early as their parents make periodicals available to them. Some even become acquainted with magazines before they are acquainted with the alphabet. Publishers, no doubt, visualize this as a splendid opportunity to capture this early interest of youth before it is lost to television.

As children grow, their interests are transferred to other magazines, usually those that are specialized to meet their day-by-day activities, such as scouting, crafts, hobbies, sports, music, and the like. Teens, too, have their outlets; as they grow older they read magazines directly aimed to high school and college-age students, to individuals entering the working world, and to those who want to indulge in the world of *Playboy-Penthouse* and/or *Ms.-Cosmopolitan-Redbook*.

Millions of readers become involved with the "Seven Sisters," as noted earlier, or with magazines designed for men in their middle years. As they grow older, a new market is waiting those in the 50-year-old and over category. Finally, along comes *Modern Maturity* and other periodicals for the so-called "Senior Citizens" in the 65-plus bracket.

Some of these periodicals are owned by publishers who have been established for years. For example, *National Geographic* established the *World* for younger readers, while *Ebony* came out with *Ebony Jr*. And other publishers have a stable of magazines with something for each age level, thus capturing an audience early and holding it for many years.

FROM THE BEGINNING

Children's Magazine, which appeared in Hartford in 1789, apparently was the first of a long list of hundreds of American publications designed for the younger readers. Although it survived only for three issues, it inspired others that followed. The Sunday School movement, for example, brought many religious-oriented periodicals and even today many children have their first exposure to periodicals in such Sunday classes.

In the early 1800s, the word "juvenile" dominated the titles, such as *Juvenile Magazine* (1802), *Juvenile Monitor, or Educational Magazine* (1811) and *Juvenile Port Folio* (1812). And there was *Parley's Magazine,* which existed from 1833 to 1844 and featured stories by "Peter Parley" (Samuel G. Goodrich) and contained items with Christian morals, articles, music, poetry, letters, serials, and numerous wood cuts.

Changes, of course, have occurred through the decades as children vary in their likes and dislikes. The more recent transition, from the 1960s to today, has been characterized by *Advertising Age* as follows: "The unwashed, uncombed, anti-establishment activities of the '60s have been succeeded by a breed that is noticeably well-groomed, conservative and future oriented."[1]

Today's youth magazine market reflects a specialization based on the reader's age and his or her special concerns, whether it be rock music, Boy Scouts, movies and television, or a desire to become better educated in the many professions or to learn more about hobbies and crafts and sporting activities.

Even before children learn to read they have available specialized magazines created to arouse their interests, improve their knowledge, inform them of religious principles and help them pass a rainy afternoon when the television set is on the blink.

For children between two and five, the *Writer's Market* notes the following: *Beehive, Children's Playmate, Children's Service, Friend, Highlights for Children, Humpty Dumpty, Kindergartner, Nursery Days, Odyssey, Our Little Friend, Primary Treasure, Ranger Rick's Nature Magazine, Story Friends,* and *Wee Wisdom.* Some, of course, overlap with the next age group, the six, seven, and eight-year olds. This group includes *Cricket, Dash, Ebony Jr., Jack and Jill, My Devotions, R-A-D-A-R, Touch, Trails, Video-Presse, The Vine, Weekly Bible Reader, Wonder Time, Young Crusader* and *Young Judaean.*[2]

The nine-to-twelve group includes *Child's Life, Crusader, Discoveries, Discovery, On the Line,* and *Young Musicians.*

Many of these are church-sponsored publications, such as the *Beehive* by the United Methodists; *Children's Service* programs by the Lutherans; *The Friend,* by the Church of Jesus Christ of Latter-Day Saints; *Young Judaean,* by the Hadassah Zionist Youth Commission; *R-A-D-A-R* for Christian Sunday Schools in general, and *Trails* for Christian girls.

Several firms that have nationally-circulated magazines for older audiences also have publications for younger age groups, seeking to capture the readers' attention early and then maintain it through the years. The Curtis Publishing Company, for example, offers *Children's Playmate* for the three to eight group; *Jack and Jill,* five to twelve; *Child Life,* seven to eleven, and *Young World,* ten to fourteen.

Parents Magazine Enterprises also competes for different groups. *Humpty Dumpty* starts with the four to eight group; *Children's Digest,* for seven to eleven; *Children's Playcraft,* seven to fourteen; and *Young Miss,* for those between ten and sixteen. Johnson Publishing Company has its *Ebony Jr.* and the National Geographic Society has its *World.*

Publishers seek endorsements from educators and teachers associations and in return bulk subscriptions are provided for classroom projects, together with materials to assist the instructors. Most publishers in this field depend on subscriptions rather than newsstand sales, stressing the excitement children experience in receiving their own mail.

Another best seller often discovered in the offices of doctors and dentists is *Highlights,* with a circulation in excess of 1,100,000. Termed, "the most educationally oriented of the children's magazines," *Highlights* is designed for those between two and twelve years old. An authoritative editorial board assists in constructing the contents for *Highlights,* which contains only editorial material. Across America there are more than 600 bonded sales representatives who answer inquiries about *Highlights,* usually after reading it in a doctor's office and removing one of the mailing coupons. Promotions also are conducted through schools. An emphasis is placed on renewals.[3]

"The magazine for children" is the subtitle for *Cricket,* published by Open Court Publishing Co. The editors offer a wide variety of articles, poems, chapters from books, drawings, and the like. Judith Duke considers it a literary magazine, "a cross between a children's magazine and a quality paperback." It is more expensive than many, yet its readers' response is heavy and the publication is profitable.

Ranger Rick's Nature Magazine is sponsored by the National Wildlife Federation for readers between four and twelve. The Federation sponsors Ranger Rick's Nature Club and members receive the magazine in addition to other benefits. The National Geographic Society has a similar arrangement for its *World* for the younger reader. Founded in 1975, the *World* is approaching a circulation of two million. Both publications are beautifully produced, with excellent articles and outstanding photographs.

Another non-profit organization, the Children's Television Workshop, has *Sesame Street* for the three to six group, and *Electric Company* for those five to eleven. Recently *Boing!* arrived, for those between eight and twelve. Established by the Children's Museum of Denver, *Boing!* went national to more than 20 children's museums. Tabloid in format, *Boing!* will be distributed free at least five times a year.

Scholastic magazines have guided millions of Americans through their school years. The organization began in 1920 with the *Western Pennsylvania*

Scholastic, which became *The Scholastic* in 1922 and *Senior Scholastic* in 1943. Through the decades, the firm has acquired other magazines, such as *St. Nicholas* in 1930. It has closed some, merged others, and renamed a few. It organized a Teen Age Book Club in 1948 and pioneered in audiovisual programs in the 60s.

Today's Scholastic Magazine Group includes *Senior Scholastic, Scholastic Voice, Scholastic Search, Scholastic Scope,* and *Science World.* These five publications, for the 14 to 18 age group, have a circulation in excess of 3,600,000. They also issue *Junior Scholastic,* for the 12 to 14 group, with a circulation over 1,000,000, and *Scholastic Newstime,* for the 10 to 12 bracket, with over 825,000 circulation. Teachers' editions are provided for classroom assistance for these bi-weekly magazines. The company reported ad volume for 1979 at $4,447,677 for 359 pages. Various combinations are provided advertisers.[4]

Juvenile publications have a promising future. They could, of course, be hurt by the same economic factors that affect other periodicals, such as cost increases in paper, postage, production and personnel. Nevertheless, they have a constant audience, one that continues to grow. Such publications will succeed if they can successfully compete with television for the young folks' attention.

For Teens and College Students

Several group publishers are involved in this broad market, that covers the teens through their college days. The 13-30 Corporation of Knoxville, Tennessee, is one of the leaders in this age bracket. The firm also publishes *Esquire,* which covers some of this age group as well. Named for the age group it serves, the 13–30 Corporation is only ten years old. It has pushed its combined magazine circulation from 6,000 to 18,000,000 in that time, earning recognition as one of the largest college-oriented publishers in America.

For example, *18 Almanac* is a manual/handbook for the graduating high school senior. In the same category is the *Graduate* for those 20 to 24. Topics include career prospects, life styles, interviewing guidelines, emotional adjustments, and other topics of concern to this age group.

Nutshell is another 13–30 Corporation product for the college community. With a circulation of 1,200,000, *Nutshell* greets the college students on hundreds of campuses each fall. The firm also publishes *Insider, On Your Own, Sourcebook, America, Sports Bulletin* and *Beginner's Guide to the Single Lens Reflex Camera.*

Seventeen

Seventeen, for young girls seeking help with their everyday problems, has been a major factor since its start in 1944. From its initial circulation of 400,000, it has reached 1,450,000, with an average readership of 6,500,000.

Life-size in the beginning, *Seventeen* followed the trend to *Time*-size, adjusting its contents to best serve the changing attitudes of American girls. From its Consumer Panel of 10,000 girls between 13 and 19, *Seventeen*'s editors and advertisers are able to keep well informed of reader preferences, both in editorial content and in the advertisements. Several questionnaires are mailed annually to girls who represent a market valued in excess of $20 billion annually. Dating and marriage problems are studied, as well as buying habits, career preferences and fashions. These topics and others are reported, including beauty and grooming, recreation, sports, hobbies, and home furnishings. Some fiction also is included. *Seventeen* has pioneered the study of the 12- and 13-year olds, who don't always behave as the 18- and 19-year-olds.

More than nine million households have at least one teenage girl. *Seventeen* is believed to reach more of these readers than any other magazine. Advertisers placed nearly $20 million worth of messages in 1979 issues. Despite its title that might limit its readership, *Seventeen* editors know from their studies that girls continue reading this magazine well into their college years.[5]

There are others competing for this teenage group, such as *16* magazine, published in New York since 1957. It reports a circulation of 320,000 in the 9 to 14 bracket.

Teen, designed for those between 12 and 19, has been available since 1957. Petersen Publishing Co. of Los Angeles reports *Teen* sells more than a million copies each month.

Teen Beat, a 1976 entry for the 12 to 16 group, is a product of Ideal Publishing Co. Teen personalities are stressed in this magazine, which sells 250,000 copies. Parents Magazine Enterprises' entry is *Young Miss,* a digest-size publication that started in 1978 and now sells 300,000 copies. *Co-ed* is distributed by Scholastic Magazines to more than a million 13 to 19-year-old students in home economic classes. It has been on the scene since 1956.

The Laufer Company competes with *Tiger Beat,* for the 9 to 14 group since 1965, and with *Right On!* for Black teenage girls. The latter, now with a circulation around 200,000, stresses stories about the entertainment world, with special attention to musicians and song writers. Charles Laufer reports that *Tiger Beat* is circulated in 80 countries. The firm notes that, "We're there for the kids to enjoy and like and when they stop liking us—well, I guess we just won't be there anymore."[6] Similar comments could be applied to any of these publications. Many of them have a limited, but faithful and devoted following. Idol worshipping groups have been around for decades.

And More Specialized Groups

Boys' Life, with a circulation exceeding 1,600,000, has been the voice of the Boy Scouts of America since 1912. Readers, generally between 9 and 16, are involved in sports, recreation, outdoor activities, science, careers, food, health, and other scouting interests. It appears to be the only magazine edited exclusively for boys.

Productions of Kiwanis International are *Circle K,* for the members of

Kiwanis-sponsored college clubs, and *Keynoter*, for the high school Key Club members.

For the agricultural groups there are the *National 4-H News* and the *National Future Farmer*. The former is the voice of the Washington-based National 4-H Council, while the latter represents the Virginia-based Future Farmers of America. Young adult leaders dominate the audience for the *4-H News*, while club members constitute the readership of the latter.

There are others, too, searching for the right mixture of contents to lure the young readers. *Ampersand* claimed more than 800,000 circulation in campus newspapers. Since 1977 it has been a supplement in 60 to 70 campus publications. *Circus* is a rock music bi-weekly, founded in New York in 1969 and with a circulation approaching 150,000, mostly males between 16 and 26. Another publication directed to rock music is *Creem*, for a male-dominated group with a median age of 21 years. Males also dominate readership of *High Times*, a 300,000-plus monthly from New York since 1974. The *Hit Parader*, a monthly from Connecticut, seeks a younger group, around 16 or 17, for those interested in top songs.

Young Athlete is a western bi-monthly founded in 1975 with a circulation of 110,000. Its audience is mixed, around 15 years of age. Other new sports magazines are *Prep Basketball* and *Prep Football*, started in 1979 in New York. These are circulated free through high schools. Parents, teachers, and students from more than a thousand schools are the primary readers.

More than 1,500,000 girls between 13 and 21 receive *Young Once*, a sampling-type publication by the 12/21 Corp. in Connecticut.

Two magazines stand apart from the others. *National Lampoon*, a New York monthly since 1970, has a circulation of 650,000 for those between 18 and 24. Male readers dominate, accounting for 80 per cent of the audience. *Rolling Stone* has been around since 1967. This twice-a-month tabloid resembles a magazine in its content, which attracts a high male readership among those in their early 20s. *Rolling Stone* claims it is "read by the largest concentration of 18 to 24 and 18 to 34-year olds of any publication measured by any syndicated research." Possibly so, since its circulation exceeds 720,000.[7]

Not exactly falling into the magazine category, yet competing for much of the same audience as these periodicals are the comic groups. The major comic groups with their founding dates include Archie (1942), Harvey (1940), Charlton (1945), Whitman (1961), DC (1938) and Marvel (1939). Their circulation figures reach into the millions. Males generally dominate the readership reports.

Another slightly different publication, started in late 1980, is *Penny Power*, by Consumer Reports, for the 8 to 12 year olds. It has been designed to evaluate products, being "proconsumer and not antibusiness," although some firms no doubt will not agree to this goal. The *Wall Street Journal* noted on Sept. 17, 1980, that *Penny Power* was to be an "alternative to the glossy consumer magazines some big companies have begun to distribute in the schools." Its initial circulation was 24,000, with a goal of 150,000 by 1984.

More recent entries include *BMX Plus* for teenagers with interest in motorcross bicycles, and *Guitar World* for amateurs.

ROMANCE AND CONFESSIONS

For the post-college-age group, there are other magazines than the "Seven Sisters," the innovative women's publications, or the special interest editions. These "others" come under the romance and confession category.

Bernarr Macfadden, who started *True Story* in 1919, created the "confessions industry." Earlier he had created the "nudity industry" with his *Physical Culture* magazine and his frequent bathing beauty contests and fitness programs, often conducted in New York's old Madison Square Garden. From the thousands of letters he received from broken-hearted men and women who read *Physical Culture,* Macfadden established *True Story* to prove "truth is stranger than fiction." Macfadden's view of his magazine was compared to a priest hearing confessions. The articles were from amateur writers and he wanted them to read that way. Editors were not permitted to edit so that the "common touch" would be maintained. *True Story,* to Macfadden, was a publication designed to teach one about life and human nature and to take one's mind off his everyday cares.

True Story obviously was a product of the times, the post-World War I period that also witnessed the expansion of sex magazines and motion picture fan publications. Tabloids reached the newspaper scene at the same time, with the advent of the *New York Illustrated Daily News* in 1919. Early articles in *True Story* contained sex-oriented passages, but if they had a strong moral ending this was permitted by critics and authorities. A group of ministers was organized as a screening committee to review these stories and thus to counter such condemnation by outsiders. In addition, Macfadden had another review group, the potential buyers of *True Story:* taxicab drivers, barbers, store clerks, and assorted individuals. If they saw some potential in a manuscript it was then considered for use in *True Story.*

One of *True Story*'s early editors, William Rapp, said: "Our stories have only the normal amount of sex that you'll find in anyone's life. They're written in the common idiom . . . you've got to remember that with people of low incomes, there's a close relation between morality and economics. Liquor, immorality, gambling, etc. destroy a wage-earner's home much more quickly and surely than they do in the homes of people who have more money."[8]

True Story conducted numerous contests. It described itself as "the new irresistibly interesting *fiction* publication," thus raising some question about its title. Macfadden called for "simple stories, simply told, of people like the readers themselves; stories with the same problems that the readers themselves

are constantly meeting.'' Some of the magazine's stories were made into motion pictures. Others found their way into radio programs. Some persons believe *True Story* made readers of the semi-literate.[9]

Macfadden capitalized on the "True" concept with other magazines such
as *True Detective, Detective Mysteries, Experiences, Ghost Stories, Love and
Romance, Lovers, Proposals, Radio Tales, Romances, Stories of Love and Romance,* and *Strange Stories.* He made millions of dollars from this basic publishing venture but spent it equally fast on other projects not so successful.

The Macfadden Women's Group today has no association with the original
Macfadden family. Members of today's group include *True Story, Photoplay,
True Confessions, Secrets, True Romance, True Experience, True Love,* and
Modern Romances. The combined circulation totals around three million. At
its peak, *True Story* sold in excess of 2,500,000 monthly, mostly at news-
stands.

Writing much later about such magazines, Nona Cleland thought "femin-
ism has found a small foothold in the confessions," but these publications were
not designed for a woman who is more concerned about a career. Her review
of the leading magazines in this field notes the lighter stories, the traditional
mother-in-law conflicts, the bored housewife and her difficulties, the standard
boy-meets-girl, boy-saves-girl, boy-gets-girl saga, and a few serious and even
political themes.[10]

While "True" might be a part of the title of such publications, this is no
guarantee all such articles fall into this category. One of *True Story*'s early
editors claimed years later that he was a top "plot man." Calling in his prolific
authors, he would map out a plot and then turn a writer loose to prepare the
"true story." Cleland tells of a Nevada woman who admits to writing at least
500 confession stories. She obtained her plots from many sources, "neighborhood happenings, newspaper clips, from radio call-in shows." For 15 years
she wrote for a firm before it folded in the late 70s.

Editors realize many such stories are written by professionals but they
justify their use on the basis that each plot is formulated on facts involving
someone someplace. Such incidents could have happened to many of the faithful, believing readers. The covers are designed to attract the newsstand buyer
with such come-on lines as these: "My baby is safe in my arms once more,"
"I loved her . . . why didn't she trust me to understand?" "Doctor, Don't let
me do it again," and "Why can't you start acting like a husband?"

In addition to the Macfadden Group, which is the largest, there are the
Complete Women's Group (*Intimate Romances, Intimate Secrets,* and *True Secrets*); Ideal Romance Group (*Intimate Story* and *Personal Romances*); and the
KMR Women's Group (*Real Romances, Teen Bag,* and *Real Story*). One quickly
observes that the reader must shop with caution if she prefers the same magazine each month. The titles are, after all, rather similar.

Thus we witness another series of publications designed to attract readers,
even a few too young to read. And once the reader is "hooked" on publica-

tions he or she can continue to find something of interest in them throughout the rest of his or her life.

Next we turn to another age group, those who have reached the prime time of their lives and are planning for even more matured years ahead.

From Prime Time to Modern Maturity

With the median age moving up steadily in America, more interest is being directed to senior citizens. According to the Census Bureau, the median age in America advanced from 16.7 in 1820 to 30 years in 1979, and it will continue upward. Another age group, those between 45 and 64, also continues to expand, and now accounts for 20 per cent of the nation's population. The 50-and-over market totals more than 54 million individuals and it, too, continues to grow. By the 80s there were more than 20 million Americans 65 and over, according to Maturity Magazines advertisements which also estimated that the over-50 group represented a total income of $355 billion. No wonder many advertising and merchandising forces now eye this segment of America.

Concern about growing old has affected humans throughout our history. Explorers came to America in search of a fountain of youth; individuals continue to move across the nation with a similar goal, seeking a panacea for their aging pains. Magazines for this group did not appear until 1935, although a few pioneer publications contained articles directed to the elderly, a term with varying interpretations. Benjamin Franklin, for example, wrote about a new method for "embalming" drowned persons, while he explored a concept that lightning might affect the resurrection of deceased persons and animals. In Franklin's time readers were more concerned about such preparations for their own resurrections than some readers appear to be today.

When the *Journal of Living* appeared in 1935, its market was the 40 and over group. It was a time when "Life Begins at 40" was a major slogan, a philosophy welcomed by millions of Americans. This publication originally served as a house organ for the Serutan Company, a laxative manufacturer. Eventually it reached a circulation of 225,000 with most copies sold on newsstands.

The *Journal of Living* was a nutrition magazine at first with articles such as these: "How to Take a Sunbath," "Menus for the Blood-Building Diet," and "We Are What We Eat." About the size of *Time, Journal of Living* began with 4,000 subscribers, all seeking to prove that "health is earned by individual effort." Readers were advised that all advertisements would "be to further the comfort, welfare and health of its readers."

According to one of its early editors, Ann White Segre, the *Journal of Living* began its shift to older people in 1950 and "by 1952 it was really a senior citizen magazine." Segre noted in 1980 that this magazine was an innovator, "for plain, ordinary people who wanted to know how to adapt to the food and the diets that were available and how to get the most out of it." Other topics, similar to many in today's magazines, covered money problems, how and where to retire, ordinary fears, and the like.[11]

Meanwhile, *Lifetime Living* arrived in May, 1952, a monthly "intended to appeal to mature men and women. The magazine will discuss problems of adjustment from the age of 40 years on."[12] *Business Week* noted that this magazine was "probably the first full-dress publication to aim specifically at the interests of 'mature' people." Thus in a sense *Lifetime Living* deserves credit for being the first periodical designed for the senior citizens. One thing is certain—the merged product that followed was the only popular magazine for senior citizens in the early 1950s. To support its claim, *Lifetime Living*'s articles included "Get Ready for Your Best Years," "Where to Retire," and "There Is Sex Life After 50." Also included were features on foods, fashions, health, hobbies, and financial planning, all staple items in today's publications.[13]

The *Journal of Living* merged with *Lifetime Living* in May, 1955, becoming the *Journal of Lifetime Living*. The merged product became digest-size with stories such as "I Live on $87.50 a Month," "How to Marry Off a Daughter," and "Watch Out for Second Mortgages!" Advertisements covered mobile homes, vitamins, cereals, and Florida real estate opportunities.

Nevertheless, the *Journal of Lifetime Living* could not be sold to advertisers, who failed at that time to recognize the potential markets these older citizens represented. The prospectus for *Lifetime Living* had noted that "A visitor from Mars, judging us by the magazines, would think nobody in America ever lived beyond 30." More than reader acceptance is necessary for any magazine to succeed so in early 1960 the *Journal of Lifetime Living* was acquired by the American Association of Retired Persons (AARP) and discontinued.

Others Are Established

Modern Maturity, established in 1958 by the AARP, took over the *Journal of Lifetime Living* subscription list. Dr. Ethel Percy Andrus, a retired California teacher, founded AARP in 1958 after having started the National Retired Teachers Association in 1947. Members of AARP receive *Modern Maturity;* members of NRTA receive the *NRTA Journal,* started in 1950. For pre-retirees in the middle-age category, there is *Dynamic Years,* started in 1965. All are bi-monthly. In addition, there are the *AARP News Bulletin* and the *NRTA News Bulletin* to keep readers abreast of latest governmental activities in their areas of concern.

Today the nation has a greater awareness of the older citizens, so *Modern Maturity,* the leader, has a circulation in excess of seven million; *NRTA Journal,* 500,000; and *Dynamic Years,* 250,000. In mid-1979 these magazines for the first time opened their pages for advertisers in an attempt to "shore up finances and take advantage of the current enlightment view of older people."[14] The three magazines, all under the same publishing organization, promised advertisers more than 12,500,000 readers over 50 years of age. Previously these publications carried an exclusive message from one insurance group, a situation that created questions about the activities of a non-profit-making organization. For the last nine months of 1980, *Modern Maturity* carried in excess of $5 million worth of advertising. Editor Hubert Pryor said, "This is due to the fact that Madison Avenue is emerging from its ante-deluvian era to recognize this sleeping giant."[15]

Each of these three magazines has its specific audience, although there is some overlapping. *Modern Maturity,* for the older individuals, features nostalgia, medical news, memoirs, and similar topics. The *NRTA Journal* provides special data about teacher legislation, while *Dynamic Years* is aimed for the still-active group, those persons employed yet already planning for their retirement.

To capitalize on this expanding interest in the elderly, other publications have been established.

Harvest Years began in 1961, also in California along with the Modern Maturity group. *Harvest Years* started as an outgrowth of the initial White House Conference on Aging in 1960. The first editor, Peter A. Dickinson, said: "The main thrust was to sell it to the corporations as a sort of retirement planning and retirement living vehicle." As Dickinson remembered, "when you were 65 (in the 1960s) you were all washed up, and also people at that time were retiring on very little money. They weren't a viable market at all."[16]

In 1972 *Harvest Years* became *Retirement Living;* six years later it acquired its present title, *50 Plus*. Editor Roy Hemming said the title explains the audience he seeks to cover with a "wide cross-section of topics—some specifically informational in terms of health care and nutrition, retirement planning, money management, travel and living environments; and some strictly for entertainment (celebrity profiles, crossword puzzles, movie and TV reviews and so forth)."[17] A typical issue noted the slowness of the Federal Food and Drug Administration to approve new drugs; the job market for retirees; cures for headaches; consumer affairs; Buddy Ebsen gets younger every year, and reports on travel, food, and health concerns.

50 Plus, with a circulation approaching 200,000 as the decade opened, has a goal of a million by 1985. In order to compete with the many advantages provided readers of the Modern Maturity group, *50 Plus* offers retirement guides and kits for the elderly. The monthly carries a wide variety of advertisements.

With the opening of the 80s, *Prime Time* arrived "for people in their prime" without specific reference to any age group. Publisher Barbara Hertz told readers she was 58, with two grown daughters and two grandchildren. "Although there are 44 million of us between the ages of 45 and 65 in this country, the media have been studiously ignoring us for years, apparently assuming that we were stick-in-the-muds," she wrote in the first edition, dated January, 1980. To counteract this myth, *Prime Time*'s first number discussed the home with the children gone, the buying of a luxury resort, exploring Mexico's golden riviera, nouvelle cuisine unscrambled, nostalgia, classic cars, and similar subjects.

Started with 70,000 subscribers and a $4 million nest egg, the publisher promised that no advertisements would be carried that might suggest mid-lifers were not in their prime. In other words, no denture cream or casket ads. The first edition messages were for wines and spirits, hotels, travel, beauty aids, and home furnishings. The magazine labels its readers the "young fogies." By early 1981 its circulation had reached 150,000.

There are other such magazines with limited audiences. For example, the Days Inn of America motel group publishes *September Days* for members. Articles are directed to senior citizens who pay a small annual membership fee and in return receive a discount when they stay in Days Inns.

There also is the *New England Senior Citizen*, published since 1970 for the 55-plus group in that area. The same concern also publishes the monthly *Senior American News*, started in 1975. Farther down the Eastern shores, the *Southern World* appeared in 1979 in South Carolina. The National Association of Retired Federal Employees has its monthly *Retirement Life* with a circulation in excess of 315,000. One must not overlook the many other periodicals designed at least in part for the 45 and older groups, yet considered for special men or women audiences with interests in homes, gardens, sports, business, and many other areas.

What's Ahead?

Since this market is sure to expand, one can expect additional magazines to appear on the newsstands. Statistics indicate that the 50 to 64-year-old segment represents persons in their highest earning years. With their children through their university years, parents have more discretionary funds available for other interests. As media director George Rosenbranc noted:

> Lawrence Welk and Walter Cronkite are no longer the only available media vehicles. New media opportunities are occurring and should increase in the very near future providing advertisers show sufficient interest and daring.[18]

"Market with a future, Retirement" is an informative study made by *Marketing & Media Decisions* that noted, "Many people now retire only partially, and delay quitting past 70." The study focused on the "discretionary spending" by those in the 55-plus market, estimated in excess of $200 billion in 1977 and obviously much higher today.[19]

There are millions of men and women in the "mature period" and, as this study indicates, magazines are there appealing to their interests and needs. The potential was revealed in late 1980-early 1981 when a new money market fund was established for members of the AARP-NRTA. More than $90 million poured into this fund each month during its initial year.

8

Mass Magazines: Life *to* People

Pictures are for rich or poor, without regard for race, class, creed or prejudice, speaking the same language . . . you use one vernacular to a truck driver, another to a bank president. But the truck driver and bank president will stand shoulder to shoulder to watch a parade. Only in the subject of pictures will their interest draw apart . . .[1]

Henry Luce, the founder of *Time* and *Life* had additional views toward the role of pictures in our lives. In his lengthy prospectus for *Life* Luce concluded that the public goals were:

To see life; to see the world; to eyewitness great events; to watch the faces of the poor and the gestures of the proud; to see strange things—machines, armies, multitudes, shadows in the jungle and on the moon; to see man's work—his paintings, towers and discoveries; to see thousands of miles away, things hidden behind walls and within rooms, things dangerous to come to; the women that men love and many children; to see and to take pleasure in seeing; to see and be amazed; to see and be instructed . . .[2]

Nearly a century earlier Americans had been told that "This wonderful art of Photography, this true child of the sun, last-born and fairest, has caught expression and traced form and feature with a more delicate and accurate pencil."[3] Thus for more than a century pictorial publications have attracted Americans. And they still do. American newspapers imitated London publications in the early 18th Century. So when magazines appeared here they too copied from abroad. The monthly *Penny Magazine* attracted English readers in 1830. Then, in 1842, the weekly *London Illustrated News* had a strong following. Magazines with the word "illustrated" in their titles were published in Paris, Leipzig, Berlin, the Vatican, and in other localities.

143

In America, *Gleason's Pictorial Drawing-Room Companion* was a "copiously illustrated family miscellany" in 1851, its style copied from the *London Illustrated News*. Four years later, an English engraver named Henry Carter issued *Frank Leslie's Illustrated Newspaper*, which survived under various titles until 1922. Civil War buffs are acquainted with the work of Mathew B. Brady, whose pictures recorded this conflict. Since magazines could not mechanically reproduce such pictures in the mid-1860s, they turned to woodcuts and steel engravings for their illustrations. Often these used pictures for their models. Newspapers began to print pictures in the 1870s; magazines adopted the practices in the 1890s. Bernarr Macfadden's *True Story* in 1919 pioneered in the use of models to pose for illustrations for his short stories, novels, and other articles.

Collier's Once a Week, which first appeared in 1889, later was renamed *Once a Week, An Illustrated Weekly*. The *New York Times* established its *Mid-Week Pictorial* in 1914 more as a war extra to stress the news photos of World War I. Between 1919 and 1924 the New Yorkers' appetite for pictures was satisfied at least in part by three new tabloids, the *News, Mirror,* and *Graphic*. Then there was a rash of newcomers, mostly around for a brief stay, including such as *Panorama, Roto, See, Dime, Focus, Pix, Click, Peek, Picture,* and many others.

During the closing decades of the 19th Century, magazines arrived directed to those interested in photography, including the *Philadelphia Photographer* (1864–1923); the *American Journal of Photography* (1879–1900); *Anthony's Photographic Bulletin* (1870–1902); *Photographic Times* (1871–1915); *St. Louis Practical Photographer* (1877–1910). There were others, too, some merely representing changes in titles.[4] In Mott's extensive study of magazines in America, he noted such periodicals as *Godey's Lady's Book, Peterson's, Ladies Repository, Electric, Appleton's Journal,* and others that featured illustrations from woodcuts and steel plates before photography arrived. By 1884, the *Century* and *Harper's Weekly* devoted about 15 per cent of their space to illustrations.[5]

Although these publications have disappeared, today's readers remember *Life* and *Look*, products of the 20th Century. Other publications today, such as *People*, feature photographs. And there are the how-to-do-it magazines, such as *Modern Photography* and *Popular Photography*, and the more recent *American Photography* that views pictures more as art.

LIFE RESTORED: THE POWER OF PICTURES

Dun-Donnelley published an interesting two-page message in *Advertising Age* in mid-1973 with a large photograph featuring three tombstones under the headline:

"*Life, Look,* and the pursuit of Circulation"

The tombstones featured *Look*, Born: 1937; Died: 1971; *Life*, Born: 1936: Died: 1972; and the *Saturday Evening Post*, Born: 1821: Died: 1969.

Dun-Donnelley's message was directed to the business press, using these failures among the mass media magazines as examples, to warn about the pitfalls of circulation battles. More concern was expressed here for "a tightly-defined, target audience at reasonable prices." In other words, "Not circulation, but market coverage."[6]

With the opening of the 70s, optimism was the key word with both *Life* and *Look*. "If the American public is to tackle and solve the problems of our day, somebody has to tell them about it, and that's what we're doing," said *Life* publisher Gary Valk. At *Look*'s offices, publisher Thomas R. Shepard, Jr., termed his magazine "a platform for all Americans to turn to, to learn about the basic issues, the real gut issues of our day, race, the environment, the SST . . . It is information and entertainment for the whole family."[7]

With the start of the 80s, *Life* had been re-established. *Look* tried again but failed in its attempt to rejoin the mass media arena.

Advertisers, Others Blamed

Life's earlier existence had been shortened by some advertisers who became disenchanted with the mass media market concept and so turned their attention to specialized publications. Roland Wolseley outlined factors he believed contributed to the decline of such publications as *Life:*

1. Production costs moved upward.
2. Distribution costs followed upward.
3. Advertising revenues were up, but not sufficient to cover 1 and 2.
4. Management attempted to absorb some of these costs.
5. Forced circulation declines (by *Look, Life, SEP,* and others) failed to bring anticipated goals.
6. Many smaller advertisers could not pay the high rates, even for demographic conditions.[8]

During its final four years, *Life* lost some $30 million, surrendering its leadership in advertising revenues to *TV Guide*. In order to overcome such problems and the fragmented audiences that had developed, the new *Life* and *Look* sought increased revenues from circulation, with more emphasis on single copy sales and less on costly cut-rate subscriptions. Such a trend had been predicted by John Mack Carter, editor of *Good Housekeeping,* who anticipated that by 1980 circulation revenue would cover about 80 per cent of production costs.[9] Although it has not quite reached objective, circulation revenues are increasing steadily today. When the *Saturday Evening Post* was the nation's best-read weekly in the early 1900s, the readers did not contribute enough to pay for the paper used in each copy. *Playboy* publisher Hugh Hefner was ahead of Carter, profiting from the start from both circulation and advertising revenues with his magazine.

In one sense, *Life* never really disappeared from the nation's newsstands when it ceased as a weekly. *Life* management said in 1972 that the publication would "suspend," not "fold." After that year ten special reports appeared, including some year-end "The Year in Pictures," "The Spirit of Israel," "The 100 Events That Shaped America," and others. In addition, two books, *The Best of Life* and *Life Goes to the Movies,* brought millions of dollars to Time Inc. and kept the name *Life* before the public.[10]

The revised *Life* arrived in October, 1978, following nearly a year of planning which involved the production of two dummies. Philip B. Kunhardt, Jr., who had been with *Life* since 1950, headed a staff of ten that produced these preview issues. An earlier dummy had been designed in 1974 but Kunhardt said "that was not the right time for bringing it back. Time Inc. was still struggling with *People* and *Money* magazines, the economy was turning bad, and the magazine business was not as interesting as it is today."[11]

When Time Inc. officials gave the "Go" signal Editor-in-chief Hedley Donovan said: "The magazine field is generally vigorous, and it seems an appropriate moment to bring back one of the great forces in American journalism. The power of the picture, which the old *Life* did so much to magnify, has never been greater than today. The new *Life* will be applying the selectivity of a monthly to spectacular news events; people, famous and not, captured in memorable moments; the beauties and mysteries of nature, science and medicine; the world of art, architecture, sport, fashions."[12]

A first-issue advertising record was established when 56 pages of the 140-page edition totaled $848,568 in revenues. Within eight months this figure passed the million-dollar mark.

The new *Life* was directed toward a smaller but more affluent audience, indicated in part by its $1.50 per copy price and no-discount subscription price of $18 a year, a far cry from the previous cut-rate policies of the earlier decades. Its projected circulation, with emphasis on newsstand sales, was only 700,000, compared with 5.5 million it had when it ceased in 1972 or its top of 8.5 million. By April, 1979, its rate base went to a million. Andrew Heiskell, Time Inc. chairman, said the monthly would have a "less newsy, higher quality, more pictorial format." Publisher Charles A. Whittingham said that *"Life* is coming out at a time when photographs are being treated like works of art. Combine that with our large size (10⅛ x 13⅛) and high quality paper and printing (rotogravure) and we've got a really bold magazine."[13]

Using its familiar but enlarged logo, *Life* featured balloons on its cover with details about this expanding sport, plus an 8,000-word extract from Mario Puzo's *Fools Die.* Unlike the earlier *Life* with its collection of the world's greatest photographers, this new edition planned to use the work of other Time Inc. publications and of freelancers around the world. One of the original *Life* photographers, Alfred Eisenstaedt, now rents space in the *Time/Life Building* in New York.

Photographers were excited over the revival of *Life* and *Look.* Hedley Donovan had stressed the plan to use predominantly four-color photographs, "varied with black-and-white photography, artists' illustrations, and a few articles and columns." Kunhardt, the managing editor, said *Life* was not "going to be running pictures because they're nice. We're going to be concerned with content and what we're saying with the pictures.'' Such statements prompted *Popular Photography* to conclude: ''The photo-journalism psychological void will partially be filled and renewed opportunities will be available for the thinking, hardworking photojournalist with imagination and ideas.''[14]

Life will be challenged as never before by other media. After its first decade of publishing, Dan Longwell, managing editor in 1946, said, ''We've done everything.'' A decade later, Heiskell asked: ''How can one be an institution and yet be new and different and surprising each week?'' Ed Thompson, managing editor from 1949–1961, however, was wrong in his 1975 prediction that there would never be another *Life:* ''Nobody's going to do it. I don't think you can find any money man who would pass a sanity test who would finance it.''[15] Thompson's magazine publishing ability is evident today with the *Smithsonian,* which he edited during its first decade.

Life has made it back, apparently in a more secure situation, with more achievable goals. It has profited from the nation's love for pictures. It no longer seeks to compete with weekly periodicals on timely news events. Rather, it will provide us with the best, material that historians will find of value in the years to come.

Life's wrap up of the 1970s netted sales of 1,600,000 copies of the December, 1979 edition, well above its million guarantee. This was its best sales record since its rebirth.

LOOK: HERE TODAY, GONE TOMORROW

Look magazine initially folded on October 19, 1971. It folded again in August, 1979. *Look* had appeared in 1937 from the Midwest, the product of Gardner C. (Mike) Cowles, Jr. and John Cowles, who had established their journalism careers on the Des Moines *Register and Tribune,* a family-owned operation. *Look*'s founders carefully monitored the development of the newcomer *Life* before the Cowles' published their adless monthly magazine, using techniques developed at least in part on the Sunday *Register*'s picture story format. George Gallup's pioneer research, tested on the Des Moines papers, had called for a greater use of pictures to lure more readers.

Sensationalism became associated with *Look,* with its emphasis on death, sex, and violence, its use of cheaper pulp paper and its rotogravure printing. *Life*'s glossy stock and letterpress printing stood out in contrast. Later *Look* became a fortnightly, widely quoted, with a peak circulation of nearly eight million in 1967. With more than 30 million readers, *Look,* like *Life,* won numerous major awards before its death. Between its start and finish, *Look*'s executives also gave the public the miniature *Quick* (1947–1953) and the unusual *Flair* (1950–1953).

Look pioneered in 1959 with Magazone, a new concept in regional advertising. First offered in seven areas, the plan expanded to 75 to help combat the invasion of television. In 1969, *Look* introduced Top/Spot, the first "geo-demic" issue limited to specific zip code zones with high median incomes. Eventually, some 160 separate editions of some *Look* issues were developed. Other publishing innovations involved its Kromatic printing, a high-speed color process combining the best of letterpress and gravure without requiring plates. Its Krome covers offered better reproductions, with less chance of ink smearing and smudging. Three-dimensional reproductions at high speed came through *Look*'s Xographic process.

By 1962, *Look* had passed both *Life* and the *Saturday Evening Post* in circulation with more than 7 million. Its "publishing event of the decade" was William Manchester's "The Death of a President," in four installments. This series on John F. Kennedy, which created considerable controversy as well as litigation, attracted nearly 70 million readers.

Meanwhile, problems developed after advertising revenues of $80 million in 1966 began to decline. In its "Record of the *Look* Years," the publisher noted these losses, together with the decline in subscription sales on the door-to-door installment basis, higher operating costs including projected postal rate hikes, and television. *Look* shifted its circulation to the top metropolitan markets, cutting off a million subscribers to reach 6,500,000 to attract advertisers. But it didn't work. Gardner Cowles said the termination was "even more painful" because "readership surveys and the response to *Look*'s subscription and renewal offers have never been better." His heart said "keep it going" but his head said "suspend it."[16]

During its existence, *Look* stressed people over things, but did not stress spot news or fiction. It had a more personal, first-person approach, a maximum of photographs with a minimum of text.

Some seven years later a new *Look* arrived. Daniel Filipacchi had been successful in his restoration of *Paris Match*. A disc jockey at 28, Filipacchi founded *Jazz* magazine in Paris in 1955 and eventually added other magazines to his group. He recognized the United States as the center of the magazine profession, a place where one could make money as well as lose money. He had witnessed the investment of Gruner + Jahr, a German firm, in *Parents, Humpty Dumpty,* and *Handy Andy,* as well as the investment by Rupert Murdoch, of Australia, in *New York* and other enterprises.

A pilot issue for *Look* appeared in September, 1978, featuring a story on John F. Kennedy about "Revealing Boyhood Letters." Another story asked: "Can Carter Survive?" Television's "Sexist Season" featured photographs of a "bevy of career-minded females all vying for top ratings." The cover stressed a woman dressed in a fighting Marine uniform. Filipacchi promised "the new *Look* will combine something of the old *Look,* something of the old *Life,* something of *Paris Match* and something new."[17]

When the initial public issue appeared February 19, 1979, four months after the restoration of *Life, Look* had East/West covers. Editor-president Robert Gutwillig placed a photo of Nelson A. Rockefeller, who had just died, on the East cover, while Patty Hearst, recently released from prison, was on the West edition. The magazine, with its odd 9 x 12 size, was printed in four cities. Later *Look* obtained exclusive rights to the wedding story of Patty Hearst and spread the material over three issues.

Similarities were seen to *People. Newsweek* observed the emphasis on celebrities. "There is more text than in *Life.* But the accent is on pictures, and *Look*'s lush, color photography and crisp, black-and-white layouts provide a tempo and texture that compare favorably with popular European magazines like *Paris Match* and *Stern* in Germany."[18] James Brady, *Advertising Age* columnist, noted that neither *Life* nor *Look* was so different from *People* "except that *People* is out every week, *Life* every month, and *Look* somewhere in-between." Gutwillig said "It's the old *Life* come back as a bi-weekly for a new time." Although it had originally been planned for weekly publication, financial difficulties turned it into a fortnightly picture newsmagazine before its public appearance. Later it became a monthly for the same reasons. Some writers felt the shift from weekly to bi-weekly created initial staff problems; many experienced editors and writers had been hired for weekly planning. Gutwillig was anxious about early issues and had reason to be. Sales reached between 750,000 and a million, with circulation guarantee of 600,000 to advertisers. Frequent firings occurred as Gutwillig sought "compatibility" on his staff.[19] The French financial backers had mentioned an initial investment of $25,000,000, yet when losses appeared faster than anticipated, they became more cautious. They paid $250,000 for the use of the logo *LOOK* from Cowles Communications. Losses soon reached $8 million and Filipacchi transferred the editor-publisher title from Gutwillig to Jann S. Wenner, the successful founder of *Rolling Stone.* Within a few days some 100 staffers were dismissed, while others resigned, including Gutwillig. Wenner sought a new mass public; he was not concerned with restoring the old *Look.* The July issue, first under his leadership, noted a shift in "emphasis from gossip and spot news coverage to features offering in-depth profiles of people whose lives reflect the diverse trends of our society." Wenner assured *Look* readers that the magazine would "revive the tradition of hard-hitting photojournalism that captures the essence of stories and events as no other medium can."[20]

Within six weeks, Wenner, too, was gone. Some reported that the losses by this time had reached $10 million, a figure others claim was "overblown," Wenner projected a need for three more years and $5 million more to turn the magazine into black-ink operations. The backers rejected this concept.

Despite rumors that *Playgirl* and other publishers were "involved in several negotiations" to take over *Look,* the resurrected picture magazine failed to survive 1979. The French sources withdrew their financial aid and *Look* went down for the second time, thus failing to reach the 80s. Will another attempt at revival be made in the 80s? It is doubtful.

For the general public *Life* will remain the leader. For others there are the how-to-do-it publications, such as *Popular Photography* and *Modern Photog-*

raphy. And there are dozens of others that will profit, at least indirectly, through the return of *Life.* [21]

FOR THE PHOTOGRAPHERS

The camera hysteria of the mid-30s, highlighted by the arrival of *Life, Look,* and the 35mm camera and its devotion to candid photography, brought other periodicals to the scene. For most Americans, photography became a hobby and they wanted to read more about this new activity.

In mid-1937 *Popular Photography* arrived, primarily to inform readers about new equipment and developments. The initial edition acknowledged the influence of *Life* and *Look,* which it classified as picture magazines. "These publications go in for the story in the picture. We're not as interested in the story in the picture as we are in the story behind the picture—who took it, how, what camera, what stop, what film, what exposure." [22]

At that time when nude photographs were generally confined to the art world, this magazine and others that followed published such pictures, providing, naturally, significant information about camera used, lens, film, exposure, and other useful facts should the amateur photographer want to try such activities.

Popular Photography eventually absorbed other magazines, including *Prize Photography, Photo Arts, Camera Magazine,* and *American Photography.* Since 1955 it has carried its present title, reaching a circulation of nearly 850,000 monthly. Founded and still published by the Ziff-Davis Publishing Company, *Popular Photography* issues annuals. Since its inception, the publication has invited readers, both amateurs and professionals, to submit letters and articles about their photographic experiences. Many readers consider this and other periodicals in this classification as their teachers, providing the knowledge necessary for one to move from the beginners' field to the professionals' world.

Modern Photography, likewise founded in 1937, aims for a similar audience of photographers and hobbyists. Its circulation at the start of the 1980s was 610,000. Both of these publications carry extensive advertising, especially of camera stores in the major cities. *Modern Photography* is published by the ABC Leisure Magazines, Inc. In 1981 it started *Photo America.*

In June, 1978, a newcomer, *American Photographer,* hit the market. Editor Sean Callahan wrote: "It is not a camera magazine. It is not a picture portfolio-type of magazine either. *American Photographer* is a magazine about photography and the men and women who have made it an American idiom . . ." He termed photography "the most democratic of all the arts." Considering the tremendous sale of cameras and equipment, the editor believed "photography has transcended its rather primitive alchemic origins; it has progressed from being a hobby or a profession to the point where it is now a vital fact of daily life. It has become one of the most pervasive and influential forces in our art, culture, and commerce. It informs, entertains, enlightens, sells, and indulges us with images real and imagined.'' Henry Luce would have said ''Amen'' to those words. In less than two years, *American Photographer*'s circulation passed 160,000, mostly through subscriptions.[23]

Other specialized publications are available, each with its own audience. For example, the *PSA Journal* is designed for members and affiliates of the Photographic Society of America, Inc. It has been on the scene since 1934, truly a pioneer. In 1956, *Camera 35* arrived to present ''photography as a medium of visual communication.'' Similar to the others, it has book reviews, picture essays and portfolios, articles on innovations and the changing techniques.

In the more limited areas there are *Darkroom Photography, Functional Photography, Industrial Photography, Lens, Photographic Processing, Photographic Trade News, Photo Marketing, Photomethods, PhotoWeekly, Professional Photographer, The Rangefinder, Studio Photography,* and *Technical Photography*. Several of these also publish directories and annual editions.

Photography, obviously, is here to stay.

And this wide interest in photography has inspired, at least in part, the return of the mass-circulated magazine.

MASS MAGAZINE RETURN

After a lapse of some twenty years, a periodical directed to the mass market arrived on March 4, 1974, with the initial issue of *People,* ''a magazine whose title fits it perfectly.'' It would ''focus entirely on the active personalities of our time—in all fields. On the headliners, the stars, the important doers, the comers, and on plenty of ordinary men and women caught up in extraordinary situations.'' Mia Farrow appeared on the cover, while inside were photographs and articles about the Randolph Hearsts, Marina Oswald, *Exorcist* author William Peter Blatty, a MIA family picketing the White House, and other topics.

After a pilot issue had been tested the previous August in 11 cities, *People* editors determined they wanted their magazine to be ''fun to pick up and both easy and worthwhile to read—page after page, cover to cover.'' It was not to be a revived *Life;* rather, it was to be a new concept with a new format, the first Time Inc. publication to undergo marketing research before reaching the newsstands. Initially, it was available only on newsstands, thus providing some 100,000 locations. Apparently Time Inc. recalled problems associated with the inaugural of *Life,* when circulation so rapidly outpaced the rates charged advertisers that millions of dollars were lost before new rates could be established.[24]

Nora Ephron claimed there was a debate about who selected the title. ''Some people, mainly Clare Boothe Luce, think it originated with Clare Boothe Luce; others seem to lean toward a great-idea-whose-time-has-come theory, not unlike the Big Bang, and they say that if anyone thought of it at all (which they are not sure of), it was Andrew Heiskell.'' Whoever made the choice obviously deserves considerable credit for the magazine's success.[25]

Robert L. Liddel, of Compton Advertising Agency, said *People* was a success because it provided entertainment for the mass audience. ''When *Life, Look,* and the *Post* folded the small-circulation special-interest magazine books took over and nobody noticed that there was nothing left for the general amusement. It wasn't until the *National Enquirer* got away from the 'deformed baby' type of thing, and began selling 3 million copies a week, that somebody realized there was a broad market for fun.''[26]

''We always want to leave people wishing for more'' was the goal set by managing editor Richard B. Stolley. This helped to account for the maximum of 1,500 to 2,000 words for articles. It has been estimated that the entire issue of *People* may total about 15,000 words, about a third of *Time*'s content. Women would be the target, according to preliminary surveys that predicted they would constitute 65 per cent of the buyers and nearly 60 per cent of the readers. Stolley considered this a major factor for the poor sale of the issue with Howard Cosell on the cover. ''Women don't like him, or they were striking back at professional football by not buying his cover,'' he noted. Others who did poorly were Mary Tyler Moore and Helen Reddy, while Gregg Allman and Cher, Elton John, Bob Dylan and Mick Jagger were early winners. These choices no doubt reflect the 18 to 34 age audience the publication seeks.

People has surprised early critics with its success. Two years after its founding, the *Wall Street Journal* noted the magazine had turned from red to black ink within 18 months, a situation unheard of in the publishing field.[27] ''There's an X factor, too, of mystery and intrigue, something about that person that the reader doesn't know, but wants to know . . . There's a three-second decision to buy, and we need a figure who will sell,'' said Stolley, speaking of the supermarket buyer as she approaches the cash register where *People* usually is positioned. And Mal Ochs, with Time Inc.'s magazine development group, said of *People:* ''You can pick it up, thumb through it, start anywhere, stop anywhere. Its impulse usage is analogous to its impulse purchase.''[28] On the other hand, ''If *People* has one widely criticized fault, it is blandness. Press critics, noting that more than half of *People*'s readers are under 35, say that perhaps this blandness befits a generation reared on television,'' so Stephen Grover, in his *Wall Street Journal* article, wrote. Another approach, by Nora Ephron, may augment Grover's views. She believes the magazine is ''for people who don't like to read'' and who have the ''shortest attention spans in the world.''

Unlike early Time Inc. publications, *People* started with and has continued to operate under a low-budget operation requiring minimum personnel, while depending heavily on free lance writers and photographers. In its earlier years, writers received $1,500 for full profiles and photographers $350 for cover shots.

After its introduction to the advertising world, reactions were mixed. ''We'll have to look at it because *Time* does it'' was a general reaction. The majority were cautious, although many neither questioned nor criticized its goal, as *Advertising Age* noted. "Some media men consider *People* a raving success. Some grouse about how Time could produce what they see as drivel. But most are cautiously sidelining final judgments." Although Stolley said the expectations were low at the start, *People* attracted more than 1,000 pages of advertisements in its second year.[29]

"Personality journalism" is the label applied to *People.* Stolley, who spent 20 years with *Life* before taking over *People,* admitted "A better society is *not* our goal, nor our problem. I'm not sure that it should be any publication's. A *better informed* society certainly is our objective—the better information a society has, the more intelligent and humane its choices ought to be." And he added that "If vindication of personality journalism was ever needed, Watergate provided it. Without responsible keyhole reporting on the Watergate figures, how would we ever have comprehended the enormity of their misbehavior or the absence of their remorse?"

Another problem encountered by *People* concerns the "disturbing countertrend among celebrities to gain control of stories written about them," according to Stolley. *"People* will never bounce the galleys back to the celebrity for approval. Once you give in on this, you have to do it for everyone . . . For this reason, we've lost covers that we'd have liked to have run." And privacy presents another major problem for such publications that deal with personalities. "Every story is an invasion of somebody's privacy, basically. And when you're dealing with the kind of journalism we deal with, dealing only with people, you're invading privacy . . . So the celebrities desire, demand, control of the story in exchange for allowing us to invade their privacy," noted Stolley. Yet the managing editor stressed the need to retain control over all articles, feeling that any relaxation of the rule would lead to repeated requests for similar treatment by other personalities.[30]

Within five years *People*'s circulation reached 2,300,000. From 1,046 advertising pages the first full year, 1975, its annual advertising pages grew to 1,920 in 1976, 2,710 in 1977, 3,177 in 1978, and 3,520 in 1979. Total advertising revenues likewise reflect spectacular growth during these five years, from slightly over $8 million in 1975 to more than $90 million for 1979. *People* ranked in the top 20 in circulation and fifth in consumer magazine advertising pages, according to Publishers Information Bureau reports. Its initial per copy price of 35¢ climbed to 75¢ during this period, while circulation passed another Time Inc. success, *Sports Illustrated.*

Looking to the 80s, *People* publisher Richard J. Durrell anticipated no editorial changes, although the magazine will "remain flexible to adapt as things evolve . . . Two-thirds of our readers are 18 to 34. The one thing that may change is our demographics as we keep tracking this group as they go."[31] Durrell had noted in 1976 that "This is a magazine devoted *entirely* to people—we do not deal with issues; we don't deal with events; we don't deal with debates. We deal *only* with human beings."[32]

After five successful years under its current format, one wonders why anyone would consider changing *People*'s approach to its readership, still about 85 per cent newsstand buyers.

People was a pioneering magazine in establishing a floating or variable rate base for advertisers. Termed IBIT for "Issue by Issue Tally," *People* charges advertisers for actual circulation. Other magazines that depend heavily on fluctuating newsstand sales have started to follow *People*'s system. In 1980, *People* added more regional and metropolitan editions for advertisers.

Brunette stars bring better profits, reported the Associated Press in a late 1980 story about magazine cover pictures. Valerie Bertinelli, young television star, appeared on both *People* and *Us* covers in 1980 and brought top sales for both. *People* sold 500,000 more copies than its normal sales of 2.3 million, while *Us* sold 850,000 copies of that issue compared with its average of 712,000.

Sometimes the decline of a television show can result in the decline of magazine sales when such stars are featured. *Us* discovered this when it placed Cheryl Ladd, of "Charlie's Angels," on its cover.

On other occasions the combination of a noted personality and tragedy can increase magazine sales. No doubt many publications increased their sales with cover pictures of John Lennon as they had earlier with Elvis Presley.

And Then Came Competition

People's success brought competitors, "The People Perplex" as *Time* labeled them. Two years after the birth of *People,* the New York Times Co. published *Us*. After two issues were tested in several cities, the first number arrived May 3, 1977, featuring Paul Newman on its cover. It contained a collection of odds and ends, from "Nixon's TV Comeback" to "Helen Reddy and husband; ten years of making up." One wonders, however, why a magazine with such emphasis on illustrations failed to stress its article on famed photographer Ansel Adams on its cover. The 80-page issue had nearly 30 articles and divisions. In less than a year *Us* claimed a circulation of 885,000.

"We hope to make *Us* editorially distinctive in the scope and quality of our reportage. *Us* will be devoted not simply to people in action but to the action of people—to the dramatic and inspiring events of the day that can be captured by the eye of a camera. We believe that the growing millions of better educated young adults will respond to superior photo journalism." Thus did *Us* introduce itself.

Us began with a rate base for advertisers of 750,000 but this was cut to 500,000 as sales fell below expectations. John Mack Carter said it wasn't that *Us* tried to imitate *People*, "it was that *Us* is not a very good copy." Carter also said insufficient enthusiasm by the publisher was another handicap, as was the biweekly schedule. Insufficient color advertisements resulted in too many dull black-and-white editorial layouts; grayer paper stock also failed to come up to *People*'s appearance. Newsstand sales, which still account for about 75 per cent of its circulation, often fell to about 30 per cent of those available on the racks.[33]

People and *Us* were classified as "soft-news" picture magazines by Fred Danzig. *Us* used a "Future Takes" section, noting upcoming television shows, movies, concerts, books, and the like. *People* at the same time started its "People Picks" with similar goals, informing readers of future highlights.[34]

Before *Us* completed its first year, rumors of its possible sale appeared in trade publications. *Advertising Age* claimed the New York Times Co. was disappointed. Management personnel were shifted about in a search for a successful combination. Apparently they feared additional losses of millions of dollars before any profits could be expected. However, executive William H. Davis said, "We've revised our forecasts and expect to lose less money than we'd budgeted for. We expect to be in the black in our fourth year," which would have been 1981. In order to improve editorial content, *Us* recruited stringers in 20 cities, searching for top feature writers.[35]

As the decade opened, conflicting messages appeared in the trade journals. *Advertising Age* noted that *Us* claimed "the young money," noting its appeal to that circulation group. At the same time a news story predicted its sale and shortly after that Peter J. Callahan, president of the Macfadden Women's Group, acquired the publication.[36] The publisher of *True Story, True Confessions, Secrets, Photoplay,* and *Cheri* is said to have paid about $5 million. Most of this, however, represented circulation liabilities he assumed.

Some reports indicated the magazine was selling more than a million copies of each issue and "edging into the black and improving editorially" at the time. *Newsweek* claimed "The *Times* board was originally split over adding such a tacky product to its roster of sport and service magazines." Losses were estimated at $10.5 million through 1979. Both CBS and the *National Enquirer* passed up the property. The new owner promised "to keep *Us* firmly fixated on Cheryl, Cher and the other *People*-type people—the very folks whose news never quite fit comfortably at the *Times*." [37] In commenting on the sale, *Times'* executive Sydney Gruson admitted the firm "did not know enough about that branch of publishing. Our expertise is in service magazines, and we think it will be best to invest in that area." In early 1981 *Us* was guaranteeing advertisers a million circulation. With its circulation gains, *Us* was considering a weekly frequency, possibly in 1982.

Another imitator was *In the Know,* a monthly that arrived in May, 1975, for a brief career. Sam Schwarz & Co., publishers, said the pictorial and feature magazine would be "an attempt to get back to *Life*" yet would be similar to *People.* John Wayne's picture occupied the cover with such stories as "Jackie: Aftershock of a Greek Tragedy," "The Schneiders: Romy—on scandal, Maria—on bisexuality." "Inside Judge Sirica's Wastebasket," and miscellaneous features.

Advertisements were sold only for the inside and back covers. Black-and-white photographs reproduced on cheap paper stock failed to impress sufficient readers and Schwarz's prediction of a 500,000 circulation within a year failed to materialize. So *In the Know* disappeared about as quietly as it had arrived after Schwarz sold the magazine to Irv Munch's Challenge Publications in California.

9

City, State, and Regional Magazines

AMERICANS long have had the opportunity to read magazines that appealed to their particular local and regional interests. Some such publications have established their boundaries to include a few states, such as *Sunset* for the western area, and *Southern Living* for the south. Others have drawn the boundary lines a bit more narrow, such as *Arizona Highways*. Today the lines have been made even tighter with many cities sporting their own publications, not only for the general public but for home owners, sports enthusiasts, gardeners, and other interest groups.

Advertising Age reported in 1979 that the "localization of publishing in America has arrived," yet actually it wasn't that new in our history. Only the emphasis was. Ben L. Moon researched early city magazines for his University of Florida thesis and noted that "the first American publication of magazine format that concentrated its editorial content primarily on a city was perhaps *Town Topics,* founded by Colonel William Mann in New York City before 1900." It collapsed in 1932 after providing readers with society news, gossip, and general light news.[1]

Nearly a decade ago John Peter wrote about "The rise of the city magazine," correcting the impression many individuals had that such publications were "amateurishly edited, local chamber-of-commerce puff organs." Peter admitted a few were still the old-fashioned boosterism type for local business leaders, but he noted the successful publications had secured professionals to handle the operations.

"City magazines are another example of the shift from general to special-interest publications," Peter wrote. And he added, "You don't always have to have the numbers (circulation) if you have the *right* numbers," noting the high income and sophistication of the reading audience. And among the general characteristics of city magazines is the inclusion of *lists:* what's going on where, where to eat, sporting events, theater, concerts, places to visit, and similar valuable information useful not only to local residents but to visitors as well. Such service features make these publications worthwhile. Clay Felker, then editor of *New York,* said, "In the asphalt jungle we live in, a magazine like *New York* is essential for survival. This is what I call 'consumer journalism.' "[2]

Association Created in 1978

City magazines appeared to be in the driver's seat as the 80s got underway. Some publishers date this development from the close of the Vietnam War; others view this as an expansion of the desire of Americans for more local coverage in all media. Others might credit it to the natural growth of magazines, such as *San Diego* established in 1948 and claiming today to be the "oldest city magazine of modern city magazine style." *Santa Barbara* publisher David Fritzen contributed his reasoning for success in this field on these points:

> For the first time since the 1920s when the *New Yorker* was born, people are free to become self-indulgent, especially the affluent who more readily make the transition from ambivalence to contentment. And for the first time in two decades, newspapers and the national media—with their heretofore mesmerizing documents of horror, terror and protest—left the door open for stories of a more provincial appeal to capture the attention of consumers.[3]

These publishing phenomena prompted the creation of the City & Regional Magazine Association in 1978, with headquarters in Washington. The previous year a number of these magazines were represented at a convention in Washington where the *Magazine Industry Newsletter* editor observed that their publishers looked prosperous, were in love with their magazines and were "independent, fractionated, unstandardized in page sizes, rate cards, binding techniques, circulation claims."[4]

During the 1978 organizational session, CRMA opened its membership to audited city and regional consumer magazines. Larry Adler, of *Washingtonian* magazine, the group's first president, called for more consistency among the member publications, with professional research designed to attract additional advertisers. In explaining the rapid growth from the 22 original members, Adler credited the selectivity of the audience. "We are pretty similar in format, but we're talking to our own markets and zeroing in on a special audience. That keeps our readers coming back and also our advertisers coming back month in and month out." In addition, *Texas Monthly* founder Michael Levy credited "the quality of the editorial product that the successful folks in the field have managed to turn out," noting those that have won national awards. His own magazine has been a leader in this category.

These magazines seek to "make life better for the reader," while providing "the story behind the story." *Nashville* publisher Turney Stevens Jr. added: "We can't tell what happened last night, but we can sure tell why there has been a rash of arsons in the city over the last few months and what's behind all that—the story behind the story."

To retain its independence, CRMA's members voted in 1980 to continue their separate organization rather than become an adjunct of the Magazine Publishers Association. More co-operative efforts were called for, especially in paper purchasing and printing, as these publications sought a larger share of the national advertising budgets. In its first survey of readers, CRMA publications claimed the average subscriber's income topped $45,000, with a median of $34,640. The median age was 39, with most readers married and with children. The majority have a college education.[5]

Many city magazines began merely as the voice of a local chamber of commerce, with emphasis on puffery and support of local activities, while offering guidelines to the best the community had to offer in hotels, restaurants, shows, museums, the arts, resorts, and the like. The *Boston Better Business* and *Greater Philadelphia* were among the World War I publications. In the 1930s, for example, the *Bystander* and *Parade* appeared in Cleveland. But it was after World War II that the pace increased. This continued throughout the 1960s and 1970s, when a rash of newcomers arrived, a few to survive for only a few issues.

These publications provide newcomers with an opportunity to learn about their new environment, where to shop and eat, what places to visit, who the leaders are, and similar useful data. In addition, many of the consumer-orientated stories have prompted older newspapers to broaden their coverage of local affairs. As Bernard McCormick, publisher of *Gold Coast of Florida,* noted: "Good city magazines make local newspapers better, more alert and competitive. Even when good papers exist, there is room for a good local magazine."

Advertising obviously is a major factor that determines whether any magazine will succeed or fail. These magazines appear to be more serious contenders for the national dollars, in addition to their ability to lure local revenues. Some ad agencies are aware of the concentrated circulation and their affluent level of readers. Other agency personnel, however, consider such magazines "a drop in the total ad bucket" because of their limited circulation. Since these magazines have formed the CRMA agencies now can place the same ad in many publications across the nation, reaching an expanded audience with minimum bookkeeping efforts. Other advertisers have adopted a delaying game, waiting for these magazines to "prove their vitality in the market place." In late 1980, CRMA members turned to efforts seeking more co-op advertising, a type appearing in many newspapers.

Expansion in this area continues with today's publications more directed to special interest groups within a city or a state, including women, sports enthusiasts, business leaders, homemakers, gardeners, and others. Such fragmentation of the market might limit potential advertising on a national basis, yet it could more readily attract local merchants.

THE NEW YORKER

Long before the majority of today's city and regional magazines appeared, the *New Yorker* was established

> . . . to be a reflection in word and picture of metropolitan life. It will be human. Its general tenor will be one of gaiety, wit and satire, but it will be more than a jester. It will not be what is commonly called sophisticated, in that it will assume a reasonable degree of enlightenment on the part if its readers. It will hate bunk.[6]

Thus the 1920s received the announcement of Harold Ross' new publication that in numerous ways established the format and objectives for today's city magazines. Rather than be compared to a newspaper, it would be interpretative rather than stenographic. It would cover contemporary events and people of interest, presenting "the truth and the whole truth without fear and without favor, but (it) will not be iconoclastic." Prose and verse, short and long, humorous, satirical and miscellaneous items were included. Among the early contributors were Robert Benchley, Dorothy Parker, Robert Sherwood, Heywood Broun, Alexander Woollcott, Marc Connelly, Edna Ferber, Rea Irvin, George S. Kaufmann, Laurence Stallings, and later E. B. White, James Thurber and others.

Ross entered an arena that was dominated by *Vanity Fair, Smart Set, Judge, Punch,* and the original *Life.* In varying degrees, these magazines appealed to a similar audience that Ross sought to entice to the *New Yorker.*

Ross' training had been acquired on newspapers and magazines, with his editorship of the World War I *Stars and Stripes* his major achievement. As a member of the Algonquin Round Table, a group of famous writers of the post-World War I era, Ross met with individuals who eventually helped to make the *New Yorker* the distinctive magazine it remains today.

The first issue on February 21, 1925, had a press run of 15,000 with a price tag of 15¢. That aristocratic gentleman, Eustace Tilley, made his appearance in his high choker collar, wavy side whiskers, and curl-brimmed high hat that set him apart from other such symbols in existence. Financial assistance came from Raoul H. Fleischmann, who would lose some $700,000 before the *New Yorker* turned into one of the nation's more profitable magazines. His son, Peter F. Fleischmann, is today's largest stockholder, with 26 per cent of the shares. John Peter Toohey is credited with providing the name, based on the concept that it was to be a metropolitan magazine about New York.[7]

"The *New Yorker* concentrates its attention on those centers of amusement on which smart New York focuses its interest, and reports the anecdote and chat of clubs and theaters and hotels, of drawing rooms on Park Avenue and shops on Fifth, sports in vogue at night clubs—and at country clubs," according to early announcements.[8]

Its famous and oft-quoted comment that it would be "the magazine which is not edited for the old lady in Dubuque" provided another guideline for today's editors. Early contributors wrote under nicknames and pseudonyms, some, no doubt, wondering if the publication would succeed. Ring Lardner once noted that he would rather write for the *New Yorker* for a nickel a word than for the *Cosmopolitan* for a dollar a word. The magazine in 1933 published its "Code of Publishing Practice," with suggestions for "good usage among publications which enjoy a recognition of leadership." The booklet concluded:

> Let no advertiser write, and let no publisher publish, any advertisement which is not conceived for the best interests of the prospect and the reader.
>
> Let the product be trustworthy, the presentation honest and in good taste.

Cartoons were barbarous by today's standards, often exaggerated. Yet through the years Helen Hokinson made plump women famous, Peter Arno's aristocratic old gentleman chased the young girls to entertain readers, while Gardner Rea, Otto Soglow, Charles Addams, William Steig, and others added much to make the *New Yorker* a weekly entertainment publication. Charles E. Martin has drawn more than 160 covers over a 35-year period. At the start Dorothy Parker, a good friend of Ross', "regarded the magazine as a joke," yet lived to see it succeed. From the start it featured The Talk of the Town, Goings on About Town, profiles, and comments about the press.

This "unique chronicler of American life and American people" has another distinguished record; it has had only two editors in more than half a century. Ross served until his death in 1951; William Shawn became the editor in 1952. In comparing the editors, E. B. White thought Shawn "laughs with his mind, not his belly; he is quiet, intellectually interested in everything that comes along, works 24 hours a day, and is wholly receptive to new talent." Shawn is responsible for such excellent fiction and non-fiction accounts as those on Hiroshima, insecticides, race riots, Vietnam, and other political and social issues. More than 850 books have originally appeared in the *New Yorker,* including classics such as Truman Capote's *In Cold Blood,* Rachel Carson's *Silent Spring,* Charles Reich's *The Greening of America,* James Baldwin's *The Fire Next Time,* and others.[9]

Hardly noticed by the magazine was its 50th anniversary, although it did reprint the cover featuring the immortal Eustace Tilley, an annual event. New York Mayor Abraham Beame issued a proclamation. The *New York Times* called the magazine that "Mannerly Maverick at 50," noting its profitable operation for the Fleischmann family. *Newsday* termed it funny, decent, and civilized. If any changes occur, Shawn told the *Times* they "take place as the result not of formal decisions but of the magazine's sensitive reaction to the changing thoughts and feelings, the changing interests and inclinations, of its many individual writers, artists, and editors. We try to keep the magazine's frame spacious enough to allow for experiment and idiosyncrasy, and, more crucial, to permit each person to follow his own bent. Innovations, even mutations, occur, but often they take us by surprise. Our finest changes come unbidden.''[10]

Time magazine, also reflecting on changes in the *New Yorker,* noted: ''The cartoons are no longer classic—but oddly enough they are funnier. The younger contributors, from John Updike to Woody Allen, have tended to displace rather than replace their predecessors. And the *New Yorker* itself? Well, as George Orwell aptly observed: 'At 50 one has the face one deserves.' '' The writer, Stefan Kanfer, concluded:

> The current golden-anniversary issue once again exhibits the profile of Eustace Tilley. But it is no longer the true face of the magazine. Another visage somehow hovers behind the columns, a face no longer young but not old, a wise, ironic face that has learned to tell a joke as well as take one; a face that can turn grim, because contemporary distress can no longer be answered with a riposte; a face that has resolved its youthful conflict. 'If you can't be funny, be interesting.' The advice no longer applies. The face at long last manages to be both—and a little more.[11]

Shawn admitted ''there is less humor today than a decade ago, but if the *New Yorker* has become more serious, it's not the result of any conscious policy change.'' Such gradual changes can be expected, Shawn added, with more serious topics today. On the other hand, the *New Yorker* today publishes more cartoons than ever before. Meanwhile, the magazine continues to publish humor and to nurture new humor writers.[12]

New York Joins Market

When the *New York* magazine appeared some felt it would appeal more to a younger group, that select 18 to 34-year-old bracket, a group ''the *New Yorker* either ignores or makes fun of.'' However, it appears there is a market for both publications. The *New Yorker* continues along its successful path, attracting its usual half-a-million subscribers and newsstand readers each week while earning a strong annual profit.

New York magazine appeared in April 1968, as a spinoff from a Sunday supplement in the New York *Herald Tribune* which had folded earlier. Surveys had revealed the majority of the newspaper readers bought the Sunday edition for this supplement. Clay Felker, as editor, made it a sophisticated and imaginative publication, with its exposure of happenings in the city. Felker had among his staffers Tom Wolfe, Jimmy Breslin, Judith Crist, Gloria Steinem, Dick Schapp, and others. Milton Glaser became art director and George A. Hirsch publisher. The initial press run was 250,000 with 60,000 charter subscribers.

New York, viewed by some as a competitor to the *New Yorker,* stands apart from many city magazines. Both are weekly, however, rather than monthly, and both have a higher sales record outside their metropolitan area than many of the other city-oriented publications. Early *New York* became a trend-setter, "a magazine of both local controversy and national impact—as likely to publish stories on war in the Mideast and gourmet food in France as to mugging in Manhattan and cheesecake in Brooklyn," according to David Shaw.[13]

New York's success was its ability to win "the loyalty of Manhattan's influentials—the affluent residents of the Upper East Side," according to *Time*, which observed early that some critics "find *New York* excessively slick and too often frivolous" but yet it "undeniably generates excitement."[14]

In many ways Felker's editorial statement for *New York* is typical of the hopes expressed by publishers of other city magazines. He wrote:

> We want to cover everything in New York.
>
> We want to attack what is bad in this city and preserve and encourage what is new and good.
>
> We want to be *the* weekly magazine that communicates the spirit and character of contemporary New York.
>
> We want to have a direct involvement in this city. We want to be inseparable from it. We want to be its voice, to capture what this city is about better than anyone else has.

Felker in many ways made *New York* synonymous with the New Journalism. By 1970 the magazine was in the black. Yet in "one of journalism's strangest, swiftest coups," the magazine was sold to Rupert Murdoch, who also acquired the *Village Voice* and *New West* in 1977 in a series of stormy transactions.[15] Murdoch replaced Felker with James Brady, who vowed no drastic changes under the new owner. By 1979 other changes had Joe Armstrong as president-editor and Cathleen Black as publisher. In 1980, *Cue* magazine was merged with *New York,* hiking the circulation to 400,000. Armstrong was succeeded by Edward Kosner, formerly editor of *Newsweek*. Murdoch reportedly paid $5 million for *Cue*. The firm's *New West,* launched in 1976 amidst a conflict over who owned that title, continued to expand its every-other-week publication in California, until it was sold in 1980 to Michael Levy and his *Texas Monthly*.

Conflicting Reports

Advertisers were singing, "We Love *New York*," according to a late-1980 account, while another magazine reported "Trouble in Paradise," referring to the *New Yorker*.

Advertising Age reported that "A magazine publisher recently likened the marriage of *New York* magazine and *Cue* to 'merging a man with no arms with a man with no legs.' " Fiscal 1979 was reported to have been *New York*'s best year. After a slow start in 1980, the magazine's revenues climbed and management predicted 1981 would be even better.

The *New Yorker* has its highest circulation ever, 480,000, yet *Time* fears there are problems, primarily because of a shortage of talented writers. Thomas

Griffith thought some "book reviews miss the irascible authority of Edmund Wilson . . . movie reviews often seem longer than the films themselves." He adds, however, "Thank heavens for the cartoons."

Along with the rest of the magazine world, the *New Yorker* will wait for any change that might come when the magazine's second editor in its 55-year history, William Shawn, steps down. But it will be difficult to change a landmark.

Texas Monthly Big Too

The *Texas Monthly* has been so successful that it has received national and international recognition while attracting numerous competitors in the Lone Star state. On a National Broadcasting Company "Today Show" on May 4, 1979, Gene Shalit said *Texas Monthly* was the best in that state. "Its thoughtful, tough young writers and editors produce a good-looking periodical that is savvy and sophisticated and slick in the best sense of those words." The NBC critic was impressed by the age of the publisher-editors, in their late 20s and early 30s. Another national writer, David Shaw of the Los Angeles *Times,* likewise has been impressed by the youth involved in the city/regional magazine field. Shaw wrote that "these men have brought a fresh, crisp approach to the magazine. They have attracted what is generally regarded as the finest group of writers now available to any city magazine. They generally give their readers a higher gravity/frivolity ratio than any other city magazine."[16] *Business Week* reported it was the "third largest and reputedly the most profitable of the city and regional magazines."

Texas Monthly publisher is Michael R. Levy, a graduate of the Wharton School of Finance and Commerce at the University of Pennsylvania and of the University of Texas School of Law. Before founding *Texas Monthly* in February, 1973, Levy worked for the United Press International and the *Philadelphia* magazine. Editor William Broyles, a graduate of Rice University and Oxford in England, also has had newspaper and magazine training. In the initial issue of *Texas Monthly,* Broyles set the stage for the success of this publication, noting:

> If our readers have ever finished the daily paper or the six o'clock news and felt there was more than what they were told, then they know why we started *Texas Monthly.* We designed it as an intelligent, entertaining and useful publication for Texans whose culture, sophistication and interests are largely unrecognized and unserved by existing media. All of Texas will be our province, but our major focus will be on the metropolitan triangle of Austin, Dallas, Fort Worth, Houston and San Antonio. Our only banner is one of integrity, fairness and quality writing.

Texas Monthly has been described as "the envy of all the other city magazines" and this envy appears justified. It has won dozens of awards, not only for its excellent editorial content but for its art work as well. The awards have come from its home state and from national associations as well. Its writers, too, have been cited for achievements in their specialities. Awards have recognized the magazine's outstanding business reporting, medical writing, women's features, and the like. The American Institute of Graphic Arts Show, for example, has given *Texas Monthly* several citations, as have other art groups in Houston, Dallas, and New York.

Texas Monthly has received international recognition as well but its success remains with its home-state following who show their appreciation by the steady circulation climb from 41,500 in early 1974 to some 250,000 in 1980. In late 1980 one issue contained 201 pages of advertisements, bringing in more than a million dollars. This has been achieved through fine writing and in-depth reporting. Writers are paid well and are granted ample time to research articles Texans enjoy to read. For example, editor Broyles wrote about The King Ranch and the October, 1980, issue devoted more than 40 pages to the story, including an excellent collection of photographs. There was sufficient material there for another television show to match "Dallas," and could aptly be called "The King Ranch."

In addition to the major stories, *Texas Monthly* provides the basic raw material found in many city/regional publications, with its guide to entertainment and events around the state. ADWEEK'S editors selected *Texas Monthly* as the hottest consumer magazine for 1980, based on its 46 per cent gain in advertising revenues and 13.9 per cent gain in advertising pages. The magazine has published books as well, such as *Texas Monthly's Guide to Mexico, The Best of Texas Monthly, Texas Monthly's Political Reader, Lone Stars: A Celebration of Texas,* and others.

The magazine has expanded to California, acquiring *New West* in 1980 for a reported $3 million. The new owners noted that "Texas and California are mythic places. Legends abound in both states and they excite the imagination of both editors and readers." It was reported that the magazine (*New West*) had lost a million and a half in 1978–79.

There are, of course, many, many other city and regional publications as noted later in this chapter. Each has its own audience; each has its own goals. But each has its desire to succeed as *Texas Monthly* has. There also are some magazines that cover a much wider area, a section of our nation, such as *Sunset* and *Southern Living*.

Sunset in the West

An 80-year-old love affair between a magazine and the surrounding states best describes *Sunset,* an innovative publication in many ways. The magazine's history is divided into three units, with the present ownership responsible for *Sunset*'s success. Founded in 1898, *Sunset*'s first objective was to promote the West as a place to live or at least to visit, especially if the trip were made by train. The magazine was named after one of its owner's most famous trains, the Southern Pacific's "Sunset Limited."

YOSEMITE AND THE HIGH SIERRA IN THIS NUMBER.

May 1978   95 cents

Sunset

The Magazine of Western Living

Powwows

Indian Gatherings
Across the West in 1978
You are Welcome P 106

80th BIRTHDAY ISSUE

1898–Looking Back P 120
1978–Sunset Garden P 196

FEBRUARY 1929

SUNSET

10 CENTS

By 1915 the railroad apparently was satisfied with the magazine's success so *Sunset* was sold to its editor, Charles K. Field. He changed the content to an emphasis on political and literary subjects, promoting western authors. Famous writers were published, including Jack London, Bret Harte, Sinclair Lewis, Kathleen Norris, Zane Grey, Earle Stanley Gardner, and others. This change, however, failed and *Sunset* was near bankruptcy in 1928.

Today's *Sunset* really began in early 1929 when a new publisher, Laurence William Lane, took control. A midwesterner, Lane learned the magazine business while working in Des Moines for the Meredith Publishing Co., which owned *Better Homes and Gardens* and *Successful Farming*. Lane, who traveled the west as Meredith's sales manager, soon became an enthusiastic promoter for the area's future, much as the original had before the turn of the century. In late 1928, Lane and several associates at Meredith arrived in San Francisco. The first issue under Lane's ownership, which appeared the following February, noted:

> *Sunset* will cover the whole range of home-life and family interests with timely and practical suggestions on gardening, building, home-decorating and furnishings, cooking and home management, traveling, enjoying outdoor life, and a host of other subjects of equal interest to men and women.

Shades of *Better Homes and Gardens?*

Circulation was 70,000 for the monthly that sold for 50¢ a year. By 1932, there were three regional editions, a pioneer move in magazine publishing. That same year the audited circulation reached 203,000, mostly by subscription. Within a few years the magazine began to publish books about cooking and gardening, some used as bonus items to attract more subscriptions.

A landmark in advertising was started in 1935 with its "*Sunset* Shopping Center." This involved a collection of small ads with each offering something to purchase by mail. Similar layouts appear today in *Southern Living* and other publications.

Expansion in editorial and advertising continued as *Sunset* improved its contents. A photograph was used for the first time on a 1936 cover. The cover design was redone in 1938, the first year Lane reported a profit. Liquor advertisements had been rejected from the start and by 1940 Lane had banned tobacco and beer messages as well.

During World War II *Sunset* suffered from the paper shortage, not an unusual occurrence among magazines in war times. However, paper was available for the *Sunset Vegetable Garden Book,* obviously viewed as an aid to help the nation overcome the food shortages of the early 1940s.

In 1951 the company moved to new quarters in Menlo Park, in facilities surrounded by gardens. *Advertising Age* once described the "sprawling buildings of adobe, brick and timber" as "more like the home of a wealthy California rancher than headquarters of a publishing company." These gardens attract so many visitors today that guides are provided to handle the tourists.

Sunset's unique subscription plan tends to keep contents and readers closely allied. The magazine serves "Western Living" in four major areas: food, travel, building, and gardening. It serves 13 states: Alaska, Arizona, California, Colorado, Hawaii, Idaho, Montana, Nevada, New Mexico, Oregon, Utah, Washington, and Wyoming. Copies are available on newsstands only in the West. Subscribers outside this "covered territory" pay extra.

Similar to Meredith's success with cookbooks and those concerned with other topics, *Sunset* has published more than 100 titles with total sales beyond 70,000,000. Half of these volumes have sold more than 500,000 each. Early in its publishing career *Sunset* promoted the sales through supermarkets and specialty stores. Today it has been estimated that books alone account for some $10,000,000 annual income for the publisher.

Sunset's circulation has climbed steadily since the Lane family took control, reaching its first million in 1971 and 1,350,000 as the 80s opened. Its renewal rate is extremely high, reflecting its devoted audience. Today's publisher, Bill Lane, said:

> We are excited about the future, and determined to stay down-to-earth and useful. Our task is to be sensitive enough to bridge the old and the new. In a world where it seems we're all being leveled by computers, *Sunset*'s policy is to recognize all of you as distinctive individuals. We are in a very personal business. Serving your interests is what *Sunset,* the Magazine of Western Living, is all about.

Sunset has proved that specialization can succeed. It has developed a faithful following in one section of America. By limiting its audience it has permitted itself to better serve those persons. The exotic subjects have their place, but "the guts of the magazine" still includes the service features.[17]

Southern Living Successful

An oft-expressed negative attitude toward the South was at least partially responsible for the founding of *Southern Living* in 1966. From its start, *Southern Living* has served the South, has reflected its good elements and has offered positive reasons for living there. Like *Sunset, Southern Living* planned a highly selective editorial pattern, with its circulation designed for Southern families. Advertisers, obviously, have focused on Southern products for Southerners.[18]

Southern Living began as the title of the home section of *Progressive Farmer,* one of the nation's leading publications, established in 1886 in North Carolina. Later it moved to Birmingham, Alabama. *Southern Living* was tailored more for the urban and suburban audience rather than for readers of *Progressive Farmer.* Nevertheless, to capture recognition from its godfather, the line "An edition of *Progressive Farmer*" appeared under the *Southern Living* logotype at the start. Originally *Life*-size, the magazine today is *Time*-size. Its first cover featured a home scene in Mobile, with azaleas, towering Southern pines, a carefully manicured lawn, and a Cadillac barely showing in the background.

Emory Cunningham is president-publisher of *Southern Living* with Gary F. McCalla, editor. Cunningham said *Southern Living*'s concept began in 1964 "as a result of our confidence in the future development of the South . . . we knew there would be much more growth in our region (16 states) and we wanted to help influence the direction of that growth." He has been described as the Norman Vincent Peale of publishing for his enthusiastic views toward his magazine and its Southern audience. He seeks to steer "the magazine toward what our readers can accomplish in their own towns." Like *Sunset, Southern Living* charges subscribers more if they live outside Dixie.

In defense of charges that *Southern Living* avoids "advocacy journalism," Cunningham replies: "We have a special interest in helping people without preaching."[19]

Within two years *Southern Living*'s circulation reached 500,000. Today it has passed 1,750,000, well ahead of its founder, *Progressive Farmer*. In five basic subject areas the magazine portrays active and gracious living in the South: Features, travel and recreation, homes and building, garden and landscape, and food and entertaining. Special sections relate to football in the South each September; "The Future of the South" each January; and to travel in states or regions from time to time. Golf, too, receives excellent coverage as well as other events associated with the area. McCalla feels the emphasis is to stress the South's "differences—differences in geography and climate, in foods and ways to entertain, in plant materials and gardening."

To Cunningham, "The South is a state of mind. Although much of the South has become urbanized, it still is the most rural part of the country in terms of its thinking and traditions. There is more open land, a longer growing season and a wide-spread interest in outdoor activities.''

Southern Living and *National Geographic* have at least one situation in common—readers are reluctant to throw copies away. And with its circulation approaching two million, *Southern Living* has proved that partisan advocacy has its place in the magazine world. The magazine practices what it preaches about environmental problems. In 1973, when the firm moved into new head-quarters in southern Birmingham, the trees were left within inches of the building. Today slash pines, azaleas, crepe myrtle and other flowers and plants surround the structure, making it almost invisible to those who pass by on the adjoining four-lane highway. Even the Appalachian topsoil was retained around the building.

And Other Regionals/City/State

Yankee magazine was founded in 1935 in the midst of the Depression. Today it also publishes *The Old Farmer's Almanac,* established in 1792, and the *New Englander,* 1953, as well as *Yankee Magazine's Guide to New England,* 1971, and other sectional publications.

Originally housed in a one-room building described as an over-sized red chicken coop, in Dublin, New Hampshire, *Yankee* continues to grow as it tells the world about New England. Nearly 200 persons are employed to prepare the monthly which has 850,000 subscribers. More than 63 per cent of the sales are in New England and Middle Atlantic states, although more than 30,000 copies reach California, many, no doubt, to former New Englanders.

Contributors have included Pearl Buck, Archibald MacLeish, Ted Kennedy, Sherman Adams, and others. Founder Robb Sagendorph wrote in 1935, ''*Yankee*'s destiny is the expression and perhaps indirectly the preservation of that great culture in which every Yankee was born and by which every real Yank must live.''[20]

The Old Farmer's Almanac passed four million circulation in 1979 as it continues to offer weather forecasts and helpful information for the entire nation. Its accuracy continues to baffle the scientists who have made forecasting their business.

DIRECTORY

Regional and city publications available in early 1981:

Arkansas Times; Afro-Denver; Aloha; Anchorage; Atlanta; Atlanta Business Chronicle; Atlanta City; Austin Home & Gardens; Austin; Avenue (New York); *Back Home in Kentucky; Baltimore; BFLO* (Buffalo); Baltimore *Maryland Center; Bay View; Big Valley* (California); *Bay Life* (Florida); *Beverly Hills; Birmingham; Boston; Boston Fashion Trend; Broward Life* (Florida); *Brown's Guide to Georgia; Buffalo Spree; California Business; Capital District Business Review* (Albany); *Central Florida Scene; Charlotte; Chesapeake Bay;*

Chicago; Chicago Business; Chicago Sports Report; Chicago Sport; Chicago and Midwest Home/Garden; California Business; Chicago Elite; Cincinnati; City (Kansas City); *Chicago North Shore; Cleveland; Cleveland Business; Colorado; Colorado Business; Colorado Woman; Colorado/Rocky Mountain West; Columbus Monthly; Commonwealth* (Virginia); *Connecticut Trends; Connecticut; Connecticut Business Journal; Corporate Report* (Minneapolis); *Corporate Report* (Kansas City); *Country Journal* (Vermont); *County Life* (Pennsylvania);

D (Dallas); *Dallas/Fort Worth Business Journal; Dallas/Fort Worth Home & Gardens; Dallas; Dallas Vision; Dayton USA; Delaware Today; Delaware Valley Business; Denver; Denver Monthly; Denver Business World; Monthly Detroit; Detroit Fifty Six; Down East* (Maine); *Erie; Exclusively Yours* (Wisconsin); *Fairfield County* (Connecticut); *Family Style* (Chicago) *Flint; Florida Trend; Florida Sportsman; Gold Coast of Florida/Indian River Life; Focus/Philadelphia Business Weekly; Fort Collins; Fort Wayne; Grand Rapids; Gulfshore Life; Hampton Life* (New York); *Honolulu; Houston; Houston City; Houston Business Journal; Houston Home/Garden; Houston Public Times; Hudson Valley; Indiana Business; Indianapolis; Indianapolis At Home; Hudson Home; Indianapolis Home & Garden; Jacksonville* (Florida); *Jackson* (Mississippi); *Kansas City; City* (Kansas City); *Kansas Business News; Kentucky Business Ledger; Knoxville; Lansing; Living,* with editions in Austin, Dallas, Fort Worth, Denver, Florida, Houston, Phoenix and San Antonio; *Long Island; Los Angeles; Los Angeles Business Journal; Long Island Business Review; Louisville; Louisville Today; Madison* (Wisconsin); *Memphis; Metro* (Newark); *Metro, Magazine of South East Virginia; Mesa* (Arizona); *Metro Business Monthly* (Washington, D.C.); *Miami; Milwaukee Impressions; Montana; Minneapolis-St. Paul; Minnesota Monthly; Nashville; Naples Now* (Florida); *New England Business; New Florida; New Hampshire Profiles; Nevada; New Jersey Monthly; New Mexico; New Orleans; New West; New Worlds* (California); *New York/Cue; New Yorker; Northern Ohio Business Journal* (Cleveland); *North Shore* (Chicago); *Northwest America* (Idaho); *Now in Stark County* (Ohio); *Ohio; Oklahoma; Oke* (Oklahoma); *Omaha; Orange County Home & Garden; Orange County Illustrated* (California); *New Worlds of Orange County; Orange County Forum; Fifty; Orlando-land; Oregon; Pacific Northwest; Palm Beach Life* (Florida); *Palm Beach Social Pictorial; Palm Springs Life* (California); *Park Avenue Social Review; Philadelphia;* Philadelphia-*Delaware Valley Agenda; Phoenix; Phoenix Home/Garden; Pittsburgh; Pittsburgher; Playsure* (Houston); *Portland; Richmond-Lifestyle; Roanoker* (Virginia); *Rocky Mountain; Routes* (New York); *SA* (San Antonio); *San Diegan; Sacramento; San Diego; St. Joseph* (Missouri); *St. Louis; St. Louis Living; St. Louis Nine; Sandlapper* (South Carolina); *San Francisco; San Francisco Focus; San Francisco Business Journal; San Jose; San Fernando Valley; Santa Barbara; Sarasota Town & County* (Florida); *Seattle Business Journal; Seattle Nine; Shenandoah Valley* (Virginia); *The South* (Florida); *South Bay* (California); *South Florida Outdoors; Southern Accents; Spokane; Spring-*

field/Hartford; Stark County (Ohio); State (North Carolina); Texas; Texas Monthly; Texas Business; Texas Homes; Texas Sports; Texas Woman; Tampa Bay Life; Topeka; Town Squire (Kansas City); Tucson; Twin Cities (Minneapolis); Triad (North Carolina); Tulsa Home/Garden; Utah Holiday; Valley Monthly (Pennsylvania); Viva New Mexico; View of Puget Sound (Washington); Virginia Lifestyle; Washington Calendar; Washington Dossier; Washington Capital Shopper; Washingtonian; Washington Monthly; Westchester Illustrated; Westchester Traveler; Westways (California); Wichitan (Kansas); and Yankee (New Hampshire).

Cuisine introduced its Cuisine's New York in 1980 and announced plans for similar localized editions in Los Angeles and Chicago for 1981. Eventually there would be ten such local Cuisines.

Meanwhile, the city-state-regional lists fluctuates weekly.[21]

10

Sports Magazines for Everyone

The beauty of the sports field is that this is one of the last things a family is going to cut out. Expensive vacations go first—and that creates a greater interest in sports at home.

This comment by E. Dan Capell, publisher of *Inside Sports,* sets the stage for a study of sports publications for the 80s. Capell appears correct in this prediction that sports will escape much of the setbacks other areas might experience in the bleak economic picture. Capell could have included the additional leisure time Americans now have as well as the increasing number of retired persons with their involvement in sports, from participation to viewing and listening.[1]

Especially during the past decade Americans have engaged in a health campaign that has involved a considerable interest in sports. Besides turning to diets and seeking to curb their smoking, many Americans also have turned to sports. This has created a new audience for publications. This national fitness crusade has prompted millions of Americans to jog, walk, swim, and to engage in other sporting activities. Thus the related sports publications have profited from the potential audiences, and equipment makers, clothiers, travel agents, and others have joined in the bonanza. Their advertisements have made many sports-orientated periodicals possible.

Sporting activities often involve many members of the family, so magazines have developed to serve these specialized interests. Such growth has been evident since the appearance of *Sports Illustrated* and the expanding coverage of sports provided by television. It appears that the more the public witnesses on television, the more that public desires to read and see stories and pictures of the same events in periodicals. And for others who acquire a desire to participate there are magazines to provide the how-to-do-it guidelines. No doubt many of the millions who have viewed the Boston and the New York marathons on television have taken up jogging for their own physical benefit.

Such enthusiasm has lured advertisers, including some from the fringe areas. For example, the Yashica and Canon camera firms depend heavily on well-known sports personalities in their commercials, usually showing them taking pictures of sporting events in which they are participants.

Three of the more then 300 sports-directed periodicals appeal to the general sports audience, a mass market in a way. They include the older, and currently financially-troubled *Sport;* the broader-based *Sports Illustrated,* and the newcomer, *Inside Sports.* According to a *Sports Illustrated* researcher, the 300 magazines account for sales of 65,000,000 copies each month, a figure that has doubled within the past decade.

Sport

Sport, a monthly hero-worshipping publication, was founded in August, 1946, by the Macfadden-Bartell firm. The initial issue sold 350,000 copies and in the process of appealing to a younger audience with a median age of 30, *Sport* has passed 1,200,000 in circulation. Forty percent of its readers are college-educated and some 95 per cent are themselves active in sports.

"*Sport* mixes depth coverage of professional sports with personality pieces and splash photography. Its layout is less impressive but still attractive. It covers a wider spectrum of sports than *Inside Sports* and its approach is likely to become more eclectic," according to Jeff Sommer, who noted that the publication has added sports fashion coverage. Sommer believes sports fans would not hesitate to buy both *Sport* and *Inside Sports.*[2]

In late 1980, *Sport* was to be sold by the Charter Corporation to CBS, who would assume the subscription liabilities, which could be high considering *Sport* has more than a million subscriptions. However, at the last moment Bill Paley, CBS chief, vetoed the deal, raising some questions about the autonomy of the CBS publication division.[3]

Sport was sold to Ray Hunt, a stepbrother of the famous silver-Hunts of Texas. Mr. Hunt also owns *Texas Homes, D* magazine and *Houston City.*

Sports Illustrated

Sport almost became the property of Time Inc. when that firm was planning a new sports-orientated periodical in the early 50s. Henry Luce offered the Macfadden firm $200,000 for *Sport* but refused to meet the $250,000 asked by the publication. Instead, Luce acquired the title *Sports Illustrated* for $5,000 from Stuart Scheftel. A magazine under that title had a two-year existence in the 1930s and another brief revival after World War II.

Today's *Sports Illustrated* began on August 16, 1954, after first issuing two dummies to excite potential advertisers and sports writers across America. It was estimated that more than $3 million was spent on these dummies during 13 months of planning. Twenty-five years later its anniversary promotional booklet reprinted the 1,250 covers, providing an information pictorial summary of sports across the years.

In its first year, *Sports Illustrated* reached a circulation of 575,000, a million by 1962, and more than 2,250,000 today. By 1974 it had become America's fourth largest magazine in advertising revenues.

Founder Henry Luce said "There has never been a National Sports Weekly. Furthermore, it has been brilliantly proved that there never can be . . . (and he added)

People's interests are too varied . . .

Maybe. Maybe that's the way it was. Maybe that's still the way it partly is. But one thing is sure; the world of Sport is a wonderful world and everyone enters it with Joy . . .

You don't have to read it—not any of it. Sport is Liberty Hall. It compels nobody. You don't have to read about it in order to be a better executive . . . But you'll surely want to have a look at this new magazine . . . You may find that it makes more enjoyable what you already enjoy . . . And *that* could have consequences.

One consequence could be that, at last, America will have a great National Sports Weekly.[4]

Luce also said "the new magazine will be a re-evaluation of sport—not an over-evaluation—to put it in its proper place as one of the great modes of expression."

At the beginning the word SPORTS appeared in large type, with ILLUS-TRATED in smaller type. For some time the magazine advertised itself in trade journals as "the third news-weekly," behind *Time* and *Newsweek* and ahead of *U.S. News & World Report*. Some readers questioned this comparison, although the publication prefers to be listed with news weeklies rather than sport periodicals in the Standard Rate and Data Service reports.

Sports Illustrated seeks to prove its claim as *the* authoritative sports publication. Its photographers want to avoid the typical shots so they go after new angles. The magazine also uses paintings and drawings to illustrate the features. Eventually the society phase of sports gained space, as did dog shows, show horses, and similar "classy" topics not generally found in earlier publications for sport fans. *SI* labels itself "the magazine of performance," offering sports as information as well as entertainment, in illustrations and in words.

Television viewers want more than a glimpse of the action; they want more of the "why" which *Sports Illustrated* seeks to provide. It is written in a non-newspaper style with the stress on the feature approach. Half of its readers are college-educated with a median age of 31.6.

Inside Sports

In 11 metropolitan areas in October, 1979, the premier edition of *Inside Sports* appeared. With a promise from its owner, Newsweek, Inc., of $10 million to see it through the first two or three years, *Inside Sports* is after the "upscale audience." The first official issue arrived in April, 1980, with a rate base of 500,000. After its first years, its circulation base was 550,000.

Covers vary from two to six each month, focusing on more localized interests. The editorial content, however, does not vary. The pre-testing period, conducted especially in the Eastern markets, helped staffers in planning the content.[5]

Publisher E. Dan Capell said in the initial issue that *"Inside Sports* will concentrate on the big four sports—baseball, football, hockey, and basketball—because we know, as fans, that those are the sports you care more about. Our editorial format will provide the fund of information we believe you won't get anywhere else; in-depth coverage of the players and teams you want to know better and the issues that matter most. Sure, we'll touch on other sports, but only if we can give you a new insight into the loves of the people who play, coach, and are in some way a part of the spectator-sports scene." Earlier Capell had said, "There's a lot of sport magazines on the market and room for a lot more."

John Walsh, the first editor, admitted he was competing against "one of the best magazines in America—*Sports Illustrated.*" Walsh felt that weekly sports magazines and daily newspapers "don't have space to satisfy the demand for features, analyses and background articles created by the explosion of interest in sports in recent years." It has become more than the games. "Sports involve business, medicine, gambling and many other aspects. There are a lot of hardcore spectator sports fans out there" and Walsh predicted *Inside Sports* would cater to them as fans.[6] Financially, *Inside Sports* lost $12 million in 1980.

Specialized Pack, Big and Little

A part of the mass national sports scene is *The Sporting News,* a pioneer in the field. As a tabloid it doesn't really belong with this group, yet it has been around since the Spinks family in St. Louis established it in 1886. For years it was devoted only to baseball, but now has expanded to include football, basketball, and hockey. In 1977 it was sold to the Times-Mirror Co. A presenter of many nationally recognized awards in sports, the *Sporting News* has a circulation of 450,000, with a median age of 33 for its readers. However, its greatest role no doubt is the influence it has had on other sport publications.

Now to some of the others.

There are the giants, such as *Sports Illustrated,* and there are the midgets in the sporting world. These periodicals do have their faithful readers, eager for the latest word from their heroes or inside details about recent developments in their activities. And statistics, too, are sought after. Some magazines represent associations, such as the *American Rifleman* and the National Rifle Association of America. Some conduct special contests across the country and others, such as *Golf Digest*, gain international publicity by offering $50,000 to men and women golfers who establish record scores in the U.S. Open Tournaments.

Field & Stream is one of the giants, with its circulation of over two million. It was founded in 1895 by John P. Burkhard and Henry W. Wack, who thought of the idea to support conservation while sitting in a duck blind. The magazine, now owned by CBS Publications, experienced survival pains in its early years before it became successful. In addition to the monthly edition, *Field & Stream* also publishes annuals, such as *Bass Fishing, Deer Hunting, Fishing, Hunting,* and others. *Field & Stream* since 1977 has used local inserts in five regional editions.

Although it is older, having started in 1887, *Sports Afield* has not kept pace with *Field & Stream* in the circulation battle. Now a part of the Hearst organization, *Sports Afield,* with its circulation in excess of half a million, sponsors many state fishing awards programs.

Sports Afield claims "the best educated and best heeled male audiences of any major outdoor publication in America." Its studies conclude that American sportsmen annually spend over $6.5 billion on hunting and fishing, plus another $14 billion for food, lodging, transportation and entertainment. The magazine improved its graphics in 1978, seeking to reverse a series of profitless years.

In addition to graphic changes, *Sports Afield* also cut its circulation from a million to 500,000. The management cited these reasons:

> During the 1970s, we witnessed a tremendous explosion in the outdoor marketplace. One by-product of that explosion was the emergence of a new breed of outdoor enthusiast. His needs and wants had changed. New marketers had entered the arena; traditional marketers had adjusted to meet these new needs and wants. As the marketplace had changed, it became evident to us that we were not giving this new breed of enthusiast the type of magazine that he needed and wanted, so we made changes not only for the benefit of our readers, but for the benefit of our advertisers as well.

Thus the magazine seeks to "interest more and more Americans in hunting and in fishing by displaying each month what is best, what is beautiful and what is inspiring in the out-of-doors."[7]

Outdoor Life is among the near-giants, one of some 50 periodicals directed to the outdoor arena. It was started in 1898 by John A. McGuire, a Westerner with a great love for the outdoors. His son, Harry, eventually edited it for many years before it was sold. The Times-Mirror group operates it today with a circulation of 1,750,000.

Outdoor Life announced in 1980 that it would split-run the magazine over five geographic regions, tailoring the editorial content to specific audiences. It likes to call itself "a national magazine with regional appeal." The magazine noted that today there are more than 33 million fishing licenses and 28 million hunting licenses purchased annually. In addition, there are estimates of from 10 to 15 million saltwater fishing fans. Obviously, *Sports Afield* and *Outdoor Life* like to quote statistics.

Stuart Bernard, *Outdoor Life* publisher, reflected the situation today when he noted that the "sportsman is not only more plentiful, he's better educated and more sophisticated in various ways than he was in the past. To reach and keep this reader, we've had to provide more targeted and more sophisticated articles."[8]

In 1976 there was *Mariah* and in 1977 there was *Outside,* born "for people who love to play, work, live in, or just plain enjoy the great outdoors." Two years later they were merged into *Mariah/Outside.* Later that year the magazine purchased *Backpacking Journal,* giving *M/O* a circulation base of 200,000.

The *American Rifleman* is in the million-plus category. Its sponsorship by the National Rifle Association of America assures this circulation. Designed for persons "who have a strong hobby or professional interest in firearms, the *American Rifleman* reports on activities of the Association as well as NRA-sanctioned tournaments. It is active in lobbying activities in Washington, where it is edited.

There are others along this line such as *Guns and Ammo* (1958) with more than 500,000 circulation. There are the *American Hunter* (1973), *American Handgunner* (1976), *Guns* (1955), *Gun Week* (1937), *Gun World* (1960), *Hunting* (1973), *Rifle* (1968), *Shooting Times* (1960), *Skeet Shooting Review* (1947) and others.

Arnold Palmer and President Dwight Eisenhower combined with television to increase the nation's enthusiasm for golf. Palmer, who has maintained a large following on the links, became the nation's hero when television began to cover the major tournaments. As a president, Eisenhower represented millions of amateurs in the golf world. Such development obviously helped magazines.

Golf Digest, part of the New York Times Magazine unit, reached a million circulation in 1980, the 30th year of its existence. It claimed a monthly readership, however, of 2.4 million. Its nearest competitor, *Golf,* owned by the Times-Mirror Magazine network, has a circulation of 710,000, with a readership of 2.2 million. *Golf* began in 1959.

In addition, there are *Golf Illustrated* (1973), *Golf World* (1947), *Fore* (1968), and *Country Club Golfer* (1972), and others for the more business-oriented followers such as *Golf Business* (1927) and *Golf Shop Operations* (1963).

Many For Tennis, Too

Leaders in the tennis market include *World Tennis,* started in 1953, which capitalized on the boom in the late 70s and reached a circulation of 475,000 by 1980. This CBS Publications magazine has been challenged for the circulation leadership by *Tennis,* a New York Times magazine established in 1965. *Tennis* claimed a higher circulation than *World Tennis,* with ABC reports to justify its figures. Some reports indicate there are 25 million tennis players.

Nearly a million copies of magazines directed to skiers are sold monthly, with *Skiing* (1948) and *Ski* (1935) the leaders. Also for these fans are *Skier* (1952) and *Far West Ski News* (1970). There also are annuals, such as *Skiers Almanac* and *Skier's Guide.*

Soccer is comparatively new for Americans but it is gaining rapidly in acceptance by fans. At least four publications were started in the 70s, with more expected in the 80s. *Soccer World* (1974), *Soccer Corner* (1977), *Soccer Digest* (1978) and *American Soccer* (1976).

With an estimated 25 to 30 million runners in America today it is only natural to expect publications for this market. The leader, *Runner's World* (1966), reported 475,000 circulation for 1980. It became involved in a dispute with a major shoe manufacturer over the magazine's annual rating of runners' shoes. With a $250 million shoe market at stake, a long debate is assured over the verdicts. The *Runner* began in 1978 and reached 85,000 within a year. Its current circulation has exceeded 120,000. Among the contributing editors are Bill Rodgers and Frank Shorter, noted marathon winners. It is designed for the mile-a-day jogger as well as the marathoner. The magazine promised readers it would provide them with "the feeling of the runner." When women became involved in running, the potential audience increased by millions.

Since 1948 the *Track & Field News* has been published. The bimonthly *Karate Today* made its debut in early 1981.

Also gaining fantastic popularity as the 70s ended and the 80s began was racquetball. Magazine fans had a wide selection to choose from, including *National Racquetball* (1972), Racquet Club (1976), *Racquet* (1976), and *Racquetball Illustrated* (1978). The pioneer in this field is *Racquetball,* established in 1968. There are some 10 million participants in this sport and the number is growing.

The *Motorcyclist* has appeared since 1912. However, Ziff-Davis' *Cycle* (1952) has become the circulation leader for this special group that has gained many new members during the last decade. Motorcycling continues to attract more believers with the increasing cost of gasoline. Not only are the manufacturers placing more ads in the cycle magazines, but they also are using *Playboy, Penthouse, Sports Illustrated* and others. For example, the following have circulations in excess of 100,000: *American Motorcyclist* (1947), *Dirt Bike* (1971), and *Easyriders* (1971). In addition, with lesser circulation, there are *Custom Bike* (1980), *Choppers/Big Bike* (1968), *Modern Cycle* (1964), *Motocross Action* (1973), *Rider* (1974), *Road Rider* (1969), *Street Chopper* (1969), and *Touring Bike* (1976). *Bicycling* (1980) is a recent entry.

For individuals with more interest in automobiles of varying styles and designs there are dozens of publications. Some of the major firms have several such periodicals, including CBS Publications with *Road & Track* (1947), *Cycle*

World (1961), and *Packup, Van & 4WD* (1972), with a combined circulation of 1,190,000. There also is specialization within specialization, with this special group: *Dune Buggies & Hot VWs* (1967), *4x4'a and Off Road Vehicles* (1976), *Four Wheeler* (1962), *4 Wheel & Off-Road* (1977), and *Popular Off Roading* (1976).

Hot Rod (1948) has a remarkable 850,000 circulation, while *Motor Trend* (1949) has 750,000. *Car and Driver* is a Ziff-Davis publication with 725,000 circulation for this 25-year-old magazine. There are others with circulations over 100,000, including *Car Craft* (1953), *Owner Operator* (1969), *Racing Pictorial* (1959), *Road King* (1964), and *Scholastic Wheels* (1977).

Among other periodicals with some limited appeal are *Auto Week* (1958), *Car Collector/Car Classics* (1968), *Cars and Parts* (1957), *National Dragster* (1960), *Racecar* (1975), *Rod Action* (1971), *Sports Car* (1944), *Stock Car Racing* (1966), *Street Listing* (1975), *Street Rodder* (1972), *Super Stock & Drag Illustrated* (1964), *Mini Trucks & Pickups* (1975), *Truckin'* (1975), and *Van Pickup & Off Road World* (1973). The Popular Argus Group includes *Popular Hot Rodding, Super Chevy, Off-Road, VW & Porsche,* and *Sport Trucking,* all started between 1969 and 1976.

Water Appeals to Many

Millions of Americans prefer sport activities associated with water. More than 30 such publications are listed by Standard Rate and Data Service. Among the circulation leaders are *Yachting* (1907), with 150,000; *Motorboat* (1973), 130,000; *Motor Boating & Sailing* (1907), 135,000; *Sail* (1970), 170,000; *Salt Water Sportsman* (1939), 115,000; and *Sea* (1908), 165,000. There are some with special appeal and a few with general appeal in special sections of the country, such as *Chesapeake Bay* (1971); *Cruising World* (1974); *Ensign* (1914); *Florida Sportsman* (1969); *Lakeland Boating* (1945); *Marine Business* (1978); *Marine and Recreation News* (1962); *Pacific Skipper* (1974); *Pleasure Boating* (1973); *Popular Performance Boat* (1976); *Powerboat* (1958); *Sailing* (1966); *Small Boat Journal* (1979); *Soundings* (1963); *Southern Boating* (1972); *Trailer Boats* (1971); *Waterway Guide* (1947); *WoodenBoat* (1974); and *Yacht Racing/Cruising* (1961).

For those who prefer closer contact with the water there are the *Surfer* (1960); *Surfing* (1964); *Water Skier* (1952); and *Spray* (1976).

Fishermen, too, have a wide assortment to choose from, depending on whether they have local or national interests, or whether they are concerned with fishing in general or fishing for specific species in particular locations.

For example, there is *Angler* (1974) as well as *Bassmaster* (1968). *Fishing World* (1955), *Outdoor America* (1922), and *Fishing Facts* (1963) could have broader interests. Others include the *Texas Fisherman* (1973); *Fishing and Hunting News* (1944); *Fly Fisherman* (1969); *Fur-Fish-Game* (1905); and *Southern Outdoors* (1953). There are some group publications, including *Fishing in Maryland* (1953), *Fishing in New Jersey* (1977), and *Fishing in New*

York (1979). Another series for fishermen was started in 1963 for those in New Jersey, Long Island, and New England. And there are *Trout* (1960); *Waterfowler's World* (1977); *Salt Water Sportsman* (1930); and *Ducks Unlimited* (1937).

Archery World (1952) and *Bow & Arrow* (1963) have their strong devotees. *Bicycling* (1963) represents another growing sport with its 125,000 circulation.

There are dozens of state and local sports publications, some serving as the official voice of conservation units. The *Michigan Out-of-Doors* (1947) has a circulation of 114,000. The *Wisconsin Sportsman* (1972) has an area approach while *Western Outdoor News* (1953) and *Western Outdoors* (1960) both cover a wider area.

Sports professionals also are represented by such magazines as *Athletic Journal* (1921); *Coach and Athlete* (1938); *Texas Coach* (1957); *Referee* (1976); *Scholastic Coach* (1931) and others.

The horse has earned recognition across the country. Some Americans have special interests, as reflected in such magazines as *Appaloosa News* (1946); *Arabian Horse World* (1960); *Harness Horse* (1935); and *Thoroughbred Record* (1875). Others represent associations, including *Backstretch* (1962); *Chronicle of the Horse* (1937); *Hoof Beats* (1933); *Horsemen's Journal* (1949); *Quarter Horse Journal* (1948), and *Rodeo News* (1961). In 1981, *Centaur* was started, with indepth reports and elaborate photography.

The *Western Horseman* is the circulation leader, with 165,000. It is also one of the oldest, dating from 1936. Others with more than 100,000 circulation include *Classic* (1975); *Equus* (1977); *Horse Action* (1978); *Horse Care* (1978); *Horseman* (1956); *Horse, Of Course!* (1972); *Horse & Rider* (1962); and *Horse World* (1970).

There are others, too, including *Blood-Horse* (1916); *Horse and Horseman* (1972); *Horse Illustrated* (1976); *Horse Lover's National* (1936); *Horsetrader* (1960); *Horse Women* (1978); *Hub Rail* (1975); *Practical Horseman* (1973); *Quarter Horse Track* (1975); *Quarter Horse Record* (1961), and *Saddle and Bridle* (1936).

To a sports fan there is no such classification as "miscellaneous." Yet in this study there are a few publications that stand out in their fields, although they don't have too much competition as yet. For example, the *Skin Diver* (1951) has 168,000 circulation. The *Woman Bowler* (1936) reaches more than 156,000 subscribers. *Official Karate* (1968) can depend on more than 160,000 regular sales. *Baseball Digest* (1942) with 240,000 circulation has been a leader for years. The Century Sports Network publishes seven periodicals, with a combined circulation of nearly 890,000. They include *Auto Racing, Baseball, Basketball, Football, Hockey,* and *Soccer Digests,* plus the Century Sports Network.

Business Publications Represented

In addition to the many consumer-oriented publications there are dozens of others directed to the business phase of sports, to the merchandising of products to supply the fan's needs. *Advertising Age* considered this interest sufficient to provide its readers with a special section on "Sports Marketing." The magazine noted in mid-1980 that while the country's economy might be tapering off, "The manufacturers, the advertisers, the media, and the retail outlets say consumers' burgeoning interest in sports should keep business strong."[9]

Under the heading of Sportings Goods, the Standard Rate & Data Service Business Publication rate and data book lists the following audited magazines:

American Firearms Industry (1972), *Camping Industry* (1966), *Fishing Tackle Retailer* (1980), *Fishing Tackle Trade News* (1952), *Selling Sporting Goods* (1948), *Sporting Industry* (1956), *Ski Business* (1961), *Skiing Trade News* (1954), *Snow Goer Trade* (1966), *Sporting Goods Business* (1968), *Sporting Goods Dealer* (1899), *Sports Merchandiser* (1968), *SportStyle* (1978), and *Tennis Industry* (1972).

Among the non-audited periodicals are *Action Sports Retailer* (1980), *American Hockey & Arena* (1973), *Archery Retailer* (1975), *Bowlers Journal* (1913), *Bowling* (1960), *Bowling Proprietor* (1954), *Golf Industry* (1975), *NOON-National Outdoor Outfitters News* (1976), *Racquetball Industry* (1977), and *Swimming World-Junior Swimmer* (1960).

Sports lovers thus can keep occupied, through participation in their favorite activities or through reading about what's going on.

Football fans have *Football Digest* (1971) and *Football News* (1939), while hockey fans have *Hockey News* (1947), *Hockey Pictorial* (1955) and *Hockey Digest* (1972).

Possibly the Oldest?

Claiming the title as the oldest sports magazine in the world is *Ring*, founded in 1922 by Nat Fleischer. Its monthly circulation is about 150,000, which includes the Spanish-language edition, *Ring Espanol*. For years *Ring* was the gospel for national boxing ratings, but in 1977 a scandal that involved ABC-TV, Doug King, and the magazine hurt its reputation. Critics at the time noted that "If *Ring* is the bible of boxing, boxing needs a new testament."[10] The magazine's new owners include Bert Randolph Sugar, who sought investors with no boxing connection "because there's too much conflict of interest in the sport as it is."

Another magazine that encountered some problems is *Vital*, designed for healthy living. In 1979, it died after two issues but was scheduled for revival later. Its owners were still optimistic, predicting a million circulation by the mid-80s.

11

Science Publications Expand

Sci Anxiety and the consumers' thirst for knowledge have stimulated an expansion in science and science-related periodicals. Americans, bombarded by newspapers and the electronic media with strange and exciting reports of scientific occurrences, feel that some accounts verge on science fiction or fantasy. They observe that "New science magazines have come into being recently with a burst of energy that resembles the suddenness of Biblical Creation more than the gradualness associated with Darwinism."[1] An advertisement by *Science 80* probably presents the picture better when it claims, "The more aware you are, the more severe the symptoms."

Recently the public has acquired an interest in pure science as well as "near" science, bringing success for many publications, such as the *Smithsonian, Discover* or *Science Digest*.

Such intense interest has been attributed to the almost-daily news accounts of incidents from Three Mile Island, Love Canal, genetic engineering, and Skylab to the many activities allied with the nation's struggle to solve its energy and environmental problems. Science as such has become a more personal topic for readers to pursue. Once considered of interest only to the specialists, science news now reflects our expanding concern and expectations from spectacular discoveries and developments. Motion pictures such as "Star Wars" and "Close Encounters of the Third Kind" contribute to readers' desire to learn more about the unknown world around us. Charles Darwin's theory of evolution has experienced a revival in public interest after being dormant for decades. *1984* is nearer and what once seemed impossible no longer seems so. Calculators, first the exclusive tools for specialists, now are used by shoppers as they tour supermarkets and by youngsters who consider them as necessary as pencils, paper, and books for classroom assignments. *Magazine Age* once noted, "science has become something to worry about as well as to wonder about."

With the opening of the 80s, the nation witnessed an almost staggering expansion of science-oriented periodicals. *Newsweek* termed it "the heaviest proliferation of science journalism since the coverage of the manned space flights in the mid-1960s." Many of today's potential readers lived through this era when science and technology became the normal part of their day-to-day discussions. David Perlman, science editor of the San Francisco *Chronicle,* said, "TV has stimulated the public's interest in science. People get their first exposure there. Those who want to know more turn to newspapers, then magazines."[2]

Jack Godler, who developed the "Sci Anxiety" promotional campaign for *Science 80,* offered three reasons for this growth:

> First, his "intellectual shortfall" concept that makes us realize we know very little about the "staggering array of advancements in technology that affect so much of (our) life."
>
> Second, the "data deprivation" view that requires us "to judge fateful public and private questions based on information that seems incomplete, confusing or even contradictory."
>
> Third, the "gnawing disappointment" feeling we have when we cannot find the answer so we seek "accurate explanations in terms (we) can understand."[3]

Public Broadcasting, too, has contributed to this situation through such programs as "Nova," "The Ascent of Man," and the many excellent productions sponsored by the *National Geographic*.

Science as a subject has expanded its coverage today, from the longtime leader, *Scientific American,* to *GEO, Natural History, SciQuest, Omni, Next,* and others. In addition, there are dozens of magazines devoted to more specialized scientific areas, such as *IEEE Spectrum,* a product of the Institute of Electrical and Electronics Engineers, Inc., to those concerned with the broad arena dominated by complex computers. Some stress today's happenings; others concentrate on the future, apparently bound only by the editors' wildest dreams.

"With the new explosion in science journalism it is unlikely that science will ever again be regarded as too mysterious—or too complicated—to interest the public," according to *Newsweek*. Carl Sagan believes, "We are a society based on science and technology in which very few people know anything about its essential elements. It's a prescription for disaster."[4] However, some magazine publishers apparently believe they can better prepare their readers to avoid such disasters. And it is possible that some of these periodicals have so stretched the interpretation of "science" that even advertisers face complications in determining just where to place their messages.

Scientific American

Scientific American has been described by its publisher, Gerard Piel, as "the highest brow magazine published anywhere in the world. There is a spectrum of intensity and intellectual energy required to read *Scientific American*— as well as high motivation and intellectual muscle."[5] Founded in 1845 as a weekly newspaper, *Scientific American*'s first publisher, Rufus Porter, said his aim was "to furnish the intelligent and liberal workingman, and those who delight in the development of those beauties of Nature, which consist of the laws of Mechanics, Chemistry, and other branches of Natural Philosophy, with a paper that will instruct while it diverts or amuses them, and will retain its excellence and value, when political and ordinary newspapers are thrown aside and forgotten."[6] The magazine grew while America's technological developments advanced. For years the publication's emphasis was on industry, and the ways in which science and technology affected Americans.

Owned by the Orson D. Munn family for more than a century, *Scientific American* suffered through the Depression and in 1947 was sold to Gerard Piel, Dennis Flanagan, and Donald H. Miller, Jr. Piel and Flanagan had been science editors for *Life*. The new owners changed the focus, assuring readers that *Scientific American* now would report on all branches of science, physical, biological and social, and tell how these areas affect Americans. Not only did they seek to attract scientists, doctors, engineers, industrial leaders and others, but they also wanted to lure those interested laymen and other concerned readers to their periodicals. They promised articles that would be in plain English, understood by intelligent laymen rather than limited to scientists. Through the 50s innovations served to increase its circulation, a sure sign of its successful transition to the new trends. Its 80,000 circulation in 1950 grew to more than 615,000 as the 80s opened.

Scientific American's influence extends well beyond America. The Chinese for years published an unauthorized edition until recently when Piel and the government there reached an agreement on rights. A similar situation existed in Russia yet Piel feels "science is a world culture" that should be encouraged. The magazine also publishes special sections on German and Japanese technology, and in other countries as well.

Scientific American claims today to be "the magazine of discovery, attracting a growing number of newsstand buyers and subscribers around the world. Each month it reaches over two million people who make the future happen." Nevertheless, there are other publishers who believe there are millions of potential readers who desire even more readable magazines with broader interpretations of science. Such magazines, on slick paper with beautiful illustrations and exciting layouts, compete for the nation's readers.

Science Digest

Founded in 1937, *Science Digest* was acquired by its present owners, the Hearst Corporation, in 1958. It, too, has undergone changes that reflect the new trends. Its original digest size was discontinued in late 1980, when a larger format was adopted. The publisher looked upon this change as creating a "new" magazine and offered advertisers special deals. From a bimonthly, the magazine moved to monthly frequency in March, 1981.

Science Digest, a "magazine created by scientists and journalists working together," seeks to be the place "where facts are even more exciting than fiction," according to its trade ads. For many years *Science Digest* shared the market with *Scientific American* when readers weren't as plentiful as today. The new enlarged version seeks to blend photographs and illustrations to produce a more attractive publication for its circulation of 500,000, dominated by college-educated men readers.

The broadness of its coverage is seen in a late-1980 issue with topics on Your Brain's Reptile Heritage, Cannibalism in American Today, Beyond Darwin, Amazing Machines, The Case for UFOs, No Jealousy for Amorous Lepcha Tribe, Liquid People, Science of Live Sex Research, H-Bombs on Mars, and Star of Bethlehem. Obviously, a bit of science mixed with a bit of sensationalism. And possibly some topics about sex as well.

Science 80 (81, 82, etc.)

Science 80 celebrated its first anniversary in November, 1980, with a shift from bi-monthly to 10-times-a-year frequency for its 600,000 subscribers expected in early 1981. Established "not to be stuffy or academic," but "to bridge the distance between science and citizen," *Science 80* is published by the American Association for the Advancement of Science, a non-profit organization founded in 1848.

Science 80's general manager, Owen Lipstein, told *Madison Avenue* staffers that: "We're delivering a receptive audience. They're reading our magazine because they are people who are curious about events related to technology. Companies with corporate stories—like Exxon and Gulf—are after people who have a known level of interest in scientific developments."[7] When asked by *Magazine Age* about his latest competitors, Lipstein said: "They're going to have to define themselves to us. We are the standard."[8] A year earlier, Lipstein told *Advertising Age* that " 'Science 80' would fill a gap between *Popular Science* and *Scientific American* . . . our competition was surprised at our professionalism. They pictured us as stuffy professors bumping into each other in the hallways."

AAAS went to court in 1980 to prevent Hearst's *Science Digest* from using a logo with the word "Science" appearing much larger than "Digest." The court ruled that "Digest" must be at least 75 per cent the size of "Science." The *Digest* then put both words in the same type size.[9]

Jack Schneider, media supervisor of McCaffrey & McCall, believes, *"Science Digest* appeals to a slightly less affluent audience, *Science 80* to the more affluent, and *Omni* falls somewhere in between."[10] Its publisher, AAAS, also issues *Science,* founded in 1880 by Thomas Edison, and now a weekly newsmagazine for scientists. The publisher believes *Science 80* offers "in-depth articles and quick wrap-ups of discoveries, advances, ideas, insights, controversies and personalities in today's science and technology" as it seeks "to introduce its readers to scientists who transcend the ordinary," according to its trade advertisements. Readership, like others in the field, is male-dominated, with some 88 per cent college educated. Originally sent only to subscribers, *Science 80* turned to newsstand tests in late 1980 in five cities, searching for more well-educated affluent Americans. Its name, obviously, will change with the years. William Bennett feels the magazine is "rigidly structured."

Science 81 upped its rate base from 600,000 to 675,000 in 1981. The magazine has also produced an experiment series for radio.

Omni

"There is a universal architecture of infinite elegance and logic from which all things animate and inanimate seem to derive," according to *Omni* founder, Bob Guccione, better known in the publishing field for his financially successful *Penthouse*. Started in October 1978, *Omni* represented a boyhood dream for Guccione. It was a creation of pure joy, he said. The title, taken from its Latin root, means all or everywhere. This can be seen in the variety of topics offered in *Omni*.

Planned as "an original if not controversial mixture of science fact, fiction, fantasy, and the paranormal" by Guccioni, it has upset some readers who are disturbed to find that fact and fiction appear side-by-side. In his Collector's edition, October, 1978, Guiccione wrote about the

> . . . inevitable and tragic collision between science and religion, between knowledge and faith. Man cannot shed one discipline without taking another in its place. The frontiers of human knowledge and experience are forever changing, forever expanding, and we, who are living at the very dawn of time, must make our common peace with change if we are to survive the next 1,000 years.

Still there were critics. "How can a reader trust a publication that on one page seriously tries to inform him, but in the next story features fantasy?" one asked.[11]

Omni, in some ways a pioneer among the slick science books, reached 650,000 copies after its first year, and today's rate base is 800,000. Its policy is to "afford paranormal phenomena the simple dignity of a proper, ongoing scientific inquiry." *Scientific American* publisher Gerard Piel believes *Omni* "features the nonsense (such as UFOs) but is careful to say that it is nonsense." Editor Kathy Keeton says *Omni* "is intended to stimulate and evoke curiosity," while *National Geographic* takes readers to unusual places around the world *Omni*'s publishers admit it is an entertainment magazine, with an editorial mix that appeals to a slightly younger audience than some of the longer-established scientific publications. It was selected as Magazine of the Month by the *Gallagher Report* because of its ability "to combine a realistic look at the future with helpful hints for problems of today's society."[12] Its fiction is often "delectable and occasionally even nourishing." *Omni* contains 60 per cent science fact, 30 per cent science fiction, and 10 per cent paranormal phenomena.

GEO

GEO's elaborate mailing campaign set the stage for one of the most beautiful magazines on the market. Originally published in Europe, *GEO* acknowledged it would be more expensive and would require more of the readers' time than other periodicals. It would bring "consequential events into focus—whether they be of science, nature, the arts, our physical environment, our political and social climates—the world of human behavior, human problems."

According to publisher Igor Gordevitch, it would combine "extraordinary photography with sophisticated and stimulating writing," as it sought an above-average audience, preferably from persons well acquainted with such periodicals as *Harper's, Natural History, Smithsonian, Scientific American* and the *New Yorker*. Its audience, according to Simmons 1979 studies, included readers in the professional/management field, with most college-educated, a median age of 39 and incomes averaging more than $41,000.

Some readers view *GEO* and *National Geographic* as competitors for some of the same reading public. Both are noted for the beauty and quality of their photographs. *National Geographic* has won numerous major prizes through the years in photo competition. *GEO*, however, won several awards in the 1979 Picture of the Year national competition, cited for Best Use of Pictures for a Magazine and one of its staffers, Susanne Walsh, was cited as winner of the Magazine Picture Editor's Award.

It was predicted that *GEO* would "change your perception of the world." This magazine encountered difficulties after its initial year, a time when losses were estimated at $5 million. According to *Newsweek,* its renewal rate was below the hoped-for 70 per cent and it was having a problem establishing a clear identity.[13] Meanwhile, *GEO* advertised that it "defies any pat description," which apparently disturbed some potential advertisers. Others claimed *GEO* did not reach its goal of superb writing, graphics, or photography. Gruner + Jahr, the German owners, were said to be willing to commit $20 million to make *GEO* a success in America, following its success in Germany and France. However, by mid-1980 a retrenchment policy resulted in more material being used from the German edition, with less material created in America. Charging $4 a copy, *GEO* claimed to be neither a travel nor a geographic magazine, or even a newsmagazine. *Magazine Age* did not consider it a science magazine in its special study of this medium.

Next

Next joined *Omni* in offering readers stories concerned with the future, in economics, lifestyles, politics, technology, military strategy, health and medicine, psychology, culture, the environment, law, and philosophy. It promised to "give an idea of what to expect, of the consequences of what's happening today." And, when necessary, to offer alternatives.

According to the *Media Industry Newsletter, Next* is the brainchild of *Medical Economics'* president, Carroll Dowden, working with editor Al Vogel, veteran editor of *ME*. It was seen as a magazine that would appeal to Alvin Toffler and his *Future Shock* and *The Third Wave*. Some readers believe *Omni* and *Next* seek audiences interested in the experimental and avantgarde approach to science.[14]

Litton Publications offered this bi-monthly as a magazine of the future and the magazine of discovery, the latter possibly a takeoff on the new Time Inc. publication, *Discover*. The initial issue in March–April, 1980, which followed a preview edition the previous September, reached some of its goals, but to others it was difficult to categorize. In its Preview Issue *Next* noted:

> We don't believe that a magazine about the future has to be far-out; indeed, we believe it *can't* be far-out if we are to deal with the matters that will affect your life and the lives of the people around you. . . .
>
> We want to talk about things that are likely to happen two, five, 10 years down the road rather than to speculate about what may happen 100 (or 1,000) years from today. . . .

For example, a mid-1980 issue discussed such topics as "If the inflation rate tops 25 per cent," "The Robots Are Coming," and "Fellini's Once and Future Woman."

In a heavy advertising campaign, *Next* said it "takes up where *Time* and *Newsweek* leave off." In other words, the near-future. Goals were set for a circulation of 400,000 with monthly publication planned by September 1981. However, in 1981 *Next's* career came to an end.

Discover

Stressing timely subjects as what readers might expect from a Time Inc. product, *Discover* arrived in October 1980, the firm's biggest venture since *People*. A monthly with an initial circulation of 400,000, *Discover* had sections titled Essay, Profiles, History, Science People, Gallery (photos and illustrations), New Inventions, Critical Eye, and News. The premier edition featured "Computers as artists" with a cover picture of DNA molecule drawn by a computer.

After observing its success with science-related stories in *Time,* and the firm's success with books on nature and science, the publisher spent 18 months testing the *Discover* concept. It is believed Time Inc. spent more on this experiment than on any of its other magazines. Promotional material sent to some 10 million potential subscribers claimed *Discover* would be the first "to capture the full range of the scientific adventure for the intelligent, educated, curious layman. Timely, topical, without jargon." It would be the newsmagazine of science, a science publication for non-scientists, but admittedly for better educated lay persons. There would be only a two- to three-week time lag between events and newsstand sales. By early 1981, *Discover* could guarantee advertisers a circulation base of 600,000.

Discover's claim of being the first to approach science as news was disturbing to the publisher of *Science News* in Washington. E. G. Sherburne, Jr. noted that in 1981 his magazine would celebrate its 60th consecutive year of publication and at the same time *Science News* had only a one-day deadline for copy, compared with the longer time *Discover* announced.[15]

Science News

Originally called the *Science News-Letter* when it was founded in 1921, the magazine's title was shortened to *Science News* when it underwent a facelift in 1966. In its issue of September 23, 1966, the magazine described itself as "a weekly letter that tells you succinctly, in words and pictures, the exciting and important progress of science research and technology." It was designed to be read in one sitting. Its circulation is 185,000 for the 16-page weekly. Its success comes partially from its frequency with its ability to be current in topics offered. It is directed to a more science-oriented audience, as its readership study shows.

SciQuest

Published by the American Chemical Society, *SciQuest* was started in 1964 under the title *Chemistry*. It was designed for high school teachers; however, when it was renamed it sought additional subscribers among high school students and literate adults. It, too, seeks to be informative, provocative, and entertaining.

The Sciences

Similar in size to *TV Guide* when it was started in 1961, *The Sciences* switched to full-size format a decade later. Published by the New York Academy of Sciences, the magazine reports on current research in a provocative and readable manner.

HISTORY AND SCIENCE MIXED

Smithsonian

Celebrating its 10th anniversary in March, 1980, the *Smithsonian* represents one of the major success stories of the 70s. Edward K. Thompson, the first editor, formerly edited *Life*. He helped to put into published format the concept of this newer publication: "It's about things in which the Smithsonian in interested, might be interested or *ought* to be interested." Thus, the *Smithsonian* covers man's cultural, intellectual, social, and physical environment and, as the *Magazine Industry Newsletter* reported, "everything from ecology, science and urbanology, to art, history, nature, and leisure activities."[16]

Interesting incidents of the early years were reported by Edward Park for the anniversary number. He cited, "The marriage between professional journalism and the serene, scholarly world of curators and researchers was as uneasy at first as the hasty liaison with the bookies" who permitted staffers to use their phones in the early days. Computer difficulties once resulted in a subscriber receiving 400 copies of the same issue, prompting him to complain that the *Smithsonian*s prohibited him from entering his own living room.

S. Dillon Ripley, secretary of the Smithsonian Institution, greeted readers in April, 1970, in his regular "View from the Castle" page with this comment:

> It should be the task of our magazine to add to the sum of public knowledge within the mandate of this Institution for every portion throws light on all the others as (James) Smithson asserted in the beginning.

This 80-page issue featured courting elephants on the cover. The 10th anniversary issue, a hundred pages larger, featured a reprint of all 120 covers. Thompson took a sabbatical from his editing chores and Don Moser became the managing editor.

Smithsonian's initial circulation of 163,596 passed the million figure within five years. Since then it has grown to 1,900,000, including a large number of college-educated readers with high median incomes. In its promotional advertisements, the *Smithsonian* claims "no other magazine has achieved such widespread acceptance at the top of the market." It has become "the first popular class magazine." The Gallagher Report labeled it the Magazine of the Month in 1979 for its coverage of a variety of modern cultures, with sharp, bright photography and effective layouts. Increases in subscription and advertising rates have failed to deter the publication's growth. Subscribers become Smithsonian Associates and receive special benefits, including discounts on services and merchandise offered at the Institution.

The *Magazine Industry Newsletter,* attempting to explain the magazine's success, noted:

> *Smithsonian*'s editorial premise is that their "new" category of reader is really "an educated generalist." This audience, which is upscale and more affluent than most others, appreciates balanced writing (with no biases or opinions masquerading as facts) and in-depth reporting that presents all the available information so that the reader can reach his own conclusions. One of the guiding dictums is "the editor is no smarter than the reader."[17]

No doubt this magazine will continue to share in the benefits of an ever-increasing traveling America, including millions who make the Smithsonian in Washinton one of their major tour sites. Either before, or shortly after that trip to Washington they will read the *Smithsonian*.

Natural History and *Museum*

Natural History, the official publication of the American Museum of Natural History, observed its 80th birthday in 1980 with a circulation approaching

500,000. Edited for laymen, *Natural History* is designed for a "well-educated, ecologically aware audience," including professional people, scientists, and scholars.

Early in 1980 a newcomer, *Museum,* published its premier issue. It featured articles on the National Gallery of Art, Walt Disney's Museum of the Future, and How Ancient Royalty Sought Immortality. Also featured on the cover was Art Buchwald's Six-Minute tour of the Louvre and Diana Vreeland on Dazzling Hapsburg Court Fashions. Obviously, a varied diet for the hoped-for 120,000 sales.

Museum also had a goal to inform travelers about what to look for in museums around the world. Its initial editorial concluded: "There are heavens, it would seem, waiting to be explored by those who would journey to them. If you are one, let *Museum* take you there."

Other Interests Served

For more than eight decades, the National Audubon Society has waged a continuous struggle to gain an uncontaminated environment and to crusade to save our endangered species, such as the bald eagle, whale, and snail darter fish.

Through its well-illustrated bi-monthly, *Audubon,* the society reaches more than 320,000 readers. Human interest articles, many written by free-lancers, normally present both sides in each case before the magazine takes its stance.

The society, organized in 1899 to protect birds, continues to expand its goals. Its concerns have been enlarged to include the conservation movement and related subjects.

National Wildlife

Organized in 1936, the National Wildlife Federation seeks to educate Americans about conservation, including the protection and restoration of wildlife habitats.

Jay N. "Ding" Darling founded the Federation. Known to many Americans for his editorial cartoons, Darling was at one time chief of the Bureau of Biological Survey under President Franklin D. Roosevelt. Darling's fight to save the wildlife population led to the creation of the Federation.

The *National Wildlife,* started in 1969, often is critical of governmental actions. It operates from membership dues and donations. Members, and the readers, are concerned with the improvement of our water and air, and prevention of chemical pollution problems, as well as the protection of endangered wildlife species.

And More Science Magazines

More publications for the science-reading public appear regularly. In the past several years *321 Contact* appeared for children who watch "Sesame Street." The monthly is issued by the Children's Television Workshop.

Probe appeared in late 1980 as a bimonthly. *Science & Living Tomorrow* also arrived in 1980 as a monthly. For eight months a year *Fun & Science* was started in 1980 for children.

Miscellaneous With Special Appeals

There are dozens and dozens of magazines with circulations from a few hundred into the hundreds of thousands. A number are the products of scientific associations and societies. Others are designed for professionals who need up-to-date information about their special interests. Some are highly technical in content and in the writing; others are seeking that "better-educated layman" who has recently acquired an interest in a newly developed scientific tool. And a few are amateurs, representing a potential mass market for the publisher who discovers the proper approach to capture their interests.

There is, for example, *Archaeology* which was founded in 1948 and represents the Archaeological Institute of America. It reports on recent excavations around the world, on discoveries, and on ancient cultures. From a circulation of 22,000 in 1978, *Archaeology* reached 50,000 two years later, when it started to take advertisements.

Astronomy likewise has a special appeal. Started in 1973, this magazine is designed for the "scientifically-oriented public" with regular reports on celestial events, augmented with sky maps and constellation closeups.

In 1930, *Electronics* arrived, with a circulation of 5,983. For its 50th anniversary edition, the magazine carried 389 worldwide advertising pages, plus 278 editorial pages, and reached a circulation of 100,000. Nearly 24,000 of these readers live outside the United States. A review of its half-century history offered an excellent account of the change from "electron tubes—their radio, audi, video and applications" to "the living record of a technology". These are slogans used in 1930 and in 1980.

High Technology, started in 1980, is a bi-monthly with a circulation of nearly 200,000. Once the magazine stressed electronic research but later aimed its contents between straight science magazines and the how-to books. After five issues, it was sold to *Inc.* and stopped. United Marine Publishing bought it in 1981 for a relaunch with 200,000 circulation. The same firm introduced *Technology Illustrated* in late 1981.

BYTE is another widely-circulated technical publication, with some 18,000 subscribers in foreign countries. The other 142,000 are in North America. It was started in 1975 for the "personal computing enthusiast." It labels itself "The world's largest personal computer magazine," with 85 per cent of its readers involved in full-time work in the computer system world. The title refers to a part of a computer memory which contains "bits." The magazine carries ads from microcomputer equipment and computer software manufacturers and from technical publications.

Technology Review is a pioneer, having started in 1899 by alumni of the Massachusetts Institute of Technology. Eight issues a year go to nearly 60,000 readers, informing them of new developments in science, engineering, architecture, planning and related social sciences. It is less specialized than some of the more technical magazines discussed in this chapter.

Personal Computing, on the other hand, is a newcomer, arriving in 1976 and now claiming 25,000 circulation. It is designed for those who use microcomputers in offices, businesses, and homes, as well as in schools.

Creative Computing has a slightly larger audience, 70,000, for those interested in computer applications and software, for games, household management, and similar activities. It was started in 1974.

Fusion is concerned with nuclear energy, its progress, performance and future. Started in 1975, it now reaches more than 50,000 readers monthly.

InfoWorld is a California-produced bi-weekly that since 1980 has gained a circulation of 28,000 among those who use microcomputers and are interested in the trends and events new in this industry.

Interface Age claims to be the "only computing magazine on the newsstand nationally," while it seeks an audience concerned with computing technology as used in businesses, homes, and educational centers. Started in 1975, the magazine now has a circulation of 76,000.

The list goes on and on. *Kiloband Microcomputing,* which started in 1977, is for the computer hobbyists and the small businessmen. So far, it has reached a circulation of 82,000. *80 Microcomputing* has somewhat of a similar appeal. The 1980-production has reached 40,000 individuals concerned with the use of small computers in business, education, sciences, and the home.

Another of the New Hampshire-produced magazines is *onComputing,* a 1979-quarterly that has material of a more general nature—designed for the beginners, the educators, attorneys, doctors, and others who are starting in the computer area. It has a lower technical level than many of the others. *onComputing* changed to a monthly with a new name, *Popular Computing,* in mid-1981.

Computers Well Represented

In Standard Rate and Data Service's publication, *Business Publication Rates and Data,* there are many publications listed under Electronic Engineering, as well as under Science, Research and Development. In addition, there are still more specialized magazines listed under Energy Application & Management, Engineering & Construction, Power and Power Plants, and Product Design Engineering. All have some direct, or indirect, relationship with the world of science or technology.

These are limited in their audience appeal. Thus their circulation varies from 5,000 to nearly 200,000. Only a few of the more widely circulated magazines are listed here. However, one should not overlook these listings in his search for a periodical that meets his professional demands or his interests as a hobbyist or a home-consumer. In addition, there are other listings for periodicals that do not carry advertisements.

Computer Design (1962) has a circulation of 68,000, while *Computerworld* (1967) has more than 107,000. *Design News* has been around since 1946 and has built a circulation of 150,000. *EDN* (1956) is a publication for engineers and engineering managers. With a circulation of 107,000 *EDN* reports an increase of 2,000 advertising pages during the past five years.

EE (Electrical Equipment) is another oldtimer, started in 1941. Its circulation now approaches 100,000. The *Electronic Engineers Master* (1958) has 86,000. Two products of the 50s include *Electronic Component News* (1956) with 95,000 circulation, and *Electronic Design* (1952) with 104,000.

Electronic Engineering Times (1972) has reached 100,000 while *Electronic News* (1957) has 70,000 and *Electronic Products* (1956) has 94,000 subscribers.

First in circulation, advertising and editorial pages is *Machine Design,* a 1929 periodical which now reaches 160,000 circulation.

There also is a series of *Electronic News,* including special editions under these regional titles: *Northern California, Southern California, Southwest Electronic News, Mountain States Electronics & Industrial News,* and *Pacific Northwest Electronics & Industrial News.*

The American Chemical Society has a number of publications, including: *Biochemistry, Chemical Reviews, Inorganic Chemistry, Journal of Agricultural & Food Chemistry, Journal of the American Chemical Society, Journal of Chemical Information and Computer Sciences, Journal of Medicinal Chemistry, Journal of Organic Chemistry, Journal of Physical Chemistry,* and *Marcomolecules.*

In 1969, the *American Laboratory* was started and since has reached 100,000 circulation, while the *American Scientist,* a real oldtimer with a 1911 starting date, has 125,000. The *Chemical and Engineering News* (1932) has a weekly circulation of 122,000, slightly ahead of the *Industrial Research & Development* (1959) circulation of 105,000. *Laboratory Equipment* (1964) has 80,000 and *Physics Today* (1948) has 70,000. There are others below these figures.

There's Fiction, Too

A related area is science fiction, which has displayed tremendous growth in recent years. Although hundreds of paperback books cover this topic, there are some magazines with devoted followings. Movies and television series have contributed to this expansion of interest. Among the better-selling magazines are *Analog, Galileo, Heavy Metal,* and *Omni.*[18]

The digest-size *Analog* has been on the market since 1933 and sells 60,000 copies monthly. *Galileo* is similar but with a more recent start, 1979. *Heavy Metal,* for adults, appeared in America in 1977, following its success in France. Some 140,000 copies are sold monthly. *Onni* prefers not to be listed in the fantasy category, although it does offer a broad range of fiction and non-fiction.

Fantasy & Science Fiction celebrated its 30th anniversary in 1979 with a 320-page retrospective double issue.

Energy Also a Concern

Americans daily are reminded of energy problems, whether they are gassing up their cars, making plans for a new home, or paying a utility bill. Many expect scientists to solve these problems for the nation.

There are, of course, magazines designed to serve this situation. *Advertising Age* considered some of the major periodicals to include the weekly *Oil & Gas Journal,* published since 1902 and with a circulation of 58,000 today; and *Petroleum Engineer International* (1929) with 15 issues a year and circulating in nearly 110 countries. [19]

The Standard Rate and Data Service *Business Publication Rate and Data Book* lists more than 50 periodicals under Petroleum and Oil. There are others listed under Chemical and Chemical Process Industries, and some under other classifications, such as *Coal Age* (1911). Many have industrial and supply connections.

What's Ahead?

In looking ahead for the media, *NEXT* had the following comment about the science area, which sums up the situation as the 1980s got underway:

> A new breed of magazine may have already begun to respond to that need to believe. Science and Technology have been our post-modern religion, appropriately for the century of Freud, Einstein, Kettering and Ford. Sci/Tech, we are told in *Omni, Science Digest, Science/80* and *Discover,* will solve the problems that Sci/Tech has created. These magazines promise us a serene future above the clash and clamor of our conflicted, OPEC-spooked daily lives. Directly or subliminally, they present a future dreamscape of salvation with peace and a good sex life. [20]

And as the writer, Edwin Diamond, adds: "Three magazine people can't gather anywhere today without one of them dropping what's supposed to be the print equivalent of the atomic bomb: What's going to happen with the coming telecommunications revolution? And the chance that people will be getting video magazines on their television screens by punching up commands on their key pads?"

12

Home, Shelter, and How-to-do-it Magazines

CONDO AND APARTMENT OWNERS, do-it-yourself addicts, and individuals fascinated by homes built in the 18th and 19th centuries all have magazines directed to their interests. City residents, as well as those in smaller communities or on farms, have periodicals that reflect their preferences in living habits. Amateur mechanics as well as growing millions of Americans who now find it necessary to make their own home repairs and improvements also have magazines that guide them in their projects.

There is no limit to publications designed for Americans who continue to move about this nation, to tour homes around the world, or who attempt to redesign their residences to accommodate changing environment and energy needs. Some are more concerned with art objects or antiques; others are excited by architectural developments. Some love contemporary designs, while others prefer the colonial traditions. With tighter economic conditions, Americans are learning more about ways to make those home repairs rather than wait for the expensive specialists.

Thus this chapter has a variety of publications, although the primary object is concerned with the living conditions of Americans.

Better Homes and Gardens

The best known and most widely circulated magazine in this category is *Better Homes and Gardens*. Other periodicals may be older, and most are more specialized, yet *BH&G* continues to dominate the market with its 8,000,000 circulation.

Better Homes and Gardens first appeared in Des Moines, Iowa, in 1922 under the title, *Fruit, Garden & Home*. Its owner, Meredith Publishing Company, had developed *Successful Farming* 20 years earlier so the decision to start a new magazine was not a hasty one. As early as 1913, a proposal for a "magazine for town and city home-owners" had appeared in *Successful Farming*.[1]

Since its conception, *BH&G* has been service-oriented, concentrating on practical subjects with help for readers. In its initial issue an article explained "What $50 Will Do in the Backyard." In addition, Meredith wanted its magazine to serve as a forum for readers to exchange their ideas, experiences, and practical information, all for 35¢ a year, or three years for a dollar.

Through the years *BH&G* continues to initiate service projects such as landscape planning, money-back guarantee of articles advertised, test kitchens for food recipes, and others as the need developed. It has assisted such groups as the General Federation of Women's Clubs in projects related to homes and gardens. Its most notable success has been its *Cook Book,* first offered in 1920 as a premium for *BH&G* subscriptions. In 1941 it became available in bookstores. Frequently updated to include changes in cooking, including the use of microwave ovens and the metric system, the *Cook Book* reached its 20,000,000th copy in 1978. This particular copy was presented to the Library of Congress for its Rare Book and Special Collections Division. While the Bible and dictionaries have exceeded this in total sales, no single publisher has surpassed Meredith in selling any one book. As the company noted, *"BH&G* editors helped make both important on the American scene," the magazine and the *Cook Book.*

BH&G, with its circulation placing the magazine among the "top 10," maintains its philosophy "to serve husbands and wives who have a serious interest in home and family as the focal point of their lives . . (with) the editorial responsibility to move these husbands and wives to action." Reader involvement continues to be significant as witnessed in 1979 when more than 300,000 responded to its American family questionnaire, expressing great faith in the future of the marriage institution. The company notes that *"BH&G* didn't invent the family room or the barbecue grill, but *BH&G* editors helped make both important on the American scene."

BH&G is staff-planned, staff-written and staff-edited. It does not depend on Eastern-oriented editors, a policy its founder, E. T. Meredith, set in 1923. The magazine keeps abreast of the times, serving its faithful audience in the manner in which readers want to be assisted with their daily problems and activities. The magazine has been so successful that the name *BH&G* has been sufficient to ensure success in spinoffs, including dozens of special-interest books as well as in a real estate operation.[2]

BH&G began an experiment as an electronic magazine in late 1980, feeding supplementary editorial material to the Columbus, Ohio, computer time-sharing network, CompuServe. Eventually, it is believed that the entire magazine may be put on the computer so terminal users may dial for useful information. *BH&G,* which will receive a fee, will be able to determine reader interests and thus improve future editions.[3]

Apartment Ideas to *Metropolitan Home*

Meredith in 1969 started *Apartment Ideas,* first as an annual publication. A new title was applied four years later, *Apartment Life,* when frequency shifted to bimonthly. In 1977 it became a monthly. Then it was designed for a contemporary audience of active and on-the-move young individuals with a median age of 29.

Apartment Life's success was evident when its circulation grew from 200,000 to 835,000. However, to adapt to changing times, Meredith changed its title to *Metropolitan Home* in April, 1981. Explaining the change, publisher Harry Myers said:

> At the beginning of the decade, everyone born after 1946 lived in apartments. There was a life style homogeneity there that we addressed ourselves to, and we did quite well. But that started to split. Some opted in, and those are the ones we are going after. The shirkers opted out, and haven't decided to move up. We had to make a choice of who we are going to go with. . .
>
> (We will go after) the brightest and the best of the post-World War II generation . . . whether in a condo, co-op, townhouse, loft, brownstone, as well as rented apartment.[4]

Metropolitan Home was introduced with a rate base of 700,000 paid circulation. Promotional material claimed the magazine was preparing readers for the emerging 80s, noting that their "lives is the *city,* the powerful magnet for work and play, culture, education, shopping and sport that uniquely attracts and holds your best markets." Its new format included a heavier paper stock, similar to the classy *Town and Country.*

For the Homes and Gardens

A pioneer service magazine is *House Beautiful* which remarked in its first issue in late 1896 that "It is a source of never-ending amazement just why so many houses are built for the neighbors and so few for the owner thereof." Owned for 20 years by the Atlantic Monthly Company, *House Beautiful* was acquired by the Hearst Corporation in the 1930s. Still designed for those who are concerned about their homes and the furnishings, the magazine has a circulation in excess of 800,000.

Magazine historian Ted Peterson relates that the founder, Eugene Klapp, a Chicago civil engineer, called for simplicity in architecture and home decorations if one were to achieve beauty. Unlike some of today's periodicals, *House Beautiful* in 1904 carried a series on "The Poor Taste of the Rich." The stories argued that money was not essential in achieving taste in homes, since obviously "many of our richest citizens' homes are furnished in execrable taste." Along the way, *House Beautiful* acquired *Indoors and Out, Modern Homes, American Suburbs,* and *Home & Field* and merged all into today's survivor.[5] Like some of the other service publications, *House Beautiful* also publishes guides, such as *Home Decorating, Home Remodeling, Building Manual, Houses & Plans,* and *Kitchens/Baths,* varying in frequency from quarterly to annually.

House & Garden, calling itself "The magazine on the move to the eighties," is another pioneer, dating to 1901 in Philadelphia. Founded by three architects, it was devoted to the development of the country home, with special material on architecture, decoration, and gardening. Acquired in 1909 by Condé Nast, *House & Garden* was combined with *American Homes & Gardens.* With a circulation today exceeding a million, the magazine attracts the 25-to-49 age group with incomes more than $35,000 in the professional and executive categories. Topics have expanded to include creative crafts, sports, travel, wine and food, as well as the more staple subjects found in similar magazines. And it too offers guides, such as *Decorating Guide, Building & Remodeling Guide, Kitchen & Bath Guide,* and *Plans Guide,* varying from quarterly to annually.

A more recent periodical with a special appeal is *Colonial Homes,* started by Hearst in 1975. The magazine is of interest to those preferring 18th and 19th Century American homes, either to restore or to visit. The pursuit of this traditional design and classic home furnishings has inspired a circulation in excess of 450,000 for *Colonial Homes.*

New Shelter began in 1980 for the do-it-yourself homeowner. Published by the expanding Rodale Press in Pennsylvania, *New Shelter* calls itself "The magazine of home efficiency that can help you build yourself an 'ark' for the future while you get your ship together today." Expecting a circulation of 530,000 for its first anniversary, the magazine focuses on low-cost, low-energy, ecological living. Latest developments will be presented, those involving alternative energy, solar greenhouses, productive mini-farms, and other experimental projects both for the beginning handymen or the skilled craftsmen. Rodale Press also has another periodical in this area, *Organic Gardening,* started in 1942 and growing monthly as Americans turn more to home gardening and to a great concern with organic products.

Hudson Home made its debut in early 1981, describing itself as "a practical magazine to help you Make your Dream Home come true" and a "consumer shelter monthly magazine devoted strictly to the home."

Hudson Home planned to start with 250,000 subscribers and newsstand readers, with a median age of 29 and median income of $29,000. It is designed to help owners with home repairs, remodeling and improvement, expanding, and decorating, while offering stories on home plans, new products and ideas.

Interest in Architectual Projects

More Americans are expressing interest in architectual projects during the 80s, both those involved in the professional world and those interested as amateurs or hobbyists.

Architectual Digest is a California-based monthly that "showcases residences throughout the world." Established in 1920 and with a circulation base of 450,000, this magazine fascinates its affluent audience that travels extensively and entertains frequently. One would expect this when the average income is nearly $90,000.

Architectual Record, a McGraw-Hill publication with a history dating back to 1891, has won many awards. Among its circulation of 65,000 are architects and engineers who are concerned about the Dodge Reports and Statistics on construction, and about the other topics covered, including building studies, individual building presentations, technical articles, news, products, literature, costs and economics, and trends within the industry.

Also of major interest are three other publications, with varying audiences: *AIA Journal, Building Design & Construction,* and *Progressive Architecture.* The American Institute of Architects has published *AIA Journal* since 1913. It now reaches more than 90,000 monthly with the latest data on developments affecting the architectual profession.

Cahners publishes *Building Design & Construction,* with its circulation of 30,000. Started in 1958, *BD&C* is directed to architectual/engineering firms, contractors, design construction departments, institutions, government agencies, utilities and others.

Progressive Architecture is a product of Penton/IPC. With a history dating to 1920, *Progressive Architecture* has a circulation of nearly 80,000, recording considerable gains both in circulation and in advertising pages in recent years. It has won numerous awards in graphics and editorial contests.

An interesting publication for a number of years was the *Architectual Forum.* Started in 1892 as the *Bricklayer* [6], it was renamed in 1917 to *Architectual Forum* and in 1932 acquired by Time Inc. Henry Luce kept the publication for more than three decades, although it was never profitable. He wanted it "to bring together, around the central art and science of architecture, all the influences which will build a new America." It was renamed *The Magazine of Building* in 1950 and two years later divided into two periodicals, *Architectual Forum* and *House & Home.* The latter was eventually sold to McGraw-Hill, while the *Forum* was suspended in 1964. It was early concerned with urban development.

For the Mechanical-minded

Popular Science monthly for more than a century has been the bible for millions of Americans, with its devotion "to exploring and explaining to a nontechnical but knowledgeable readership the technical world around." Founded in 1872, *Popular Science* provides up-to-date coverage of new products with instructions for many home workshoppers. Its circulation of 1,800,000 comes mostly from subscribers, men with interests that includes automobiles, boats, engines, tools, garden/home/lawn equipment, television, electronics, photography and recreational items.

Today *Popular Science* is a part of the Times-Mirror magazine network, which includes *Outdoor Life, Golf,* and *Ski.* It was acquired in 1967. During its earlier years it competed with *Scientific American* for readers. However, in more recent times it has appealed to home owners and to the younger readers as well.

Popular Mechanics was established as a weekly in Chicago in 1902. It continues to compete with *Popular Science* for the circulation readership and today has more than 1,600,000, mostly male subscribers. It covers areas similar to those in *Popular Science*.

Hearst acquired *Popular Mechanics* in 1958. Today the magazine has a strong interest in science, exploration and adventure, with reports on new and unusual developments. Free-lancers are told to be specific in explaining what makes their subjects new, different, better, or more economical. In other words, how will this article assist the readers? The magazine is "for the new achievers," according to trade advertisements.

Mechanics Illustrated is another of the Big Three, with its 1,680,000 circulation. Younger, having started in 1928 under the name *Modern Mechanics, Mechanics Illustrated* has become a CBS Publication with its emphasis on youth.

It, too, has a broad appeal, covering inventions, novel means of transportation, weapons, health and health management, alternative energy, science and technology. Its editors seek to keep the articles as non-technical and practical. Unusual occupations provide human interest coverage, as well as articles about workshop projects and ideas.

Readers, similar to many who take *Popular Science* and *Popular Mechanics,* are interested in receiving simple tips on home construction projects, such as boatbuilding, furniture and the like, including outdoor subjects. The magazine adopted a new logo in 1980, when it eliminated hunting, fishing, and financial coverage.

Science & Mechanics also appeals to the home fix-up fans with their varied concerns. Started in 1937, this Davis quarterly has a 115,000 circulation. Its broad profile also includes space explorations, medicine, electronics, and the usual how-to-do-it topics.

Popular Electronics, founded in 1954, is a Ziff-Davis monthly that directs its contents to electronics experimenters, hi-fi enthusiasts, computer hobbyists, CB'ers, and hams. Its circulation of nearly 400,000 is widely spread across the nation. The firm also publishes the *Electronics Experimenter's Handbook.*

There are others, too, such as a number issued by Davis Publications, including *Budget Electronics* (1975), *CB Magazine* (1961), *Communications World* (1971), *Electronics Hobbyists* (1975), *Electronics Theory Handbook* (1975), *99 IC Projects* (1979) and *101 Electronic Projects* (1970).

Newcomers continue to arrive. *Radio-Electronics Special Projects* and *Video Action* planned late 1980 publication. Some associations have their magazines, including the Radio Amateurs' Journal, *CQ,* started in 1945 and now serving 100,000, plus the American Radio Relay League's *QST* (1915) for 150,000 subscribers.

And the list goes on, including *Ham Radio Horizon* (1977), *Ham Radio* (1968), *Home Video* (1979), *Radio-Electronics* (1929), *73 Magazine* (1960), *S9/Hobby Radio* (1962), *Video* (1978) and others.[7]

More For Homeowners

There are other periodicals for those who do their own work around their homes. For example, the *Family Handyman* is published 10 times a year by the Webb Co. Started in 1951, *Family Handyman* has profited from current trends, with its circulation reaching a million, primarily through subscriptions. Emphasis is placed on home improvements with detailed instructions for amateurs to follow. The magazine claims it is "not a science and mechanics book, not a traditional book, but a homeowner's magazine that bridges the gap between them." Webb also publishes the quarterly *Consumer Life,* started in 1975, with a million circulation for those interested in a variety of topics about the home, credit, insurance, banking, investments, recreation, and entertainment.

Blair and Ketchum's *Country Journal* is a Vermont monthly reaching more than 220,000 subscribers. Publisher Bill Blair says self sufficiency is stressed, "But not from a Messianic point of view. The tone of the magazine is affable and off hand."[8] Median age for readers is around 49.

A different type of publication in this area is the bimonthly *Homemaker,* started in 1977. It represents the National Extension Homemakers Council, reporting its activities and club projects to some 120,000 subscribers.

With a slightly broader base, *Americana* seeks to tell more about home life in articles on crafts restorations, travel, cooking, gardening, and the like. This emphasis, however, is on America's past more than the present. Started in 1973, it reaches 250,000 monthly.

Lifestyles change constantly in America, although a sizeable group remains more concerned with maintaining the nation's heritage. There has grown a segment of individuals with a preference for "voluntary simplicity," as *Marketing & Media Decisions* magazine termed it.[9] This group, described as being in the 25-to-40 age category, is evenly divided between male and female, with emphasis on the well educated, urban type and generally singles. A decade ago, they "were dismissed as freaked-out hippies or out-of-touch eccentrics." In the 80s the situation has been reversed. Some of the serious changes came with the *Whole Earth Catalogue.* And today the advertisers are giving more attention to these individuals, thus making it possible for more publications to survive.

13

Specialized Farmers
Go Specialized

THE CHANGING STATUS of the American farmer and the agricultural world in general has had its influence on farm publications. There has been a "shift away from the production end of farming toward the management and marketing aspects," according to *Advertising Age*. This review also observed that "Readership has fallen sharply because of television's penetration into rural areas, and the trend to larger farms has reduced the number of farm families."[1] There are others who still believe the real strength of today's farm magazines is the coverage of production agriculture.

Farmers and their families have become more cosmopolitan in their outlook. They want the information available from federal and state agencies through numerous periodicals, many in direct competition with the more traditional agricultural magazines.

Farm publications have existed for more than a century and a half in America. In the 18th Century many scientific and mechanics publications contained features aimed to the farmers. In 1810, however, the *Agricultural Museum* appeared in Georgetown, D.C., to become the first periodical aimed entirely toward agricultural interests. Another pioneer was the *American Farmer*, which appeared in Baltimore in 1819. Its long career might be attributed to such men as Jefferson and Madison, who endorsed its contents.

Other pioneers included the *Plough Boy, The New England Farmer, The New York Farmer,* and the *Southern Agriculturalist*. Even then the readers were encouraged to adopt business-like methods for their operations. By 1856, there were at least 44 American periodicals devoted to agriculture. Only a few were started during the Civil War era but after that conflict farm publications expanded as did other magazines.[2]

Farm publications suffered along with others during the Depression of the 1930s, when much of America was in a stagnant situation. While local farmers bartered produce and livestock for newspaper subscriptions, such trades were not utilized for magazine payments. According to some directories more than half of these magazines failed between 1928 and 1938. Since World War II there has been some additional decline. *Ayer Directory of Newspapers and Periodicals* listed 654 farm publications in the early 70s but only about 500 a decade later.

Specialization Trend Shown

In recent times this category of periodicals has joined in the specialized growth pattern, with regional and state publications designed for varied agricultural interests. In no place is this clearer than in the Standard Rate and Data Service listings in its *Consumer Magazine and Farm Publication* rates and data book. Recent copies note these divisions:

> Dairy and dairy breeds; Diversified and farm home; Farm education and vocations; Farm electrification; Farm organizations and cooperatives; Field crops and soil management; Fruits, nuts, vegetables and special products; Land use, irrigation and conservation; Livestock and breed; Newspaper-distributed farm publications; and Poultry.

Many of these magazines provide geographic and/or demographic editions, offering variations both in editorial and in advertising content. Staffers are sent into the field to maintain contact with farmers and to learn more about their current needs for information. Polls also provide data useful in planning subject matter. Many of these magazines belong to the Audit Bureau of Circulation, Business Publications Audit of Circulation, Inc., and/or the Verified Audit Circulation Corp. The Agricultural Publisher's Association in Chicago represents some of these periodicals.

There are a number of group publishers, usually with periodicals in a particular section of the nation. Then there are publications that join to obtain national advertising accounts. For example, there is the Midwest Farm Publications, six independently-edited periodicals with a combined circulation of nearly 700,000. This unit includes the *Farmer, Nebraska Farmer, Prairie Farmer, Indiana Prairie Farmer, Wallaces Farmer,* and the *Wisconsin Agriculturist.* There also is the Western Unit Farm Publications, with seven locally-edited magazines involved in improving their advertising content.

With the Midwest Unit, *Wallaces Farmer* may be the best known, since it began in 1855 and now has 125,000 subscribers. It is typical of many such magazines, since it limits its coverage to Iowa farm business and farm family living, with coverage of such topics as taxes, government programs, legislation and regulatory affairs, families' home management needs, and similar subjects for those who farm in Iowa.

In Cleveland, the Harvest Publishing Company, a part of Harcourt Brace

Jovanovich, has five magazines with good circulations. These include the *Pennsylvania Farmer* (75,000), *Ohio Farmer* (102,000); *Michigan Farmer* (74,000); *Kansas Farmer* (62,000), and *Missouri Ruralist* (74,000).

There are others, too, such as the Miller Publishing Co. in Minneapolis, a part of the American Broadcasting Companies, Inc., operations. Miller publishes *Dairy Herd Management* (65,000); *Feedlot Management* (20,000); and *Hog Farm Management* (47,000). In addition, the Miller firm has a number of more specialized magazines in the business publication category.

In nearby St. Paul, the Webb Company has a variety of publications, including some for the farm audience. The firm in early 1981 was publishing these magazines: *Beef, Consumer Life, Family Handyman, Family Food Garden, The Farmer, Farm Industry News* with Midwest/South/West editions, *Irrigation Age, KOA Handbook and Directory for Campers, National Hog Farmer, Passages, Snow Goer, Snow Week,* and *TWA Ambassador.*

From time to time these major firms will either acquire a publication from another company or start a new one. For example, Miller launched *Farm Money Management* in August, 1980, for "high-income agricultural producers and lenders." Its initial circulation was 63,000 non-paid.

There are other publishers tapping this tremendous market. Some of their magazines are circulation-controlled, free to qualifying farmers. Others are directed to farm management, such as *Agri Farmer* and *Big Farmer,* which discuss taxes, loans, cost accounting methods, cash flow and investment topics. In addition, there are other excellent magazines published by large cooperatives and agribusiness companies that compete for the farmers' readership.

There are three publications that are generally better known across the country: *Successful Farming, Progressive Farming* and *Farm Journal.* These aren't the oldest—that title may belong to the *Michigan Farmer,* which dates from 1843 when it began as a general service weekly aimed for the rural audience. The *California Farmer* has 125 years of service.[3]

Successful Farming

The Meredith Corporation in Des Moines, Iowa, started *Successful Farming* in 1902. The firm is better known for its successful *Better Homes and Gardens,* yet its "brother publication" provided the foundation for its position in the publishing world.

Successful Farming is considered a manual of "means, markets and methods," a guide to a more profitable, workable, convenient farm life, according to its publisher. Originally it focused on the specialized, highly-mechanized farms of the heartland of America, the Midwest. The publisher offers news from the latest discoveries in agricultural research to the latest in Washington's determination of farm policies. It is, of course, concerned with the know-how, the how-to, and the why types of informative articles.

Circulation, now at 700,000, is divided among 14 regional editions and three demographic editions. Special material is provided for hog, beef, and dairy interests. In 1980, the magazine said its philosophy was "to have a broad base of information useful to all of our readers, with specialized inserts to readers in various categories." Publisher Bruce Boyle also noted the trend toward farm consolidations, with larger yet fewer farms. This has created a greater concern for management topics.

Successful Farming provided the cornerstone for Meredith, with the 1902 premier edition of 16 pages going to 500 subscribers. The company reported that one man carried all of the copies to the postoffice in a single bag weighing 34 pounds. When it celebrated its 75th birthday, *Successful Farming* said it could, through the use of computers, theoretically put out 472 regional editions, but normally it was about 150.[4]

During the 70s, *Successful Farming* eliminated its home service editorial, considered by some to be a dangerous move. At the same time, it eliminated its non-farm subscribers. In addition, publishing schedules were augumented to provide the magazine when the farmers needed the information rather than strictly on a monthly basis. This resulted in 13 issues, eight during the first six months. Circulation has been expanded from the Midwest to the South, as seen with the *Successful Farming in the South* edition started with a base of 77,000 subscribers. This move came after 76 years of emphasis on the more northern states.

In explaining this move southward, the magazine claimed there would be no change in its basic subject matter. "The articles that appear will continue to fall in the following classifications: soils and crops, machinery and automotive, buildings and equipment, livestock, economics in management and marketing." The Southern edition carries its own distinctively Southern cover and features different copy. Articles will be directed to the new readers, such as "Hog Management in the South."[5]

Successful Farming is more than a service publication for today's farmers. It keeps up with changing times and with the shifting emphasis, not only with crops and animals but with the more rapidly changing economic picture.

Progressive Farmer

The *Progressive Farmer* made its debut on February 10, 1886, in Winston, North Carolina. Founder Col. Leonidas L. Polk wrote:

> A properly conducted weekly journal devoted to agricultural and other industrial interests of our people is a public necessity. Encouraged by the opportunity presented and by the gratifying indications of general support in the undertaking from all sections of our state, I assume the task and will devote to this, my chosen lifework, all of the energy and fidelity of which I am capable.

News of world and national affairs was reprinted from other journals, while the articles had appeal to all members of the family. Some items told about the management of tobacco crops, others about teaching daughters housework, with hints on washing, cleaning a stove, or making cookies. Obviously, the age of specialization had not yet arrived in North Carolina.

Polk was elected president of the National Farmer Alliance in 1889. He recognized the need for institutions of higher learning and was at least partially responsible for North Carolina Agricultural and Mechanical College, founded in 1887.

Polk edited the magazine for six years before his death. From the cotton fields of North Carolina came Clarence Poe, who, at the age of 22, acquired *Progressive Farmer*. He and four other men paid $7,500 for the magazine in 1903. He remained president of the company until 1953 and kept an active hand in its operations until his death in 1964.

Along with other Southern leaders, *Progressive Farmer* staffers called for a better balance between crops and livestock. The magazine arrived during a period when such publications were rapidly expanding along the Atlantic coast, increasing from 29 in 1880 to 83 by the end of the century. Many of these disappeared in the 1930–50 era because of economic factors. These publications sought to bring the South back as a major agricultural region, a position it lost temporarily during the Civil War.

Along the line, other magazines were absorbed into *Progressive Farmer*. Eventually it was moved to Birmingham, where in 1959 the company acquired what is now known as the Oxmoor Press, the largest commercial printers in a four-state area. The printing plant was expanded and modernized. In 1967 a new building was erected.

Emory Cunningham, who joined the sales staff in 1948, became the firm's president 20 years later. Today, *Progressive Farmer* provides readers with 17 editions, varying in editorial and advertising content. Some features appear in all editions, such as "What's Ahead" and "Washington." Articles are directed to special readers, those with interests in peanuts, tobacco, cotton and/or pork. It was a pioneer in the use of regional editions, having started the practice more than 60 years ago.

Progressive Farmer's editors have been placed in areas where they get the "feel" of their communities and thus become a part of the area they serve. The magazine is directed to the farm family. Its circulation of 1,400,000 in the 1940s has been cut to around a million today, affected no doubt by the exodus from the farm to the urban communities. Also, when these individuals moved to the cities they were informed they would receive the newer magazine, *Southern Living,* once a unit of *Progressive Farmer.*[6]

As Cunningham noted, a magazine has to prove itself to subscribers, who vote by check at least every three years when they decide about renewals. *Progressive Farmer* has this regular problem, since it is not sold on newsstands. It expects readers to share more of the costs, relieving some of the pressure on advertisers. Staffers are instructed to prepare their material "not to impress but to express" their ideas so readers can fully understand. At the same time, they are not to underestimate the intelligence of these readers. Staffers are selected from applicants who have the ability to write effectively and to understand their subjects, those who have been reared on a farm or ranch, and those with agricultural training with some specialities. *Progressive Farmer* seeks to become the reader's Bible. Its circulation extends from Maryland and Delaware through Florida and across to Arizona. The magazine also has market reports and trend analyses four times daily on a radio network.

Farm Journal

"The most complicated magazine to print in the world" is the description given *Farm Journal* by its printers, the Donnelley firm. In October, 1979, for example, it had more than 300 variations. Lee Alexander, vice president for sales, predicted that in the 80s it would have the capacity to provide copies on a personalized basis, a trend also predicted for newspapers and some other magazines. As with *Progressive Farmer,* the *Farm Journal* also has an extensive radio network.

To be able to publish individual issues, the *Farm Journal* has asked all 1,250,000 subscribers to furnish data concerning their farm operations. This is computerized so editions can be sent to those with matching interests.[7]

Publisher Dale Smith said in early 1980 that "If a farm magazine is to be important to farmers, it must report and interpret much more than the nitty-gritty of plowing, planting and picking." Smith said his magazine is the only farm periodical with a full-time Washington editor and a staff economist.

Farm Journal was founded in Philadelphia in 1877 by Wilmer Atkinson. By the 1880s it had a circulation of 200,000 and a century later it reached 1,500,000. Its first press run was 25,000 copies; by 1955 it peaked at 3,800,000; in 1969 this dropped to 3,000,000, still more than twice the subscribers it had 10 years later as publishers reduced numbers to mainly full-time commercial farmers.

It, too, has long provided specialized editions, with extras from time to time of interest to the hog, beef, dairy, and cotton farmers. As Alexander noted, "It's quite possible for neighbors across the road from each other to pull out different *Farm Journals* from their mail boxes."[8]

Folio magazine reported in late 1980 that *Farm Journal* was the leader in total revenue (nearly $30 million) and in advertising revenue ($23 million) among publications in the Farm Marketshare category.

Both *Farm Journal* and *Successful Farming* provide demographic studies to the Audit Bureau of Circulation. *Farm Journal* data appear more up-to-date. There may be some overlap of readership between these two that advertisers often feel the necessity to alternate their messages between *Farm Journal* and *Progressive Farmer.*

If there is such a thing as mass magazines for the farm market, these three obviously are representative. In some areas they are general in content, yet they manage to capture the advantages offered through specialization.

Country Gentleman

For many years the major magazine for a segment of America's rural population was the *Country Gentleman,* acquired by the Philadelphia-based Curtis Publishing Company in 1911. The magazine had a long history, dating to 1831 as *The Genesee Farmer,* founded by Luther Tucker at Rochester, N.Y. He added other publications and in 1853 started the *Country Gentleman,* which he eventually merged with these earlier magazines. Three generations of the Tucker family owned the magazine until it was sold to Curtis.[9]

Following the collapse of the Curtis firm, this magazine disappeared until its revival in 1975 by the new Indianapolis-based Curtis company. Now a quarterly, the *Country Gentleman* is directed toward the affluent farmers as well as to city dwellers who also maintain country homes. Its circulation is approaching 180,000 under the leadership of its new owners, Beurt and Cory Ser Vaas, who acquired the Curtis name.

Mother Earth News

Whether *Mother Earth News* belongs here or in some other section is a question. Obviously, it is not the type of publication that commercial farmers will take. It is, no doubt, more environmental-designed, yet in the long run it no doubt has similar goals for the treatment of the land.

In 1970 a new magazine was started in Ohio; a decade later *Mother Earth News* had a circulation in excess of a million, following its move to Hendersonville, N.C. Its founders, John and Jane Shuttleworth, feel the bimonthly serves those "seeking personal fulfillment through increased self-reliance, ecologically sound growth, and individual accomplishment." It is a service for many do-it-yourself fans interested in food, gardening, energy uses, home improvements, and the like.

The Shuttleworths started *Mother Earth News* on $1,500 with 147 subscribers. It was called "a magazine for a gentle revolution" that was timed appropriately to take advantage of an ecology-conscious society. Since its founding the firm has added a mail order operation, a book division, television and radio programs, as well as syndicated columns for newspapers. The value of the magazine to its readers is reflected by the monthly demand for some 45,000 back issues. The publishers feel *Mother Earth News* never goes out of date. Through research projects, the publishers learn about subjects that concern their readers, especially in areas related to the energy crisis.

For experimental work, *Mother Earth News* publishers have developed a 622-acre model energy community near Hendersonville. Its registered trademark is "more than a magazine . . . a way of life." And today it proclaims itself "the most relevant magazine in America."[10]

State Farm Magazines

The majority of the nation's farmers no doubt subscribe to their own state farm periodicals. A number of these have organized into the State Farm Magazine Bureau, with periodicals covering 34 states. These include:

> *American Agriculturist, California Farmer, Kansas Farmer-Stockman, Oklahoma Farmer-Stockman, Texas Farmer-Stockman, Kansas Farmer, Missouri Ruralist, Ohio Farmer, Michigan Farmer, Pennsylvania Farmer, The Farmer, Nebraska Farmer, Prairie Farmer* (Illinois), *Indiana Prairie Farmer, Wallaces Farmer, Wisconsin Agriculturist, Arizona Farmer-Ranchman, Colorado Rancher and Farmer, Washington Farmer-Stockman, Oregon Farmer-Stockman, Montana Farmer-Stockman, Idaho Farmer-Stockman,* and *Utah Farmer-Stockman.*

According to a study of the agri-market, *Madison Avenue* magazine in 1980 noted the long history of these periodicals and credit such success to the ability of the editors to meet the needs of their readers.

"Each state farm editor is faced with a different set of concerns based on climate, growing conditions, type of farm enterprises and other factors," according to *Madison Avenue.* There is, naturally, competition between this group of magazines and the Big Three, those mass-circulated periodicals. This may concern the advertisers more than the writers and editors, since both groups are staffed with specialists appropriately trained for their subjects to be covered.[11]

There is no doubt that the potential markets are there. Agriculture is America's largest single business, according to Earl L. Butz.[12] "It is the major aggregate user of capital. It is the most capital intensive of any major U.S. industry. Its increase in output per worker in the last quarter century so far outdistances the other sections of the economy that comparisons are often embarrassing." Butz added:

> The miracle of American agriculture is based in large part on the family farm structure. It is from this trinity of owner, operator and manager, in a single family unit, that entrepreneurship flourishes. It is here that incentive for excellence is strong. Here, the profit motive encourages innovation, hastens change, increases efficiency, lowers production costs, and feeds 220 million Americans remarkably inexpensively.

Another approach has been added by David S. Bennett, manager of marketing services for the Miller Publishing Co., in discussing the future of the periodicals that will serve this special American public. In noting some changes of ownership, especially the acquisition of smaller firms by larger corporations, Bennett wrote:

> This is because publications are generally entrepreneurial efforts and once the entrepreneur is at retirement age, he has to do something with his baby. Since it usually is his life's work, it generally is all he has and the only way he has of harvesting a return from his investment is to sell. Very, very few

entrepreneurs are of the sort who will take in someone, train them and then let them buy or even take over the business. They are too dominant and forceful an individual to ever allow someone else to "meddle" with what they know is best. Thus, the answer is to sell to an outsider . . .

And also significant is this observation:

Magazines are unlike newspapers as they do not serve a "community." Magazines serve markets and the economy is such that markets can form at any given time under the pressures of innovation and product development. Therefore, magazines will continue to spring up throughout our history as long as the innovative force lives.[13]

Most farm families receive numerous publications so there is considerable competition for readership. On the business side there is great competition for advertising.

14

In the Name of Religion

TREMENDOUS INFLUENCE was exercised by religious publications upon the early settlers of America. No doubt some influence continues today through the hundreds of church-sponsored and independent, non-denominational periodicals.

Some of these are widely known, such as Norman Vincent Peale's *Guideposts,* with its 3,300,000 circulation; Billy Graham's *Decision,* which reaches three million, and the Methodist-published *Upper Room,* which goes to more than two million readers each month. There are others designed basically for limited readership within a denomination, prepared for persons of all ages. Many periodicals designed for use in Sunday School classes use the magazine format.

The pioneer among these periodicals is *The Christian History, Containing Accounts of the Revival and Propagation of Religion in Great Britain & America,* published weekly in Boston in 1743. Its publisher was Thomas Prince, Jr., son of the minister and historian at the old South Church.[1] The publication was announced in the *Boston Weekly News-Letter* on March 3, 1743, when plans were revealed that it would cover the activities of ministers, contain letters, news of revivals, and other church-related topics, not only in the colonies but in England and Scotland as well. It would be religious in content, obviously, not secular.

A forerunner of today's non-denominational periodical was *The Christian's, Scholar's, and Farmer's Magazine* in New Jersey in 1789, the nation's first bi-monthly. It would contain five departments: literature, theology, agriculture, poetry, and foreign and domestic news.[2]

The *Arminian Magazine* in 1789–90 defended the Methodist doctrine and philosophy of John Wesley. Published in Philadelphia, this monthly was edited by Methodist bishops. As the first Methodist publication in America, it was a pioneer in denominational journalism.[3]

The *New-York Missionary Magazine* began in 1800 as the first distinctively missionary organ, according to Frank Luther Mott. It furnished articles on missionary societies and revivals, as well as accounts of missionaries abroad.[4] Others soon followed, as did many religious newspapers. One report said that in the 1840s there were some 60 religious publications in New York City. The 1850 Census noted 191 such periodicals in the United States, including newspapers. Today similar periodicals continue with their basic object to interpret themselves to their constituencies. In this endeavor, they often are more relevant to today's world than those in the earlier decades.

Such early magazines, as well as others that followed, were expected to defend the beliefs of their sponsors and at the same time provide inspirational and historical comments designed to encourage continued support from readers. Some definitely avoided secular topics. Although some editors discouraged personal reflections or controversial topics, others thrived on such subjects, seeking to keep the readers stirred up. Most editors focused their attention on home topics, although some articles about foreign nations were published, especially if they concerned religious activities in England or Scotland.

Such publications have their counterpart today among those that advocate specific doctrines of denominations and those that provide news of contemporary controversies while reinforcing current beliefs. Some serve a national market while many are regional in their scope. There also are those that support Christianity, or some basic faith, in general.

It is difficult to know exactly how many periodicals exist in this field. One of the longtime experts, Roland E. Wolseley of Syracuse University, appraised the religious press for many years. He agreed closely with James L. C. Ford, who wrote *Magazines for Millions,* with an estimate of approximately 1,700 periodicals. This would include 150 to 200 Jewish, 400 to 500 Roman Catholic, and some one thousand Protestant periodicals.[5]

Standard Rate and Data publications list only those that carry advertisements, which in this instance represents only a small minority. The *Writer's Market* notes more than 100 such periodicals that accept outside contributions, although the majority are either staff written or contain material prepared by members of the sponsoring church. A decade ago the *Magazine Industry Newsletter* estimated there were more than 1,200 such publications, with a total annual circulation of 1,600,000,000. In addition, *MIN* figures there were another 1,100 for which no circulation numbers were available.[6]

One major problem concerns the definition of a religious magazine. Ford thought such magazines should represent the voice of a religious belief, an appropriate concept. However, many of these periodicals are tabloids, such as the numerous state and community periodicals, while others are more akin to newspapers in format and content than to magazines.

Major Religious Organizations

Organizations that serve the church press include the Associated Church Press, which includes newspapers, magazines, and newsletters published in the United States and Canada. It maintains a postal consultant in Washington, publishes an annual directory and a newsletter, and conducts its annual Award of Merit program to encourage excellence in religious journalism.

The ACP began in 1916 in St. Louis and adopted its present name in 1937. Originally it was the Editorial Council of the Religious Press. More than 100 publications are now members, representing a combined circulation approaching 15 million. The ACP "constitutes a powerful force for informing and influencing public opinion on religious, economic, social, political, national, and international issues of our time," according to the group's program. One ACP member is the *American Baptist,* which claims to be the oldest religious magazine with continuous publication in the Western Hemisphere.

In addition to ACP there are other groups: The Catholic Press Association in New York; Canadian Church Press in Ontario; Evangelical Press Association in Kansas; American Jewish Press Association in Philadelphia.

Nashville is headquarters for the Protestant Church-Owned Publishers' Association started by 24 such concerns in 1949. As a trade association it seeks "to share effective ways of relating the publishing ministry to other ministries of the parent denomination, to increase mutual understanding, appreciation and utility" along with other cooperative projects. Liaison is encouraged among the members, as well as with other groups and associations. It includes the major publishing houses.

Among the major publishing houses in Nashville is that operated by the Southern Baptist Convention. Their publications likewise are designed for specific audiences, such as *Home Life* for the young marrieds; *Home Mission,* with in-depth stories about innovative missionary efforts; *Commission,* for foreign mission work; *Outreach* for Sunday School leaders; *Contempo,* for women between 18 and 39; *Church Administration,* for pastors and religious education leaders; *Baptist Program,* for ministers; *Accent,* for pre-teen girls; *Church Singles* and *World Mission Journal* for special groups; *Probe* for boys.

There are other specialized areas covered by *Deacon* and *Proclaim* for pastors, while *Search* is an intellectual journal about trends, doctrine and related topics. The *Quarterly Review* profiles serious material, including statistical and other vital information for church leaders under its subtitle: A Survey of Southern Baptist Progress. There are still others, with each serving a major age group and with specific objectives.

Independent Protestant Periodicals

The *Christian Century,* published in Chicago, is a pioneer, having started in 1884. It is "for college-educated, ecumenically minded, progressive church people, both clergy and lay." The weekly reports a circulation of 30,000.

The *Christian Herald,* another pioneer that started in 1878 and is published in Chappaqua, N. Y., reaches some 270,000 subscribers monthly. It is a general magazine for church-going families, with stories emphasizing religious living. Some 100,000 receive the monthly *Christian Life,* which began in 1939 and is designed for the "whole man."

Christianity Today is another Illinois magazine, started in 1956. A Gallup survey said this magazine, with its 188,000 subscribers, "led the list of the ten most widely read magazines by clergy." It emphasizes the orthodox, evangelical approach.

There are, of course, many others, mostly with limited audiences such as the *Journal of Church Music,* published in Philadelphia for organists and choir directors in small- to medium-sized churches. On the other hand, the Moody Bible Institute in Chicago sends its *Moody Monthly* to more than 300,000 subscribers, those considered to be conservative evangelical readers.

For anyone interested in "Charismatic renewal" there is the *Logos Journal,* a bimonthly since 1971, with a circulation of 56,000. The Tyndal Press publishes the bimonthly *Christian Reader,* going to nearly 205,000 subscribers. Founded in 1963, it contains "reprints and condensations of articles from theologically conservative periodicals and occasionally from secular sources that provide information, Biblical insight, and spiritual inspiration to evangelical readers."[7]

Church-Sponsored Periodicals

The *Catholic Digest,* founded in 1936, today reaches nearly 550,000 subscribers monthly. For Knights of Columbus members and others the monthly *Columbia* has more than 1,250,000 subscribers. Directed to Catholic families since its start in 1920, the *Catholic Digest* has been termed a *"Reader's Digest* with a halo."

Catholic laymen are responsible for *Commonweal,* a biweekly with 20,000 circulation. This New York magazine aims its articles to the college-educated audience and has been compared to the *Nation* and the *New Republic* in its appeal to a small but influential group of readers. It is quoted extensively. It doesn't always agree with the policies voiced by the Pope or other Catholic leaders. It was started in 1924.

Catholics also publish nine editions of *Our Sunday Visitor,* with a weekly combined circulation of 400,000. Contemporary problems are reviewed, while feature articles reflect the Catholic principles. Designed for family reader, the magazine began in 1912.

Another well-known Catholic publication is the *Sign,* published by the Passionist Fathers and Brothers in New Jersey. This 60-year-old magazine has a circulation of nearly 140,000. School administrators and teachers are provided *Today's Catholic Teacher* to assist them in their duties. For Catholic families there is *St. Anthony Messenger,* established in 1893. Now reaching more than 300,000 subscribers monthly, it is prepared by the Franciscan Friars in Cincinnati.

The Reformed Church in America has a number of publications, including the *Church Herald,* a biweekly with 73,500 circulation. Dating from 1826, it is certainly a pioneer among today's religious periodicals. It serves church workers, Christian families, and the clergy.

Presbyterians, too, have many periodicals, such as the *Presbyterian Survey,* published monthly in Atlanta for more than a century. The 120,000 copies stress articles on general and contemporary issues. There also is *A.D.,* published in two editions: *United Presbyterian A.D.* and *United Church of Christ A.D.* Started in 1972, their combined circulation is nearly 270,000. *A.D.* "addresses itself to the hurt and hunger of the world, the malfunction of society, and the nature of the mission of the church in the world."

The *Lutheran,* with many regional editions and a 22-times-a year schedule, has a circulation approaching 600,000. A general interest publication of the Lutheran Church in America, it began in 1896. The *Lutheran Standard,* started in 1842, is aimed for families of the American Lutheran Church. This semi-monthly has a circulation of 565,000. For the middle-age and older audience there is the *Lutheran Journal* with 105,000 circulation. This conservative quarterly began in 1937. For another specialized group the *Lutheran Women* reaches 40,000 with topics of interest to mothers "related to the contemporary expression of Christian faith in daily life, community action, international concerns."

Episcopalian monthly is approaching 300,000, reaching members of the Episcopal Church. Started in 1836, the *Episcopalian* is published in Philadelphia.

In South Carolina the Jacobs Religious List has a number of publications, with varying frequencies. With a combined circulation of two million, this list includes 16 Southern Baptist papers, 13 other Protestants, seven Methodists, three Jewish, and one Catholic. These vary from weeklies to monthlies.

The Campus Crusade for Christ organization publishes its monthly *Worldwide Challenge.* This California-based, interdenominational Christian movement works with youths across the nation. Also on the West Coast is the Gospel Light organization, started in 1933, that issues many periodicals, books, and study programs. The Salvation Army's *War Cry* is more like a newspaper.

For advertising purposes a number of the church publishing concerns have united to form the Interfaith Network. They include: *A.D., Catholic Digest, Christian Herald, Episcopalian, The Lutheran, The Lutheran Standard, Presbyterian Survey, St. Anthony Messenger,* and *Sign.* Their combined circulation, mostly through subscriptions, reaches in excess of three million.

Guideposts

For more than 35 years, *Guideposts* has "shown the way toward spiritual fulfillment and moral and honorable and decent behavior," according to John Mack Carter, commentator on today's magazine scene.[8] Norman Vincent Peale and Raymond Thornburg raised $1,200 from such men as Frank Gannett and

Branch Rickey to start *Guideposts*. The initial issue featured a four-page article by Eddie Rickenbacker titled "I Believe in Prayer."

Today, with a staff of 450, the monthly *Guideposts* has more than 3,300,000 subscribers who contribute in excess of $12 million annually for this digest-size inspirational periodical. More than 75 per cent renew each year. Celebrities join with "ordinary folks" to share their religious experiences through messages of faith and hope.

Quest

Started in March, 1977, as *Human Potential, Quest* has had an up-and-down career during its brief existence. Herbert W. Armstrong, founder of the Worldwide Church of God in California (a group of 100,000 members with headquarters in Pasadena), started *Human Potential* under the sponsorship of the Ambassador International Cultural Foundation.

Originally, *Human Potential* was "to explore all aspects of man's accomplishment and creativity—the constructive, noble side of man—past, present, and future." Before its first year of publishing ended, the magazine became *Quest/77*. Staffers no longer were only church members with journalism training. Professionals, not necessarily church members, were brought in to direct the operation. Art Murphy, an alumnus of Time Inc., became the publisher. He, in turn, brought in Robert Shnayerson, with 20 years experience on *Time, Life,* and *Harper's*. Shnayerson became the editor.

Some of the confusion also exists about the magazine's goals. It is not listed with other religious publications. Rather, it is included with the General Editorial group.

Ironically, with the opening of 1981, the public became confused. Thousands received promotional letters from *Quest/80* written by Shnayerson. His message, which required six printed pages, claimed "every issue a collector's item" so subscribe now.

Yet at the same time, newspaper and magazine accounts told of Shnayerson's resignation, along with five of his editorial colleagues. The editor claimed Armstrong directed him to print a cover story which would undermine "a basic premise that the magazine was independent of the church." The article concerned President Anwar Sadat's plans to build a peace center in Sinai.

The Worldwide Church of God apparently was not upset by the resignations. According to *Time,* a spokesman said:

> We have always had the prerogative to interfere with the magazine. It doesn't matter to us if people have resigned.

Editor Shnayerson replied: "I feel very sad about the loss of some good work. It is sort of like walking up to a painting and putting your foot through it."[9]

United Methodist Publishing House

In 1789, John Dickins, a Methodist preacher, opened the Methodist Book Concern in Philadelphia. In 1854, the Nashville operation was started. Today it is the largest church-owned publishing house in the world.

Controlled by the church conference, this operation has these objectives: To advance the cause of Christianity, to promote Christian education, and to publish, manufacture and distribute for the church. Profits from the approximate $50 million annual gross income are placed in the ministerial pension funds. Within this operation are the publishing, retail sales, and manufacturing divisions.

The Graded Press produces the literature for the entire church, including curriculum periodicals for all ages. Millions of copies of these periodicals go to Methodists around the world. The Abingdon Press handles the books and multi-media operations, with Cokesbury retail stores in 21 states.

The United Methodists do their own printing, with the major work performed in Nashville. In today's publishing world it is rare to witness such an organization, one that completes the full gamut from the planning stage through the completion of magazines, books, and other periodicals.

In 1977, the Parthenon Press, the Methodists' manufacturing division, converted to the new cold-type computerized copy-processing system. The next year a new high speed adhesive bindery system was installed at a cost of $1,250,000.

The church publishes 340 separate titles, including 280 printed and 60 audiovisual. Each working day two freight car loads of paper and a thousand pounds of printer's ink are used. Much of this material, of course, is for Sunday School curriculum. More than 100 new book titles are published yearly. Among the publications are these major magazines, in addition to the *Upper Room* mentioned earlier: *Circuit Rider,* for ministers; *Newscope, Mature Years,* and *Christian Home,* all with special audiences.

Problems Faced Today

George Gallup spoke to the Catholic Press Association convention in 1978 and summarized the problems faced by many church periodicals. He told the audience that

> In order to survive, a publication must deal with the key needs of its readers. In theory, at least, every person should read at least one daily newspaper each day, and would if the newspaper touched upon an important and immediate concern of his—how to meet the next mortgage payment, what to do about a child that is flunking school, a father-in-law who has to be moved to a nursing home, a wife who has undiagnosed illness . . . the Catholic press could play an important role as "preserver of the family unit" . . . It is important for the Catholic press to respond to and anticipate trends, but it is also important to create trends, to be pacemakers.[10]

Gallup need not limit such advice to the Catholic press. The entire magazine world can apply his suggestions.

15

Newspaper Magazines/Tabloids

THERE ARE SOME periodicals that challenge classification. Some persons refer to them as newspaper magazines, as Sunday supplements, or merely tabloids. There are, obviously, debates about their status. For example, are they magazines or newspapers? Obviously, they represent a mixed breed. They tend to look like newspapers because of their size and/or format. Yet in contents they are more magazine oriented, with little interest in news as a timely product. They are generally more feature oriented, providing additional material about previous incidents, more of the human side of the stories.

Three of these publications are quite well known to the grocery shoppers of America, since it is difficult to get past checkout stands without seeing copies of the *National Enquirer, The Star,* and the *Midnight Globe.* As a result of their prime position near the supermarket checkout counter, these publications sell more than nine million copies each week. Their headlines, photographs, and color photography lure the potential shopper as she waits in line. Their prices are still within reach of most shoppers, usually costing around 40 cents a copy. Thus they are included with grocery items, increasing still more the purchaser's complaints about the high costs of food.

Since these three publications sell upward to 80 per cent of their total sales under such conditions, they are anxious to maintain this distribution channel. *National Enquirer,* for example, maintains a large sales force across the nation to see that this weekly is placed in a good position in the stores and that copies are always available for customers.

Since the majority of these sales are in exposed positions in stores, these magazines have been forced to reduce the sensationalism that marked their front pages several years ago. That is not to say they still aren't sensational; it

223

is to say the sensationalism previously reached through gore, gruesome pictures and headlines has changed to an "acceptable" sensationalism concerning celebrities and their love and children problems, new diets, medical breakthroughs, predictions for the months ahead, and similar subjects.

The majority of the readers are middle America, with high school diplomas. Their incomes tend to be slightly below the nation's average, but their families tend to be larger. The publishers fight to retain their checkout priority, since other magazines and comic books strive for this bonus position. The margin of profit for the groceryman on magazines is much higher than that on his food products so he, too, is anxious to place them where they will sell. He need not worry about inventory controls, loss by spoilage, or other problems. He continues to collect at least 20 per cent of the selling price, with usually a bonus for the use of priority outlets near the cash register. "The tabloid industry is working hard to gain even greater consumer acceptance of tabloids as they exist today, and they plan to keep their sales nothing short of sensational," reports *Profit Ways*.[1] These publications also continue to spend millions of dollars, especially through television commercials, to stimulate still more sales.

In addition to these three nationally-circulated weeklies, there are a number of magazines, more subdued, better edited and designed, that appear with Sunday daily newspaper. These include the prestigious *New York Times Magazine* and those in other newspapers with total circulations well in excess of these three national tabloids.

American Weekly and This Week

It is reasonable to trace the beginning of these publications to the *American Weekly,* which began Nov. 15, 1896, in the Hearst newspapers. It was the first such periodical to reach a circulation of 10 million. However, it died Sept. 1, 1963.[2]

Morrill Goddard, the "father of the Sunday newspaper," made the *American Weekly* famous. Although the publisher claimed the articles must be authentic, many of them were wild. There was less sensationalism after a noted Chicago editor, Walter Howey, took control.

The *American Weekly* once sold 100,000 reprints of a cover picture of Jack and Jackie Kennedy. It also raised $250,000 in the pioneer days of Danny Thomas' St. Jude Hospital for children in Memphis.

Death, however, came to Hearst's pioneer because of too much competition for the advertisers' dollars, as well as too much competition from television. The circulation had dipped to four million at the end.

This Week is another pioneer that has left the scene. It originally appeared in a 16-page tabloid format in early 1935 and by 1950 had surpassed the *American Weekly* in circulation and advertising revenues. But it too suffered from competition and died in late 1969.[3]

Parade

Parade celebrated its 40th anniversary in mid-1981, having started on July 13, 1941 when it entered the market against *American Weekly* and *This Week*. At that time the publishers, the Field enterprises in Chicago, believed there were sufficient three-newspaper markets to justify the gamble with *Parade*. Apparently Marshall Field was correct.

The Newhouse organization purchased *Parade* in 1976. At the start of the 1980s, the periodical had a circulation of 21.6 million, the nation's largest. Its regular features include "Personality Parade," "Intelligence Reports," and "Keeping Up With Youth."

Family Weekly

Another major Sunday newspaper supplement today is *Family Weekly*, started on Sept. 13, 1953, by the Downe Publications. In 1978 it celebrated its 25th birthday with a review of the dramatic events that helped to shape people's lives, from the transistor to television to microcomputer. It also reviewed the changes in medicine, and the major inventions, with a look ahead to the year 2000.

Family Weekly was sold in 1976 for a reported $21 million to a company representing four newspaper groups: Small Newspapers, Donrey Media Group, Holies Newspapers, and Howard Publications. In late 1979, the periodical was sold to CBS Inc. for about $50 million. CBS Inc. termed it "a prestige, premier publication."

Appearing in more than 350 newspapers, with a circulation of 13.3 million, *Family Weekly* publishes more service and how-to articles, with less emphasis on national or international news. There are articles on money management, food, health, sports, and similar topics of family interest.

The New York Times Magazine

About the same time Hearst established the *American Weekly*, the *New York Times* was starting its own Sunday magazine, in 1896. Obviously, it had a more in-depth approach from the start. And it has remained only in the *Times*, while the *American Weekly* was sold to other newspapers in cities that lacked a Hearst newspaper.

Appearing in the *Sunday Times*, the magazine has a circulation of 1,500,000. Its profile claims it includes "indepth articles that range across the spectrum of current affairs, from science and sports to foreign affairs and changing life styles." There are interpretative stories as one would expect from any part of the *New York Times*. There are stories about fashions, food, interior design, child care, training, plus humor, crossword puzzles, and other topics.

The *New York Times Magazine* is one of the nation's leaders in total advertising pages, competing with *Business Week* and the *New Yorker* each year

for the top position. Its readership represents many college graduates who occupy managerial/professional-type positions.[4]

When the 80s opened there was a trend toward more locally-produced
Sunday supplements, publications more like the *New York Times Magazine*.
Some of the national periodicals, such as *Parade,* were offering local advertisements, and making provisions for more local control to head off the competition that might result in the loss of a major outlet.

Some of these Sunday supplements have tremendous circulations, such as
the *New York News Magazine* and those in the *Los Angeles Times* (*Home Magazine*), Washington *Post,* Chicago *Tribune,* San Francisco (*California Living*),
and others. A number of the major dailies use the supplement *Sunday,* which
provides opportunities for more local editing and advertising controls.[5]

SUPERMARKET TABLOIDS

Millions of Americans read Sunday newspapers and the majority place
their supplements aside for more perusing later. Often these magazines are
clipped for their ''how-to'' articles, their games or puzzles, or their recommendations for better home management. These are often localized, with coverage
for city or regional audiences.

On the other hand, there are three major national tabloids that appear weekly
on thousands of newsstands and in thousands of supermarkets. They have a
tighter publishing schedule than the newspaper-produced supplements and often
can provide features on later news-breaking events. These are the *National
Enquirer, Midnight Globe,* and *The Star.*

National Enquirer

New York area readers were offered another dose of sensationalism in
1926 when William Randolph Hearst's new publication, the *New York Enquirer,* arrived. It featured gruesome criminal pictures and detailed stories characteristic of the ''roaring twenties.'' It also arrived at a time when three dailies
were engaged in the tabloid battle of the century. Most of the 18 million readers of today's *National Enquirer* are unaware that Hearst had founded it, and
are equally unconcerned. Under Hearst, however, the publication reached only
17,000 circulation and its only claim to fame was the fact that the city had no
other Sunday afternoon paper.

Things began to change in 1952 when Generoso Pope, Jr., bought the
weekly. His family was involved in the concrete business and the operation of
Il Progresso, the Italian-language newspaper founded by his father. Most of the
$75,000 was borrowed and Pope later said he spent the next six years borrow-
ing more funds to maintain the publication.[6]

In the first issue under Pope, he claimed his paper would ''fight for the
rights of man—the rights of the individual, and will champion human decency

and dignity, freedom and peace.'' Nevertheless, the era of gore continued a few more years. Within a decade, Pope reached a million circulation. To continue this upward trend, Pope visualized the potential if major supermarkets handled the *Enquirer*. To achieve this goal he had to eliminate much of the gore. Pope shifted emphasis then to the celebrity stories and to the unusual ''gee whiz'' type. He added more offbeat topics, including self-help stories, new treatments for such diseases as cancer and arthritis, the continuing story of UFO's—do they or don't they exist?

Pope moved the *Enquirer* to Lantana, Florida, in 1971, where it has prospered. The publication does not try to make news; rather, it claims to give people what they want to read, without any deathless prose nor Pulitzer-prize writing. Apparently, he has been successful. Today, the weekly sells in excess of five million copies. It ranked 16th in total gross sales among the *''Folio 400''* publications in 1980 and it pays the highest editorial salaries of any publication in the nation, starting its reporters at $41,000. Pope once declared that ''if we're making money, they (staffers) deserve a part of it.'' In return they are expected to have high productivity, travel extensively, and be able to withstand pressures. There are 164 full-time editorial and research employees, plus some 1,000 regular freelancers.

The *Enquirer* switched to color in mid-1979, changing its black-and-white printing in Florida to rotogravure plants in Buffalo and Dallas. In part, this was to meet the competition from *The Star*. To utilize the Florida presses, Pope planned a new tabloid with a different approach, the *Weekly World News*.

The magazine received national publicity with its coverage of Elvis Presley's death, selling 6,688,563 copies, or 99.4 per cent of its press run. The other copies were damaged, frequently by fans fighting to buy them. This total was a million above previous bestsellers, those that told about ''Roots'' and the death of Freddie Prinz. Twenty staffers covered the Presley story and one person, still not publicly identified, obtained a picture of Presley in his open coffin.

Pope maintains an active sales force that checks on supermarkets to see that the *Enquirer*'s racks are filled. His goal is to sell 80 per cent of the print order. In reaching this, Pope sees his major competition as magazines, not newspapers.

Early in his career, Pope was charged with many inaccuracies in his publication, especially on a ''60 Minutes'' CBS network segment by Mike Wallace. In attempting to answer Wallace, the editors ''found themselves trapped between the boss's demand for accurate and detailed reporting and his demand for increasingly provocative headlines,'' according to John Mack Carter.[7]

The *Enquirer* was in the news in 1975 when one of its freelancers was caught with five bags of trash taken from Secretary of State Henry Kissinger's home. In a reverse action, a Palm Beach, Florida reporter carted off some of the *Enquirer*'s trash and found a memorandum to the staffers from Pope that explained what stories should include. They were to be ''packed with color and

emotion . . . must make readers react. We should touch our readers' souls
. . . cause them to smile, to get lumps in their throats, to break down and cry
. . ." They were to have such appeal as two famous classics: "Yes, Virginia,
there is a Santa Claus" and the Boys' Town slogan, "He ain't heavy, Father,
he's my brother."[8]

More than a million dollars has been raised for families and individuals in
need through *Enquirer* stories. In addition, thousands of letters have been sent
to encourage others. For example, an account of Joe Louis' suffering from a
stroke resulted in 20,000 letters and cards to the champ. Celebrities do fight
back over gossip stories. In mid-1980 at least seven were angered enough to
sue the *Enquirer,* including Carol Burnett, Paul Lynde, Phil Silvers, Rory Cal-
houn, Ed McMahon, Shirley Jones, and Marty Ingles. There have been times
when it wasn't wise to sue. For example, it was reported that Steve McQueen
was planning to have his attorney ask for a retraction on a story that he had
cancer. McQueen died of cancer a few months later.

Carol Burnett won $1.6 million in suit against the weekly. She said the
verdict, which is being appealed, "puts publications like the *Enquirer* on notice
that those of us in the public eye have rights."

With the opening of 1981, the *Enquirer* had seven lawsuits pending against
it. The firm's public relations consultants noted that at the same time *"Newsweek* has 15; and in Los Angeles alone, the Los Angeles *Times* has three, NBC
seven, and ABC five. The *Enquirer* has not paid a libel judgment in 20 years
and fully intends to stand behind all it prints."

A former *Enquirer* reporter wrote a "confessional" about his experience
there and made the following comments about his work there and his feelings
after leaving.

> . . . in the uppermost councils of dead-serious journalism the *National
> Enquirer* has become fashionable. It has made money and increased circulation
> while more respectable formats could not. Indeed, most major dailies now
> maintain desks that, whether they admit it or not, follow the *National En-
> quirer* formula—without the *Enquirer* pizzazz. . . .
>
> . . . in its narrow field of interest, the *National Enquirer* is the most
> carefully edited, methodical and accurate journalistic product in the United
> States. To be sure, accuracy is a relative word at the *Enquirer,* but it still is a
> word. For example, a faith-healing experience . . . requires at least three
> affidavits from physicians familiar with the case. The affidavits are necessary
> to ensure the editors that the patient did not recover from conventional medical
> treatment . . .
>
> . . . one must understand that its staff is the *creme de la creme*—jaded,
> black-hearted and unscrupulous *creme de la creme,* perhaps, but still *creme
> de la creme.* Mr. Pope made it a point to pay the highest wages in the industry
> on the principle that he saved money in the long run. It worked. The level of
> competence at the *Enquirer* was such that nobody did anything twice. There
> were pressmen said to have made $80,000 a year.
>
> (The *Enquirer*) goes with the flow. It is a marketing device that follows

the classic marketing principle—don't give people what they need, give them what they want.

Good news, no matter how much we wish it otherwise, is blessedly hard to document in this world. But the *Enquirer* found it, or at least appeared to find it—amazing cancer cures, friendly flying saucers, life after death, movie stars more miserable than their fans, and on and on.[9]

Midnight Globe

In the mid-1950s, the *Midnight Globe* arrived "for an audience interested in a wide range of non-fictional human-interest stories, contemporary in nature, with particular emphasis on the human condition."

The *Globe,* seen as "racy" by some readers, has reached a circulation in excess of 1,500,000. It attracts an audience that includes mostly women over 40 who desire gossip about Hollywood and television celebrities, as well as articles about health and medical developments. There is considerable interest in the occult, with predictions of what's ahead for the world. They tend to believe in miraculous cures and become excited about those who have conquered physical and mental obstacles.

The Star

A newcomer, having started in 1974, is *The Star,* originally called the *National Star.* It terms itself a newsmagazine for the entire family, with contents similar to the others—health, astrological predictions, celebrities from Hollywood and the television world, dress patterns, diets, and service features.

In its first issue, it termed itself "a new kind of newspaper . . . for all the family. Whatever your interest, it is catered for in these compact, fun-packed, fact-packed, IMPACT pages."

Owned by Rupert Murdoch, *The Star*'s readership is mostly women. It also likes the title, "A weekly entertainment magazine," and currently it is second to the *National Enquirer* with its weekly 3.3 million circulation. In 1980 it developed a syndicated "TV Star" television program, using material from the magazine.

The Star's goals include this major objective: "Not be politically committed, not be a killjoy, not be bullied, not be boring."

In addition to these, there are other publications, some similar in content and format, yet none has achieved the circulation of these three.

16

Medical Publications Most Numerous

MEDICAL JOURNALS are so plentiful that it is difficult to reach any exact figure for their numbers today. *Advertising Age* in 1979 noted they numbered nearly a thousand, with industry observers predicting an expansion rate of 5 to 10 percent at least through 1983.[1] Others have estimated there are some 3,500 medical publications in America, including, no doubt, many city, regional, and state periodicals, along with the better-known and more widely distributed magazines.

When Rowell's *American Newspaper Directory* made its debut in 1869, it listed 40 medical periodicals. Frank Luther Mott estimated there were 300 to 400 in the post-Civil War era, 1865 to 1885. This reached a thousand by the turn of the century. Specialization apparently stimulated such expansion, with many local organs of city or state medical societies, hospitals, or medical schools. Others were designed basically for medical study and practice, as are many today.[2] The middle Nineties experienced a period of competition in the medical journalism field. Additional magazines appeared for public and private health groups, dentistry, and pharmaceutical interests.

First Appeared in 1797

Three New York physicians provided medical journalism a big push in 1797 with the establishment of the *Medical Repository,* proposed as a quarterly but with an irregular existence until its death in 1824.

These men possessed varied backgrounds. In addition to being a doctor, Samuel L. Mitchell also was trained in law and served in Congress for 12 years. Elihu Hubbard Smith was one of the Hartford wits who in his spare time wrote an opera. Edward Miller was a "gentleman of social gifts and scientific and literary acquirements," according to Mott.[3]

Medical Repository promised special attention to "the study of epidemics (the nation then was experiencing a yellow fever epidemic), to the connection between climate and health, and to diet," topics still discussed in similar periodicals. Other physicians contributed articles on science, geography, agriculture, natural history, and related topics.

Another early magazine was the *Philadelphia Journal of the Medical and Physical Sciences,* founded in 1820 and continued after 1827 under the title, *American Journal of the Medical Sciences.* Mott claims it was established by Dr. Nathaniel Chapman to answer an attack in the *Edinburgh Review,* which asked: "What does the world yet owe to American physicians and surgeons?"[4]

In 1812 the oldest of the medical publications available today, the *New England Journal of Medicine and Surgery and the Collateral Branches of Science,* was started. There had been other medically-oriented magazines in New England but the majority had short careers.

Two Boston doctors, John Collins Warren and James Jackson, were the founders. From its start it has been the voice of the Massachusetts Medical Society. Today, edited from offices in the Harvard Medical School, it continues to be the first to inform the world of many major discoveries and treatments. In 1846, for example, it told about the use of ether and in this century announced pioneer developments concerning hysterectomy and ruptured spinal disc surgery, as well as the use of L-dopa to treat victims of Parkinson's disease. These were among its many "firsts."

Medical historian Dr. Joseph Garland wrote in 1968, in reviewing this magazine's history, that

> Scientific achievement, which may, perhaps fancifully, be called a product of the brain, will continue to advance, and it must be matched by a continually expanding social consciousness, which is a product, according to a long-cherished sentiment, of the heart. The virtue of an all-purpose journal is that it must give space to both.[5]

In 1952, Garland concluded another historical presentation with a comment by Oliver Wendell Holmes, who spoke before the same medical group in 1860, saying a major goal should be to achieve the following:

> To cultivate that mutual respect of which outward courtesy is the sign, to work together, to feel together, to take counsel together for the truth, now, always, here, everywhere; for this our fathers instituted and we accept, the offices and duties of this time-honored society.

It is believed that one of the best-read units is the Letters section. Some of these are mini-studies, complete with detailed footnotes. Social and economic aspects of medicine also provide many articles. It often gains worldwide attention with its news reports dealing with new drugs and/or treatments.

Its current circulation of some 200,000 includes nearly 83,000 physicians and 32,000 residents in the United States. In addition, nearly 30,000 copies go to foreign physicians, and a like number to medical students. Others are distributed to manufacturers, hospitals and libraries. All specialities are represented among the subscribers, with a heavy concentration among those concerned with internal medicine. About half of the nation's physicians subscribe.

The Lancet

Probably the oldest medical journal in the world, *The Lancet,* was started in London in 1823. By the 1980s, *The Lancet* had a larger circulation in North America than in its home country. Dr. Thomas Wakley, the founding editor, set forth his aims in the first issue.

. . . to produce a work that would convey to the public and to distant practitioners, as well as to students in medicine and surgery, reports of the Metropolitan Hospital lectures . . .

. . . to give a correct description of all the important cases that may occur, whether in England or on any part of the civilised continent.

Wakley added, "We hope the age of 'mental delusion' is passed and that mystery and ignorance will shortly be considered synonymous . . . Ceremonies and signs have now lost their charm; hieroglyphics, and guilded serpents their power to deceive."[6]

Dr. Wakley early aroused interest from the medical world as well as the lay public with attacks on the Royal College of Surgeons and on the accepted medical practices of the times, especially the activities of quacks and bodysnatchers, who sold their loot to medical schools. He was critical of the appalling conditions within mental institutions and infirmaries, as well as the contamination and adulteration of foodstuffs and water. He took an active interest in political affairs, campaigning for higher pay for the working classes and for other changes in London. He was a friend of William Cobbett, an American editor during the Revolutionary War who fled this country to escape a libel suit won by a Philadelphia physician, Dr. Benjamin Rush. Some sources say Cobbett urged Wakley to start a magazine, seeking "justice to poor, downtrodden doctors."[7]

A study of *The Lancet* files provides a tour through history. During its first half-century, reports appeared on the rise of physiology, the start of biochemistry, and the influence of Darwin's work on medical aims. Other accounts discussed the use of chloroform in operations, the treatment of wounds on antiseptic principles, accounts of treatments for plague, malaria, sleeping sickness, and yellow fever. These helped to make the magazine a major newsbreaker for important research projects.

In mid-1966, *The Lancet* made a major move with the establishment of a North American edition, to be printed in Boston. The editorial content was the same, although the advertisements were for American companies. Originally some 6,000 subscribers in the United States and Canada took *The Lancet.*

On its 150th anniversary in 1973, *The Lancet* admitted it was not as sharptongued as in the past and thus it had not encountered as many libel suits. Yet it continued to oppose some actions of the British Medical Association, and to express its views on such varied topics as boxing, euthanasia, nuclear tests and heart transplants.

Unique in another way, *The Lancet* has had only eight editors in its long existence, four being Wakleys. Its world distribution today reveals that 44.5 per cent of the circulation is in North America, 24.7 per cent in the United Kingdom, 16.1 per cent in Western Europe, and the rest scattered to more than 100 countries.

AMA Publications

JAMA is one of the best known medical publications in America. The *Journal of the American Medical Association* is issued four times monthly to provide material relevant to medicine. First appearing on July 14, 1883, *JAMA* has had only 13 editors, including Dr. Morris Fishbein, who served the longest, 1925 to 1949.

JAMA's goal is education, informing its readers of progress in clinical medicine and medical research. Other developments that interest physicians also are reported. Today *JAMA* has a circulation of 239,000, with editions in French, Japanese, Portuguese and Spanish. In the magazine listing in SRDA, its circulation is broken into 83 categories. During its first 70 years, *JAMA* published more than 100 medical classics and it remains the most quoted of all AMA periodicals. For example, it was cited nearly 22,000 times in 1979 in the world's scientific literature.

From its start, *JAMA* rejected "all advertisements of proprietary, trademark, copyrighted, or patent medicines." A major attack on patent medicine began on April 21, 1900, with an article on "Relations of Pharmacy to the Medical Profession." Later other magazines, especially *Collier's* and the *Ladies' Home Journal,* joined the crusade against quack medicine. Mott credited Fishbein with "hard-punching editorials" and "chatty and too personal 'Dr. Pepy's' Diary" style of writing.[8] Fishbein's comments brought many libel suits as he attacked quacks and frauds. One of his major targets was John R. Brinkley, the Kansas goat-gland man. As early as the 1930s, *JAMA* published articles on socialized, or state medicine.

The American Medical Association publishes other magazines. The *American Journal of Diseases of Children* began in 1911. With a circulation of 25,400, this monthly likewise is widely quoted, with more than 5,300 citations in periodicals around the world in 1979.

The *Archives of Dermatology* began in 1920. In its earlier days it was known as the *Archives of Dermatology and Syphilology*. Its circulation of more than 17,000 brings it before many medical specialists. It, too, is widely quoted.

In 1919 the *Archives of Neurology and Psychiatry* was established, to be renamed the *Archives of General Psychiatry* in 1959. With a circulation of nearly 21,000, the *Archives* was cited nearly 7,000 times in the world's scientific literature in 1979.

One of AMA's older publications is the *Archives of Internal Medicine,* established as a monthly in 1908. Its goal was

> . . . devoted to the publication of original studies carried on at the bedside or in the laboratory, on clinical medicine and of all the physiological and pharmacological researches that relate to the diagnosis or treatment of this class of conditions.

Fifteen medical classics have appeared in the *Archives of Internal Medicine* since 1940. With its circulation of 54,200 it continues to be read around the world. It was cited more than 7,300 times in 1979.

The *Archives of Neurology and Psychiatry,* noted above, was started in 1919 and in 1959 was superseded by two separate journals: the *Journal of Neurology* and the *Archives of General Psychiatry. Neurology* today has a circulation of 13,300 and it, too, is widely quoted.

Both English and German language editions of the *Archives* of *Ophthalmology and Otology* appeared in 1869. This monthly magazine became part of the AMA operation in 1929, under a shorter title, *Archives of Ophthalmology.* Its circulation is more than 15,000.

A younger AMA magazine is the *Archives of Otolaryngology,* started in 1925. Today's circulation exceeds 11,000.

Another AMA magazine is the *Archives of Pathology and Laboratory Medicine,* started in 1926. It was designed to advance the science of pathology and to advance professional applications to human pathology and laboratory medicine. Although its circulation is around 8,700, the publication was quoted more than 5,300 times in journals in 1979.

The *Archives of Surgery,* with more than 44,300 circulation, has been published monthly since 1920. Its first issue set the objectives, with an editorial by Dr. William J. Mayo:

> The *Archives of Surgery* will attempt at least to enlarge the surgical horizon and assist in establishing surgery on a sounder basis. Unpleasant as it may be, the editors will not hesitate to comment editorially on the papers published in its columns in order that both sides of a moot question may be considered. The reader will be given an opportunity to peruse surgical fads and fancies if such be presented, but if the subject matter introduces questionable material it will not be allowed to go unchallenged.

This magazine accepts papers dealing with experimental surgical problems as well as clinical problems. In 1979 it was quoted more than 7,000 times.

AMA publications reach a total audience of some 450,000.

Medical Economics

"If you don't manage your practice and personal investments properly, you'll never be a successful doctor." That was the philosophy of *Medical Economics,* founded in 1923. The publication added: "The more efficient your office methods, the more patients you can see, and the better the medical care that you can dispense."

The first issue, 48 pages, went to 100,000 physicians. In its early days, *Medical Economics* encountered *JAMA* editor, Dr. Morris Fishbein, who urged pharmaceutical companies not to advertise in the newcomer. He was critical of the magazine's controlled circulation policy, which sent copies free to concerned readers. Later, however, *JAMA* introduced its own medical economics section.

Its publisher, the Medical Economics Company, calls itself a firm "acknowledged as a leader in useful, unbiased research, and (one that) has provided more authoritative and innovative data as a service than any other publisher in the health-care field."[9] In 1958 the company worked with Alfred Politz in developing medical publication research techniques.

The company also publishes *CLR/Clinical Laboratory Reference, Contemporary Ob/Gyn* and *Contemporary Ob/Gyn Technology, Diagnosis, Diagnostic Medicine, Drug Topics, Drug Topics Red Book, MLO-Medical Laboratory Observer, MLO Direct Response Cards, Nursing Opportunities,* and *RN*.

Its best seller is the *Physicians' Desk Reference,* a book published annually and sent to doctors, hospitals, pharmacists, dentists, nurses, veterinarians, nursing schools, nursing homes, advertisers, lawyers, police, and others. Many individuals are now buying this annually to learn more about the medicine prescribed for them.

Early in 1981 Litton's publishing interests which include Medical Economics Co., were sold to International Thomson Organization Ltd. for $60 million cash and $30 million payout over the next five years.

Prevention

Some medical leaders might object to the inclusion of *Prevention* in this chapter, yet this is a periodical that they cannot ignore.

One finds it difficult to separate this comparative newcomer from its founder, J. I. Rodale. In some respects the early career of Rodale may be compared with the life of Bernarr Macfadden, who introduced numerous health concepts to the American public through his *Physical Culture* magazine and numerous books that he published during the first four decades of this century.

Rodale, a successful electrical manufacturer in Emmaus, Pennsylvania, in 1935 began to collect health articles, publishing them in *Fact Digest*. He briefly experimented with two other magazines, *You Can't Eat That* and *True Health Stories*. Rodale was more successful in 1942 with his *Organic Gardening and Farming,* which now has a circulation of 1,250,000. His interest in health habits continued and he once wrote:

> I began to browse in medical journals (such as *JAMA*) and was amazed
> to find out how much valuable nutritional data of a preventive nature was
> hidden away there, mouldering, which the medical men were not disseminat-

ing to their patients . . . I became infected with a strong desire to dig out this information and present it to the public.[10]

Thus in mid-1950 *Prevention* arrived. Rodale editorially said, "We hereby formally appoint ourselves the representative of the public to seek out wherever it may be any information that will show people how to prevent themselves from becoming sick and how to be extremely happy while doing so."

Prevention from the start has waged war on food additives, refined white flour, and sugar, among many other items. The 50,000 original subscribers grew to more than one million by 1971, when Rodale died. After 30 years, *Prevention* has passed 2,413,000, a figure it quotes in trade advertisements as placing it ahead of *People, Sports Illustrated,* and *U.S. News & World Report,* making it 17th in circulation among the consumer magazines. Obviously it is taking advantage of the nation's interest in health and the well-being of individuals.

Prevention's growth has been overlooked until recent years. Rodale, a unique publishing firm, still operates in Emmaus, a community of 6,000 and to some it remains a "publishing curiosity." Advertising agencies encounter many taboos, since *Prevention* rejects messages for commercially prepared foods, alcoholic beverages and cigarettes, as well as some household appliances and toiletries that the publication fears do more harm than good.[11] In 1980, however, a more favorable public image was sought, through the employment of a New York public relations firm. In addition, the firm started *New Shelter* in 1980 and turned more to newsstand sales for added revenues.

Today the Rodale publications are audited and advertising is taken more seriously. Since its annual volume exceeds $65 million, Rodale has become a major publisher. Perhaps its articles in *Prevention* will take on a more serious reaction from the public as well.

"*Prevention* is a health magazine, or a medical magazine for laymen, rather than a science publication," according to John Feltman, managing editor.[12]

Vital Comes Alive

Vital, under its slogan of "the lively magazine of healthy living," reappeared in 1981 after a brief two-issue career in 1978.

Signature Publications, the publishing arm of Montgomery Ward, acquired the title and plans to focus the contents on the total well-being with a "Look better, feel better, live better" concept.

Vital was presented to the public through a $10 million sweepstakes campaign in late 1980. An initial press run of 100,000 is predicted with a projected circulation over 500,000 within five years. The publishers are seeking a position between *Self* and *Prevention* with bimonthly publication shifting to monthly in 1982.

Signature also has *Crossroads* for Montgomery Ward auto club members and *Going Places* for the firm's travel club.

Many Well Known

In the midst of these hundreds of medically-directed publications some obviously are better known than others.

For example, *Family Health,* established in 1969, now has a regular circulation of more than 800,000 subscribers. Published by Family Media Inc., *Family Health* reaches an audience primarily middle-class and mainstream America in its outlook. Readers are concerned with what might be described as basic problems today, including food and nutrition, baby and child care, preventive medicine and self-help suggestions, diet, exercise, beauty, good grooming, and other departments. The magazine conducts annual Nutrition Seminars and presents Nutritional Advertising Awards annually.

Modern Healthcare, on the other hand, reaches an audience of 60,000, which is controlled. Within this group are those personnel concerned with the business aspects of healthcare management, obviously a growing industry in America. This Crain publication concerns itself with finance, purchasing, legislation, labor, planning, construction, patient care, government affairs, fundraising, technology, marketing and management, all topics of vital concern to the administrators of the nation's health centers. The publication's analysis of its circulation is broken into more than 50 categories.

C. V. Mosby Company

There are a number of publishers with many medical publications coming from their presses. With 17 magazines the C. V. Mosby Company of St. Louis represents these groups. With its total circulation more than 261,000, the firm's magazines vary in circulation from 4,000 for the *Investigative Ophthalmology & Visual Science* to more than 60,000 for *Heart and Lung: The Journal of Critical Care.*

Fifteen of Mosby's publications have some organization affiliation. For example, the *American Journal of Obstetrics and Gynecology* represents some 40 organizations across the nation. Some of these are national in scope, although the majority are state or city groups.

All of the Mosby publications are sold by subscriptions. There is no controlled circulation. The firm believes in paid circulation, saying, ''To be worth a busy physician's time, we must offer an editorial product which meets his professional standards, provides needed, useful information, and does not duplicate something else he already receives.''[13] Although many of these publications have the highest subscription rates in their specialty areas, these magazines report an average renewal rate of 87 per cent.

The editorial content averages nearly 75 per cent for the 17 publications. The highest editorial rate is 97 per cent news versus 3 per cent advertising in the *Journal of Laboratory & Clinical Medicine.* This magazine is affiliated with the Central Society for Clinical Research.

Advertisers are provided detailed breakdowns of the subscription lists, with each specialty identified, along with numbers of copies sent to libraries and other institutions.

The Mosby publications include the following:

Journal of Laboratory and Clinical Medicine; American Journal of Obstetrics and Gynecology; Journal of Allergy and Clinical Immunology; Heart and Lung: The Journal of Critical Care; Journal of Hand Surgery; American Heart Journal; Oral Surgery, Oral Medicine and Oral Pathology; American Journal of Orthodontics; Journal of Pediatrics; Journal of Prosthetic Dentistry; Surgery; Journal of Thoracic and Cardiovascular Surgery; Clinical Pharmacology and Therapeutics; Investigative Ophthalmology & Visual Science; the EMT Journal; Journal of the American Academy of Dermatology, and *American Journal of Infection Control,* formerly *APIC Journal.*

Other Leading Publishers

Among the many publishers of medical journals there are several with many magazines. For example, the J. P. Lippincott Company publishes the following periodicals, many with association affiliations:

American Journal of Clinical Pathology, American Surgeon, Anesthesiology, Annals of Surgery, Cancer, Clinical Nuclear Medicine, Clinical Pediatrics, Clinical Preventive Dentistry, Diseases of the Colon & Rectum, Hospital Pharmacy, Investigative Radiology, Laboratory Medicine, NITA, Ophthalmology, Review of Surgery, Spine, and *Transfusion.*

The Charles B. Slack, Inc., firm is a medical publisher with periodicals for doctors, nurses, and allied health professionals. In this fairly specialized market, Slack has these magazines:

American Journal of Medical Sciences, Infection Control, Journal of Allied Health, Journal of Continuing Education in Nursing, Journal of Gerontological Nursing, Journal of Nursing Education, Journal of Pediatric Ophthalmology Strabismus, Journal of Psychiatric Nursing & Mental Sciences, Occupational Health Nursing, Ophthalmic Surgery, Orthopedics, and *Today's OR Nurse.*

Technical Publishing Company has three medical publications among its many magazines, including *American Journal of Cardiology, American Journal of Medicine,* and *American Journal of Surgery.*

Another major medical publisher is Williams & Wilkins Company. Its magazines include the following: *American Journal of Physical Medicine, Endocrinology, Investigative Urology, Journal of Biological Chemistry, Journal of Clinical Endocrinology & Metabolism, Journal of Histochemistry & Cytochemistry, Journal of Immunology, Journal of Investigative Dermatology, Journal of Nervous and Mental Disease, Journal of Pharmacology and Experimental Therapeutics, Journal of Trauma, Journal of Urology, Laboratory Investigation, Microbiological Reviews, Neurosurgery, Obstetrical & Gynecological Survey, Plastic & Reconstructive Survery, Stain Technology, Survey of Anestheology,* and *Urological Survey.*

17

Minority Publications
Led by Ebony

"BLACK-OWNED MEDIA can be proud of what they have achieved. But it has to be a bitter pride."

Black Enterprise editor-publisher Earl G. Graves so described the opening of the 1980s. "Black media exist out of necessity," added John H. Johnson, owner of the Johnson Publishing Company, the leading Black publisher who was called "The man who turned Ebony into Gold" by *Reader's Digest.*

With a population of 25,000,000, Johnson calls attention to this single largest minority group in our country. He believes "Blacks tend to go to their own media to find what they believe to be the truth." He also feels many Blacks have an uncertain feeling that they are not always receiving the whole truth from white media, a feeling often voiced toward the white policeman in the Black neighborhood. The "Believability problem" offers the Black publishers an edge with the Black audience that white publishers may not enjoy, Johnson feels.[1]

In the mid-70s the Black magazines were becoming more pragmatic, and those that earlier had leaned more toward Black nationalism were now leaning more toward a non-racial stance, according to a Los Angeles *Times* writer, J. K. Obataka.[2] He noted that such magazines as *Ebony* and *Jet,* both published by Johnson, earlier placed a high value on light skin, but in recent years the "dark-skinned Afro-Americans have more effect on middle-class life than previously, when it seemed a more or less natural assumption that Afro-Americans with lighter complexions would predominate in social, political, and cultural affairs."

After reviewing the emphasis change "from integration to separatism in the 1960s" and the 1970 shift toward non-racialism, Obataka concluded:

> The changes at *Ebony, Black Scholar* and other magazines reflect a grow-
> ing realization among Afro-Americans that Blacks and other Americans are
> still faced with some complex and serious problems which are not likely to
> yield to simplistic solutions—no matter how strongly we believe they will.

When one thinks of Black publications he first thinks of *Ebony,* the circulation leader and the most successful. John Johnson moved from Arkansas
to Chicago when quite young, having visited the 1933 World's Fair in the
Windy City. When he was 25 he founded *Negro Digest* on $500 borrowed on
his mother's furniture.[3] His three-man staff included artist Jay Jackson, and a
white man, Ben Burns, his executive editor. Within three years *Negro Digest*'s
circulation had reached 110,000, providing funds needed to start *Ebony,* designed to "mirror the happier side of Negro life—the positive, everyday
achievements from Harlem to Hollywood. But when we talk about race as the
number one problem in America, we'll talk turkey."

Johnson said *Negro Digest* eventually ran out of steam. He noted that a
publisher cannot really determine what goes into a true digest magazine. He
also learned that readers apparently didn't desire an all-serious publication. The
magazine eventually became *Black World* but after its failure to earn a profit it
was discontinued.

Twenty years later Johnson wrote that *Ebony* has "become a spokesman
for the full and equal treatment of all Negroes in this day and age." Johnson
also wrote that *"Ebony* is based on the principle that what is best for the Negro
is best for all America, and vice-versa."

From an initial press run of 50,000 in 1945, *Ebony* has grown to its present circulation of 1,300,000. *Newsweek* called the first issue "a 25-cent slick-
paper job crammed with pictures" with "photo-sequences of blacks and whites
mingling." *Newsweek* pointed out "lax editing, loose writing and inaccuracies."[4] *Time* said *Ebony* seemed to imitate *Life*'s format, and *Life* said it was
"a Negro picture magazine which is a frank imitation of *Life.*"[5] Johnson was
a friend of Time Inc. owner, Henry Luce.

Ebony circulates across America, an ethnic magazine appealing primarily
to urban, middle-class Blacks. Johnson's growth in the Black magazine market
reflects the tremendous efforts he placed on this finished product. *Ebony* became a pictorial Who's Who in Black America. Through the years it has dealt
with war on poverty, riots, the heritage of the Blacks, and their future. In the
process, *Ebony* has become the "spokesman for the full and equal treatment of
all Negroes of this day and age."[6]

"It had a real problem with the quality of the products being advertised
and the ad content. Until the magazine established a wide audience, it was
forced to accept ads from mail order houses and producers of novelties and
gimmicks," reported Victoria L. O'Hara, in a study of Black consumer magazines in 1974.[7] At that time many firms believed they had to "talk down to
Negro readers."

In its second year, when *Ebony* began to accept advertising, it experienced difficulty in attracting some of the major firms to its pages. Today's ads, however, reflect the rising Black middle-class. In the transition, the magazine pioneered in the use of Black models in advertisements, opening up a new area of employment for them. Today Black models appear regularly in magazines, mail order catalogs, and in other periodicals.

Other Johnson Publications

Jet was started by Johnson to utilize the material he couldn't fit into *Ebony*. The pocket-size weekly now sells more than 750,000 copies. *Tan Confessions* was another Johnson entry. It survived, as did other romance-type publications, by promising readers tidbits of love and sex, with the details omitted. However, when magazines such as *Playboy* and *Penthouse* began to fill in the missing words, with more pictures added, confession-type periodicals suffered circulation-wise. So Johnson replaced *Tan* in 1950 with *Black Stars*. The magazine reached out into the Black world for stars from many facets of life, from the musical and theatrical worlds, and from other areas, such as sports, where Blacks have been successful. However, *Black Stars* folded in 1981.

Ebony Jr. was started as a service and inspirational magazine for children. Originally it had a sub-title, "For Black Children," but after Johnson learned that many white children were regular readers he dropped this line. No advertisements are carried so the magazine, much like *Jet,* must survive on its circulation revenue. It has become an excellent educational medium, widely used in schools.

Johnson, as the most successful publisher in his area, has been the subject of articles in *Harvard Business Review, Organizational Dynamics, Reader's Digest, Nation's Business,* and other periodicals. He feels his success has come from meeting a long-unmet need for Black-oriented publications and from being persistent from the start. Johnson never viewed failure as an option. Unable to obtain sufficient advertising in the early years, he depended on circulation revenues, a trend many magazines are adopting today. The company operates from a well-designed 11-story building on Michigan Avenue in Chicago, where Johnson has amassed a fine collection of African art. In this building he also has his radio station and his cosmetic firm, Fashion Fair, which is managed by his wife. The publishing firm has offices in New York, Washington, and Los Angeles, while the cosmetic products are sold in more than a thousand outlets across the nation.

In his advice to young Blacks, Johnson told *Nation's Business* they should set small goals and not expect to start at the top. "One needs confidence in business. One must move from one plateau to another, each time gaining greater confidence."[8] Johnson, an office boy in a large Chicago insurance company in his early years, today is the chief executive officer for that same firm. He and his organization have won numerous awards and Johnson has served three U.S. presidents in official assignments. He once told the *Harvard Business Review* that he believes it is his "obligation to try to be a successful model, to build businesses, to contribute to the community in other ways, but I don't believe it's my obligation to invest every time some guy believes he's got a good idea."[9]

Readers of Johnson's publications have been surveyed by several major research organizations. For example, a 1979 Simmons demographic profile of *Ebony* indicated a total audience of nearly seven million, with slightly more (52.5 per cent) women. Nearly 88 per cent are Black, with a median age of 32, with heavy concentration between 18 and 34. The great majority, nearly 88 per cent, live in metropolitan areas. A Roper study in 1978 concluded that "The profile of the *Ebony* reader is decidedly upscale. Seventy-one per cent of young Blacks with some college education read the magazine, 64 per cent of professional, managerial and white collar workers, 60 per cent of persons making more than $15,000 a year read *Ebony*." They believe Blacks can improve their conditions through voting and politicial activities. Roper added:

> *Jet* magazine, however, has a flat profile, appealing about equally to all income groups and to high school graduates (who are in the majority). Both magazines appeal more to women than to men.
>
> By way of contrast, *Black Stars* magazine is a decidedly downscale magazine having much more popularity among persons making less than $7,000 a year, men, singles, non-high school graduates, blue collar workers, the unemployed and swingers.

Roper's study noted that the Blacks preferred Black periodicals. While great numbers read *Ebony* and *Jet*, only 10 per cent read *Playboy*, 6 per cent *Cosmopolitan*, 14 per cent *People*, and 25 per cent *Time*. Simmons, on the other hand, reported the same for *Playboy* but 21.8 per cent for *Playgirl*, 8.7 per cent for *Cosmopolitan*, 9.3 per cent for *People*, and only 8.3 per cent for *Time*.

Essence

The first magazine designed exclusively to attract the Black woman is *Essence,* established in May 1970. Initially to be called *Sapphire,* after the precious stone, the founder later said, "Black women told us that was a putdown. *Essence* was more to the mark." In addition to its appeal to a select audience, *Essence* has been termed "the first of the new breed of Black magazines in the 1970s with its roots to the Black power movement of the previous decade," according to its long-time enthusiastic editor, Marcia Ann Gillespie.

One of the founders, publisher Edward Lewis, says *Essence* seeks to "make Black women feel good about themselves." He believes the advertisements, stories, and reports in other women's magazines address themselves more to a white audience. A bank management trainee at the time he had the idea for such a publication, Lewis acquired three partners: Clarence (Larry) Smith, Jonathan Blount, and Cecil Hollingsworth. In addition to their own money, they received financial support from several Eastern banks and other concerns and, in 1970, from Playboy Enterprises.

John Mack Carter, *Good Housekeeping* editor, recalled *Essence*'s planning period when he and other magazine leaders offered guidance to the four men in their objective. John Veronis, George Hirsch and personnel from Time Inc. and Young & Rubicam also helped with advice.[10]

In *Essence*'s 10th anniversary edition in 1980, Gillespie announced her resignation, saying she was "Gonna step out and write and travel and be open to my life's journey. Gonna let go and be a pilgrim." She credited her years with *Essence* with providing "the chance to explore myriad dimensions of our collective and my individual being." She was succeeded by Daryl Alexander. The anniversary edition included 192 pages, heavy in advertising featuring Black models.

Gillespie had first taken over as managing edition and later became editor. Only 26 at the time, she had worked as a researcher for Time Inc. She feels "the Black career woman should learn to love, treasure and give of herself to self." She recounted some of the early problems in a luncheon talk to the American Society of Magazines Editors Feb. 14, 1975:

> Potential advertisers had to be convinced that Black women possessed sufficient buying power to make them a worthwhile market.
>
> Black women had to be convinced that a Black magazine would last through a one-year subscription.
>
> The expectations and idealism of the Black community created difficulties. *Essence,* the prototype in the field, had been expected to espouse every Black cause and point of view, an obvious impossibility.

And, finally, she explained the "awareness sessions" *Essence* held with advertisers as well as other potentially-interested groups, such as college students. There she "sold" the significance of her publication.

In reviewing the decade in the anniversary edition, Bonnie Allen wrote: "Created to satisfy 12 million upwardly mobile/poverty-stricken, man-hungry/lesbian, hippie/Muslim/revolutionary Black women, *Essence* really tried to make us all happy." She concluded: "If there's a ray of hope in the future, it's that the children of the sixties, the Youth Generation, are now well into their thirties and forties, and finally mature enough to assume leadership positions."[11]

Like *Ebony, Essence* is geared to the Black middle class, which Gillespie terms the "strive-a-class." Its content, like some other women's publications, is geared specifically to the Black woman, with topics such as hypertension, a great killer among Blacks. One-subject issues are regularly presented, on topics such as beauty, careers, home sewing, travel, college, and the like. The majority of *Essence*'s stories are by Black free-lancers whenever possible, as well as Japanese and Puerto Rican photographers.

Gillespie told *Folio* magazine in 1976 that she "didn't want little Black girls growing up as (she) had, thinking only white women were beautiful. (She) wanted them, through *Essence,* to see and to feel what Black women really are." In her early career days she viewed the women's magazines as representative of three broad categories: "What I call the 'better-mama, better-homemaker' magazine; the 'how-to-get-him, how-to-hold-him' kind; and the one that straightly 'let's-be-chic.' "[12]

Gillespie's product represented her—it is gutsy, a term she enjoyed using as she sought to break through stereotypes about Blacks. Seeking to make *Essence* "the best magazine out there that happens to be for Black people," Gillespie sought consistency and quality. In the mid-1970s it had become the fastest growing woman's magazine in America. The pioneer achievements by *Ebony* with some of the nation's major advertisers helped *Essence*. Nevertheless, there were still many firms, especially in the cosmetic field, that failed to recognize this potential market. *Essence* has, on occasion, rejected ads which used only white models.

The *Essence* woman in the 1970s was defined by researchers as "a young, Black lady in her late twenties with a college education." The head of the household is employed in business or government; many are professionals. Her household income is higher than the average for the country as a whole. She is an avid consumer. Another study noted that Black women read *Ebony*, *Jet* and *Essence* in that order, all well above the "Seven Sisters" of the more traditional white-oriented publications, as well as other Black magazines. *Essence*'s guaranteed rate base was set at 650,000 in early 1981.

Black Enterprise

The *"Fortune* of the Black world," *Black Enterprise* began in 1970 as "the only magazine specifically geared to reach Black businessmen and women, professionals, and administrators, on a nationwide basis." In its goal to foster Black economic development, it annually presents the *"Black Enterprise 100"* issue, similar in its coverage to the *Fortune 500*. Motown Industries in Los Angeles usually leads the list of Black-owned or operated businesses, followed by the Johnson Publishing Co. The annual compliation contains not only financial data but profiles and additional information about the personnel involved.

Editor-publisher Earl G. Graves noted in 1979 a problem peculiar to his people in their business operations and their planning for the future. "What is the mood of the country toward Blacks?" was Graves' question, which he says "can have more to do with Black business' profits and losses than anything the owners of the company can do." And with setbacks in the nation's economy, the Black workers frequently are the earliest and hardest hit when companies cut back on employment.

Graves, noting the $100 billion Black consumer market, fears that "the mood of this country toward equal opportunity for Black Americans and Black-owned businesses is getting worse, not better." He did note that the top 100 firms broke the billion-dollar barrier in 1978.[13]

Designed as a how-to-do-it magazine for Black men and women, *Black Enterprise* encourages more Black merchants. In its earlier years, it was aimed more toward the "Mom and Pop" operation. Being the only publication in its field, *Black Enterprise* must cater to a wide variety of interests. Special issues in addition to the "100 edition" concern careers, travel, opportunities, money management, travel, and similar areas of concern to the readers. It assists new Black firms in their recruiting efforts and in their particular problems that are not always reflected in the "white business world." The magazine has been able to attract some of the large corporate advertisers. It, too, seeks to use Black models in these messages. Some readers compare it to *Business Week* since both tend to be general business publications. However, *Black Enterprise* carries more personality sketches than other business-oriented periodicals.

Black Enterprise seeks to stress "class, not mass" with its class being the influencers and opinion molders among the nation's Black leaders. It sponsors annual achievement awards to recognize those Blacks who have succeeded in business.

Chicago Mahogany was started in Chicago in late 1980 as a monthly general interest, black-style magazine. Its initial circulation was 30,000.

Crisis

The National Association for the Advancement of Colored People established the *Crisis* as its official publication in 1910. For a quarter of a century its editor was W. E. B. Du Bois. Today it claims to be the nation's only magazine devoted primarily to civil rights and race relations.

Crisis has some 116,000 subscribers today, with 32 per cent under 45, and an even mix between male and female readers. Some 67 per cent are college graduates.

Crisis has been generous in opening its pages to new writers as well as those with established reputation. H. L. Mencken, Langston Hughes, Vachel Lindsay, Oswald Garrison Villard and others have written for *Crisis*.

In 1977 its largest issue to date was an anthology of the works of Roy Wilkins, published to honor his services at his retirement.

Crisis, like some of the other periodicals that stress opinions and views, reaches a large number of influential leaders in the Black community, as well as other national leaders.

There are other Black publications, although these three, *Ebony, Essence*, and *Black Enterprise*, represent the leaders in their categories. They have come a long way since Blacks had their first newspaper, *Freedom's Journal*, in 1827, and their first magazine, *Mirror of Liberty*, in 1837.

Black Collegian

A five-times-a-year publication designed for college students and recent graduates is the *Black Collegian*, started in 1970. At the end of its first decade its circulation had reached 257,000.

Preston J. Edwards, publisher, was on the Southern University faculty in Baton Rouge when he became aware that his students were unaware of what really occurred on other college campuses. His brother was a New Orleans printer and his early staffers were volunteers who worked without pay. "We survived on the confidence that we would survive," Edwards said. And on experience gained with each issue.[14]

Edwards feels his readers must be prepared to grab what opportunities exist after graduation. *Black Collegian* helps them make contacts. Each issue had a specific theme, including careers, money, engineering, jobs, graduation. Advertising revenues continue to improve.

Main Man

A newcomer in 1980 was *Main Man,* designed for the college-educated man between 21 and 46. It is a magazine that offers "fashion and life styles for the international Black man." It was four years in the planning stage by Dick Barnett, a former professional basketball player.[15]

With bi-monthly circulation, Barnett hopes for 100,000 newsstand sales and a subscription list of 50,000, mostly from heavily Black urban areas. It covers fashions, profiles, grooming, health, interiors, money management, music, sports, travel and other topics that "accent the positive."

Nuestro

The magazine for the Latinos is *Nuestro*'s advertising slogan. This magazine first appeared in March, 1977, in New York, with Daniel M. Lopez publisher. The title translates to *Ours*.

Aimed for a market that Lopez estimates between 2.6 and 3.2 million households, and growing at a more rapid pace than other American families, *Nuestro* appears in English, with a brief Spanish synopsis for major articles. The great majority of the Latinos in the United States are literate in English. Lopez, born in Chicago the son of Mexican parents, said that "out of every 14 Latinos in this country, nine are Mexicans and four are Puerto Ricans." They are mostly urban dwellers, on the East and West coasts.

With two former *Time* staffers, Philip Herrera and Jose Ferrer, as co-managing editors, *Nuestro* reached a circulation of 205,000 after three years. An offshoot, *Nuestro Business Review,* was planned as an insert with the possibility of becoming an independent publication later.

An interesting result was reported in the magazine's promotional booklet, Marketing Concept:

> The largely bilingual Latino market preferred to listen to Spanish radio and to a lesser extent watch Spanish TV and read Spanish newspapers, but that reading was done predominantly in English.

Early summaries revealed that two-thirds of the readers were male, 80 per cent had some college education, with the median age 35. More than half are either professional/technical or managers/officials/proprietors. In early 1979, *Nuestro* published a list of the top 100 Latino companies in America.

Jewish Publications

There are dozens of Jewish publications in America. These started in 1823 when Solomon Henry Jackson founded a quarterly, *The Jew*. This English-language publication warned its readers to beware of Christian missionaries. The publication survived only two years.

Rabbis were usually the men who started these periodicals. In his several volumes on *The History of the American Magazines,* Frank Luther Mott devoted only a few pages to the Jewish press. However, it noted some of the pioneers, such as the *Occident* (1843–1868); *Hebrew Leader* (1848–1906); *Jewish Messenger* (1857–1903); *Chicago Occident* (1873–1893), and others.

There were numerous newspapers, too, in English, German, Hebrew, and Yiddish. Some of these periodicals were radical, others conservative, and many slanted toward socialism. "The Yiddish press has been the greatest education and cultural force in American Jewry," according to some writers.[16]

The English-language Jewish press grew as the Yiddish press declined. In 1930, there were more than 80 Jewish periodicals in the nation, mostly weeklies. The Jewish students participated in the 1960's "social explosiveness" and "rebelled against Jewish establishment. Some went to communes, others turned to Hasidism and many started periodicals" such as *Response,* founded at Brandeis University in 1967.[17]

Ulrich's International Periodicals Directory in 1980 listed nearly a hundred Jewish interest publications. Many are city-oriented, others cover a single state or a specific region.

Still More for Everyone

In addition to those already mentioned, there are many Black periodicals serving cities and states. Some of these are more newspaper types, while others have a magazine approach to their contents. The majority are in the East. Among some of the titles are *African Enquirer, African Mirror, Black Affairs, Black Scholar, Gentleman of Color, Miss Black America, Negro History Bulletin, Soul, Soul Teen, Black Law Journal, Black Perspective in Music,* and *View South,* "a Black view of today's new South."

Indians, too, have their periodicals. The majority are directed to special tribal concerns, such as the *Aroostook Indian, Cherokee Advocate, Choctaw Community News, Fort Apache Scout, Navajo Times, Northwest Indian News, Ute Bulletin, Wotanin-Wowapi,* and others.

Many language groups have periodicals in America, generally published in larger cities where the population is sufficient to support their magazines and newspapers.

There are many Spanish periodicals, from *Agenda* to *Latin* to *Tribuna.* Many appear in California, where there is a large Spanish-speaking population. In the East there are some Italian periodicals, such as *Attenzione, I-Am, Parola Del Popolo,* and others.

Publications also are available for Armenians, Arabics, Assyrians, Asians, Croatians, Czechs, Chinese, Danish, Estonians, Finnish, Germans, Greeks, Hungarians, Irish-Americans, Latvians, Koreans, Lithuanians, Norwegians,

Polish, Portuguese, Russians, Scandinavians, Scottish-Americans, Serbians, and others.

Bilingual Publishers

There are many American magazine publishers who have editions in foreign languages. In the 1930s, for example, *Reader's Digest* and *Time* launched Latin American editions, followed later by *Newsweek*. *Newsweek* did not last too long in its initial attempt, but in 1978 resumed *Newsweek Latin America,* printed in Florida, where *Time* also is printed.

National Geographic, Billboard, and others have entered this market. And, as indicated elsewhere in this book, there are other periodicals with special editions around the world. The magazine world certainly reflects the "One World" concept.

18

Media Publications

IN CELEBRATING its 50th anniversary, *Advertising Age* observed that "prolif-eration, localization, specialization mark media trends." Herbert Zeitner, a Crain Communications Inc. vice-president, predicted more growth "as more local-ized media become available and pin-pointing of specialized markets intensi-fied," in reviewing the 1930–1980 era.[1]

Zeitner added, "Magazines as a category are enjoying unprecedented prosperity but in an importantly changed environment. Many national maga-zines can now provide an almost bewildering number of geographic and de-mographic split runs, and scores of narrowly focused special publications come on the scene each year to carve out particular, specialized markets for appro-priate advertisers."

The value of such information to the media as well as to historians can be tremendous. Anniversary editions are prized by those who enjoy a review of the past plus the chance to predict the future. In addition to these anniversary editions, media publications in their regular weekly or monthly editions inform the world about what's going on behind the scene, what is changing, and what is seen for the future. Without such files, historians would only have limited sources to utilize in preparing books and articles.

Not only do these publications recount highlights of the day-by-day activ-ities within media, but some more general publications recognize that many Americans also are interested in the background of sources that supply such information. For example, *Time* and *Newsweek* contain media sections; *TV Guide* appeals to millions, in part because of its treatment of the individuals and or-ganizations behind the scene; Hollywood-type publications have for decades satisfied a hunger on the part of millions for the "inside dope" about their heroes. Serious students and critics of media want more information than radio, television, newspaper and magazine sources can provide. The professionals within media want more information about their business operations, their competitors, their sources of supplies and equipment, and the like. Thus they often turn to media publications. Although the circulation of these magazines is not high, the readers include leaders and workers within each medium, the persons who occupy influential positions.

Editor & Publisher

One of the pioneers, *Editor & Publisher,* traces its history to the *Journalist,* founded in 1884. It went through a series of mergers that involved *Newspaperdom* and *Fourth Estate,* justifying its claim as "The oldest publishers' and advertisers' newspaper in America." The weekly has established a series of significant off-shoots, such as its *International Year Book* (1921), its tabulation of newspaper lineage and other mechanical requirements (1922), annual Syndicate Directory (1924), annual Market Guide (1925), Newspaper Promotion Awards (1933) and Color Awards (1956).[2]

Since 1912, when James Wright Brown acquired controlling interest, *Editor & Publisher* has been operated by this family. However, all has not been peaceful in the relationship between *E&P* and its public, including the American Society of Newspaper Editors. Some ASNE members asked: "What's Wrong with *Editor & Publisher?"* The magazine was faulted for its "inadequate reporting about major trends and issues, reporting that is too often inaccurate and superficial. A poor sense of design. An apparent lack of direction and mission." A limited staff, with no full-time writer on the West Coast, prompted another complaint. Its circulation of 26,000 in an industry employing 400,000 was considered too low. President-editor Robert U. Brown noted that his magazine is "the only newspaper industry-wide news magazine that continues to pay its own way even after 95 years." In defense of the charge of excessive use of puffery, Brown noted that 60 per cent of *E&P* is staff produced.[3]

Advertising Age

Advertising Age arrived January 11, 1930, a dollar-a-year weekly. In its 50th anniversary edition, *Ad Age* noted the "endless struggle against bankruptcy and failure," while reprinting the entire 12-page initial issue. Family-owned by the Crain Publishing Co., *Advertising Age* entered a field then dominated by *Printer's Ink* and *Tide.* Friends warned G. D. Crain, Jr., that he was crazy to attempt such a publication, especially in Chicago during the Depression.

"Presenting the news of advertising—a business of widespread interests and ramifications, involving expenditures of two billion dollars a year—has never been the primary, exclusive function of any advertising publication," *Advertising Age* noted, claiming its basic function was to correct this deficiency.

Through the half-century *Advertising Age* has published numerous special issues. In 1963, for example, it told about "The World of Advertising" in a 340-page issue. In 1964 the centennial of J. Walter Thompson Co. was celebrated. Of special interest to historians is the April, 1975, bicentennial issue, "How It Was in Advertising, 1776–1976." Annual reports detail advertising expenditures in all media, the top agencies by volume, the leading advertisers, as well as its 280-page review of the 1930–1980 era. Frequent supplements offer specialized background data on agencies, foreign advertising, magazines, youth markets, agribusiness, and other topics. Editor-in-chief Rance Crain believes "advertising is one of the greatest democratizers our society has ever known, for its brings to the masses information on new products and services formerly reserved for the elite." Crain added, *"Advertising Age*'s coverage of the ebb and flow of the advertising business has changed and modified with the times, but what hasn't changed is our desire to keep you abreast of the news and nuances of this everchanging business."[4]

The Crain firm now publishes 14 other magazines, including its latest, the *Collector-Investor,* designed to explain the international markets, from fine arts to stamps to other collectibles.

Broadcasting and Other Media

Broadcasting, established in 1931 as a newsweekly for the broadcasting and allied arts world, is published in Washington, where major decisions are made concerning this industry. *Broadcasting* also has a number of special issues, such as the Top 100 Companies in Electronic Communications, Top 50 agencies, and the Top 100 records.

Designed for a wide audience, *Broadcasting* includes material on cable television and video cassettes, as well as the growing elements of the electronic communications industry. In its annual media report, *Broadcasting* noted its editorial content was divided into 80 per cent news, 15 per cent feature articles, and five per cent departmental reports.

This magazine is designed for "advertisers, agencies, sales representatives, networks, engineers, equipment manufacturers, program producers and distributors, talent, promotion experts, financial specialists, media brokers, government officials, students and teachers in communications sequences." Its circulation is 35,000. The firm also publishes *Broadcasting/Cable Yearbook.*

Marketing & Media Decisions is a New York monthly that "examines, evaluates and chronicles in depth the factors involved in deciding where national and regional ad dollars go." Started in 1966, it recently added "Marketing" to its title to more accurately define its audience, which includes nearly 20,000 advertiser and agency decision makers. Guest editors regularly relate to current advertising problems. All major media are covered.

Madison Avenue is another informative monthly, "edited for the advertising industry and targeted to the client." In each issue the magazine conducts a "sales call" to provide vital data about a special publication or a major association. *Madison Avenue* began in 1958 and has a circulation of 32,000.

Yes, magazine publishing is publishing

For many years, magazine publishers were like the proverbial shoemaker's children who had no shoes. Magazine publishers had no business magazine of their own. Then, in 1972, FOLIO: THE MAGAZINE FOR MAGAZINE MANAGEMENT was started by Joe Hanson, an experienced magazine publisher and executive.

Today, FOLIO is a successful, thriving magazine that provides magazine publishers and key executives with news of changing developments in magazine publishing as well as innovative ideas in Magazine Management, Circulation, Pro-

duction, Editing and Writing, Magazine Design, Advertising Sales, Research and Promotion, etc.

Like many other magazines, FOLIO markets a wide variety of other information services . . . special issues, books, seminars, trade shows, mailing lists, newsletters, etc.

In a sense, FOLIO is a microcosm of the modern magazine publishing organization—an information and educational center which markets a wide variety of additional services to its readers and to the market it covers.

SPECIAL ISSUES

The Folio Annual Directory of Magazine Suppliers is the magazine industry's major buying guide. This comprehensive Directory provides important information about major suppliers of the products, services and equipment purchased by magazines.

The Folio 400 Study of Magazine Performance— Published annually, the Folio 400 is the industry's authoritative guide to magazine performance and industry growth. A special "advertising community" edition is distributed to 20,000 advertising executives.

magazines. But it's also the sale of additional information services.

FOLIO: PROFESSIONAL BOOKS FOR MAGAZINE EXECUTIVES. Book publishing can be a profitable venture for magazine publishers. Folio publishes professional books for magazine executives and markets them through its own magazine pages and magazine mailing lists.

MAILING LISTS. Mailing lists of the nation's 10,830 magazines and approximately 50,000 magazine executives are available from Folio's Magazine Industry Databank. To keep the Databank up-to-date, Folio maintains the nation's second largest magazine library (after the Library of Congress).

SEMINARS AND TRADE SHOWS

FOLIO sponsors FACE TO FACE: The Annual Publishing Conference and Exposition, the world's largest combined meeting of magazine and book publishing executives. FOLIO also sponsors Magazine Publishing Week, a weeklong program of professional seminars on key publishing subjects.

FOLIO: The Magazine for Magazine Management is published by Folio Magazine Publishing Corporation, P. O. Box 697, 125 Elm Street, New Canaan, CT 06840.

Folio, "the magazine for magazine management," is designed more for executives. Established in 1972, *Folio* has become a major voice within this medium, especially through its seminars and workshops and from its tabulation of the leading publications as reflected in their circulation, advertising, and total revenues. The introduction of the "Folio 400" in 1980 represented a landmark in magazine history.[5]

Magazine Age, begun in 1979, is aimed for the more than 37,000 top advertisers, their agencies, and others concerned with this medium. Each issue features a special editorial presentation of a major advertising market. It concentrates on consumer, business, farm, and newspaper-delivered magazines, calling itself "the only publication devoted exclusively to magazine advertising, covering every aspect of our four billion dollar business" and "the journal of print power."

Two useful sources but with more limited appeal are *Publishers Auxiliary* and *Publishers Weekly.* The former is a weekly tabloid designed primarily for members of the National Newspaper Association. Published in Washington, it has been in business since 1865, seeking to keep readers up-to-date on activities in the nation's capital that affect their operations. Its coverage tends to emphasize smaller dailies and weeklies.

Publishers Weekly has an indirect interest in the magazine world, although designed basically for those associated with the book industry. However, many magazine owners today also operate book publishing units and their businesses overlap. A major example is Time Inc., which owns the Book-of-the-Month Club Inc., as well as book publishing concerns. *Publishers Weekly* has been the bible of the book industry since 1872.

Journalism Reviews

In a related area, the *Columbia Journalism Review* is one of the few survivors of many such reviews started in the 1960s. Published bi-monthly by the Columbia University Graduate School of Journalism, the *Review* is a "national monitor of the media." It seeks to keep its readers informed of both the good and the bad within media, providing in-depth studies along with brief "darts and laurels" aimed toward media. Its initial goals were voiced in the Fall, 1961, pilot issue:

> To deal forthrightly with what it finds to be deficient or irresponsible and to salute what it finds to be responsible, fair, and professional.
> To discuss all the means that carry news to the public, thus viewing the field whole, without the customary partitions.
> To provide a meeting ground for thoughtful discussion of journalism, both by its practitioners and by observers, to encourage debate, and to provide ample space for responsible dissent.
> To attempt systematic studies of major problems in journalism, drawing not only upon published sources but upon new research and upon correspondents here and abroad, including many of the school's alumni active in the profession.

To recognize that others (like *Nieman Reports, Journalism Quarterly,* the *Saturday Review* and, in some ways, trade publications like *Editor & Publisher* and *Broadcasting*) have been doing part of the job and to acknowledge their work in the *Review*'s pages.

SRDS Publications

It would be impossible for the media world to operate without the publications of the Standard Rate & Data Service, Inc. The company's current periodicals, with founding dates, and current circulation, include the following:

Business Publication Rates and Data (1919) 7,500.

Community Publication Rates and Data (1945), semi-annually for buyers of weekly papers/shopping guides. 2,700.

Consumer Magazine and Farm Publication Rates and Data (1919) 6,580.

Direct Mail List Rates and Data (1967) 4,250.

Direct Mail List Bulletin (1967), issued 24 times a year 4,250.

Network Rates and Data (1,045).

Newspaper Rates and Data (1919) 6,860. There also is the *Newspaper Circulation Analysis* (1958) annual.

Print Media Production Data (1968), published quarterly, and *Print Media Production Data Bulletin* (1968), published eight times a year, 5,526.

Spot Radio Rates and Data (1929), monthly, and *Spot Radio Small Markets Edition,* semi-annually (1976), 5,000.

Spot Television Rates and Data (1947), 4,580.

SRDS also publishes a weekly *Change Bulletin Group* (1971) to handle five of the major books. Circulation varies from 2,000 to 3,250.

Other Publications

Publications concerned directly or indirectly with media, including a number with limited regional interests, are listed among the more than 3,000 periodicals in SRDS's *Business Publication Rates and Data,* such as:

Advertising & Marketing: *Ad Biz, Adcrafter, Ad East, Ad Media, Advertising & Advertising World, Adweek Network, Agri Marketing, American Demographics, Art Direction, Communication Arts, Creative, Graphic Arts Buyer, Graphics Today, Graphics USA, Incentive Marketing, Industrial Marketing, Journal of Advertising Research, Journal of Marketing, Journal of Marketing Research, Marketing Communications, Marketing News, Marketing Times, Medical Marketing & Media, New England Advertising Week, Potentials in Marketing, Premium/Incentive Business, Print, Publishing News, Public Relations Journal, Signs of the Times, Specialty Advertising Business, Television/Radio Age, Variety, Watch,* and *ZIP*.

Books and Book Trade: *Book Production Industry & Magazine Production, Bookstore Journal, Choice, Christian Bookseller, Marketing Bestsellers*.

Journalism & Publishing: *Missouri Press News, PNPA* (Pennsylvania), *Production News, Quill, Technical Communication, Writer, Writer's Digest, Washington Journalism Review*.

Radio & television: *Audio & Electronics Digest, Audio Times, Audio Trade News, Audio Video International, BM/E Broadcast Management/Engineering, Broadcast Communications, Broadcast Engineering, Broadcast Equipment Exchange, Cablefile, Cablevision, Communications, Communications-Engineering Digest, Communications News, Consumer Electronics, Educational & Industrial Television, Electronic Distributing, Electronic Servicing, Electronic Technician/Dealer, High Fidelity Trade News, Key Account Retailer, Mart, Merchandising, Mobile Times, P.D. Cue, Personal Communications, Popular Electronics, Radio-Electronics, Radio & Television Weekly, Recording Engineer/Producer, Satellite Communications, Sight & Sound Marketing, SMPTE Journal, Sound Arts Merchandising Journal, Sound & Communications, Television/Radio Age, TVC, Videography, Video Systems, Video Trade News, Pro Sound News,* and *Watch.*

As many of these titles indicate, these publications usually appeal to a limited audience. Some have controlled circulation, while others offer free copies to those with specific corporate titles with paid subscriptions for "outsiders."

Media Industry Newsletter

The "oldest continuously published media/marketing newsletter" is *MIN*— Media Industry Newsletter. Started in 1947, *MIN* was edited for more than 20 years by Roy Quinlin, who died in 1967. Earlier he was associated with J. Walter Thompson Co.

Leon Garry became the new editor and through the years other editors have included John Hillock, Ralf Brent, Mitchell Danow, and Terence Poltrack.

Owned originally by Business Management, Inc., the newsletter was sold in 1977. At that time its circulation was announced as 1,511 paid. However, the new management, Media Industry Newsletter, Inc., said its circulation had climbed 25 per cent within a few months of the changeover. Current publisher is the MIN Publishing, Inc.

In addition to major news coverage of the media world, *MIN* provides continuous statistical data on circulation totals as well as boxscores on advertising pages for the leading periodicals. Interesting commentaries are provided by Dr. Tony Schwartz of Environmental Media Consultants, Inc.

In recent years *MIN*'s appearance has improved with smaller type size permitting more coverage. The normal weekly edition is eight pages with extra pages when needed. *MIN* provides excellent background material for historians seeking data on new publications with their financing and staffing difficulties, on periodicals that have departed the scene, and on current periodicals that might be in trouble. Unlike *Gallagher*'s *MIN* places less emphasis on the inside gossip. Nor does *MIN* operate a placement bureau.

Gallagher Report

There are mixed feelings about the *Gallagher Report,* a weekly newsletter addressed to "marketing, sales, advertising and media executives." In Bernard

Gallagher's promotional material he quotes many executives with such comments as "must reading," "accurate and to the point," "you feel naked if you don't read it," "has had a significant impact on advertising industry," "invaluable source of information," and on and on.

On the other hand, Gallagher has his critics. In a *Wall Street Journal* article in late 1980, Daniel Machalaba quoted critic Chris Welles as saying, "Much of the *Gallagher Report*'s opinions stem from Bernie's feelings about people. People who slight Bernie are often the subject of an attack."

When *Reader's Digest* stopped its contract with Gallagher's World Wide Publications, Inc., the *Report* later carried articles such as *"Reader's Digest* Fights 'Loser' Image" and "'Trouble in *Reader's Digest* Paradise?"

Gallagher refused to be interviewed by the *Journal* writer, thus there is no accurate record of the newsletter's circulation. The reporter estimated it was 15,000 in the late 1960s, possibly 10,000 now, yet postal authorities provided a much lower figure, slightly above 5,000 in 1980.

Weekly reports tell of changes in the media world, while providing blind listings for jobs paying at least $35,000. There are at least 30 supplements annually that provide readers with valuable information about circulation, advertising revenues, and similar topics. Gallagher has a fascination about salaries.

19

Collectors, Educators, Artists, Nature Lovers, Others

ANY ATTEMPT to consolidate the hundreds of American periodicals into a few chapters obviously creates difficulties. Too often magazines just "don't fit" into neat packages or classifications.

In recent years, for example, there has been a surge of interest in collectibles. Thus we witness more readers who are concerned about the nation's past, stimulated in part by our widely-celebrated bicentennial programs. Millions continue their faith in almanacs and their concern for museums and other art centers, history, the military, and other topics.

Interest in the outdoors has sparked more concern about our environment, from bird watching to sky viewing. The consumer movement continues to focus readers' attention on several magazines, while other persons continue to enjoy mysteries, whether in magazines, books, or on the screen. With a major slice of our budgets devoted to educational expenses, more attention is being focused on magazines that tell about trends, problems, and developments in this area.

Other specialized magazines include civic publications that inform millions of Americans about what their service clubs are doing.

In this and the following chapters an assortment is offered, which may be confusing at times. The goal, however, is to inform readers about as many magazines as possible, with sufficient data to encourage additional probing on their part. It is not intended in any way to be all-inclusive. No one book could perform that task.[1]

Almanacs

The oldest publications on the newsstands today are the almanacs, still read faithfully by millions of Americans who like to check the weather predictions and to utilize other vital information that might affect their day-by-day activities. Others like to study the miscellaneous data they all offer, thinking back two centuries to some of the original sayings Ben Franklin wrote for his successful *Poor Richard's Almanac*.

Old Farmer's Almanac has been on the scene since 1792. Nearly three million copies are sold annually on newsstands of this Yankee, Inc., guide produced in New Hampshire.

Another 18th Century periodical is *J. Gruber's Almanack*, established in 1797. Like others, it provides data on the sun, moon, planets, weather, and the like. Today it sells more than 175,000 annually. Although somewhat younger, *Grier's Almanac*, started in 1807, today sells more than three million copies. It is directed to small towns and rural areas of 12 Southern states. It emphasizes farming topics along with good health and grooming tips.

The *Ladies Birthday Almanac*, established in 1890, is the best seller in this group, with some 4.7 million sales. It, too, comes from the South, published in Chattanooga to cover 14 states.

Trail Blazer's Almanac and Pioneer Guide Book began in 1934 and today reaches more than 1.2 million buyers. On the other end, the *Moon Sign Book*, started in 1905, has 200,000 sales. A more recent entry, the *Old Moore's Astrological Almanack*, began in 1965 and now reaches 200,000.

More of a regional periodical is *Blum's Farmers & Planters Almanac and Turner's Carolina Almanac*, published in North Carolina, where it began in 1828. It sells more than 400,000 copies, appealing to all members of the family.

These almanacs normally include articles on agricultural interests, household hints, handicrafts, family concerns, health and grooming, cooking and sewing. Often there are jokes and cartoons as well to ensure more readership. In addition to these, there are many others issued as advertising promotions by larger companies.

Antiques and Art

The post-World War II interest in antiques is confirmed by the founding dates for many of today's magazines devoted to this business, or hobby. For example, the *American Collector* with a circulation of 150,000 began in 1970. The monthly *Antique and Collectors Mart*, with 90,000 circulation, began in 1976. It is for investors and collectors in many areas, artifacts to stamps to coins. And more recently, in 1978, the *Antiques World* arrived. It now sells 38,000 copies monthly for those involved in the international antiques world. That same year *Art & Antiques* arrived and now reaches 48,000 with its slogan, "The American magazine for connoisseurs and collectors." It covers the period from 1600 to 1940.

One of the oldest on this market is the magazine *Antiques*, started in 1922. In addition to stories for collectors of antiques and works of art, this monthly tells about exhibitions, museum acquisitions, new books, along with features for individual collectors with their diverse concerns. With a circulation over

53,000, it is owned by Straight Enterprises, under a trust created by Dorothy Whitney Elmhirst.

Others with their devoted followers include *Antique Monthly* (1967) 92,000 circulation; *Antiques Journal* (1946) 50,000; *Antique Trader Weekly* (1957) 92,000, and some regional periodicals such as the *Maine Antique Digest*.

There also are art magazines, such as *American Artist* (1937), *Art in America* (1913), *Art/World* (1976), *Fiberarts* (1975), *North Light* (1969), *Portfolio* (1979) and *Today's Art* (1952).

Civic

Americans are "joiners" and their magazines reflect this attitude. They love to review the past, see what others with like interests are doing today, and then look ahead to what their clubs can do for the betterment of their communities.

V.F.W. magazine was established in 1914 and *American Legion* began in 1919. With a lower potential membership, the Veterans of Foreign Wars publication reaches 1.6 million readers while the *American Legion* has 2.5 million. Both publications are sent to members and in many ways may be classified as general magazines.

Service clubs are represented by magazines that carry their titles. Circulations vary annually, depending upon the clubs' membership gains or losses. The magazines are sent to paid-up members as part of their dues expense.

The *Elks* (1922) and the *Moose* (1910) magazines have the largest circulations, 1.6 million and 1.3 million respectfully. Along the same classification there are the *Eagle* (1913) with 685,000 circulation; *Lion* (1918) 670,000; *Rotarian* (1911) 460,000, and *Kiwanis* (1917) 280,000. All of these publications are designed for the members, furnishing current news, forecasts for the future, features designed for this specialized audience, and other items of interest.

Columbia, created for members of the Knights of Columbus, started in 1893 and today reaches 1.2 million monthly. It is, however, more of a general family magazine rather than directed to club, or group activities.

Another group with a monthly magazine is the General Federation of Women's Clubs' *Clubwoman,* started in 1917. In addition to the usual club topics, this magazine assists the members in their planning and selection of local projects.

The official organ for the United States Jaycees is *Future,* a bi-monthly designed to assist these young members in community projects.

Typical of magazines of other groups is *Hadassah,* the official publication of The Women's Zionist Organization of America. However, it calls itself a magazine for American Jewish families, with coverage of social, economic, and educational subjects. Started in 1925, it now reaches more than 360,000 subscribers.

There are, of course, hundreds of publications representing other clubs, lodges, fraternal groups, and the like.

Consumers

Consumer Reports, with a circulation of two million, is the voice of the Consumer Union, founded in 1919 after a group of employes left Consumers Research, Inc., and its magazine, *Consumers Research.*

Consumer Reports' readership includes those in the higher income and better educated groups. They tend to read more and be more rational in their buying habits. They are consumer "activists" who continue to demand more product testing and consumer education.

The magazine has tested thousands of products and in the process had become involved in a number of court cases. However, it has never lost such a case. In 1972, Consumer Union established The Center for the Study of the Consumer Movement, with headquarters in Mount Vernon, N.Y.

Consumer Research continues to be published in Washington, New Jersey, and has a circulation of 200,000.

Consumer Life, a Webb publication started in 1975, is a quarterly with more than a million subscribers. However, it is less involved in research than the others, being more concerned with home service functions.

Education

Change, the magazine of higher learning which appears ten times a year, has a circulation of 25,000 and provides information about university life, research projects, academic leaders and institutions. Published since 1969, *Change* contains many philosophical pieces.

Among the dozens of periodicals concerned with education is *Today's Education,* started in 1913. As the official publication of the National Education Association, it has a circulation of 1.7 million. Another group publication, the *American Educator,* appears quarterly for the half-a-million members of the American Federation of Teachers.

The monthly *American Teacher* is also published by the same union. Started in 1916, *American Teacher* goes from Washington, D.C., to 530,000 members.

Others have more limited audiences, such as *Learning,* established in 1972 to serve elementary and junior high school educators and administrators, and *Teacher* (1882) for those associated with classes from kindergarten through the eighth grade. In addition, there are numerous state and regional publications plus another large group directed to business and administrative functions in the world of education. There are magazines devoted to camps and camping, adult training, motivation and development, as well as individual areas, as indicated in these titles: *American Biology Teacher, American Libraries, Arithmetic Teacher, Voc Ed.,* and *Wilson Library.*

Four publications of the R. R. Bowker Company are related to libraries, acquisitions, operations, etc. The best known is *Publishers Weekly,* founded in 1872 and reaching 37,000 today. It is the "must" magazine for the book industry, reporting trends, promotions, new books, best sellers, and other valuable data. Other Bowker magazines include *Library Journal* (1876) with 28,000 circulation; *School Library Journal* (1954), 44,000; and *Previews* (1972) with 12,500 circulation to those who use non-print material in their school work.

History

Four publications of the Historical Times Magazine Group reach more than 600,000 subscribers across America. These are directed to special interest groups except for *American History Illustrated* (1966) with its 154,000 circulation. Since 1962, the *Civil War Times Illustrated* has appeared, stimulated by the centennial celebration of this conflict. More than 101,000 Civil War buffs read this magazine.

British History Illustrated (1974) reaches 65,000 while *Early American Life* (1970) is the group leader, with 342,000 circulation reflecting the nation's concern with its past.

Horizon, founded in 1958, was acquired in 1978 by Gray D. Boone of Tuscaloosa, Alabama, who promised: *"Horizon* will continue to report on these mirrors of our lives, sometimes extending the effectiveness of the mirrors and, hopefully, occasionally functioning as one of the mirrors itself.'' The monthly has a circulation of 105,000. Boone also owns *Antique Monthly.*

Americana, started in 1973, is designed for those with interest in crafts, collecting, restoration, travel, decorating, cooking, gardening, and other topics related to the country's past. The bi-monthly, with 250,000 circulation, has how-to-do-it instructions and practical information.

There are many journals, especially quarterlies, devoted to history, usually sponsored by associations for their members.

Museums

Although a number of the more widely circulated periodicals, such as *Smithsonian,* provide features concerning the nation's museums, at least three magazines now cover this topic.

Museum News, started in 1958, is a bi-monthly appearing in Washington, D.C., designed for the museum industry rather than for the casual reader.

Museum, established in New York in 1979, has 120,000 subscribers interested in art, history and science museums. The magazine plans to sample the treasures of more than 24,000 museums around the world.

Museums New York is another recent magazine with more limited appeal. With a circulation of 60,000 this two-year-old magazine covers the 50 museums in New York, telling of their events, exhibits, and other activities.

Humanities, Labor, Unions

The *American Scholar* appeals to a general audience through non-technical articles with emphasis on the contemporary scene. It is a quarterly, started in

1932, by Phi Beta Kappa, honorary scholarship society, and sent to 30,000 members.

Commentary, noted earlier under religious publications, is also concerned with a wide range of political and social issues. Cultural topics are offered regularly by this American Jewish Committee monthly that was started in 1945.

Labor unions have their own periodicals. For example, the Labor Press is a group of regional and international AFL-CIO union periodicals. Including 100 newspapers and magazines, the group has a total circulation of 3,700,000. The magazine unit, with nearly a million circulation, includes these periodicals: *Actors Equity News, American Federation Television and Radio Artists, American Teacher, Journeyman Barber and Beauty Culture, International Musician, National Postal Alliance, Railway Carmen's Journal, Signalman's Journal, Typographical Journal,* and *American Postal Workers.* These are mostly monthly. Others such as the *Guild Reporter* and *U.M.W. Journal* are designed for specific union memberships.

HUMOR

Mad

Started as a comic book in 1952, *Mad* has attracted millions of readers through the years. Although *Time* magazine quickly predicted a short life for *Mad,* it has been "must" reading for young Americans for nearly three decades. Richard Reeves once wrote that *"Mad* may be the most influential magazine in the United States—if you assume teenagers and other children are worth influencing."

The man behind *Mad* is William M. Gaines, who calls himself a maniac. His father, Max Gaines, started the idea of putting together newspaper comic strips into book form. In 1947, the younger Gaines took over Educational Comics following his father's death. These early "comics" were so gruesome that the government and distributors brought them to a halt.[2]

Young Gaines then started *Mad* as a 10 cents-a-copy comic book. The early editor was Harvey Kurtzman, who eventually joined *Playboy,* working with that magazine's "Little Annie Fannie." These early issues today are collector's items, some worth $160.

Alfred E. Neuman is the magazine's symbol, with his "What, me worry?" slogan and his appearance as a "lop-headed, jug-eared, gap-toothed idiot boy."

In 1955, the magazine adopted a new format and upped its price to 25 cents. A cover read:

"The new *Mad* magazine has a vitally important message inside." The inside message? "Please buy this magazine." This helped *Mad* acquire another title, "irreverent."

Hustler magazine described Gaines as "full of contradictions. He is at once extremely generous yet embarrassingly cheap. He is an egomaniac and yet also big-hearted. He dresses like the world's messiest slob; yet he runs his little empire with astonishing efficiency and control."

Obviously there are no sacred cows nor any political point of view expressed in *Mad*. It once wrote that *"People* magazine is a great publication for those who never learned how to read hard things, such as two-syllable words."

Mad frequently receives national recognition. When Barry Goldwater, Jr., proposed in 1980 that the government sell space on postage stamps to advertisers to help wipe out the department's deficit, he was reminded that 14 years earlier *Mad* had made the same proposal. The only difference? *Mad*'s idea was voiced with tongue in cheek; Goldwater was serious.

Mad is published eight times annually. "Folio 400" in late 1980 credits the magazine with a circulation of 1,850,000, mostly from single-copy sales. This brings more than $11 million to *Mad*. In addition, the *Mad Specials,* with a circulation of 1,162,000, contribute another $5.8 million to the company.

The *Mad* "spirit" is displayed in the *Super Special Summer 1981,* which included 14 car and home window stickers, with double meanings. For example, one was as follows:

In small type	If you want to be
In much larger type	SAFE
In small type	Don't Ride with this
In much larger type	DRIVER

Mad appeals more to boys than to girls, and more to the early teenagers than those in the older age brackets. As the *New York Times* noted in early 1981, *"Mad* was the first satirical magazine for children, a sort of an easy-to-read Junior Swift, the first to deal with children's reality—their parents, schools and the general adult culture around them."

Editor Al Feldstein was quoted as saying

> What we did was to take the absurdities of the adult world that youngsters were facing and show kids that the adult world is not omnipotent, that their parents were telling the kids to be honest, not to lie, and yet they were cheating on their income tax. We told them there's a lot of garbage out in the world and you've got to be aware of it. Everything you read in the papers is not necessarily true. What you see on television is mostly lies. You're going to have to learn to think for yourself. . . .

In the 1960s, *Mad*'s focus "turned to more and more difficult concerns—adult hypocrisy, sexuality, women's liberation, divorce, the drug and alcohol scene . . ."

National Lampoon

Both *Mad* and the *National Lampoon* were influenced by the original *Life,* a humor magazine. The *Lampoon,* of course, traces its development from the century-old *Harvard Lampoon,* which became famous with its parodies of national publications.

Celebrating its 10th anniversary with the February, 1980, 128-page edition, the *National Lampoon* then recalled that the first five issues were "monumental flops. The public didn't buy it. The company that distributed it didn't think it was funny. The advertising community snarled when our salesmen came in to try to sell them space.''

National Lampoon claims its editorial policy is dictated in part by a philosophy that says, ''It can be sick—but it must also be funny. Don't try to get a laugh just by being shocking.'' As a result it has encountered lawsuits. The first came after a parody on Minnie Mouse in September, 1970. Then Charles ''Peanuts'' Schulz objected to some of its contents, to be followed by complaints from George Wallace, an unnamed movie actress, 1960s-radical leader Mario Savio, and others. An automobile company objected to an ad that said: ''If Teddy Kennedy drove a Volkswagen, he'd be president today.'' The ad showed a VW floating on water. Despite these charges the magazine has lost only one suit, that to a South Carolina midget.

Douglas C. Kenney told an audience of magazine editors in 1974 that the *National Lampoon* has three major objectives:

First, to make money. Second, to make people laugh. Third, as a boon to those young people who still know how to read, the magazine ''sensitizes their bull shit detectors.'' The magazine ''sells'' sex, political satire and cartoons, with its editorial content described as ''paralegal and faintly obscene.''

One of the best selling books published by the *National Lampoon* is its *High School Yearbook Parody,* first issued in 1964. It has sold several million copies and continues on the market.

Readership is about 80 per cent male, in the 18 to 24 age group. Some 80 per cent of the copies are sold on newsstands, especially in university communities. In 1974–75, its circulation reached 900,000, and then dropped to 500,000. Today it is about 650,000, while its publishers visualize a circulation of 750,000 to 800,000 within a few years. ''Folio 400'' reported its income as $12.9 million, with about $2.7 from advertisements and the rest from circulation.

The godfather *Lampoon* at Harvard profits tremendously from royalty payments. The national edition became famous in the production of its movie, ''Animal House.'' It has published other parodies and plans one on Sunday newspapers. It also projects another movie, ''Animal House II.''

In promoting itself as an advertising medium, the *National Lampoon* says it is: ''Known by the companies we keep—DuPont, Lever Bros., Seagram, Panasonic, Heublein. There's nothing funny about the way it sells.'' It profiles itself as a ''literate contemporary magazine of humor, satire, and parody,'' usually with a different but timely subject for each issue.[3]

Mystery, Adventure, Science Fiction

Television and the movies have helped to keep Americans interested in mystery stories. And, of course, the nation's exploration programs and such movies as ''Star Trek'' have combined to lure millions of readers to a group of magazines and books.

The variety of periodicals under this category is indicated by the titles.

The *American West* since 1964 has been recalling the nation's frontier heritage. It also reviews the many books about our past. *Frontier Times* (1923) contains "documentary articles and stories on badmen, lawmen, range wars, trail drivers, cowboys and ranch life, mining, Indians, lost treasures, the gold rush" and other frontier subjects. Its circulation is over 115,000. The *Real West* (1957) reaches over 130,000, while *True West* (1953) has nearly 150,000. *Old West* (1964) has similar objectives for its 112,000 circulation.

For adult fantasy fans there is the *Epic Illustrated,* established in 1980 seeking a goal of 200,000 readers. It covers science fiction, heroic posters, sorcery, humor, and offers novellas. *Fate* is another magazine for mystery fans, with "true stories of the strange and unknown." Ancient civilizations and religions are studied, along with other mysteries of history. It began in 1948 and today had a circulation of 115,000.

Ellery Queen's Mystery Magazine appears 13 times a year for nearly 250,000 readers. In addition to publishing mysteries of its own, the magazine keeps its readers abreast of hardcover and paperback books that should interest them.

Heavy Metal is the unlikely title for an adult illustrated science fiction fantasy magazine published by a subsidiary of *National Lampoon.* The monthly was started in 1977 and today has a circulation approaching 190,000. Its contents are both contemporary and futuristic in theme.

Isaac Asimov's Science Fiction magazine is another newcomer, started in 1976. Short stories, book reviews, editorials, and science puzzles are included for the 135,000 readers. *The Magazine of Fantasy and Science Fiction* explains its contents through its title. It also carries a science column by Isaac Asimov.

More traditional mystery fans turn to the official detective group, which includes *Master Detective, Official Detective Stories, True Detective, Front Page Detective,* and *Inside Detective.*

Nature, Ecology, Physical Sciences

Audubon is one of the major periodicals with a wide readership, distributed to 320,000 subscribers across America. It is also one of the oldest, having started in 1899 under the sponsorship of the National Audubon Society. The *Bird Watcher's Digest* (1978) is another bi-monthly, with similar concerns, but a much smaller circulation, 10,000.

The Sierra Club reaches its audience through *Sierra,* a bi-monthly bulletin founded in 1892 and now reaching 158,000. Also from California comes *Oceans,* started in 1969 and now telling 66,000 subscribers what happens in, on, above, below and around the sea. Assisting in publicizing conservation projects is the *National Parks & Conservation Magazine,* an association periodical for 35,000 members.

Among the business publications there are others more concerned with nature. For example, *American Forests* (1875) relates to the lumber and forest industries for its 70,000 subscribers.

Others are interested in the sky so they read *Astronomy* (1973). This is a monthly for professional astronomers and the scientifically-oriented public. There are 100,000 concerned readers. *Sky and Telescope* (1941) also reaches lay persons and professional scientists who want news about current advances in astronomy and the space sciences. It has a circulation of 76,000 amateur and professional astronomers.

Archaeology, on the other hand, has a circulation of nearly 50,000 for those interested in recent discoveries, excavations, and related topics. Information also is furnished for those readers planning such trips.

Psychology Today

Started in May, 1967, *Psychology Today* and its early associates, Nicholas H. Charney and John J. Veronis, have had an exciting career.

The magazine's philosophy was established by Charney in his opening issue editorial, where he noted in part:

> I am irritated with pompous unnecessary vocabularies generated by some psychologists in their attempts to be objective and precise. Certainly a specialized language is essential to rigorous thinking; but jargon sometimes prevents the identification of communication of important principles and all too often merely cloaks trivial thinking.
>
> Though it can be cold and impersonal as a science, psychology is a fascinating and alive subject. Current research always creates controversy. We intend to print current research . . . I hope to make *Psychology Today* lively, clear, and technically accurate. . . .

Today the magazine is owned by Ziff-Davis and has a nationwide monthly circulation of nearly 1,200,000. Readers are mostly in the 18 to 44 age bracket, college-educated, professional-managerials. It claims to be for social scientists and intelligent laymen who are concerned with the behavior of society and individuals.

20

For the Good Life:
Travel, Eating, Crafts, Pets

AMERICANS LOVE TO TRAVEL, whether by plane, boat, automobile, recreational vehicles, or on foot. They not only desire to tour other areas in the United States, but they often want to see the rest of the world, visiting the major tour sites and out-of-the-way islands and nations as well.

Magazines are designed to assist travelers in making necessary plans, for pilots who fly for business or for fun, and for those who seek epicurean delights. For the thousands who drive recreational vehicles, magazines and directories are available. All travelers, of course, want to be entertained. Some prefer the unusual, others the famous. And while the Metropolitan Opera still has its devotees, country music fans are growing by the millions. In the midst of all of this, there are single persons seeking guidance.

A minority are into "society" while another small group turns to such publications as *High Times* for comfort. For others who have considerable spare time or who desire a little extra money, there are many crafts available. The growth of interest in hobbies and in collecting has been reflected in the expansion of magazines to encourage such activities. There always have been millions of Americans who own dogs and cats, some for the pure joy of their companionship, others for show purposes or for breeding.

A market of its own concerns the "military family," estimated to involve at least 11 million Americans. Officers and enlisted personnel have their periodicals, while their families at home also receive help from specialized magazines.

Travel Agencies

More than 17,000 travel agencies are available to help Americans spend more than $20 billion annually. Although their growth has expanded in recent years, some have been around for a half century or more.

The American Society of Travel Agents' publication, *ASTA Travel News,* began in 1931. It calls itself a business management magazine for travel agencies, tour operators, and other travel concerns. It reaches more than 16,000 agencies.

Travel Trade (1929) is another pioneer with 25,000 circulation. It is aimed more to the industry's sales force, the agents, with updated data designed to improve their business. It is published in two editions: one is a weekly newspaper, the other is a monthly magazine.

Travel Scene has the largest circulation, 129,000, with its three monthly editions: *Travel Agent, Airline/Interline,* and *Business Travel.* These serve the professional travel planners. *Travel Age* has several special editions, including *TravelAge Southeast, TravelAge East, TravelAge West,* and *TravelAge Mid America.* All are published by a division of Official Airline Guides, Inc., a Dun & Bradstreet Co. operation. The "Age" group reaches 45,000 sales specialists.

Travel Agent is a twice weekly publication dating to 1929. With a circulation of 32,000, it serves agents and tour wholesalers. *Travel Weekly* is a semiweekly with nearly 45,000 circulation that started in 1958. It is more of a business-oriented newspaper.

Others are more specialized, such as the *Pacific Travel News* (1957), with its circulation of 25,000 directed to those agents serving Asia/Pacific destinations. Departments are devoted to specific areas or countries in this part of the world. *Business Travel* (1978) reaches more than 25,000 monthly, assisting agents in planning meetings, working with commercial accounts, and allied projects.

There are many official guides such as *Official Airline Guide Worldwide Edition* (1962), *Official Hotel & Resort Guide* (1963), *Official Railway Guide Passenger Travel Edition* (1974), and *Official Steamship Guide International* (1932). They vary from monthly to annual frequency.

Individual Travelers

Four travel magazines with a combined circulation of 3.5 million help Americans as they tour the nation and foreign countries. Each represents a sponsoring organization, or club.

More than 1.1 million members of the Montgomery Ward Auto Club receive the bimonthly *Crossroads.* In business since 1974, *Crossroads* advises readers about car maintenance, protection from thieves, proper clothes for travel, and similar worldwide subjects.

Travel & Leisure originated in 1971 as a free publication for American Express credit cardholders. It reached 5 million before plans were developed to change it to a paid subscription periodical. By 1976 it had a circulation of 800,000 and in 1981 had 935,000. Readers are mostly males, age 25 to 54, with a median household income of over $33,000.

Signature (1956) is the voice of the Diners' Club. This monthly is sent to 600,000 subscribers, mostly male (83 per cent) with a median income of $33,000. The National Travel Club publishes *Travel/Holiday* for 750,000 subscribers. It has 58 per cent female readership, with a median age of 47. The magazine *Travel* and the once Curtis-owned *Holiday* merged in 1978. *Discovery* is a quarterly published by Allstate Enterprises, Inc., covering all aspects of travel. It has more than a million subscribers.

The American Automobile Association has many magazines in addition to its famous tour books for members. For example, the AAA Midwest Publications Group includes 12 state periodicals with a combined circulation exceeding two million. More than 22 million AAA tour books were distributed free to AAA members in 1979. *Casino & Cabaret International* was started in 1981 to help vacationers at these centers.

In addition to these there are many regional periodicals, such as *Keystone Motorist* (1911) for 233,000 subscribers; *Michigan Living* (1917), 806,000; and the *Yankee Magazine's Guide to New England* (1972) 150,000.

Adventure Travel (1977) is a monthly reaching 100,000 who "demand more than routine itineraries." It offers many first-person travel features. For hotel and motel guests in many cities, there is *Travelhost* (1968) with localized television programming. These are placed in the rooms. A recent newcomer, *Going Places* is designed for international travel, sponsored by Wards Wide World of Travel. It started in 1980 with a circulation of 125,000.

Millions of Americans in their travels come in contact with *Travelhouse,* a weekly for hotel guests in many cities; *Where* magazine, another weekly to tell them what to see, where to eat, places to visit; and *Leisureguide,* an annual available to hotel guests in eight major cities.

Cruises have become more popular, obviously influenced by the successful television program, "Love Boat." In 1980 six publications appeared to serve steamship lines, including *Embark* for Princess Cruises; *Azure Seas* for Eastern Steamship Lines/West; *Emerald Seas* for Eastern Steamship Lines/East; *Sunway* for Home Lines; *Golden Odyssey* for Royal Cruises; and *Sea Scene* for Paquet. These are designed for the affluent readers, with their high family income and their desire for leisurely travel. These magazines assist them while on the ships as well as while visiting on land.

Cruise Travel (1979) is a bimonthly with a limited circulation, 1,250, with data for those planning such tours.

In learning more about air travel the readers also have many choices. There are publications for pilots, from the beginner to the seasoned professional. There are inflight magazines for customers enroute.

Aviation

Pilots, plane owners, and aviation enthusiasts have periodicals to keep them well versed in today's happenings. *Aero* (1968) is a monthly for 75,000 owners of fixed wing aircraft, informing them of equipment evaluations, safety methods, travel reports, and news of current concern.

The Air Line Pilots Association has its monthly, *Air Line Pilot,* keeping 44,000 persons aware of safety and industrial developments, features, editorial comments, technical talk, and biographical sketches. The association celebrated its 50th anniversary in 1981 with articles citing members' contributions during a half century of air travel.

With a circulation of 154,000, *Air Progress* (1941) is designed for pilots, aircraft owners, businessmen and others interested in planes for pleasure or career purposes. Articles discuss evaluations, designs, construction techniques and applications, as well as government activities and aviation as a career.

Pilots and plane owners also have *Flying* (1927), a Ziff-Davis publication with a circulation of 375,000. It updates FAA regulations, industry news, flying safety, books, and films. There are semi-technical and feature articles of interest to many pilots. The magazine also has an annual, *Flying Annual & Buyers Guide. Aviation* is a 54,000-circulated magazine for plane owners.

For enthusiasts in sports aviation there is *Homebuilt Aircraft* (1975) with a 35,000 circulation. It includes items on antique, classic and military planes, as well as experimental air craft.

The official publication of the Aircraft Owners and Pilots Association is *AOPA Pilot,* reaching 240,000. Light plane owners, from beginners to seasoned veterans, have *Private Pilot* (1965), with a circulation of 92,000. Another publication for general aviation topics is *Plane & Pilot* (1965), reaching 53,000 concerned with upgrading equipment and other vital topics.

There are others who view flying as a sport. For them there is *Sport Aviation* (1953) with items designed for pilots, designers and builders of amateur-built aircraft. Readers see flying as fun and seek technical data to assist them in design and construction projects. *Sport Flying* (1967) also concerns itself with recreational aviation, for both modern and vintage aircraft. Some emphasis also has been placed on photographs.

A regional publication is *Western Flyer* (1959) for owners and pilots with news on government actions, new products, antiques, homebuilts, and the business use of planes.

Frequent Flyer entered the scene in 1980, a monthly consumer magazine for those individuals who use the air frequently, who often rent cars at airports, and who spend an average of 85 nights a year in hotels while earning an average $52,000. It began with a guaranteed circulation of 225,000 for a predominately male audience (92 per cent), college-educated (85 per cent), and average age of 40.

Inflight

Inflight magazines began in America in the late 1950s and expanded slowly. By 1970 only eight airlines had such periodicals. Today there are many more, with the majority published by three groups.

Pan American Airways was the first to provide customers with such a magazine. In those early days these periodicals generally were prepared by the airline's public relations department. Today the majority are professionally produced, with well-written articles and good photographs, along with considerable advertising. They are subjected to research as to their readers with their likes and dislikes, and how many of them take copies home, as they are encouraged to do. Likewise, their educational and monetary status are researched.

In the late 1970s Air Group One was organized as a selling affiliate for a number of these magazines. Today it claims first place, with a combined circulation of 1,312,000 for TWA *Ambassador*, Frontier *Frontier*, Northwest Orient *Passages*, Delta *Sky*, Braniff *Flying Colors*, and American *American Way*.

The East/West Inflight Network claims a circulation of one million, including United *Mainliner*, Eastern *Review*, Continental *Extra*, Ozark *Flightime*, PSA *California*, Hughes Airwest *Sundancer*, and Texas International *The Texas Flyer*. The network includes the New England *Flying Your Way* for joint advertising purposes.

A new group in this area is the Ziff-Davis network, which includes the Pan Am *Clipper* (a merger of the former National *Aloft* and Pan Am *Clipper*), US *Air*, Republic's *Scene*, and Piedmont *Pace*. Its circulation is more than 545,000.

Jeffrey S. Butler, founder and president of Nugent Communications, formed the East/West Network in 1968. Butler had previously developed PSA *California*. By combining this with other inflight magazines, Butler developed his network and created the inflight market. Advertisers, who now spend more than $30 million annually in these publications, obtained a strong market to reach what Butler determined to be highly mobile, upper-management, business executives.

Readership surveys vary with the publications and with the researchers. Audits & Surveys Inc. used questionnaires to quiz passengers over 18 and found that the great majority (73 per cent) of the passengers are men, with 42 the median age. Their income is much higher than the average and they have a more impressive college background. This study noted that 24 per cent of the passengers took copies with them, as they are encouraged to do. Other studies differ in percentages, yet the overall picture remains the same.

Contents vary in these publications with interesting subjects designed to relax the passengers. A review of several copies revealed such topics as "George Burns: Not the Retiring Sort;" "You're Fired: What Next?;" "Ridin' Ropin' and Rodeo;" "The Folk Art Boom in Pueblo Country;" and "Careers For The

1980s.'' There often are special topics, such as ''That Sunny Florida Style,'' obviously of interest to many air travelers.

In addition there are other publishers. *Air California* magazine serves Air California. Halsey Publishing Co. handles Braniff's *Flying Colors* and *Delta Sky*. F. M. Hitshew & Associates publishes *Western's World;* Summit Publishing has Southwest's *Southwest,* and Seattle Northwest Publishing Co. has Alaska Airline's *Alaskafest*. Titsch Publishing Co. has *Tailwinds* and Webb publishes Northwest's *Passages*.[1] *Skylite* arrived in 1981 as a controlled-circulated bimonthly for 40,000 executives who own or lease corporate jets.

Campers, Recreational Vehicles

When Americans travel the nation's highways they quickly become aware of the wide interest in campers, mobile homes, trailers, and recreational vehicles. Whether the high price for gasoline will diminish this volume remains to be seen. Americans, however, are a mobile people and as millions retire earlier and live longer, one can expect to witness more recreational vehicles crisscrossing the continent. And everyone has his own periodicals to keep up with developments, travel centers, technical advances, and other useful data.

Some have organized, such as the Family Motor Coach Association, with *Family Motor Coaching* (1964). With a circulation of 28,000 this magazine reports news, meetings, travel routes, new products, and industry data. More than 106,000 owners of self-propelled vacation vehicles turn to *Motorhome Life* (1968) for guidelines and directory data.

There also are annuals with similar objectives, including the *Recreational Vehicle Directory, Woodall's RV Buyer's Guide, KOA Handbook and Directory for Campers, Wheelers RV Resort & Campground Guide,* and *Woodall's Campground Directory*.

Woodall's RV Travel is one of the oldest, started in 1935, and most widely circulated, 282,000. It contains current reports, maps, lodging data, and other features helpful to travelers. The American Automobile Association also publishes campbooks.

There are the regionals, too, such as *Adirondack Life* (1970) for northern New York state; *Alaska* (1935), published in Washington for 185,000 readers; *Appalachia* (1976) for the Appalachia Mountain Club. Backpacking has become one of the major outside activities and in 1973 *Backpacker* arrived. It now reaches 125,000. That same year *Canoe* appeared and now goes to 45,000. *Camping Journal* (1962) is a family camping periodical, with a circulation in excess of 285,000. It is published eight times a year.

Epicurean

Three leading magazines in this category are *Bon Appetit, Cuisine,* and *Gourmet*. Their combined circulation exceeds 2,600,000. In some ways their goals seem similar, yet each has a distinctive flavor of its own and attracts a slightly different audience.

Gourmet is the oldest, first appearing in 1940 for those who prefer "good living," not only in the home preparation of foods from scratch but in choices of places to dine out. It has been called the "food purist," for those who happen to be affluent. Some studies indicate more *Gourmet* readers own homes valued at over $100,000 than readers of any other publication. Cities are explored and travel features supplied for the 655,000 subscribers. Histories of foods are offered as the magazine tries to include more than 100 recipes, many intricate, in each issue. People often save *Gourmet,* as they do some other favorite publications, and frequently have the copies bound. *Gourmet* likes the unusual and once featured meals for a bachelor to cook for his last dinner before marriage.

In 1956 *Bon Appetit* arrived for those "who relish cooking and entertaining." Originally it was a give-away promotional magazine. Today elaborate meal preparations are reviewed with more than 100 recipes in each number. With a circulation of 1,145,000, *Bon Appetit* claims more than 2.8 million ambitious cooks among its readers. It is the most successful of fine food magazines. Some feel that *Bon Appetit* is more informal editorially than the other two major magazines.

Cuisine, the youngest with its start in 1971, has 800,000 circulation and a readership of 2.2 million, including individuals concerned with "adventurous cooking, baking, home entertainment," along with recipes, book reviews and ideas for entertaining. It says it is not as "elegant" as *Gourmet,* not as "casual" as *Bon Appetit.* It began as *Sphere,* the Betty Crocker magazine. It also has been termed a "practical and exciting adventure" with entirely realistic recipes.[2]

There are others with more limited and specialized audiences, such as *Wine World* (1971) for both industry and consumers among its 42,000 circulation. *Pleasures of Cooking,* published by the president of Cuisinart, carries no advertisements, yet often its recipes appropriately call for a food processor. The *Cook's Magazine* is a bimonthly started in 1980 and designed more for cooking techniques rather than recipes.

Entertainment

Across America there are special entertainment publications for thousands of readers. Arts & Leisure Publications offers magazines for San Francisco, Los Angeles and Chicago theaters. *Bravo* is the official program for theatrical centers, opera house, symphony and the ballet in Denver. New Orleans entertainment seekers have *Go.* In Washington and Baltimore there is *Forecast* for those active in musicals and fine arts. And in at least 25 cities the traveling public finds *Key* magazines in numerous places.

American Film appears ten times a year, providing behind-the-scene coverage of film and television art. This comes from the John F. Kennedy Center for the Performing Arts. The Metropolitan Opera Guild in New York publishes the *Opera News* (1936) and *Ballet News* (1979) 20 times a year. From the Film

Society of Lincoln Center comes *Film,* a bimonthly since 1962. And since 1926, *Dancemagazine* has kept some 50,000 subscribers alert to changes and developments.

Music

Another broad category may be titled music, which obviously overlaps education, entertainment, literary, book reviews and writing, as well as television and radio communications.

Billboard, the pioneer in this area, started in 1894 and reaches 46,000 weekly from its Los Angeles base. *Billboard* labels itself the all-around music and big entertainment book, as it covers the international music/record/tape industry. Its departments review the major divisions of the music world, such as classical, country, gospel, soul, and others.

Movie and television viewers are well aware of the growth of country music from the South to all corners of America. This is also reflected in the magazine market as well. *Country Music* (1947) prints ten issues a year for enthusiasts in this category who desire more inside interviews with personalities and more news about what's going on. Its 1981 circulation was 450,000. The *Music City News* from Nashville, started in 1963, today reaches more than 170,000 fans and professionals. *Country Style* is another monthly for fans, musicologists, and recording artists and those concerned with the industry in general. It began in 1976 and now has a 400,000 circulation. *Country Song Roundup* (1947) has grown to 125,000 copies monthly.

There are specialists within this specialized category. For example, there are the *Drum Corps World* (1971); *Guitar Player* (1967); *Keyboard World* (1972); *Singing News* (1969), and *Songwriter* (1975).

Some 375,000 copies of *High Fidelity* are sold regularly, along with the annual buying guides published by this ABC-owned magazine. *Modern Recording* (1975), with 70,000 monthly sales, also issues buyer's guides.

Stereo Review, a Ziff-Davis publication, has been around since 1958 and now reaches more than 540,000. In addition, its buying guides have a wide audience.

Hit Parader and *Song Hits* (1942) are two widely sold monthlies with top song lyrics in each issue, plus many other features. *Sheet Music* (1976) reproduces both words and music of many songs in addition to other divisions of interest to amateur and professional musicians. Appearing nine times a year, it has 210,000 subscribers.

Rolling Stone Different

In its first issue on Nov. 9, 1967, *Rolling Stone* editor Jann S. Wenner wrote:

> *Rolling Stone* is not just about music, but also about the things and attitudes that the music embraces. We've been working quite hard on it and we

hope you can dig it. To describe it any further would be difficult without sounding like bullshit, and bullshit is like gathering moss.

Wenner explained that the title came from a song by Muddy Waters, and the publication was "sort of a magazine and sort of a newspaper."

In its 10th anniversary edition, Dec. 15, 1977, Wenner recounted some of the transitions. "We've been through many changes and considered many ideas. *Rolling Stone* is now some 140 staffers and a $16 million a year enterprise. We've moved from San Francisco to New York City . . . music has a magic that can set you free, and rock & roll will stand. Despite success, flashy publicity, maturity and new disguises (it took on a new logo) we're still up to the same old tricks."

Dr. Hunter S. Thompson, long a major writer for the magazine, wrote the lead story and 50 pages were devoted to photographs by Annie Leibovitz that highlighted the decade. Her first cover picture was John Lennon; during that decade she had 58 cover shots. On its Jan. 22, 1981, cover, *Rolling Stone* ran a picture of a naked John Lennon, cradled in the protective arms of a clothed Yoko Ono, who apparently approved of its use.

Early in 1981 *Rolling Stone* took on a new image, describing itself as a "streetwise magazine with a range as wide and churning as the culture it covers." Music coverage was moved to the back of this every-other-week periodical with its 700,000 circulation. Upfront features were about politics, personalities and issues, movies and reviews. Then came the music highlights. Fiction, losing out in many magazines, was started in February, 1981, as another attempt to broaden the magazine's appeal. At the same time the publication shifted from tabloid to magazine-size, printed on a combination of newsprint and slicker paper.

The magazine said *"Rolling Stone* has always been a magazine in concept, but tabloid in its physical format. It's not like we're becoming a glossy magazine or anything, we're just growing up." In the 1970s the magazine won more than 40 graphic design and journalism awards.

College Papers, a twice-weekly publication, was halted by *Rolling Stone* and will be inserted in that magazine in April and October. Additional projects for the *Rolling Stone* firm include a syndicated 90-second radio feature and the formation of a video division. The magazine also has an Italian edition.[3]

Dancing

The spread of country music fans across America has helped to promote square dancing as well. There are two magazines, both founded in 1948, that have long campaigned for more such dancing.

American Square Dance Magazine, a monthly, is designed for dancers, callers, teachers and leaders in the square dance movement. It reports news of their festivals and other events and even has some coverage of round dancing.

The Sets in Order American Square Dance Society has *Square Dancing* as its official magazine for 24,000 members.

Lifestyle and Society

This topic has varied interests. One entry, *Forum,* is a publication owned by Bob Guccione of *Penthouse* success. Started in 1968, *Forum* has reached 702,000 circulation as "the international journal of human relations." Interviews and case histories of human behavior are reported.

To reach the "lucrative untapped singles market," *Intro* arrived in 1980, with a prediction its circulation soon would reach 100,000. Its premier edition featured "The Dating Dilemmas of the Single Parent," "So What If She Earns More Than You Do," and "The Cinderella Syndrome—Waiting For Mr. Right." An advice column is provided, along with other departments. It does not accept sexually oriented ads. Editor-publisher Suzanne Douglas noted: "There are no wallflowers in the world. Just a lot of unhappy people who are in the wrong place at the wrong time, sharing a frustration that is never mentioned out loud."[4]

Also in this category is *Wet,* another California-produced monthly like *Intro.* It began in 1976 and reaches 50,000 customers for its reports on those Americans "with an eye on the avant garde." Each issue has a specific theme, from the humorous to the serious.

Any discussion of marijuana, as well as other drugs, is apt to create a controversy. Founded in 1974, *High Times* seeks to help solve these controversies. Its "mere existence is enough to make a lot of people who have never read it simmer with outrage," reported the *Wall Street Journal.*[5] While *High Times* will "never rate very high on parental popularity charts," it will be "a big hit with drug users themselves, including large numbers of young readers."

A more mature approach featured the magazine's contents briefly, but editorial changes in 1980 returned *High Times* to its "underground glamour" with more how-to features for home marijuana growers.

Carol Burnett claimed *High Times* influenced her teen-age daughter to get into drugs. The actress said, "I'm not for censorship, but I'm praying *High Times* will die a beautiful natural death."

A circulation high of 405,000 in 1976 dropped to around 300,000 in the 80s. A loss of $400,000 was reported for 1978–79, with additional losses expected. A former editor said, "We did with drugs what *Playboy* did with naked women and *Rolling Stone* did with rock music."

On the opposite side is the monthly *War on Drugs,* started in 1980, and dedicated "to ridding the nation of the menace of drugs." Its publisher, the National Anti-Drug Coalition, suggests that it be placed next to *High Times* to "give a kid a chance."

There are others of interest to the social sets, such as *Club Living* (1977) with a controlled circulation of 51,000. It is distributed in private clubs, as well as yacht, tennis and city clubs, at events and tournaments, and other such centers seven times a year.

Interview (1969) contains conversations with screen, art, stage, music, fashion, and society stars as they report on their lifestyles. Its 101,000 circulation is gained mostly from newsstand sales.

The "magazine for connoisseurs" is *Robb Report* (1972). It is designed for those who appreciate Rolls-Royces, Bentleys, yachts, premium properties, horse farms, art, and similar items. Its circulation is 30,000.

Crafts

Interest has grown tremendously in recent years in hobbies and crafts. Some of the major magazines, such as *Better Homes and Gardens* and *Sunset,* continue to publish books for lovers of crafts and those concerned with Christmas and holiday projects. There also are a number of business-oriented periodicals for companies that deal with crafts, games, and hobby supplies and their merchandising.

For decades there have been millions of stamp and coin collectors in America. Two weekly tabloids serve these individuals: *Linn's Stamp News* (1928) goes to 84,000 subscribers, and *Coin World* (1960) reaches 108,000. There also is *Coins* (1962), along with *Coinage* (1964) and *Numismatic News* (1952). The rise in gold and silver prices stimulated interest in coin collecting. And the Postal Service encourages individuals to turn to collecting stamps through its advertisements in magazines and on the air.

Crafts is a monthly reaching some 150,000 since 1977. For the trade, the company offers *Profitable Craft Merchandising. Crafts 'N Things* is a bimonthly for 242,000 women who are interested in their homes and apartments and other craft activities.

Playboy Enterprise Inc., in 1977, entered this market with *Games,* which now reaches 600,000. It is a bimonthly for men and women who want a challenge from games, such as chess, backgammon, and bridge, as well as original games introduced in this publication.

Millions of Americans turn to the crossword puzzles in their daily newspapers. For these and others who want more challenges there is the Charlton Crossword Group, with five publications designed for the easy to medium-talented wordsmith.

Ceramic Arts & Crafts (1955) is a monthly for hobbyists in ceramics, while *Fine Woodworking* (1975) is for the serious woodworker, whether a beginner or an expert. The rockhound has *Lapidary Journal* (1947), a monthly for 65,000. The outdoor gems' hobbyist finds this of interest as to those who use rocks in making jewelry items.

In recent years the miniature craze has hit the nation. Now there is *Miniature Collector,* with a circulation of 68,000 for those who collect miniatures on a $1/12$ scale, such as the contents of dollhouses. The magazine focuses on contemporary collecting and the craft activities involved.

Fish fans, too, have their publications, such as the *Tropical Fish Hobbyist* (1952) for those 41,000 who have recreational, educational, or commercial interest in this breed.

Railroad fans have been around for decades, including those interested in the "real thing" as well as those interested in models. *Model Railroader* (1934) has a circulation of 185,000 for beginners through the more advanced fans, with features on all gauges and scales. *Passenger Train Journal* (1968) is a monthly for 10,000 individuals interested in American and European train developments. It also tells about rail industry management. *Railfan & Railroad* is a pioneer, dating to 1906. This bimonthly now reaches 95,000. *Trains* (1940) is a monthly for laymen, management, employees, customers, and owners. Among its 72,000 readers are those concerned with the "function and lore of the industry."

Flying fans also have their interests appeased through *Model Airplane News* (1929) for 82,000 hobbyists and *Flying Models* (1927) for 33,000 enthusiasts.

Dogs and Cats

Owning a dog, cat or some other animal can become a full-time avocation. This becomes evident to those who study the nation's magazines and to all who shop in supermarkets where they observe the space given to foods and gadgets for animals.

Some magazines are for pets in general, although the majority are directed to specific breeds. Some publishers try to reach a broad market, such as *Cat Fancy* (1966) and *Dog Fancy* (1969). These two, with circulations of 78,000 and 64,000, are for professional breeders, show exhibitors, and general pet owners. They discuss proper grooming, exotic and domestic breeds, new products, and other developments.

Since 1916 *Dog World* has appeared monthly, now reaching 55,000. For more specialized dog owners there is *Hounds and Hunting* (1903), which goes to 14,000 beagle owners and beagle field trial enthusiasts. And the National Shoot-to-Retrieve Field Trial Organization, Inc., publishes *Hunting Dog* (1966) for its members. The American Kennel Club publishes the monthly *Pure-Bred Dogs American Kennel Gazette* (1970), for 30,000 members. On the other side, *Popular Dogs* (1970), a bimonthly for 103,000 has a more general appeal with its how-to articles, historical features, and dog news.

Cats has been on the market since 1945 and with a circulation of 64,000 today related to the "influence of the cat in our culture." Stories tell about breeding, selling, and exhibiting, along with other articles on the care and health of cats.

Of more general interest is *Pet News* (1975), a bimonthly with many articles written by veterinarians, and *Today's Animal Health* (1970) for owners who seek more data about nutrition, behavior, training, health and other guidelines for animals.

Military and Naval

Three of the best known military publications are the *Air Force Times* (1947), *Army Times* (1951), and *Navy Times* (1951). The publishers believe the military market includes 11 million people. These weekly publications comprise the Army Times Military Group. They are directed to military personnel and their families with data about pay, promotions, legislation, along with other useful information.

There also are camp newspapers handled on a national basis by several groups. The Base Paper Company, for example, has more than 1,752,000 copies going weekly to bases around the country. Each base paper is localized with movie news, family reports, sports, and the like. Military Media Inc. newspapers distributes some 1,770,000 weekly and the four publications of the Military Newspapers of Virginia began in 1980 in a similar operation.

There are specialized periodicals in this category, such as *Eagle & Swan* (1977) designed for Black men and women in the armed forces. Its circulation has reached 100,000. For the military wives, both stateside and in Europe and the Pacific, there is *Family* (1973) which is published ten times a year. More than 300,000 receive this magazine.

Also for military wives is *Ladycom* (1969) with its 400,000 circulation. It is designed to view the perspective of the military wife, with traditional subjects to meet her needs. These topics include health, beauty, careers, marriage, childbearing, food and entertaining, and creative homemaking.

The Fleet Reserve Association has its *Naval Affairs* (1923) for 148,000 subscribers while the Retired Officers Association's *Retired Officer* (1945) is sent to 283,000 military personnel. For the career enlisted men and women in the Air Force, both active and reserve, there is the monthly *Sergeants* (1962) with 130,000 subscribers.

Book Digest

An overnight success has since fallen upon leaner times. That tells the basic story of *Book Digest,* started in 1974. It reached a million circulation within four years. Then it was sold for $10 million to Dow Jones & Co., with Reader's Digest Association later acquiring a minority interest.

In 1978, however, the publishers slashed its circulation to 400,000 by upping subscription rates and seeking high demographic groups. The monthly publishes six to eight excerpts from best-selling books in each issue. Editorial changes in 1981 included features about earlier best sellers, such as Pearl Buck's *The Good Earth* of the 1930s. In recent years its losses have been in the millions.

Rod Serling's Newcomer

Television fans will no doubt welcome another new magazine, *Rod Serling's The Twilight Zone Magazine.* This monthly fiction publication began in

1981. In addition to original stories, it will discuss movies and new books, provide interviews with leading writers and directors, and no doubt will tell more about some of the original Serling mysteries.

These two chapters have been designed to present a broad picture of the magazine markets. They have not been intended to present the *full* picture. This would be impossible, since one could do nothing other than list the magazines in the nation and this would require a full book.

One must remember that whatever his interests might be he is assured some publication is available to satisfy his desires. If there isn't, then he and another "fan" no doubt will establish one.

Such a study also indicates that one medium may inspire activities in another medium. No single medium can operate in a vacuum. For example, millions of Americans watch the soap operas daily so we now find on the newsstands such publications as the *Soap Opera Digest,* with its appeal to some of the 35 million women said to watch such shows.

21

Major Magazine Publishers

IN TODAY'S MEDIA WORLD there are some fears voiced about the concentration of ownership within the hands of a few large conglomerates. This is especially true with newspapers. Today a handful of owners control a large portion of the dailies. At the start of the 80s there were nearly 1,780 dailies, with more than 1,100 of these under group ownership, a trend that continues.

Advertising Age statistics in late 1980 indicated there were 12 media conglomerates, with major holdings based on ad-related revenues. This represents a mixed bag, since some firms dominate the newspaper field, others the electronic media, while some lead in magazines or cable subscribers. This study by B. G. Vovovich listed these leaders:

(See chart on next page)

In the magazine world there doesn't appear to be any chance that one publisher could become the "press lord" of the industry, as the Curtis Publishing Company was at the start of the century through its ownership of the nation's leaders: *Saturday Evening Post, Ladies' Home Journal,* and *Country Gentleman.*

Today's market is too large, too fragmented and specialized and entirely too complex to permit any one firm to capture control. Some firms are well recognized by millions of readers, such as Time Inc., with its widely-distributed popular magazines. On the other hand there are many firms that are not known to their readers. And some companies are better known for other interests than for the periodicals they own, such as the American Broadcasting Company. And in the world of conglomerates today it becomes increasingly difficult to learn who owns what.

Media leaders tend to agree with the reasoning behind the increased growth of conglomerates. They have the financial backing necessary to absorb the tre-

Top 12 Media Conglomerates (by revenues)

Company	Dailies	Maga-zines	Tv	Am	Fm	Cable Sub-scribers	Other	Ad-related Revenues in Millions
ABC Inc.	—	125	5	6	7	—	207 tv affiliates, 1,729 radio affiliates	$1,984
CBS Inc.	—	10	5	7	7	—	Formed cable division, 200 tv affiliates, 387 radio affiliates	$1,981
RCA Corp.	—	—	5	4	4	—	213 tv affiliates, 292 radio affiliates	$1,377
Newhouse Newspapers	29	17	—	2	3	320,000	—	$1,200†
Gannett Co.	81	12	7	6	7	—	22 nondaily papers	$1,049
Hearst Corp.	13	20	4*	4	3	—	Formed cable division for programing and networks	$1,000†
Times Mirror Co.	7	8	7	—	—	550,000	16 foreign publications, 7 licensed foreign publications	$980
Time Inc.	1	7	1	—	—	1,200,000	HBO-5,000,000 subscribers, 30 nondailies	$979
Tribune Co.	8	3	3	4	2	37,000	Shopper and nondaily circulation over 750,000	$964
Knight-Ridder Newspapers	34	—	5*	—	—	—	12 nondailies	$943
New York Times Co.	10	5	3	1	1	55,000	6 weeklies	$601
Washington Post	3	2	4	—	—	—	—	$593

*One station still subject to FCC approval
†Privately held corporation—AD AGE estimate
(From B. G. Vovovich, "Big, Sprawling and Powerful," *Advertising Age* (October 27, 1980) S-26.

mendous initial start-up costs and the losses that often follow. They have the know-how in personnel, distribution methods, research and promotional techniques. With their funds they are able to support new developments, including the millions of dollars required for the world of computers and other electronic hardware. They also can battle the continual fight that involves higher costs for postage, paper, and personnel.

While the total number of newspapers remains static, such a situation is not characteristic of the magazine world. We already have noticed that from

200 to 500 new magazines are founded each year in America. While the majority fail to enjoy much longevity, a sufficient number do survive so that the magazine population increases annually. Advertising and circulation revenues likewise increase, aided in part by inflation.

There is another side of the picture, as indicated by Joel Davis, president and publisher, Davis Publications, Inc.

> Although it is certainly true that there is a greater concentration of magazine properties within the framework of a few major companies, the fact remains that there are over 2,000 individual titles, with huge numbers coming on the scene each and every year. The growth of regional and sectional magazines, not to mention city magazines, has revolutionized much of the publishing industry by allowing relatively less experienced firms to become involved in publishing within a designated geographical area. In my opinion, the major publishing houses would not be interested in considering such an acquisition, for it would not blend in particularly well with most major houses. What I do believe is happening is that a highly concentrated area of Special Interest titles covering one specific field will eventually result in fewer titles actually being produced, the publishing answer to the law of the jungle which pervades our industry as it does many others.[1]

Concentration in the magazine industry is displayed in part by the *Folio 400* study. In the Standard Rate and Data Service consumer, farm and business periodicals listings there are nearly 300 group publishers listed. The term "multiple publisher" is also used here along with "group" to indicate those that issue two or more separate and distinct publications with frequencies of more than semiannual. SRDS, however, concerns itself with only those periodicals that carry advertisements.

Under the *Folio 400* study, the six publications of Time Inc. represent annual advertising-circulation revenues of more than $850 million, led by *Time* and followed in order by *Sports Illustrated, People, Fortune, Life,* and *Money.*

Triangle Publications, Inc., may not be a familiar name to the average American, yet the annual advertising-circulation revenues from *TV Guide* and *Seventeen* total more than $600 million.

Another large publisher, Hearst, receives more than $340 million annually from *Good Housekeeping, Cosmopolitan, Popular Mechanics, House Beautiful, Harper's Bazaar, Science Digest, Sports Afield* and *Town & Country.* Condé Nast, with revenues approaching $200 million, is another leader with *Glamour, Vogue, House & Garden, Mademoiselle, Self,* and *Bride's* contributing to the income.

When broken down into circulation and advertising units, these companies would still be among the leaders. However, Reader's Digest Association would join the group, based on the circulation of its monthly. With its newcomer, *Families,* which appeared as a monthly in 1981, the Reader's Digest organization becomes one of the major groups. The National Geographic Society, with its famed monthly and its youth-directed *World,* forms another major group.

The following major groups are reviewed, although details about their individual periodicals appear under more appropriate chapters. No attempt is made, obviously, to cover *all* groups. The best, most up-to-date source for this information remains the listing in the appropriate Standard Rate & Data Service publications.

Time Inc.

Time Inc. remains in the public mind as a magazine publishing company, although it is heavily involved in other media. It is, as the firm admits, "by virtually any measure, the largest magazine publishing company in the world." Year after year, the magazine division accounts for the largest revenue-producing portion within Time Inc. For example:

Year	Total Revenue	Magazine Unit
1975	$ 910,700,000	$317,700,000
1976	1,038,200,000	366,300,000
1977	1,249,800,000	459,900,000
1978	1,697,600,000	571,800,000
1979	2,504,100,000	680,000,000
1980		[2]

The corporation's magazines are constantly in the limelight. For example, *Time* led all magazines in worldwide advertising revenues of $296,000,000 in 1979, and continued this trend into the 1980s. (Its debate with *TV Guide* for this leadership involves the counting of revenues only for the American edition of *Time,* not the worldwide totals.) *Life,* in its first full-time year since its revival in late 1978, reached the million-circulation mark. *Fortune* celebrated its 50th anniversary with increases in advertising and circulation for 1979, while *Sports Illustrated,* in its 25th year, ran its largest ad insert, a 64-page section on Lake Placid. *Money*'s advertising and circulation incomes also were up. *People* moved into fourth position among all magazines in ad pages and 10th in advertising revenues, while maintaining its circulation above two million.

Time Inc. also operates a consumer sales organization, Corporate Circulation. Time Distribution Services became a new subsidiary to supervise the firm's periodicals. A worldwide staff of 1,800 works in the Subscription Service Division. The Corporate Manufacturing and Distribution unit handles all the paper, printing, and distribution for the company's 800 million magazines delivered each year.

The Editorial Services Division includes the reference library, with the world's largest and most completely indexed private collection of pictures. In addition, it handles the electronic data retrieval operations and other services.

Time Inc. has a goal of a 50–50 ratio between advertising and circulation revenues for its magazines. By 1974 this had reached about 35 per cent circulation to 65 per cent advertising, and had climbed to 40–60 in 1979. The figure inches upward each year to the ultimate goal.

The corporation acquired the Book-of-the-Month Club in 1977 for a reported $65,000,000. The *Gallagher Report* noted advantages for both sides:

> Time acquires steady, profitable business to counter magazine advertising cycles. Able to expand subsidiary Little, Brown & Co.'s presence in general interest field (vs. text book). BOMC's direct mail marketing capability to facilitate Little, Brown's acquisition of book titles. BOMC gains Time's management expertise over the long haul.[3]

Time Inc. obviously plans to remain in first place.

Since all of its publications have been started within the organization, one can expect future magazines to start under the organization's supervision.

ABC One Of The Largest

Few television viewers of the ABC network shows are aware that the same corporation also is one of the nation's largest magazine publishers. ABC Publishing covers an area as broad as the network's shows.[4]

In 1979, for example, ABC Publishing acquired three other companies: Chilton, R. L. White, and part of the McCall Pattern operations. The largest is Chilton, which has four major areas:

Automotive/Transportation: *Commercial Car Journal, Distribution World-wide, The Fleet Specialist, Motor/Age, Owner Operator,* and *Truck and Off Highway Industries.*

Industrial Magazines: *Automotive Industries, Automotive Industries International, Food Engineering, Food Engineering International, Iron Age,* and *Iron Age Metalworking International.*

Merchandising: *Accent, Automotive Marketing, Hardware Age, Jewelers' Circular-Keystone,* and *Review of Optometry.*

Technical/Design: *Electronic Component News, Instrument & Apparatus News, Instruments & Control Systems,* and *Product Design & Development.*

Many how-to-do-it fanatics, as well as professional mechanics, are aware of the Chilton Auto Repair Manuals and other such guides to technical services.

Another unit of ABC Publishing is the Farm Progress Publications, including *Indiana Prairie Farmer, Prairie Farmer, Wallaces Farmer,* and *Wisconsin Agriculturist.* These all have regional appeal. Also associated with this group is the Wallace-Homestead Book Company, with its volumes and guides on antiques and collectibles.

And then there is the Hitchcock Publishing unit, that includes *Assembly Engineering, Industrial Finishing, Infosystems, Machine and Tool Blue Book, Office Products, Woodworking & Furniture Digest,* and *Quality.* This unit, bought in 1978, also operates marketing and research services.

The ABC Leisure magazines include *High Fidelity/Musical America, McCall's Needlework & Crafts Publications, Modern Photography,* and *Schwann Record & Tape Guides.*

The Miller Publishing unit involves another operations of ABC Publishing, with such specialized periodicals as *Dairy Herd Management, Farm Store Merchandising, Feedlot Management, Feedstuffs, Garden Supply Retailer, Hog Farm Management,* and *Tack 'n Togs.* This group also sponsors numerous agricultural trade shows while directing agricultural marketing and research services.

In addition to these magazines, ABC Publishing involves many other facets of communication, such as Chilton's Ad Chart, Book Publishing, International Services, Management Information Services, Datalog, Marketing and Opinion Research Services, and the Naughton-Studios-Graphics Services.

California-based NILS Publishing involves a specialized legal service, with emphasis on insurance law, environmental protection law, and hotel/motel law.

In 1979 the broadcasting firm bought the R. L. White Company, with its *Homes* magazines that are distributed monthly in 125 cities. Associated with this operation is the Multiple Listing Service Publications. Under Words, Inc., ABC has divisions concerned with books, direct marketing services, educational products, music, and records. This unit is located in Waco, Texas, and has more than 60 recording artists and 300 writers, including Billy Graham, Roy Rogers, Tom Landry, and others. Debby Boone, B. J. Thomas, and others are among the singers.

McCall's Needlework & Crafts is a quarterly with 1.5 million circulation. Another well-known acquisition is *Los Angeles,* city magazine bought in 1977. *Los Angeles* is a national leader in number of advertising pages.

ABC can justify its claim as "a diversified communications and entertainment company."

McGraw-Hill

Early in 1981, McGraw-Hill had 31 magazines, 29 newsletters, ten newswires and services, seven joint-venture magazines, and nine other media services.

Centered in its gleaming tower on the Avenue of the Americas in New York, McGraw-Hill's periodicals "report and interpret new developments in business, government, science and technology, with emphasis on 'actionable information' that subscribers can utilize immediately." Two-thirds of the McGraw-Hill magazines are No. 1 in their specialized fields.

In the late 1970s the firm fended off an attempt by American Express to gain control. McGraw-Hill, established more than 70 years ago, is divided into four major categories:

1. Advertising and Marketing Information
2. Industry Data
3. Product Data
4. Services.

President Paul McPherson has said that the firm was "only interested in properties in the embryonic or growth stages." This accounts for the acquisition in recent years of such periodicals as *onComputing* and *BYTE*. It also expressed an interest in more consumer periodicals. McPherson added that the firm's base of operations will continue in the magazine format, but McGraw-Hill will continue to push ahead to increase its nonpublishing activities, such as conferences and seminars. He worries about paper and postal problems, as most publishers do.[5]

Muse was planned in 1979 but after one test issue, the magazine was scrapped because of economic factors, such as the high circulation development costs. At the same time, *Museums New York* was launched.

McGraw-Hill operates a Research Laboratory of Advertising Performance for other magazines. These publications all provide data about their ad sell, ad call, ad performance, and ad feedback.

The firm has published an informative "Guidelines for Equal Treatment of the Sexes in McGraw-Hill Book Company publications." Words, phrases and constructions that may imply a sexist bias have been listed, together with suggestions on how they may be avoided. Calling for the recruitment of more women as authors and contributors, the booklet also calls for the avoidance of job stereotypes.

> For example, this statement was rated *NO:* "Henry Harris is a shrewd lawyer and his wife Ann is a striking brunette."
>
> Rather, this statement was rated *YES:* "The Harrises are an attractive couple. Henry is a handsome blond and Ann is a striking brunette." *OR* "The Harrises are highly respected in their fields. Ann is an accomplished musician and Henry is a shrewd lawyer."
>
> Such a term as "mankind" is replaced with "humanity, human beings, human race, or people." "Man-made" is better described as "artificial; synthetic manufactured; constructed; of human origin." "Salesman" becomes "sales representative; salesperson; sales clerk." "Foreman" becomes "supervisor."

The McGraw-Hill publications include the following:

American Machinist, Architectural Record, Aviation Week & Space Technology, Business Week, BYTE, Chemical Engineering, Chemical Week, Coal Age, Data Communications, Electrical Construction & Maintenance, Electrical Wholesaling, Electrical World, Electronics, Engineering and Mining Journal, Engineering News-Record, Fleet Owner, Fleet Owner/Small Fleet Edition, Graduating Engineering, Housing, Industry Mart, International Management, Medical World News, Modern Plastics, Modern Plastics International, onComputing, The Physician & Sportsmedicine, Postgraduate Medicine, Power, Textile Products & Processes, Textile World, and *33 Metal Producing.*

The joint-venture magazines include *American Industrial Report,* a Chinese-language trade journal; *World Medicine;* and the following in the Japanese language: *Nikkei Architecture, Nikkei Business, Nikkei Electronics, Nikkei Mechanical,* and *Nikkei Medical.*

McGraw-Hill also has many books, directories, buyers' guides, economic studies, rental lists, marketing information reports, research studies, audio-visual programs and seminars, as well as the newsletters noted earlier.

Harcourt Brace Jovanovich

Describing itself as "a world of business publications, professional journals, newsletters, and services that influence virtually every industry and profession," Harcourt Brace Jovanovich Publications is one of the nation's largest groups.

Although it may be better known to the American public as a publisher of books, HBJ has a number of magazines in these classifications:

Health care: *Geriatrics, Hearing Instruments, Hospital Formulary, Modern Medicine, Modern Medicine Practice Guide, Neurology,* and *Physician's Management.*

Energy: *Brown's Directory of North American and International Gas Companies, Energy News, Energy Week, LP-Gas, Petroleum Engineer International, Pipeline & Gas Journal, Practical Guide to LP-Gas Utilization,* and *SGA Directory.*

Merchandising: *Body Fashions/Intimate Apparel* (and its directory), *Body Fashions/Intimate Apparel Market Maker, Flooring, Flooring Contractor's Digest, Flooring Market Shopper, Gourmet Today, Home & Auto, Home & Auto APAA Show Dailes, Home & Auto Buyer's Guide, Hosiery and Underwear, Housewares, Housewares Show Stoppers, Pets/Supplies/Marketing, Pets/Supplies/Marketing Retail Pet Supply Manual, Rent All, Rent All Management, Rent All Show Dailies, RTW* (Ready to Wear), *Selling Christmas Decorations, TH&C* (Toys, Hobbies & Crafts), *TH&C Directory, Toy Trade News,* and *Hobby Show News.*

Foodservice and Processing: *Fast Service, Fast Service Action Cards, Food Management, Kitchen Planning, Quick Frozen Foods, Quick Frozen Foods Directory of Frozen Food Processors.*

Communications and Electronics: *Communications News, Electronic Technician/Dealer, Electronic Technician/Dealer's Modern Serviceshop Management, Telephone Engineer & Management, Telephone Engineer & Management Directory, Telephone Engineer & Management Fast Action Postcards.*

Dental: *Dental Industry News, Dental Laboratory Review, Dental Laboratory Review Buyer's Guide, Dental Management,* and *Dental Survey.*

Manufacturing, Distributing, and Service: *Cosmetic Capers, Drug & Cosmetic Industry, Drug & Cosmetic Catalog, Hotel & Motel Management, Hotel & Motel Management Buyer's Guide, Hotel & Motel Management Quick Order Product Directory, Paper Sales, Paper Sales Convention News, Paper Year Book, Professional Remodeling, Roofing/Siding/Insulation Incorporating Solar Contractor, Snack Food, Snack Food Blue Book,* and *Tobacco Reporter.*

In addition to these magazines, HBJ also publishes newsletters such as *Aviation Monthly* and *Real Estate Investing.* It also operates printing and phototypesetting plants as well as its bookstores and the History Book Club.

HBJ also owns the Harvest Publishing Company of Cleveland, which publishes *Pennsylvania Farmer, Kansas Farmer, Missouri Ruralist, Ohio Farmer,* and *Michigan Farmer.* Its Nebraska Farmer Company publishes *Nebraska Farmer* and *Colorado Rancher and Farmer.*

The firm also has its University and Scholarly Publishing Group; School Education Group; Magazines, Trade Books, and Broadcasting Group; Periodicals and Insurance Group, and Popular Enterprises Group.

Hearst

The name Hearst long has been associated with the newspaper industry, an area in which William Randolph Hearst dominated as a press lord. The present organization, however, is a leader in the magazine field, along with expansion and development in broadcasting, real estate, mining, livestock, and paper mills. It operates one of the leading newspaper syndicates, King Features, and it continues to look ahead for acquisition in the magazine world.

Today some 50 million readers look at Hearst magazines each month. In the general area, the firm publishes *Cosmopolitan,* with its specials; *Good Housekeeping,* with its Beauty Book, Needlecraft, and Country Living; *Harper's Bazaar; Popular Mechanics; House Beautiful,* with many specials; *Science Digest; Sports Afield;* and *Town and Country,* one of the nation's oldest. There also are the *American Druggist, Motor,* and *Motor Boating & Sailing,* with a number of specials for these.

According to the *Folio 400* study in late 1980, these general publications accounted for more than $335 million in revenue.

In addition there is the Hearst Business Publishing Group, that acquired the United Technical Publications. The periodicals include *Electronic Engineers Master, Electronic Products, IC Master, IC Update, Industrial Products Master Catalog; United Pricing Reports, United Cost Service, Office Products News, Office World News, Corporate Systems, Lens, Lens on Campus, Industrial Machinery News, Floor Covering Weekly, Noticias De Maquinarias Industriales, Black Book* publications, plus Retirement Advisor newsletters and publications.

Hearst also acquired the National Drug Data Center and plans to become involved in electronic database publishing. Frank Herrera, director of distribution for Hearst magazines, offers some unique concepts for improving the distribution system. He feels the industry is "25 years behind other industries in the way we merchandise books and magazines. Procter & Gamble, the automotive industry, the electronics industry are much more sophisticated in what they do than we do." In mid-1980 he began to explore the possibility of combining coupons with subscriptions. A subscriber would receive a book of 12 or 24 coupons and they would be redeemed at a newsstand. This would save costs in mailing, would permit the subscribers to get his magazines quicker, and would eliminate a complaint voiced by many when they see copies on the newsstands before their copies arrive at home.

Hearst, obviously, is in the market to stay. Possibly it will become as well known here as it was under its founder's control many decades ago. In late 1979, a Hearst executive told of plans for new publications. However, K. R. Brink said the company would "see if we can develop a product that someone would buy. Advertising will follow."[6]

Cahners

Cahners Publishing Company, with headquarters in Boston, also has a tremendous operation, including nearly 30 periodicals. In trade messages, Cahners claims its magazines are the "best-read in their fields. Year after year, they cover more subjects more extensively than their competitors, and win more awards for editorial excellence."

The publications include:

Appliance Manufacturer, Brick & Clay Record, Building Design & Construction, Building Supply News, Ceramic Data Book, Ceramic Industry, Construction Equipment, Construction Equipment Maintenance, Design News, EDN, Electro-Optical Systems Design, Electronic Business, Electronic Packaging & Production, Foodservice Distribution Sales, Foodservice Equipment Specialist, Institutions, Mini-Micro Systems, Modern Materials Handling, Modern Railroads, Package Engineering, Plastics World, Professional Builders/Apartment Business, Purchasing Magazine, Security World, Security Distributing & Marketing, Semiconductor International, Service World International, Specifying Engineering, Traffic Management, and *U. S. Industrial Directory.*

Curtis

Benjamin Franklin, Norman Rockwell, and the *Saturday Evening Post* are related American institutions. Although the *SEP* claims family ties to Franklin (a claim long since proved wrong by journalism historians), the magazine does have an extended history, dating to 1821. Its claim to No. 1 in America came under the ownership of Cyrus H. K. Curtis, who bought the publication in 1897.

Rockwell, who called himself the illustrator, prepared more than 300 *SEP* covers. Collections of these remain bestsellers today. The magazine, however, failed to keep up with changes in American life and became so involved in personnel disputes and reorganizations that it died in 1969. It had tried to survive by selling the plant and equipment and other publications in the Curtis family. In 1968 it also cut its circulation base from a high of 6.8 million to 3 million in an attempt to lure more advertisers.

Although it did disappear temporarily from the newsstands, in the eyes of the American public the *SEP* survived. In 1970, Beurt SerVaas bought the controlling interest from the Curtis estate and a rebuilding campaign was under way. In 1977, the new firm, no longer in Philadelphia but now in Indianapolis, published what it called the 250th birthday edition. It was a sellout.

SerVaas, and his wife, Dr. Cory SerVaas who is the president and chief executive officer, now publish *SEP* along with another Curtis revival, the *Country Gentleman*. The firm has three trade magazines: *Trap and Field, Indiana Business and Industry,* and *Plywood & Panel*. *Jack and Jill* is published under a licensing agreement with the Benjamin Franklin Literary and Medical Society.

Curtis also operates a book division, with such volumes as the *Saturday Evening Post Better Health Cookbook*.

Charter

Charter Publishing Company has several, well-known periodicals, including *Ladies' Home Journal, Redbook, Redbook's Young Mother,* and *Sport*. The firm experienced financial trouble in 1980 and placed *Sport* on the market. CBS almost bought the magazine until a last-moment "No" from higher management halted the sale. It was estimated that *Sport* had been losing three to four million dollars a year.

Redbook supposedly was losing in 1980–81. In mid-1980, the firm closed its 10-year-old *Ladies' Home Journal Needle & Craft* bi-annual and its recently established *Holly Hobbie Home Times*. The company is heavily involved in other media, including newspapers, radio stations, fulfillment, and the like.

Crain

Crain Communications, Inc., is best known for its *Advertising Age,* the leader in this field. It also has an European edition. In addition, Crain has *Business Insurance, Industrial Marketing, Industrial Marketing Media/Market Action Cards, Modern Healthcare, Modern Healthcare Product Action Cards,* and *Pensions & Investments*.

In recent years, Crain has established *Chicago Business* and *Cleveland Business,* along with the *Collector-Investor*. The last was started in 1980 for a launch audience of 20,000 of the most powerful investors in the world.

In Detroit the firm's automotive group publishes *Automotive News* and *Rubber & Plastic News*. Under another division, American Trade Magazines, Inc., Crain publishes *American Drycleaner, American Laundry Digest, American Clean Car, American Coin-Op, Product Information for Car & Truck Wash Operators,* and *Product Information for Drycleaners & Laundries*.

Crain has been moving ahead in the book publication field, although 85 to 90 per cent of the firm's revenues still come from magazines. The firm had home study courses and is looking ahead to newsletters and directories.

Fairchild

A division of Capital Cities Communications Co., the Fairchild operations include a number of newspapers along with some magazines. For example, *Women's Wear Daily* is nationally known. Some of the others have more limited and concentrated audiences.

The variety of the firm's magazines is indicated by the 13 different categories under which they are listed in SRDA. The magazines include *American Metal Market, Clinical Psychiatry News, Daily News Record, Electronic News, Energy User News, Entree, Family Practice News, Footwear News, Heat Treating, HFD Retailing Home Furnishings, Home Fashions Textiles, Internal Medicine News & Cardiology News, Men's Wear, Metal Center News, Metal Center News Metal Distribution, Metal Statistics, Metalworking News, MIS Week, Ob Gyn News, Pediatric News, Skin & Allergy News, SportStyle, Supermarket News,* and *Women's Wear Daily.*

Dow Jones

Dow Jones & Company, Inc., is best known for its "averages" and its nationally-distributed newspaper, the *Wall Street Journal.* It does, however, publish *Book Digest,* which it bought in 1978 for $10 million. It cut the base from one million to 400,000, and, after losing more than $2 million in 1979, predicted a profit by 1983. The *Digest* was acquired for its potential, according to Dow Jones. The company has been considering the establishment of a magazine of the quasi-consumer type.

Macfadden

The word *True* entered the magazine world in 1919 when Bernarr Macfadden established *True Story,* the first of its kind and the first of many to follow with *True* somewhere in the title.

Since that time, the so-called confession magazines have been selling sex, sin, and suffering. This is part of a title of a book recalling these publications, written by Florence Moriarty of the Macfadden Women's Group. It is called *True Confessions,* published in 1979.

Today the three periodicals under the Macfadden label include the still popular *True Story, True Confessions,* and *Photoplay.*

Geyer-McAllister

Ten periodicals are issued regularly by Geyer-McAllister Publications Inc. These include *Administrative Management, Administrative Management "Tools of The Office" Product Action Cards, Geyer's Dealer Topics, Geyer's Who Makes It Directory, Gift and Decorative Accessories, Gift and Decorative Accessory Buyers Directory, Playthings, Playthings Directory, Shipping Digest,* and *Word Processing Systems.*

Gralla

One of the leaders in the business press field is Gralla Publications, a successful brother act involving Lawrence and Milton Gralla. They once credited their success to unremitting hard work and a top management team plus:

> It's due primarily to the heavy and constant emphasis on the journalistic and editorial aspect of the business.

> We just don't publish and send a magazine; we become part of the in-
> dustry the magazine serves.[7]

Today they publish *Bank Systems & Equipment, Bank Systems & Equip-
ment Direct Reply Cards, Catalog Showroom Business, Contract, Contract Di-
rect Reply Cards, Giftware Business, Health Care Product News, Kitchen
Business, Meeting News, Merchandising, Multi-Housing News, Multi-Housing
News Action Reply Cards, National Jeweler, National Jeweler Annual Fashion
Guide, Premium/Incentive Business, Professional Furniture Merchant,* and
Sporting News Business.

In 1951 the brothers formed the National Trade News Service Corporation
to provide on-the-spot coverage of the trade magazines. Assignments were handled in the major American cities. The company continues to search for acquisitions, although most of their current publications were started by Gralla.

Meredith

Meredith Corporation has come a long way since its start in 1902 with
Successful Farming. Today, it is better known for *Better Homes and Gardens.*
It also publishes *Metropolitan Condo,* formerly called *Apartment Life.* Through
these three periodicals Meredith reaches into millions of homes.

The firm also publishes many specials and books under the BH&G label.
In addition, it has *Sail, Sailboat & Equipment Directory,* and *You.* And, of
course, its famous *Cook Book.*

Now in its modernized printing plant in Des Moines, and its plant shared
with Meredith/Burda in Virginia, the firm continues to print many magazines
for other publishers. For example, in Des Moines the plant takes 500 tons of
paper through the presses and turns out a million magazines each day.

All processes are used by Meredith—letterpress, offset-lithography, and
rotogravure.

The firm has many other interests, such as list marketing, mail order book
sales, book syndication, premium and specialty book sales, and Meredith newspapers under the publishing group. Other groups involve the printing operations
and broadcasting projects.

Penton/IPC

In 1976 Penton and IPC (Industrial Publishing Company) merged with
headquarters in Cleveland, where the two firms were founded and had engaged
in head-on competition. Today the firm also has a New York office and publishes nearly 30 periodicals. Calling itself "One great communications company," Penton/IPC now issues the following:

*Air Transport World, Airconditioning & Refrigeration Business, Chemical
Engineering Catalog, Energy Management, Foundry Management & Technology, Government Product News, Handling & Shipping Management, Heat-
ing/Piping/Air Conditioning, Hydraulics & Pneumatics, Industry Week, Lodg-*

ing Hospitality, Machine Design, Management Leisure Time, Material Handling Engineering, Materials Engineering, Modern Office Procedures, New Equipment Digest, Occupational Hazards, Power Transmission Design, Precision Metal, Production Engineering, Progressive Architecture, Restaurant Hospitality, School Product News, Used Equipment Directory, Welding Design & Fabrication, The Welding Distributor.

Petersen

Hot Rod, introduced by Robert E. Petersen in 1958 with a press run of 5,000, set the foundation for the west coast Petersen Publishing Co. Its appeal has been to the automotive and youth markets, as these publications indicate:

Motor Trend, Car Craft, Teens, Guns & Ammo, Skin Diver, Photographic, Motorcyclist, Hunting, 4-Wheel & Off-Road, and *Vans and Pickups.* In addition, there are the *Lakeland Boating, Pacific Skipper, Rudder,* and *Sea & Pacific Skipper.* Most of these were started by Petersen, although a few such as *Teen* and *Skin Diver,* were bought from other publishers.

Each motor magazine is aimed at a "homogenous automotive audience of its own." The action group audience has been estimated at 25 million monthly, with 70 per cent in the 18 to 24 age group. This includes all of these except *Teen* and *Vans & Pickups.*

Times-Mirror

Another group better recognized for its newspapers than for its magazines is the Times Mirror Company. Its newspapers include the *Los Angeles Times, Newsday, Dallas Times Herald, Hartford Courant, Advocate* and *Greenwich Time* in Connecticut, and the *Orange Coast Daily Pilot* in California.

In the magazine field, the Times Mirror firm publishes *Golf, Outdoor Life, Popular Science,* and *Ski. Outdoor Life* has expanded its regional operation to include *Fishing The South, Fishing The Midwest* and *Hunting The Midwest.* The firm also owns the *Sporting News* and the *Sporting Goods Dealer,* together with guides and record books for the fans.

The Times Mirror operations are approaching the two-billion-dollar mark, although magazines contribute only a fraction of the total.

Watt

Another interesting firm is the Watt Publishing Co. of Mount Morris, Ill. Established by J. W. Watt, a Scotsman who came here as a lad with nothing except ambition and talent, the firm dates from the *Poultry Tribune,* established in 1885. The firm continues to concentrate in this area, with these magazines:

American Dairy Review, Farm Supplies, Feed Management, Industria Avicola, Petfood Industry, Pig International, Poultry International, Turkey World, and *Who's Who in the Egg and Poultry Industries* with its international editions as well. Orvel H. Cockrel, vice-president and publisher, feels "almost anyone can still launch a publication, if they have an idea and the courage to do so. The investment requirements are very minimal."

Webb

Webb, a company nearly a century old, is heavily involved in many publications, both as a publisher and as a printer. In 1979, with total revenues more than $110 million, Webb received some $75 million from printing, with $35 million from its publishing and creative services.

The Webb Company long has been active in printing custom-designed magazines, such as *Sun Scene* (Sun Oil), *Living Trends* (Foremost Insurance), *Amoco Agronomics* and *Farming with Amoco* (Standard Oil of Indiana), *Mobil Farm Future* (Mobil Oil), *Cat's Pride* (Arctic Enterprises), *Easy Living* (Creative Marketing Enterprises), *Dollars Plus* (Financial Institution Services), *Better Farming Systems* (White Farm Equipment Co.), *Worksaver* (Clark Equipment Co.) and *Crops Quarterly* (PAG Division of Cargill Inc.).[8]

These have been termed "eternal house organs" and some 3,000 are listed in *Gebbie's Directory of Publications*. In a manual developed after nearly 20 years in this facet of publishing, Webb noted "that a properly designed and executed magazine makes a far deeper and longer impression on prospective customers than any advertisement can hope to do, and is infinitely more flexible."

Today the company publishes *Consumer Life, Family Handyman, Family Food Garden,* the *Farmer, Farm Industry News/Midwest, Farm Industry News/South, Farm Industry News/West, Irrigation Age, KOA Handbook and Directory for Campers, National Hog Farmer, Northwest Passages, Snow Goer, Snow Goer Trade, Snow Week,* and *TWA Ambassador.* There also are the *Pork Producer Buying Guide, Beef,* as well as *Beef Buyer's Guide.*

Ziff-Davis

One of the nation's largest producers of consumer, business and trade publications is the Ziff-Davis Publishing Co. Seven of its major periodicals reach more than ten million men each month. These include *Boating, Car and Driver, Cycle, Flying, Popular Photography, Skiing,* and *Stereo Review.*

The firm also has *Backpacker, Fly Fisherman, Modern Bride, Popular Electronics, Psychology Today, Sport Diver,* and *Yachting.*

Travel, transportation and leisure-time activities are reported through *Meetings & Conventions, Travel Weekly, Hotel & Travel Index, Official Hotel & Resort Guide, Official Meeting Facilities Guide, World Travel Directory, Aviation Daily,* and the *World Aviation Directory.* In addition, there are *Business & Commercial Aviation, Photomethods, Skiing Trade News, Travel Market Yearbook,* and *Adventure Travel.*

Some of these tend to overlap in part. *Skiing,* for example, appeals to consumers while *Skiing Trade News* has a more limited audience.

For more than two decades Ziff-Davis has engaged in research, making pioneer studies of the travel agency market, amateur photographic products and services, bridal market spending, and other areas. In 1981 it bought *Uniques* and renamed it *Unique Homes* to advertise properties for sale in the million-dollar price range.

New York Times

Like the Times Mirror operations, the New York Times Company is best known for its famous daily newspaper. However, the firm does publish *Family Circle,* one of the nation's Top Ten in circulation, along with *Golf Digest* and *Tennis.* For a few years it also published the mass-circulated *Us,* a magazine that just never did fit properly into the Times' family.

And Still More

Some of the major groups are discussed in earlier chapters, such as the American Medical Association and various farm publications. However, there are some rather specialized group publishers, such as the Army Times Publishing Co. with *Air Force Times, Army Times, Federal Times, Navy Times,* and *The Times Magazine.*

The American Chemical Society has a number of journals. Among its 18 periodicals is *SciQuest. Billboard* is the major magazine of Billboard Publications, Inc., which also publishes *Amusement Business, Aud/Arena Stadium Guide and International Directory, Interiors, Managing The Leisure Facility, Photo Weekly Buyers Handbook & Product Guide,* and *Tradeshow/Convention Guide.*

Bill Communications, Inc., has 17 magazines involved with marketing, distribution, restaurant business, sales and related areas. Business Journals, Inc., has periodicals concerned with diesel, gas, handbags and accessories, and luggage and leather goods as well as four under its *Modern Brewery* title.

Ellery Queen periodicals are among those published by Davis Publications, Inc. In addition, Davis issues *Budget Electronics, Camping Journal, C B Yearbook, Communications World, Electronics Hobbyist, Electronics Theory Handbook, Elementary Electronics, Hi-Fi Stereo Buyers' Guide, Income Opportunities, Issac Asimov's Science Fiction, Kitchen and Bath Improvements, 99 I C Projects. 101 Electronic Projects, 101 Home Plans, Science & Mechanics,* and *Today's Homes—Plans & Ideas.*

In Atlanta, Communication Channels, Inc., has magazines from *Adhesives Age* to *Trusts and Estates.* Also among their 26 periodicals are those concerning paint, real estate, shopping centers, solid waste management, and opportunities for salesmen.

Gordon Publications, Inc., is involved in 23 periodicals concerned with architectual news, chemical and computer topics, metalworking and mining as well as solar heating.

Johnson Publishing Co., Inc., is the leading firm in the Black magazine market. Its No. 1 magazine is *Ebony,* followed by *Jet* and *Ebony Jr.*

American Printer and Lithographer is a product of Maclean-Hunter Publishing Corporation, along with others concerned with boxboard containers, coal mining, concrete and rock products, paper, film and foil converters.

Magazines for Industry, Inc., publications specialize in the beverage, candy, dairy, food and drug areas. Others concern the glass industry and paperboard packaging. In addition, this firm also has catalogs and directories.

Keller Publishing Corporation has a number of foreign-language periodicals in addition to *Beverage World*.

Medical Economics Company has its leader in the magazine that provides the firm's name. In addition, it has a dozen publications in the medical field, such as *Diagnostic Medicine, Nursing Opportunities,* and others.

San Francisco-based Miller Freeman Publications has more than 20 magazines about medicine, energy, forest, pulp and paper, coal, wood, and mining. Several have Latin American counterparts.

Concentrated basically in medicine is the C. V. Mosby Company in St. Louis. Its 16 magazines vary from *American Heart Journal* to *Surgery*.

North American Publishing is more concerned with import/export news, schools, marketing bestsellers, and other topics related to printing, along with *Zip*.

Parents magazine is the major output for Parents Magazine Enterprises, Inc. The Company also has *Baby Care, Expecting,* and *Young Miss*.

Scholastic Magazines are well known to millions of American students through these publications: *Forecast For Home Economics, Scholastic Coach, Scholastic Magazine Group* for various ages, *Scholastic Newstime* and *Scholastic Wheels*.

Periodicals related to photography constitute the major output of the PTN Publishing Corporation. They include such as *Studio Photography* and *Technical Photography*.

Reed Holdings, Inc., has nearly 50 highly specialized magazines, along with directories and other reference aids. From Boston, Reed's magazines vary from *Appliance Manufacturer* to *U. S. Industrial Directory*. Others are concerned with building designs, electronic business, modern railroads, packaging, and traffic management.

Charles B. Slack, Inc., is a leading medical publisher, with 12 magazines such as the *American Journal of Medical Sciences,* and others for nursing education and orthopedics. Slack started *Orthopedics Today,* a bimonthly tabloid, in 1981.

United Business Publications, Inc., is a subsidiary of Media Horizons, Inc. The first has 13 periodicals, varying from *Audio-Visual Communications* to *Videography*.

Technical Publishing Company in Illinois has a varied assortment of special interest magazines among its nearly 50 periodicals. Some are directed to engineers in many areas, while others are concerned with medical topics. In addition, there is the *Graphic Arts Monthly* as well as others related to mining, including several editions in Chinese.

Vance Publishing Corporation divides its publications into these divisions: professional salon, wood, home center, food and agricultural; and the paper industry. The firm now has sixteen trade publications, including the *Pork Producers Reference,* a 1981 periodical to appear six times a year in magazine format for 55,000 readers. The firm also has the *Drovers Journal,* which began in 1873.

Williams & Wilkins Company publishes 21 magazines with medical interests, such as the *American Journal of Physical Medicine* and *Urological Survey.*

Lebhar-Friedman, Inc.

Lebhar-Friedman, Inc., has published trade advertisements in recent years calling attention to its role as "The voice of retailing." These have had effective headlines, such as:

"Let's go down to the store and steal a couple of sweaters."

"The cost to feed the average American family this week was $465.14."

"Welcome to the future."

These, and similar messages, are designed to acquaint the medical world with Lebhar-Friedman periodicals, such as:

Drug Store News, which has existed since 1928; *Chain Store Age Supermarkets,* termed the newsmagazine for corporate chains, co-ops and voluntaries; *Chain Store Age,* for general merchandise group; *Chain Store Age Executive,* for the busy officials; *Discount Store News; Nation's Restaurant News;* and *National Home Center News.*

In addition, the firm publishes the *Chain Store Age* in the Far East to serve Japan, Korea, and Taiwan. It also operated the *Denver Magazine.* In addition, it operates research programs, publishes books and business guides for retailers, and a newsletter, *Inside Retailing.*

In a study of magazine group ownership, two journalism professors concluded that "Despite the polemics over newspaper and broadcast ownership trends, parallel ownership patterns in the magazine industry have caused little concern." Professors Edward J. Smith and Gilbert L. Fowler, Jr., noted that, "The history of the medium is replete with examples of group, cross-media and conglomerate ownership patterns."[9]

This study was based on the best sources available for magazine research, the Standard Rate and Data Service's General Consumer and Farm and Business Publication dates and data directories, along with the Ayer's Directory.

The theme voiced in this article, and in this chapter, is that there appears no threat to the magazine world of any upcoming takeover by some "press lord."[10]

22

Research:
A Way to Success

SINCE 1911, when the first marketing research was established by the Curtis Publishing Company, magazines have turned more and more to their potential audiences for guidelines. They have probed and probed their customers until they know all about them—their age, income, education, likes, dislikes, where they live, what they buy, and on and on.

Charles C. Parlin headed the Curtis division that set out to learn more about the agricultural implement industry. Curtis had recently purchased *Country Gentleman* and the staffers were rather ignorant of the agricultural business.[1]

Parlin's study resulted in a 460-page report. But more significantly, it started him on other more intensive studies, including surveys of department stores, the automobile business, and other industries, as he sought out data concerning buying and reading habits of Americans. Editorial contents were surveyed and readership of the advertisements was probed. As Theodore Peterson noted, "Research became a weapon not only in the battles that magazines waged among themselves, but also in their warfare with rival media." Earlier research had been conducted as far back as 1879 when N. W. Ayer & Son tested advertisements in selected local publications.

During these early years there were skeptics, much as there are in the 80s. Research results can be conflicting and, at times, misleading. Obviously, each magazine seeks to present itself in the best light. During the 1970s some magazines objected so strenuously to some results that new surveys were conducted. Usually these resulted in a much brighter picture for the magazines concerned. And even with more refined techniques and the assistance of computers, magazine research remains one of the most discussed topics in the publishing world.

Magazine Age, in its first issue in 1980 noted, "The Research Battle Rages On." The magazine noted a year later, in January, 1981, that certainly the battle continues to rage on and on. "What else can one say when one service has a magazine's readership zigging as the other has it zagging? Magazine Research Inc. report for fall 1980 has *Newsweek*'s readership rising 2.2 per cent from the fall of 1979 as Simmons Market Research Bureau has it dropping 4.3 per cent in the same period. There is also a difference of over seven million readers between the two . . . and *Newsweek*'s total circulation is under three million."[2]

Media Decisions raised similar questions to those cited by *Magazine Age,* asking: "Can you count on the numbers?" The editors observed that "Sense will emerge from the ratings war only when media planners and buyers refuse to buy the inflated and exaggerated importance of one analytical tool—however critical. The numbers have indeed been oversold, overused, and overrated."[3]

One media director repeated what must have been voiced earlier in the 1920s and 1930s saying, "I don't believe them. I don't trust them." Yet this research is the best available today, fortunately or unfortunately.

Some Basic Guidelines

David P. Forsyth, McGraw-Hill Publications Company vice-president for research, noted in early 1981:

> Magazines thrive when they bend and adapt to the needs and desires of their fickle audiences. Change is the lifeblood of magazines. Yet research, the one tool that can gauge the change and provide early warnings, is too often shunted aside. In fact, magazine research has probably been the most maligned and neglected of the basic tools available to people in the magazine business.[4]

If objectively conducted, Forsyth believes "there is no substitute for magazine research." Yet it must be valid and reliable. He suggested five types of magazine research:

1. *Research available to an editor.* This includes the reader profile with detailed description of the typical subscriber or reader: age, education, marital status, size of family, etc.
2. *Research on magazine audience.* This is counterpoint to the first point, viewing the situation from the standpoint of the advertiser. Product/service concepts and who makes the decisions on purchases. Considerable qualitative data available.
3. *Research on advertising/marketing.* It has been predicted that more than 440 studies will be made in 1981 on more than 1,800 separate issues to learn more about recall of advertisements. Pretesting and post-testing will be studied.
4. *Circulation research.* This will include much from the previous categories, plus data on why readers don't renew, plus other behavior studies on why individuals buy single copies, etc.

5. *New publication feasibility research.* Major target markets are studied, questionnaires prepared, and prototype copies sent to selected audience segments with follow-up interviews.

Forsyth has developed more data concerning each of these types, raising questions researchers must answer. The complexity of the situation is shown by his chart on the general kinds of magazine research.

War: Time Inc. vs. Simmons

One of the major disputes concerning research results occurred in early 1975, when Time Inc. filed a suit against W. R. Simmons & Associates Research, claiming the publisher shouldn't be required to pay a bill for $188,346

Women reader-per-copy estimates for seven womens service magazines in through-the-book studies: 1954-1980

Researchers	Year	BHG	Fam. Circ.	Good House.	LHJ	McCalls	Red Book	Wom. Day
Politz	1954	2.3	—	2.3	1.9	1.9	—	—
Politz	1954/55	2.3	—	—	—	—	—	—
Politz	1958	2.4	—	2.1	1.9	1.8	—	—
Nielsen	1960	2.2	—	2.1	1.9	1.8	—	—
Nielsen	1961	2.2	1.5	2.2	1.9	1.8	—	1.5
Nielsen	1962	2.1	1.6	2.2	1.9	1.9	—	1.6
Politz	1962	—	—	—	—	1.9	—	—
Simmons	1962	2.1	—	2.2	1.9	1.7	—	1.5
Politz	1963	—	—	—	—	2.1	—	—
Simmons	1963/64	2.1	1.5	2.2	2.0	1.7	—	1.5
Nielsen	1963	2.5	2.1	3.0	2.3	2.1	2.0	2.0
Politz	1964	2.3	1.7	2.4	1.9	2.2	2.2	1.6
Simmons	1964	2.1	1.5	2.4	1.9	1.7	2.0	1.6
Simmons	1965	1.9	1.4	2.2	1.9	1.7	1.7	1.5
Simmons	1966	2.1	1.6	2.4	1.9	1.8	1.9	1.6
Politz	1966	2.3	2.1	2.5	2.0	2.1	2.2	2.0
Simmons	1967	2.1	1.7	2.4	2.0	1.9	1.9	1.7
Simmons	1968	2.1	1.7	2.4	2.0	1.9	1.9	1.8
Simmons	1969	2.1	1.7	2.4	2.0	1.9	1.9	1.8
Simmons	1970	2.1	1.7	2.4	2.0	2.0	1.9	1.8
Simmons	1971	2.1	1.8	2.3	2.1	2.0	1.9	1.8
Simmons	1972	2.1	1.8	2.4	2.1	2.0	1.9	1.8
Simmons	1973	2.1	1.8	2.4	2.1	2.1	2.0	1.8
Autits & Sur.	1974	2.7	2.7	—	—	—	—	3.0
Simmons	1974/75	2.3	2.2	3.4	2.3	2.4	2.2	2.3
Simmons	1976	2.3	2.2	3.4	2.5	2.6	2.2	2.3
Simmons	1976/77	2.3	2.3	3.3	2.3	2.6	2.4	2.2
Simmons	1977/78	2.1	2.2	3.0	2.2	2.5	2.0	2.2
Simmons	1978/79	2.1	2.2	3.4	2.2	2.6	2.4	2.3
Simmons	1979	2.1	2.3	3.3	2.3	2.3	2.3	2.3
Simmons	1980	2.1	2.3	3.3	2.2	2.3	2.3	2.2

(From Ed Papazian, "Mediology," *Marketing & Media Decisions,* (December 1980), 80, 82, 86.)

Simmons Primary vs. Passalong Readership Study
Selected data for 15 magazines

7 Women's Magazines (adult females only)	Total Audience % Primary	% Pass-along	Passalong Audience Place of Reading Own Home	Other Home	Work	Other*	Av. % of Test Issue Pages Opened Primary Readers	Pass. Readers
BH&G	44	56	40	20	13	27	81	73
Family Circle	50	50	43	34	11	12	83	73
Good Housekeeping	32	68	32	25	14	29	87	74
Ladies' Home Journal	47	53	32	21	13	34	83	71
McCall's	42	58	35	20	14	31	83	71
Redbook	49	51	32	16	12	40	84	71
Woman's Day	51	49	47	20	12	21	80	70
8 Men's & General Magazines (adult males only)								
Nat'l Geographic	54	46	24	25	13	38	81	73
Newsweek	28	72	16	12	31	41	75	68
Playboy	51	49	14	27	37	22	87	75
Reader's Digest	74	26	46	19	12	23	76	71
Sports Illustrated	25	75	14	21	21	44	76	66
Time	35	65	19	16	26	39	79	71
TV Guide	80	20	36	44	8	12	69	66
USN&WR	31	69	10	9	26	55	82	71

*Library, school, doctor's office, etc.
Advertising Age (April 5, 1976)

for a Simmons 1974 study that indicated the magazine's readership had declined by 13 per cent. The *Wall Street Journal* headlined the conflict: "Magazine Industry Is Jolted by Lawsuits Challenging Audience-Survey Concerns."[5]

Arguing that the report contained "biased and unreliable statistics," Time Inc. said if the 1973–74 figures were correct then it should not have to have paid the $1.4 million it had during earlier years. Later *Esquire* joined in the suit against Simmons, claiming a million dollars for damages over the "intentional" exclusion of that magazine from Simmons' field work in 1975, despite the fact it had been in all previous studies since 1962. *Esquire* earlier had complained about the 1974 study that had shown its audience to have declined by 46 per cent.

Simmons was challenged by another magazine, *Girl Talk*, that asked $1.2 million for the amount it said it had lost in advertising since the 1974 report showed its readership to be down.

Wall Street Journal writer Stephen Grover correctly concluded:

There is no sign that this preoccupation (with total audience) is abating or will be abating in the near future. There is also no sign that the controversy over the surveys will go away, whatever the lawsuits decide. But Robert J. Coen, a vice president and director of media analysis at McCann Erickson Co., the big advertising agency, says he's convinced the controversy is "all to the good." He explains: "The studies are already reliable, but there will be some changes made, and they'll be all to the better."

General Kinds of Magazine Research

Research on Advertising/Marketing

Advertising Readership
Special Issue Readership
Advertising Recall
Advertising Page Exposure
Advertising Effectiveness
    Pretesting
    Coupon and Bingo
Response
    Action Taken Follow-up
    Campaign Tracking
    Post-Testing
Advertising's Reach
Brand Acceptance & Preference
Zip Code Marketing

Circulation Research

Pinpoint Potential Subscriber
Functions in Plants
Non-Renewal Evaluation
Non-Payment Studies
Delivery Date and Condition of Issues
Single Copy Purchase Behavior Studies
Subscription Mailing Tests
Testing of Subscription Price
    on Subscription Sales
Influence of Magazine Price
    on Single-Copy Sales
Influence of Magazine Cover
    on Single-Copy Sales

Research Available to an editor

Profile or Reader Definition
Interest in Subject Areas
Reader Needs
Editorial Traffic
Publication Acceptance
Publication Involvement
Publication Positioning
Non-Reader

Research on Magazine Audience

Subscriber or Recipient Profile
Reader Quality
Product/Service Use; Purchase Decision
Syndicated Total Audience
Primary Audience
Primary/Secondary Readers
Diary Audience
Apperception/Media Image/Media Comparability
Intermedia Involvement
Audience Accumulation
Issue Life

New Publication Feasibility Research

Publication Concept
    Potential Readers
    Potential Advertisers
Prototype Acceptance
    Potential Readers
    Potential Advertisers
Quantitative Acceptance

From David P. Forsyth, "A basic guide to magazine research," *Folio* (February 1981) 46. Forsyth explains each category in this informative article, written by an expert in research.

These parties became involved in a no-win situation. If Time Inc. had won its suit, it would have been placed in the awkward position of having used inaccurate figures in selling millions of dollars worth of advertising in previous years. Many interpreted Time Inc.'s actions as being self-serving, feeling the magazine would have been content with the methodology had the results been more favorable. No doubt many publishers who suffered decreased audiences agreed with Time Inc.; others, with improved reports, disagreed.

Simmons replied with a $10 million damage suit against Time Inc., claiming libel and conspiracy to put it out of business. Simmons claimed the suit came after the researcher had refused to adjust the data. The two parties were also at odds over reports on other Time Inc. publications, *People* and *Money,* in addition to *Time.*[6]

These lawsuits were soon dropped in a Time Inc.-Simmons settlement. Meanwhile, Simmons' future contracts were changed to bar investigation by any magazine of the "field aspects" of such studies. Three years later Frank Stanton, then president of the Simmons organization, blamed publishers for the "magazine research crisis."

Time, however, still considered the 1974 readership studies "invalid" and proceeded to authorize another study, this by Audits & Surveys, Inc., to be "an exhaustive, technically complex custom study." The project was estimated to have cost $500,000 and involved nearly 5,700 person-interviews, well below the 15,000 Simmons used. *Time* explained in detail the methodology of this through-the-book study, even offering to reveal the names of respondents, interviewers, and field supervisors. *Time* used full-page advertisements in trade media to announce the results.

Time believed its study overcame some of its objections to the disputed Simmons study. The public's reactions were mixed. Some industry leaders feared it might backfire, since *Newsweek* still remained a more economical publication for advertisers on the basis of circulation and per-page ad costs. The Audits & Surveys study showed *Time* with a total audience of 22,652,000, compared with *Newsweek*'s 17,952,000. In the Simmons 1975 study, *Time* had 19,488,000 and *Newsweek* 19,013,000, although *Newsweek*'s circulation was more than a million and a half under *Time*'s.[7]

Only ten publications were used in the Audits & Surveys study, including another Time Inc. product, *Sports Illustrated,* which also gained readership over the Simmons report. The only magazine that dropped in its readership was *Newsweek.*

Should anyone believe that the conclusion of this Simmons-Time dispute had ended the controversy he had only to read the reactions to the next Simmons report. Issued in 1976, it showed a narrower gap between *Time* and *Newsweek* audiences, along with other "wide swings" when compared with the previous study. That project gave some emphasis as well to the pass-along audience. And it also asked individuals where they read magazines, at home or in "others' " homes? Adjustments also were necessary in this report, but the reactions did not involve lawsuits as before.

Meanwhile, Stanton had organized an Audit Board to supervise an independent review of the procedures used by researchers. It included publisher, agency and advertiser representatives.

The traditional disputes continued when *Advertising Age* headlined the report that appeared in late 1979:

"Controversial SMRB report boosts readership."[8]

This study was the first to combine the methodologies that had been debated for years. More than half showed readership gains despite the dip in circulation at that time. *People* magazine scored highest in readers per copy.

Merger of Simmons, Axiom

Some peace came to the research world in mid-1978 when W. R. Simmons & Associates and Axiom Market Research Bureau merged into the Simmons Market Research Bureau (SMRB). Simmons had organized his operations in 1951 but had left in 1973, claiming the "data was unreliable." Axiom had started in 1972 but had failed to make a profit with its Target Group Index, which serviced magazines, agencies, advertisers, and the major networks.

Frank Stanton became the president of SMRB, promising more attention to smaller magazines. After this merger Stanton was termed the "new research monopolist" in a *Folio* article. "His company is the most important monopoly serving major magazines," according to *Folio*.[9] Some of SMRB's operations, such as through-the-book recognition, would be limited to the larger magazines. TGI had pioneered in its "recent reading" technique. Concerning the merger, Magazine Publishers Association president George Allen said, "We're pleased with the apparent resolution of the divergency of the ratings and reporting, and trust that the execution of the merger will result in eliminating many of the characteristics with which the industry was too unhappy." Unfortunately, his hopes were not fully realized.[10]

In late 1979 the confusion continued. "Agencies tussle with research data," headlined *Advertising Age,* while *Folio* headlined its story: "SMRB report sparks anger, confusion; hope lies in ARF study." Some concerned parties objected to SMRB's techniques, especially the recent-reading concept. The debate was summarized in *Advertising Age:*

> The uproar developed because the through-the-book and recent-reading modes produced widely varying and possibly uncomparable results; because SMRB, in the view of some execs, arbitrarily realigned its recent-reading numbers to compensate for a 90% overstatement (and also bucked critics by beginning field work on the 1980 study using the controversial methodologies), and, lastly, because MRI's numbers were so much larger than the ad community's expectations as to be rendered suspect.[11]

Both *Advertising Age* and *Folio* noted that industry officials were placing some hope on the American Research Foundation's comparability study, expected in early 1980.

The American Association of Advertising Agencies also protested the 1978 report. It called for a 50-50 mix—half of the sample in each group of magazines should be measured through-the-book and the other half measured by recent-reading. Then these figures should be correlated. In the 1978 report, readership gains were posted, which for the time being buoyed the industry and temporarily calmed the opposition.[12]

Similar reactions developed when the 1980 audience study by SMRB was announced. The researchers compiled figures on through-the-book research for 44 major magazines and recent-reading figures for another 100 periodicals. Researchers tend to agree that the better of the two methods is the through-the-book process, yet this requires considerable time. And certainly it would be impossible when 144 magazines are involved in an interview.[13]

Research Role of MPA

The Magazine Publishers Association series of Newsletters of Research started in early 1973, "devoted mainly to bringing increased, usable interpretation and perspective to research which has application to or affects the role of advertising in the marketing process." Each issue presents a major theme, with the initial copy concerned with the "Working Women—A Marketing Target." Two years later another issue was devoted to "Working Women—New Insights on Communications."

In early 1976 MPA's Media Imperatives, a concept presented by Frank Stanton the previous fall, was explained through numerous statistical tables designed to impress potential advertisers about the role of magazines in America. In this study, individuals were divided into (1) heavy magazine and light television (Magazine Imperatives), (2) heavy television and light magazine (Television Imperatives), (3) heavy magazine and heavy television (dual) and (4) light magazine and light television (neither). This theme continues to be the focal point for many MPA advertisements promoting the industry in trade journals.

In mid-1977, the research newsletter forecast many media changes for the 80s. A later newsletter was devoted to the place of children, age 12 through 17, in the marketplace. The research concluded that "You cannot reach it (this youth market) efficiently with television." A newsletter in May, 1979, explained how the increase in magazine advertising affected advertisers:

> As advertising has increased, editorial articles and features have increased, so that edit-to-ad ratios have been only slightly reduced. The resulting larger magazine continues to hold the interest of readers and maintains high communication levels because magazine advertising is not confined to a 30-second time frame.

In late 1980 the newsletter observed that it had taken 234 years (to 1975) for magazines to achieve an annual advertising revenue volume of $1.3 billion. During the next four years, this doubled to $2.7 billion. The statistics also noted that since 1975 magazine circulation has expanded at twice the rate of the population growth in America.

Not everyone agrees that Media Imperatives is the best route for the industry to follow. Gabe Samuels, media research official with the J. Walter Thompson firm, is one who objects, noting that "Instead of concentrating their efforts in showing *the uniqueness of magazines* as a channel of communication, they (publishers) attempt to show how much the same they are compared to television. In other words, by suggesting that we concentrate on the fact that magazines deliver a 'quality' *audience,* they seem to tell us that the quality of *delivery* is of no importance." [14]

Other Research Organizations

In mid-1980, *Advertising Age* published its fifth annual compilation of the nation's leading marketing/advertising research firms. The total volume of the 23 firms represented reached $719 million, with A. C. Nielsen Company accounting for $302 million of this total. More than $205 million of the $719 million represented revenues from business outside the United States.

Some of these businesses are only indirectly concerned with the magazine industry, although data that involves advertisers and/or merchandising methods will be of value to some publications.

The top 23, as listed in *Advertising Age,* include the following, with their founding dates:

1. A. C. Nielsen Company (1923)
2. IMS International (1954)
3. SAME (Selling Areas-Marketing Inc.) (1966)
4. The Arbitron Co. (1949)
5. Burke International Research Corp. (1947)
6. Market Facts Inc. (1946)
7. Westat Inc. (1963)
8. Audits & Surveys (1952)
9. Marketing & Research Counselors (1965)
10. ASI Market Research (1962)
11. Chilton Research (1957)
12. Yankelovich, Skelly & White (1958)
13. Ehrhart-Babic Associates (1958)
14. National Family Opinion (1946)
15. NPD Research Inc. (1967)
16. Data Development Corp. (1960)
17. Louis Harris & Associates (1956)
18. National Analysts (1943)

19. Opinion Research Corp. (1938)
20. Elrick & Lavidge (1951)
21. Walker Research (1964)
22. Starch INRA Hooper (1923)
23. Decision Center (1965)[15]

Changes and criticism appear to be two major elements in the world of research. *Marketing & Media Decisions* noted in late 1980 that "Everybody seems to be disillusioned about magazine research except the researchers themselves."

Looking ahead, Timothy Joyce, founder of Target Group Index and now with Magazine Research Inc. (MRI), planned two new concepts for his 1981–82 studies. One would be the average page audience, a measure of ad page exposure that readers could recall. Joyce also considered it significant to know who in the household got the magazine and where he or she got it. Joyce thought this would affect the results of the primary or secondary reader's reactions.[16]

Magazine Research Survey

Folio's executive editor Barbara Love has provided an excellent collection of research projects through her thoughtful articles. She reported in early 1981 about a study the magazine commissioned McGraw-Hill Research to complete—a survey of magazines with their plans for the years ahead in research projects.

Nearly 600 publications replied to numerous questions about their types of research, their interpretation of its value, as well as how they would conduct their research and who would be responsible for it.

Among the major conclusions were these, which present a clearer picture of magazine research projected for the 80s:

1. Seventy per cent of the business magazines conduct research. Sixty per cent of the consumer magazines conduct research. These percentages are much higher (98 and 96) for magazines with revenues exceeding $2 million.
2. About 2 per cent of their gross income is spent on research, with the 1980 median $7,700. This was expected to reach $9,300 in 1981. Magazines operating their own research departments spend much more, especially consumer periodicals.
3. About one-third of the respondents have a separately-organized research department, especially the business publications.
4. Market studies have been the most widely used.
5. The second most widely used is the reader profile/demographic survey, especially by consumer magazines.
6. Fifty-four per cent conduct surveys for editorial articles and other features.

Many magazines planned to increase their research projects for 1981 and the years ahead, especially through market studies and reader profile/demographic studies. The great majority, 72 per cent, of the interviews would be conducted by mail.

There are still major problems faced by the magazine industry in conducting research. According to Love these included: Keeping the cost down, not enough time, staff limitations, poor response rate, determining cost effectiveness, getting different departments to use research, interpreting results for best use, credibility in the face of all the research out there, unsophisticated sales staff needs training in using results, getting results back when promised, and results outdated too fast.[17]

Hundreds of magazines will become involved as both *Folio* and *Marketing & Media Decisions* reported. The latter magazine often publishes lists of magazines with their studies planned.

On other occasions the other side, such as the distributors, sponsor research. For example, the International Periodical Distributors Association sponsored a study by Yankelovich, Skelly and White, Inc. to determine marketing strategy for the 80s. Among some of the conclusions published in *Profit Ways* are these:

1. The economy will grow, but modestly.
2. Economic pressures for cost containment will exist throughout the industry.
3. Impulse purchases will undergo increasing scrutiny, because consumers will be caught in the squeeze of a slower real income growth and the drive for a full, rich life and inflation's discouragement of saving, encouragement of borrowing and growing concern over the level of credit obligations.
4. Traditional media roles will blur: TV will move increasingly from entertainment to information programming, magazines will become less discursive and more pictorial.
5. Creative media strategy will rival creative content strategy—quality of audience will become increasingly important.
6. Traditional major sources of advertising revenues will remain strongly oriented to magazines.
7. Subscription cost factors will increasingly push publishers toward single-copy sales.
8. Demographic marketing. This concept is important to the industry, but although there is a lot of talk about it, there isn't much action. It must be developed.[18]

What's Ahead?

Predictions can be amusing, yet worthwhile if based on facts and well conducted research data. One of the better answers to the entire question may have been expressed by Ed Papazia in his Mediology column in *Media Decisions*.

> If we spent more time looking at what we're doing now and how we might get an edge on next year and less time peering into the clouds with dinky little telescopes, sighting castles in the sky, we might chart a more thoughtful course.[19]

Still other industry leaders, thinking of the continual struggle between researchers and publishers throughout the 70s, predict these debates would continue and would "erode the credibility of all media research." Advertising agency executive Bernard Guggenheim wrote:

> We must resolve the issue of what we are measuring when we measure magazine audiences . . . Total audience magazine research will be further complicated by increased use of regionalized covers and editorial material. Personalized magazines are probably not far down the road. Certainly the through-the-book method will have to learn to cope with these developments.[20]

Thus the 80s may not provide any clearer picture of the research confusion, or the conflict between the researcher and the publisher.

This conclusion was confirmed in a *New York Times* article in early 1981 that noted:

> The controversy over magazine-audience research reached new heights yesterday (February 2, 1981) with name calling and innuendo entering into the otherwise scholarly discussion.[21]

The account reported the results of a subcommittee of the Advertising Research Foundation that sought a comparability approach to the two methods of researching magazine audiences: through-the-book and recent-reading.

The committee's goal was to seek some calibrations between Simmons Market Research Bureau's use of through-the-book approach for the weeklies and large-circulation monthlies, and recent-reading for the smaller circulated monthlies. Scores for recent-reading often are from 60 to 100 per cent higher than through-the-book method.

Apparently no valid answer has been found. One speaker found the calibration "dangerous and error-prone," while another asked if the members understood the meaning of the words "objective and independent."

It seems that after several decades someone might come up with a new method to study magazine readership.

Readers/Reading

The Magazine Publishers Association research program reached the following conclusions in late 1980:

> Ninety-four per cent of U.S. adults read magazines during the average month. They each read an average of 11.6 different magazine copies per month.
>
> The average magazine copy earns a total of 10.6 adult reading days—split among 3.8 readers (2.8 reading days each.)
>
> There is only slight variation in magazine reading by seasons—ranging from 2 percent below average in July–September to 2 percent above average in October–November.
>
> Seventy-nine per cent of all magazine reading occurs in the reader's own home.

By day of the week, magazine reading is most prevalent on Monday, Tuesday, Friday and Saturday. Reading peaks at 13 per cent above average on Saturday.

The average U.S. adult reads 1.13 magazines per day. College-educated persons read the most magazines.

About 26 per cent of all magazine reading occurs before lunchtime; 74 per cent of reading occurs sometime after lunch.

An advertiser who runs an ad in twelve issues of the average magazine would achieve a total net reach that is 2.39 times the size of the one-issue audience. And, at the same time would achieve for the larger audience an average frequency that is five times the one-issue level.

The average magazine ad page receives 7.6 adult exposures (3.8 adult readers × 2.0 APX exposures each.)

Magazine readers are motivated to take actions as a result of reading—ranging from 20 per cent who wrote/phoned for more information on advertised product to 62 per cent who discussed a magazine article with someone.

Readers are thoroughly involved with their magazines. They not only read, but reread the magazine copy—three quarters of all readers report that they refer back/reread something, and they usually keep the issue on hand for future reference. Over half of adult readers tried an idea suggested in a magazine article; 62 per cent of women tried a recipe; 64 per cent of women clipped/used a coupon.

Magazine readers are active and involved in public & social life, politics and community. Magazine Imperatives (heavy readers—light viewers) are 79 per cent more likely than TV Imperatives (heavy viewers-light readers) to be involved in such public activities.

Magazine Imperatives are 77 per cent more likely to attend a movie and 76 per cent more likely to attend a sporting event as a spectator.

Magazine Imperatives are also more than twice as likely to take Adult Education Courses. And, Magazine Imperatives are about twice as likely as TV Imperatives to personally participate in sports and hobbies.

Magazine Imperatives are twice as likely to entertain friends and guests at parties in their homes.

23

Production and Distribution Systems

To EARN what they determine to be their rightful or expected share of the market, magazines strive to produce the best possible product at a suitable price and then provide for its distribution under the most effective arrangements.

Publishers share mutual concern over their ever-increasing production costs. They constantly review their printing processes, seeking the one most appropriate for their publications. During the past decade the continuous rise in postal expenses has prompted continuing debates between publishers and the authorities in Washington.

Computers and other electronic machines have opened up new areas that magazines must utilize to maintain their standing or suffer in the race for increased circulation and advertising revenues.

Paper can be a major problem, not only in the steady rise in its costs but on occasions, as in recent years, when shortages developed.

After all of these problems have been brought under control the publisher still does not have any real contact with his audience until the distributors have placed his magazine on the proper shelves in the newsstands across the nation. Or until the mailman, or that new alternative delivery man, has left the magazine at the subscriber's home.

PRODUCTION

With rising production costs assumed for the 80s, publishers must focus their energies on methods to curtail expenses wherever possible. Publishers review their printing processes: Should it be letterpress, offset, or gravure?

317

Two authorities, Irving Herschbein and Bert Paolucci, have summarized these processes in readily understandable terms:

(1) *Letterpress* is printing from a relief, or raised surface, generally from single-page size metal plates called electrotypes. The inked image is transferred directly onto the paper.

(2) *Gravure* uses a sunken or depressed surface for the image. The image areas consist of cells or wells etched into a copper cylinder which rotates in a bath of ink; the excess ink is wiped off the cylinder by a flexible steel blade. The ink remaining in the cells is transferred to the paper.

(3) *Offset lithography* uses the planographic method, in which the image and nonprinting areas are essentially on the same plane of the printing plate. The printing is done from a flat surface and is based on the principle that grease and water don't mix. It is called offset because the ink is first transferred from the plate to a rubber blanket, then from the blanket to paper.[1]

Their generalizations suggest that web offset is appropriate for runs up to 750,000; gravure for runs over three million. Other decisions would depend upon the number of pages involved. "Every printer reading this will have a suggestion for changing the assumption," the men wrote.

During the past decade the offset and gravure processes have gained, while letterpress has lost. For example, in 1970 52 per cent of commercial printing market was web offset; 39 per cent was letterpress, and 9 per cent gravure. By 1980, offset accounted for 63 per cent, letterpress 21 per cent, and gravure 15 per cent. By 1990 it has been predicted that 70 per cent would be offset, 25 per cent gravure, and only 5 per cent letterpress.[2]

Other factors that must be considered are typesetting, cover selections, distribution systems, and related areas involving editorial and management decisions.

Phototypesetting has replaced the long-used hot metal process. According to Professor Michael L. Kleper, in a booklet he wrote for the Compugraphic Corporation,

Phototypesetting is the most used method of setting type. It uses a standard typewriter keyboard. It is relatively simple to learn and to use. It is fast, quiet, and accessible. It is compatible in size, design, and function with office machines. It is available for as little as a few thousand dollars or up to several thousands of dollars. It offers savings in time, materials, labor and money.[3]

Typesetting will become more complex, yet still faster and more comprehensive. In a special report on production in the 80s, Frank Romano, president of Graphic Arts Marketing Associates, told *Folio* readers that all of these changes "happened because increased amounts of machine intelligence were being programmed into devices that reduced the need for human decision-making. Since typographic formatting (hyphenation, justification, page makeup) had become automated, almost any electronic device could be a source of information for typesetting. Thus, information keyed for word or data processing systems could now be used as input for typesetting without the need for re-keying.''[4]

Magazine Formats Standardized

Advance developments appear to be limitless. Lasers now create characters in digital form and transfer the images to paper. They also provide better color separation. Page makeup can also be made fully automated if the information is relatively standardized, according to Romano. Words are processed at a more rapid speed. Prices for necessary machines decline as production increases. Mini-terminals that will merge previously single operations are in use and, as Romano concludes, ''the seeds of the future are always sown in the past. Typesetting is not the end-all and be-all—it is a mirror of technology and our use of it.''

Currently more than a thousand magazines are using in-house typesetting with Compugraphic equipment. Now Compugraphic has more than 25,000 installations in more than 50 countries. There are, of course, other manufacturers in this field that continues to grow, such as Mergenthaler Linotype Co. and Autologic, Inc.

Digital Cathode Ray Tube typesetters have declined rapidly in costs. Some feel these are better than the standard electromechanical typesetters widely used. They can set thousands of lines per minute.[5]

Changes in the size of magazines have occurred during the past decade. Once a novelty because of its size, *Reader's Digest* can expect more digest-size periodicals on the market, in addition to *TV Guide* and *Jet.* The once large-size women's magazines such as *Ladies' Home Journal* and *McCall's,* and others, including *Fortune* and *Esquire,* have cut their size, saving postage, paper, and printing costs. So many periodicals are now sold on the nation's newsstands that this trend to standardization will prove advantageous to all concerned.

In such a competitive market, magazines must develop distinctive logos to lure customers their way. Titles, to be effective, must be clear, sharp, prominent and readily recognizable—such as *Time, Money, Life, Fortune* and *People,* all owned by Time Inc., which has displayed remarkable success in selecting titles. Henry Luce started it with *Time.*

When any typography or layouts of major elements inside the magazine are changed, it should be gradual so it doesn't disturb the regular readers.

Production and distribution personnel likewise are concerned with the cover story and accompanying photographs. Some magazines are sold on their logos alone to their regular purchasers who aren't influenced week by week by changing covers. Other magazines, however, depend heavily on first impressions and on the impulse-buying traits noticed at supermarket checkout counters—publishers need to remember that their covers are the ''point-of-sale'' advertisements, their messages publicizing the products.

Magazines often have ''traditional'' issues, those that sell thousands of extra copies. *Seventeen,* for example, hits a high mark with its fall back-to-school number. *TV Guide* has similar results with its fall preview edition, listing upcoming network television shows. *Fortune's 500* and *Folio's 400* are widely sought after by their followers. In addition, there are anniversary numbers and specials that draw larger numbers of readers to the newsstands. Yet now and then there is a magazine that doesn't resort to such means. The *New Yorker* never lets its readers know what's inside, nor whether it has a special or not. The same anniversary cover appears once a year. Meanwhile, *Reader's Digest* reveals all by placing its table of contents on its cover, with larger type and colors used to emphasize some major articles.[6]

DISTRIBUTION

After the stock market crash of 1929 many retailers faced a struggle to survive, and publishers as well were caught. A story is related that Catherine McNelis, then writing advertising copy for a Wilkes-Barre, Pa., store, had a concept—why not use Woolworth's 1,900 stores to sell magazines? At the start, four magazines were sold through these outlets: *New Detective, Love, Home,* and *New Movie.* The early sales averaged more than 1.2 million monthly. There were financial problems, however, and these didn't last too long; yet for many years the "5 and 10¢ store" was a major supplier of the nation's magazines as millions of customers patronized these stores.[7]

There are few, if any, other products that are distributed so widely, so quickly, and so economically as the magazines that reach some 160,000 outlets throughout the U.S. and Canada. It is a system few laymen understand. Most individuals, however, expect their favorite publications to be on their newsstands regularly regardless of any outside factors.

There are a number of major distributors as well as 500 local wholesalers who share the responsibilities for this process. The International Periodical Distributors Association (IPDA) is a group with a common mission—to expand the outlets handling their magazines and books, thus increasing sales and profits. While the members are often competitive, they also realize the need for such an association. Established in 1972, IPDA has ten members, including: CBS-Fawcett Marketing Services, Curtis Circulation Co., Dell Publishing Co. Inc., Independent News Co. Inc., International Circulation Distributors, Kable News Co. Inc., New American Library, Pocket Books Distribution Corp., Publishers Distribution Corp. and Select Magazines Inc. There are additional distributors, some that handle only one company's products and others that limit their activities. Time Distribution Services Inc. handles Time Inc. periodicals, while Triangle Publications Inc. handles *TV Guide* and *Seventeen.* Flynt Distributing Co. handles *Hustler* and other Flynt products.

IPDA publishes *Profit Ways* magazine for the trade. Profiles of leaders, agencies, and outlets are provided, along with researched articles aimed at helping members. This group pushed for the adoption of the Universal Product

Code to help with inventory and audits of sales, and this 10-digit symbol now appears on 95 per cent of all magazines. By mid-1980 more than 2,650 stores had adopted the checkout scanner system and the number continues to grow. IDPA also conducts feasibility tests to pre-determine sales and assists in audits. It has been involved in obscenity legislation, especially in local cases when various bans threatened magazine sales.

The wholesalers are the vital cog in the magazine industry. It is reported that national distributors earn about 6 per cent of the retail sales price. They handle more than 33,000 titles. Through the distributors and the wholesalers, *TV Guide* is able to move from regional printers to 150,000 markets within 36 hours of completing the press runs.

There are other groups involved in magazine merchandising and distribution. The Council of Periodical Distributors Association, which involves wholesalers, publishes the bimonthly *CPDA News*. There also is the Periodical & Book Association of America (PBAA) which represents publishers of newsstand titles. The Comic Magazine Association of America has its specialized concerns, as does the Magazine and Paperback Marketing Institute. Of area concern is the Pacific Coast Independent Magazine Wholesalers Association.

Each organization has its own goals as does each distributor and wholesaler. Kable News Company, for example, started in 1932 in Mount Morris, Ill. Today it has offices in New York City and in California and has increased its gross billings from the first year's $150,000 to more than $250 million today. Kable maintains a national field force, a marketing department, conducts trade promotions and offers advertising services and client public relations assistance. Since 1959 it has utilized electronic data processing services. Kable also has a sophisticated subscription fulfillment service and a fully computerized phototypesetting division. Other distributors may not have as many operations in this area, but each serves specific needs of the magazine industry.

Retail Display Agreement

Started in the 1950s when a national shift began from individually-operated groceries to chain-operated mass retail outlets, the "retail display agreement" (RDA) entered the magazine industry. RDA has continued to grow.

RDA involves an extra payment to a retail outlet, usually a supermarket, of 10 to 15 per cent above the normal 20 per cent profit on each magazine in return for the merchant's agreement to provide a prime display space. Shoppers are well acquainted with those magazines that surround cash registers, a prime position to take advantage of impulse buyers.

In 1978 it was estimated that publishers spent an extra $78 million for this privilege. In one way or another some 2,000 to 3,000 titles may be involved in the 145,000 to 160,000 retail outlets across the nation. Local distributors usually make such arrangements, but monitoring these displays has been labeled "logistically unfeasible and largely futile."

However, some major publishers employ their own checkers. Curtis Circulation Co., for example, regularly monitors and audits its outlets. Kable News has a computer auditing system, as do some of the distributors.[8]

Some convenience stores accept only magazines that provide this extra RDA money. Since these stores earn a higher profit on their other sales than regular stores, estimated at 28 to 32 per cent, they require an equal return on magazine sales. With RDA money they reach a 30 to 35 per cent level.

Such problems are sure to continue, with more and more periodicals turning to single copy promotions. Not only are the regulars—the weekly and monthly editions—involved but the annuals, semi-annuals and the one-shot periodicals as well. Distributors are concerned, too, about curtailing their returns by obtaining the proper mix in their placement of magazines. Stores that continually return copies often find their supplies limited as soon as computer data becomes available to the local wholesalers.

Another gimmick tested on a limited basis by some magazines is the use of store coupons to cut the individual copy price. Some publishers also test varying prices in selected geographical areas before determining their final price.

Overseas sales are still another outlet for publishers, and these are said to represent more than $50 million annually, with the men's magazines doing well, especially *Playboy* and *Penthouse*.

Supermarket Publications

As noted, the supermarkets are as essential to the magazine industry as the Postal Service, the printers, and the paper makers. Such stores have numerous specialized business publications to choose from. Four seem to stand out, including *Progressive Grocer, Chain Store Age Supermarkets, Supermarket News* and *Supermarket Business*.

Progressive Grocer is the pioneer, dating from 1922. It has become an institution in the retail food business, noted for its research on such topics as "the velocity at which items move off the supermarket shelves, how rack positions and promotions affect sales, and what stores are doing about 'shrink'— that is, spoilage and employe, vendor and customer pilferage—a sum that comes to about 1 per cent of sales, or exactly the same as the grocer's net profit."[9] The magazine's publisher also has a Magazine Resources group that sells subscriptions, and a Trade Access Group that conducts direct mail sampling. *Progressive Grocer* has always been a part of the Butterick Fashion Marketing Co. Its circulation is about 85,000.

Chain Store Age Supermarkets was founded in 1928 and today has a circulation of 102,000 non-paid. *Supermarket Business* (1946) has 92,000 controlled circulation, while *Supermarket News* (1952), the leader among this quartet in total revenues, has 58,000 circulation.

With material from these magazines, retail outlet managers can learn more about improving their sales of periodicals, much to the satisfaction of the magazine industry.

PAPER

Paper requirements are expected to continue their upward climb throughout the 80s. In its study of projected needs, the Magazine Publishers Association reported that the 1979 use of 1,441,387 tons rose to 1,482,691 tons in 1980. The projected increases to 1,586,262 tons in 1981 and 1,645,556 tons in 1982 reflect the faith publishers have for their product. Most of this will be coated paper, but only a fraction will be imported. This MPA study was based on data from 89 publishers and magazines that represent 65 per cent of the nation's paper requirements.[10]

To help meet these demands, United States paper mills will increase their capacity to produce the much-needed coated stock. One surely can anticipate annual price hikes of 10 to 15 per cent, upped in part by increased oil and energy prices as well as delivery expenses. To overcome some of this, the publishers will continue their fight to trim paper waste and obtain tighter control over newsstand distribution, to limit returns.

POSTAL REGULATIONS

Americans are well aware of problems with the Postal Service, with first-class rates touching everyone directly, while higher magazine costs hit everyone indirectly. *U.S. News & World Report* recently claimed that "if present trends continue, the giant U.S. Postal Service could become more than a pygmy by the end of the next decade."[11]

Early in 1980 additional postal regulations went into effect. These required publishers to perform more of the work in mail preparation. More changes are ahead, especially in some form of electronic mail that could affect many types of printed materials.

The Postal Reorganization Act of 1970 started a series of hikes in second class mailing costs, estimated at 413 per cent between 1971 and 1979. Throughout these years magazine publishers continued to object, voicing their opinions that the second class subsidy was part of the public service role expected from the nation's Postal Service. John F. Kennedy once said, "From the beginning of the Republic, our magazines have provided a major forum for carrying on the interior dialog of American society." However, this public service concept was eliminated in the Reorganization Act.

In a major attempt to overcome some of these increases, some magazines turned to alternate delivery systems. In 1968, Thomas W. Murray, founder of the Independent Postal System of America, told a House hearing in Washington:

> Examination of the history of the Post Office Department and of statistics related to the volume of the various classes of mail, in conjunction with a series of interviews with major users of the Post Office, indicated there was a need for an alternate service to the Post Office Department.[12]

By 1973 some magazines had already turned to another service. *Reader's Digest* delivered 5,000 copies monthly in the Los Angeles area through Inland Carriers. This process saved more than a penny a copy, signifying tremendous potential savings for a magazine with the circulation of *Reader's Digest*.

Other magazines also experimented, including *McCall's, Time, Sunset,* and *Better Homes and Gardens. BH&G* estimated a saving of 6.5 cents per copy in its Midwest experiment. In addition, part of this delivery cost was offset by the sale of advertising space in circulars that accompanied the magazines. Book publishers and record companies also have experimented with such a service as has the *Wall Street Journal,* which uses some form of alternate delivery in 90 cities.

The National Association of Selective Distributors reported that 14.5 million pieces were delivered by private companies in 1979. This was figured at 59 million in 1980, and within another three years could reach 750 million copies. More distributors are expected to join in this operation. Some services, however, have stopped, finding it unprofitable on current volume. Obviously, such alternate systems aren't suitable for every magazine.

Needless to say, postal officials are disturbed. Postmaster General William F. Bolger has promised that his service would modernize more and pass the savings along. The basic conflict involves the use of the individual's mailbox. The government says only U.S. mail can be placed there. Thus any alternate delivery service must find other means for leaving magazines at the home. Often they are in plastic bags hung on door knobs.

The future of the nine-digit Zip Code remained in doubt in mid-1981. If placed in operation, magazine publishers have been assured of improved delivery service. Such nine-digit numbers would permit more target marketing, a favorable factor for potential advertisers.[13]

Regardless of current problems, some magazine leaders see more attraction to the alternate delivery system. Newsweek Inc. vice-president David Auchincloss said "the deteriorating Postal Service is making it increasingly difficult for publishers to meet these needs through traditional channels. . . . If the delivery performance of the Postal Service continues to deteriorate, as seems inevitable, magazine publishers—especially those with time-sensitive magazines—will look to alternate distributors as a means of assuring adequate delivery standards."[14] When alternate services are used and magazines are late, publishers know exactly where to place the blame.

Hopefully, from the publisher's point of view, the Postal Service will discontinue its harrassment of private carriers. In 1979, for example, the federal agency refused to permit such deliveries to be dropped in door slots or placed on tables in apartment lobbies. For a time postal officials confiscated and returned these copies to the publisher, long after they had lost their value, resulting in irate subscribers and irate publishers.

24

Advertising and Circulation: Major Income Sources

It is the year 2020 and your grandson's wife or cohabitant has just entered her home information/entertainment room. She slips gracefully into her home information/entertainment chair. She presses the proper three buttons on the arm of the chair. This brings her favorite magazine into focus on her home information/entertainment wall. She examines the cover, presses the change-page-button and peruses the first advertising spread. It's a delicious array of wonderful desserts. She presses her print-out-food-button and a recipe goes directly into her food file, recipe scanner where it is read by her computerized-ingredient mixer. Ingredients slide down to the oven and activate the bake button. Your grandson is lucky to have a wife who cooks so well. She punches her turn-page-button and continues her magazine reading experience, much as she did in 1980.[1]

Those prophets of doom who predict the end of the printed word may find the above account challenging. While the printed word as such may undergo some transition in the decades ahead, the effects of printed words as we know them today will still be around. Whether the women of the future will read from a magazine page placed in her lap or from a gadget attached to her wall makes little difference. She will still be "looking" at words; she will still be depending on those words to improve her lifestyle. No doubt she will have more say-so about how she is going to utilize those words. She may prefer to transfer them from the "wall magazine" to her recipe file, or she may want to transfer the data to some other format to send along to her children.

The Magazine Publishers Association Newsletter also reported about an advertising agency that found that "the fact that people consume the printed word at least twice as fast as they consume the spoken word, absorb 3½ times

as much information from it and remember it longer, would indicate its continuing use by at least some elements of our future society."[2]

Magazines have been described as information machines and television as
entertainment machines. There is no reason at present to see any major shift in
this emphasis in the future.

Another factor that will remain unchanged for many decades is the fact
that much of the expense of bringing these words to millions of Americans will
be provided by advertisers. One study revealed that in 1979 advertising accounted for 55 per cent of the total revenues of magazines, while circulation
accounted for 45 per cent. As noted earlier, some publishers now strive for a
50-50 mix. On the other hand, these same magazines in 1979 contained 48 per
cent advertising and 52 per cent editorial matter.[3]

Advertising Revenues Up

Magazine advertising revenues climbed 10 per cent in 1980 over 1979
figures, slightly below the 10.6 per cent increase that total advertising recorded
for all of the nation's media. The 1980 figure of $3,225,000,000 accounted for
5.97 per cent of the total advertising volume from all sources that year. The
5.97 figure was the same as that for 1979, indicating that magazines retained
their same share of the advertisers' dollars as they had the previous year.

Robert Coen, senior vice-president of McCann-Erickson, long has been
the nation's authority on advertising statistics. His complete figures for 1979
indicated $49 billion was spent on advertising and $54.7 billion was spent in
1980. These totals include money placed in newspapers, magazines, farm publications, television, radio, direct mail, business publications, outdoor, and
miscellaneous.

Of interest to magazine leaders is the addition of $1.6 billion spent in
publications in the special business area in 1980 and the $135 million spent on
farm publications. Added to general magazines, these figures reveal that nearly
10 cents of every dollar spent on advertising in 1980 went to magazines.[4]

Advertising's role in the business world has been summarized by the Cahners Publishing Company in one of its many research reports:

> Advertising is the final link in the marketing chain supporting increased
> return on investment. Advertising of the proper frequency and quality, con-
> centrated to give maximum exposure to primary prospects (specialized busi-
> ness magazine advertising), dramatically increases brand preference. The re-
> sults are seen in increased sales dollars per call. Share of market improves
> and return on investment moves right up with it.[5]

It is easy to substitute magazine exposures to sales calls, and the share of
the market received from increased use of advertising.

Cahners makes available a number of advertising research reports, with
interest in specialized business magazines. These elements have logical application, however, to other magazines, such as these concepts:

Magazine Advertising Revenues
(In millions of dollars)

Year	Total	Weeklies	Women's	Monthlies
1980	$3,225	$1,440	$795	$990
1979	2,932	1,327	730	875
1978	2,597	1,158	672	767
1977	2,162	903	565	694
1976	1,789	748	457	584
1975	1,465	612	368	485
1974	1,504	630	372	502
1973	1,448	583	362	503
1972	1,440	610	368	462
1971	1,370	626	340	404
1970	1,292	617	301	374

(Source: Statistics prepared for *Advertising Age* by Robert J. Coen, McCann-Erickson. Material above from *Advertising Age* (September 10, 1979)   45; (February 16, 1981)   S-4.)

Magazine Advertising Cost Analysis
(Index 1961—100)

Year	Circulation	Page Cost		Cost Per Page Per Thousand	
		Black & White	Four-Color	Black & White	Four-Color
1961	100	100	100	100	100
1962	103	106	106	103	102
1963	106	109	108	102	102
1964	109	111	112	101	103
1965	113	114	115	100	102
1966	117	118	120	101	103
1967	121	122	124	101	102
1968	124	126	128	102	103
1969	122	129	130	106	106
1970	124	133	134	107	108
1971	123	133	134	108	109
1972	120	130	130	108	108
1973	121	130	130	107	107
1974	123	137	136	111	110
1975	120	145	144	120	120
1976	121	149	148	123	122
1977	120	158	159	132	133
1978	120	174	174	145	146
1979	120	189	188	158	157

(From circulation and rates for the 50 leading magazines in advertising revenue for each year. Newspaper supplements are not included. Prepared by Magazine Publishers Association.)

Magazine Advertising Cost Analysis

Year	Combined Circulation (Thousand)	Combined Page Rate		Cost Per Page Per Thousand	
		Black & White	Four-Color	Black & White	Four-Color
1961	129,624	$521,974	$717,374	$4.03	$5.53
1962	134,020	555,685	758,377	4.15	5.66
1963	137,978	568,610	775,372	4.12	5.62
1964	141,473	578,724	803,539	4.09	5.68
1965	147,080	595,143	826,879	4.05	5.62
1966	151,786	616,084	860,740	4.06	5.67
1967	156,679	635,471	887,383	4.06	5.66
1968	160,576	659,293	917,668	4.11	5.71
1969	158,510	675,018	930,627	4.26	5.87
1970	160,848	695,674	961,293	4.33	5.98
1971	159,131	692,397	958,292	4.35	6.02
1972	155,738	678,665	934,180	4.36	6.00
1973	156,971	679,836	930,286	4.33	5.93
1974	158,978	714,535	976,630	4.49	6.14
1975	155,674	754,298	1,031,318	4.85	6.62
1976	156,816	775,337	1,061,126	4.94	6.77
1977	155,129	824,443	1,142,234	5.32	7.36
1978	154,997	908,735	1,247,793	5.86	8.05
1979	155,177	986,848	1,350,364	6.36	8.70

(Based on the circulation and rates for the 50 leading magazines in advertising revenue for each year. Newspaper supplements are not included. Prepared by Magazine Publishers Association.)

Relationship of Advertising to Editorial Lineage in Magazines

Year	% Advertising	% Editorial	Total
1947	53.1	46.9	100.0
1957	49.6	50.4	100.0
1961	44.6	55.4	100.0
1964	46.4	53.6	100.0
1966	46.6	53.4	100.0
1967	46.7	53.3	100.0
1969	47.3	52.7	100.0
1970	46.0	54.0	100.0
1971	46.8	53.2	100.0
1973	49.3	50.7	100.0
1975	46.5	53.5	100.0
1976	49.3	50.7	100.0
1977	51.1	48.9	100.0
1978	51.8	48.2	100.0
1979	52.4	47.6	100.0

(From Russell Hall Magazine Editorial Reports, released by Magazine Publishers Association.)

"Have something to say. Say it briefly and to the point."

"After the advertising objective is set, try to achieve that objective with the *headline* alone. For many readers the headline is the only line read."

"Individuals with *specialized job functions* have very *special interests,* which is why they are reading *specialized* business magazines."

Cahner's other studies reveal time spent in reading specialized business magazines, the maximum reach publications have, the comparison between specialized business magazines, and the "others," such as *Business Week, Time, Newsweek,* and *Fortune.*

Magazine Advertising Pages
General Magazine

Year	Pages	No. of Magazines
1950	68,320.97	84
1951	72,230.00	83
1952	74,666.50	84
1953	77,053.22	86
1954	75,887.74	93
1955	76,427.76	81
1956	83,342.83	88
1957	80,485.00	83
1958	69,131.37	81
1959	73,954.75	79
1960	74,860.61	79
1961	68,203.14	80
1962	69,062.69	79
1963	71,995.39	81
1964	75,931.76	85
1965	80,147.22	86
1966	84,654.64	91
1967	83,482.63	93
1968	81,265.41	92
1969	81,378.67	90
1970	76,923.54	89
1971	77,008.37	91
1972	82,007.35	83
1973	85,664.82	85
1974	86,304.72	93
1975	80,735.04	94
1976	93,253.23	93
1977	103,307.18	96
1978	115,265.66	102
1979	119,832.27	102

(From Publishers Information Bureau, Magazine Publishers Association. Sunday supplements are excluded.)

Magazine Advertising Revenue
General Magazine

Year	Revenue	No. of Magazines
1950	$ 430,616,558	84
1951	480,065,294	83
1952	519,708,822	84
1953	566,440,991	86
1954	572,326,323	93
1955	622,005,729	81
1956	693,233,867	88
1957	710,785,633	83
1958	671,366,930	81
1959	760,630,046	79
1960	829,727,760	79
1961	815,015,746	80
1962	852,482,727	79
1963	906,779,205	81
1964	971,666,981	85
1965	1,048,765,191	86
1966	1,139,072,743	91
1967	1,135,334,589	93
1968	1,169,652,713	92
1969	1,221,370,544	90
1970	1,168,668,178	89
1971	1,235,175,433	91
1972	1,297,682,163	83
1973	1,309,161,028	85
1974	1,366,328,994	93
1975	1,336,313,425	94
1976	1,621,992,896	93
1977	1,965,410,809	96
1978	2,374,175,378	102
1979	2,671,052,606	102

(From Publishers Information Bureau, Magazine Publishers Association. Sunday supplements are excluded.)

CIRCULATION

Magazine publishers are placing greater emphasis on circulation. This is evident in their goal of at least 50 per cent income from this source and from their emphasis on per-copy sales. There are many ways to increase circulation revenue and some are discussed here.

Sweepstakes

More than $100 million is spent annually on sweepstakes and many of these millions are distributed by magazines. The *Reader's Digest* sweepstakes are the best known, since the magazine's first success in 1961.

These sweepstakes are just one of many such efforts to increase circulation and thus increase advertising revenues. Some of the contests have pre-selected winning numbers while others have random drawings to select the winners. And all publishers considering sweepstakes need to study the legal requirements. These often vary from state to state.

Henry Turner, a specialist in circulation, tabulated 32 sweepstakes in 1975 and 43 in 1977. No doubt this total has expanded in the 80s. Turner noted six reasons why some publishers reject this subscription promotion:

1. They feel they are too dignified for this method.
2. They don't use any promotional devices at all.
3. Can be more expensive than a straight offer.
4. Respondents may not renew as often as those who accept a straight offer.
5. Sweepstakes subscribers may not be as careful readers as other subscribers.
6. Some sweepstakes just don't pay off.[6]

Nevertheless, for millions of Americans sweepstakes can be enjoyable. It is, of course, a form of gambling and Americans love to gamble. If a publisher approaches a sweepstakes without "emotional prejudice" and with careful pre-planning, he can make it a profitable promotion.

Some publishers view this process, along with other circulation promotions, as so expensive that they place emphasis on single-copy sales. Publishers cast an envious eye toward *TV Guide, Family Circle, Woman's Day, National Enquirer, Star, Penthouse,* and a few others that dominate the single-copy system. In the process of loading the newsstands, they often waste thousands of extra copies, but they apparently are satisfied with the final results.

Store Coupons Tried

Another change being studied involves the direct purchase of a number of copies by supermarkets and convenience store chains. This apparently would solve some of the problems with returns, inventories, or audits. The chains could place these publications wherever they desired. This experiment, however, has not reached such proportions that any conclusions are available.

Magazine publishers are well aware that their products must compete with other major items in the supermarkets. Today's supermarkets often resemble department stores, with garden centers, automotive centers, dentists, beauty sections, do-it-yourself units, and sports areas. In addition to buying one's groceries, the shopper also can purchase oil for his car, golf balls for the weekend rounds, flowers for his wife, plus hundreds of other items. Magazine publishers want to be there too with their centers.

In fact, some stores are establishing family reading centers, with magazines and paperback books dominating. Many of the traditional bookstores are adding magazine sections. Magazines tend to increase the traffic in these stores, thus increasing the potential for more book sales.

Publishers are well aware of how the weather or the economy might affect their sales. Some will question how long the impulse buyer will continue to pay $1.95 for a magazine when he must count his pennies more carefully than in the past.

Cents-off coupons have been used in experiments on a limited basis. *Bon Appetit,* for example, experimented with coupons on C&H Sugar bags. Other earlier experiments have not proved too successful. However, if Americans continue to redeem millions of coupons at retail outlets, they might adopt the practice of looking for coupons that would cut the per-copy costs for magazines. Then, once a reader, they might be lured back or they might even subscribe.

Regardless of the sales approach, publishers and wholesalers have been warned of dangers from so many imitators on the market. These often crowd the newsstands so that all magazines suffer. One agency official said too many publishers work on the assumption that the more copies you put on a newsstand, the more copies will be sold. Stan Budner, president of Delmar News Agency in Delaware, said, "The leading titles give us the gross profit that allows the coattail-riders to use the system and not pay their way." He added, "Can you believe 164 girlie magazine imitators of *Playboy* and *Penthouse,* 138 car and van titles, and 146 crossword titles?" The study also revealed 83 titles concerning home, garden, and building; 99 on sports; 58 television; and 80 women's interest magazines.[7]

Subscription Methods Vary

Millions of Americans prefer to have their magazines delivered directly to their homes. They often become upset when they see the latest issue on the newsstand before their own copy arrives. They feel the subscriber has his investment in the publication and thus has prior rights to first sight.

The majority of subscriptions are still sold through the publisher's own direct mail efforts. These projects often involve the mailing of millions of advertising pieces, with the hoped-for return of 5 per cent or better. There are agencies that handle these chores for publishers, such as the Publishers Clearing House and American Family Publishers. These two contact consumers with special offers for many magazines.

There are, of course, other means for obtaining subscriptions, but most of them are expensive. Some publishers advertise their specials on television or in newspapers. They offer free telephone calls with billing later. All readers are well aware of the order cards that either are bound into the magazines or blown in. These are designed for individuals who read the magazines away from home, in the doctor's office or at the beauty parlor and so on.

Many publications have special rates for large segments of the population. Some offer college students and faculty special rates. Clergymen, too, often receive lower rates. Door-to-door salesmen haven't been around as frequently as in the past, however. Some cities have banned this technique, and in many instances the public has been suspicious of such efforts. With the expanded use of the WATS telephone system, publishers now turn to personal calls to encourage subscribers to renew and encourage others to start. Introductory subscription rates normally are the lowest, since publishers use this as bait to encourage renewals.

Readers need hardly be reminded that they are picking up a larger share of the publishing expense. Some publishers, such as *Reader's Digest,* break their bills down to indicate the amount paid for postage, obviously an attempt to shift some of the blame for the higher prices. Some filling stations have adopted this same technique—they list the federal, state, and city taxes, thus showing how little of the gas dollar the station keeps. Psychologically, it may help.

Specialists Offer Answers

John D. Klingel raised the question: "How much is too much?" when setting subscription prices. His *Folio* article tells of testing and analyzing subscription prices, with emphasis placed on consumer magazine pricing behavior.

Klingel, who heads John D. Klingel & Associates, concluded:

> Pricing strategy for a magazine is affected by competitive situations and, to a large extent, by the pricing policies of the magazine industry in total. In addition, since the economic characteristics of every publication are different, price strategy must be adapted to each individual publication and its economic situation . . .
> as a magazine's economic conditions change, so must pricing strategies . . .
> the major factors that must be considered in exploring pricing policies are profit, cash flow, and rate base. In addition, both long-term and short-term implications must be reviewed.[8]

Klingel is a magazine consultant who specializes in solving those problems that relate to circulation, promotion, and new magazine development.

Gimmicks continue to be used by publishers who seek that one answer to their particular problems. Some offer lifetime subscriptions, investing the money in high-interest money certificates. Others offer charter subscribers a guaranteed rate for a specific number of years. The majority offer a satisfaction-guaranteed or money refunded policy.

Already noted elsewhere was the effect that covers have on per-copy sales. Not only the choice of appealing persons and/or topics, but individualized covers can be helpful. *Inside Sports* and *Look* both offered sectionalized covers and *Esquire* once slanted covers to specific major cities.

Hal Speer, a circulation consultant, has been quoted in *Folio* with his 10 axioms for those involved in this continuous struggle. Several of these are designed to ease one's mind momentarily, such as "Nothing in circulation is ever exactly as it seems on the surface." And he reminded all concerned that "No one *needs* a magazine—even yours. The most desirable magazine in the world has to be *sold.*" He concluded that "Nearly any circulation problem will yield to some kind of analysis."[9]

Whatever the circulation, potential advertisers insist that the figures be audited, whether by the Audit Bureau of Circulation, the Business Publications Audit of Circulation, Inc., or some other appropriate service.[10]

Statistical Tables Helpful

The following tables, prepared by the Magazine Publishers Association, present a recent current picture of the magazine industry. As indicated, the number of periodicals and their circulation totals continue to increase. However, the circulation per 100 adults has not maintained its growth record displayed in the late 1960s and early 1970s.

Magazine readers will not be surprised at the ever-rising cost per single copy nor the hike in subscription rates. Both figures move up each year and, with inflation a way of life, will continue upward in years ahead.

The leading magazines in circulation show slight variations from year to year. The following chart shows the top ten for the past five years. The top three have maintained that standing throughout.

Magazine	1976	1977	1978	1979	1980
TV Guide	I	I	I	I	I
Reader's Digest	2	2	2	2	2
National Geographic	3	3	3	3	3
Better Homes & Gardens	6	6	4	4	4
Family Circle	4	4	5	5	6
Woman's Day	5	5	6	6	5
McCall's	7	7	7	7	7
Ladies' Home Journal	8	8	8	8	9
Playboy	9	10	10	9	8
Good Housekeeping	10	9	9	10	10

Number of U.S. Magazines

Year	U.S. Periodicals *	ABC General and Farm Magazines #	PIB Measured Magazines **
1950	6,960	250	84
1951	6,977	247	83
1952	7,050	252	84
1953	7,142	258	86
1954	7,382	259	93
1955	7,648	272	81
1956	7,907	282	88
1957	7,907	278	83
1958	8,074	270	81
1959	8,136	274	79
1960	8,422	273	79
1961	8,411	273	80
1962	8,616	278	79
1963	8,758	274	81
1964	8,900	282	85
1965	8,990	275	86
1966	9,102	276	91
1967	9,238	279	93
1968	9,400	287	92
1969	9,434	302	90
1970	9,573	300	89
1971	9,657	293	91
1972	9,062	302	83
1973	9,630	306	85
1974	9,755	316	93
1975	9,657	327	94
1976	9,872	336	93
1977	9,732	373	96
1978	9,582	369	102
1979	9,719	401	102
1980	10,236		100

(Prepared by Magazine Publishers Association, (*) data from Ayer Directory of Publications; (#) MPA Circulation iA, 2nd six months. ABC Publisher's Statements; (**) Publishers Information Bureau Inc.)

Circulation of all A.B.C. Magazines
General and Farm (Excluding Comics)
Second Six months Averages
Combined Circulation Per Issue

Year	No. Magazines or Groups	Single Copy	Subscription	Total	U.S. Adult Population (Add 000)	Circulation Per 100 Adults
1950	250	61,998,611	85,270,929	147,259,540	104,596	140.8
1951	247	64,157,748	87,345,788	151,503,536	105,159	144.1
1952	252	68,716,845	90,651,696	159,368,541	105,902	150.5
1953	258	68,109,367	94,925,139	163,034,506	106,830	152.6
1954	259	67,456,118	97,510,768	164,966,886	107,990	152.8
1955	272	71,073,877	108,891,354	179,965,231	109,342	164.6
1956	282	73,874,770	111,856,119	185,730,889	110,549	168.0
1957	278	68,305,833	113,104,515	181,410,348	111,725	162.4
1958	270	63,384,915	119,939,875	183,324,790	112,832	162.5
1959	274	62,609,711	112,979,455	185,589,166	114,091	162.7
1960	273	62,295,487	128,136,349	190,431,836	115,461	164.9
1961	273	60,696,623	134,966,829	195,663,452	117,207	166.9
1962	278	61,977,422	138,680,320	200,657,742	118,655	169.1
1963	274	62,578,172	140,645,067	203,223,239	120,072	169.3
1964	282	64,953,619	142,917,837	207,871,456	121,466	171.1
1965	275	66,538,850	148,947,898	215,486,748	123,804	174.1
1966	276	68,554,898	157,106,899	225,661,797	125,687	179.5
1967	279	71,275,957	160,848,702	232,124,659	127,536	182.0
1968	287	71,183,468	165,917,867	237,101,335	129,512	183.1
1969	302	71,587,283	170,205,937	241,793,220	131,623	183.7
1970	300	70,701,105	173,462,984	244,164,089	134,118	182.1
1971	293	73,296,562	169,157,331	242,453,893	136,659	177.4
1972	302	80,739,026	161,679,162	242,418,188	139,240	174.1
1973	306	83,947,248	161,954,594	245,901,842	141,683	173.6
1974	316	85,055,173	163,767,774	248,822,947	144,152	172.6
1975	327	85,580,704	165,250,505	250,831,209	146,800	170.9
1976	336	90,555,940	164,864,879	255,420,819	149,474	170.9
1977	373	92,757,602	171,190,950	263,948,552	152,089	173.5
1978	369	91,756,399	173,933,368	265,689,767	154,682	171.8
1979	401	89,717,939	176,936,774	266,654,713	157,529	169.3

(Sources: Circulation—A.B.C. records.
   Population—U.S. Bureau of the Census midyear estimates of the resident population 18 years and older.)

Circulation of all A.B.C. Magazines
General and Farm (Excluding Comics)
Annual Combined Circulation Per Issue

Year	No. Magazines or Groups*	Single Copy	Subscription	Total
1969	302	70,313,239	169,095,801	239,409,040
1970	300	70,231,003	174,504,070	244,735,073
1971	293	72,194,580	170,594,553	242,789,133
1972	302	77,243,489	161,861,361	239,104,850
1973	306	82,672,941	160,803,910	243,476,851
1974	316	85,156,055	164,630,113	249,786,168
1975	327	83,935,424	166,048,037	249,983,461
1976	336	89,530,500	164,829,805	254,360,305
1977	373	90,783,261	169,922,482	260,705,743
1978	369	92,812,976	173,432,472	266,245,448
1979	401	90,502,339	177,042,850	267,545,189

(*) MPA Table, Circulation 1A; 2nd six months each year.
(Sources: Averages calculated by MPA, as taken from A.B.C. publishers statements for 1st and 2nd six months each year.)

Cost of Magazines to the Reader

Year	Average Single Copy Price	Index 1960 = 100	Average Yearly Subscription Price	Index 1960 = 100
1960	$ .39	100	$ 4.58	100
1961	.41	105	4.68	102
1962	.41	105	4.79	105
1963	.42	108	4.89	107
1964	.46	118	5.25	115
1965	.46	118	5.32	116
1966	.49	126	5.51	120
1967	.51	131	5.60	122
1968	.55	141	6.05	132
1969	.58	149	6.52	142
1970	.63	162	7.16	156
1971	.63	162	7.38	161
1972	.64	164	7.57	165
1973	.68	174	7.72	169
1974	.81	208	8.98	196
1975	.87	223	10.14	221
1976	.98	251	11.52	252
1977	1.09	280	12.70	277
1978	1.21	310	14.86	324
1979	1.33	341	16.30	356

(Base: The single copy and one-year subscription prices reported to the Audit Bureau of Circulations, in effect Dec. 31st of each year, for 50 leading magazines in advertising revenue for that year. Prepared by Magazine Publishers Association.)

100 Leading A.B.C. Magazines

(Based on average circulation per issue, 1st six months of 1980)*

Rank		Circulation	% Change vs 1979	Rank		Circulation	% Change vs 1979
1	TV Guide	18,870,730	− 3.4	26	Southern Living	1,812,834	+ 4.2
2	Reader's Digest	18,193,255	+ 0.5	27	Outdoor Life	1,714,138	− 1.0
3	National Geographic	10,560,885	+ 3.0	28	Popular Mechanics	1,695,733	+ 3.6
4	Better Homes & Gardens	8,057,386	+ 0.6	29	V.F.W. Magazine	1,686,754	− 0.9
5	Woman's Day	7,574,478	+ 0.5	30	Today's Education	1,674,413	− 1.5
6	Family Circle	7,366,482	− 3.2	31	Mechanix Illustrated	1,669,808	− 4.6
7	McCall's	6,256,183	− 3.8	32	Elks Magazine	1,648,809	+ 0.4
8	Playboy	5,746,536	+ 3.7	33	Hustler	1,641,080	+ 3.6
9	Ladies' Home Journal	5,403,015	− 4.0	34	Globe	1,572,476	− 0.4
10	Good Housekeeping	5,138,948	− 0.7	35	Workbasket	1,561,727	− 8.7
11	National Enquirer	5,013,475	0.0	36	Boys' Life	1,537,601	− 3.8
12	Penthouse	4,502,810	0.0	37	Parents Magazine	1,489,507	+ 3.3
13	Time	4,451,816	+ 3.2	38	Changing Times	1,482,863	+ 4.3
14	Redbook	4,234,141	− 4.8	39	Seventeen	1,455,561	+ 6.0
15	The Star	3,380,779	+ 6.9	40	Life	1,410,273	+ 8.9
16	Newsweek	2,952,515	+ 0.6	41	Sunset	1,405,685	+ 1.5
17	Cosmopolitan	2,812,507	+ 1.6	42	True Story	1,369,634	−16.0
18	American Legion	2,591,644	+ 0.2	43	Farm Journal	1,276,443	− 4.4
19	Sports Illustrated	2,343,380	+ 2.4	44	Nation's Business	1,272,173	+ 2.7
20	People Weekly	2,308,635	− 0.1	45	Ebony	1,270,143	− 0.1
21	U.S. News & World Report	2,085,229	+ 0.8	46	New Woman	1,253,868	+17.3
22	Field & Stream	2,019,102	− 2.2	47	Sport	1,204,086	− 1.3
23	Popular Science	1,913,879	+ 6.2	48	Psychology Today	1,171,362	− 0.3
24	Smithsonian	1,890,466	+ 4.1	49	Bon Appetit	1,155,303	+ 3.5
25	Glamour	1,846,691	− 0.8	50	1,001 Decorating Ideas	1,104,698	+41.8

#	Magazine	Circulation	%
51	Teen	1,054,920	+ 7.0
52	Vogue	1,053,181	+ 8.5
53	House & Garden	1,050,733	+ 1.4
54	Family Handyman	1,038,783	+12.8
55	Discovery	1,013,765	− 0.5
56	Book Digest	1,012,875	+ 2.1
57	Us Magazine	1,006,188	+18.6
58	Golf Digest	1,005,812	+ 3.6
59	Travel & Leisure	944,222	+ 1.8
60	Mother Earth News	939,056	+45.4
61	House Beautiful	929,532	+ 7.6
62	Mademoiselle	922,049	− 0.8
63	Hot Rod	921,049	+ 5.1
64	Scouting	900,030	− 6.5
65	Grit	879,908	−12.1
66	Popular Photography	868,980	+ 4.5
67	Decorating & Craft Ideas	859,947	+ 7.2
68	Oui	851,960	− 1.9
69	Progressive Farmer	851,370	−12.5
70	Yankee	850,371	+ 6.3
71	Omni	843,538	+11.9
72	Money	837,436	− 0.9
73	Weight Watchers Magazine	826,205	+ 0.4
74	Apartment Life	818,980	− 1.3
75	Business Week	816,366	+ 1.3
76	Michigan Living—AAA Motor News	810,035	+ 1.8
77	Self	809,937	+34.8
78	Family Health	809,469	+ 0.9
79	Junior Scholastic	804,648	−10.9
80	Co-Ed	801,453	− 0.1
81	Cuisine	800,981	+ 3.6
82	Playgirl	784,935	+10.2
83	Motor Trend	756,644	− 0.2
84	Soap Opera Digest	741,739	+26.1
85	Golf	737,714	+ 4.0
86	Car & Driver	724,636	− 0.4
87	Jet	711,804	+ 0.9
88	Scientific American	705,124	+ 2.8
89	Forum	702,488	−12.4
90	Successful Farming	696,320	− 3.9
91	Forbes	690,258	+ 2.0
92	Rolling Stone	690,198	+10.5
93	Eagle	685,971	+ 0.9
94	Fortune	677,642	+ 0.2
95	Workbench	673,950	+ 3.6
96	Gourmet	671,178	+ 0.5
97	Esquire	651,596	0.0
98	National Lampoon	647,653	+ 5.3
99	Harper's Bazaar	634,997	+ 2.0
100	Modern Photography	631,962	+ 3.5

*Includes general and farm magazines of the Audit Bureau of Circulations. Groups and comics not included.

The leading 100 A.B.C. magazines for the first six months of 1980 show 0.6% increase versus leading 100 for the same period in 1979.

Distribution of Circulation

Year	Single Copy Sales Number	%	Subscription Number	%	Total Number	%
1961	60,696,623	31	134,966,829	69	195,663,452	100
1964	64,953,619	31	142,917,837	69	207,871,456	100
1967	71,275,957	31	160,848,702	69	232,124,659	100
1970	70,701,105	29	173,462,984	71	244,164,089	100
1973	83,947,248	34	161,954,594	66	245,901,842	100
1976	90,555,940	35	164,864,879	65	255,420,819	100
1979	89,717,939	34	176,936,774	66	266,654,713	100

(Source: ABC reports on General and Farm magazines (excluding comics and newspaper supplements) for the second six months of each year/MPA. Printed in MPA Magazine Newsletter of Research (August 1980) 2.)

Magazine Circulation by Circulation Size Groups

Circulation Size	Number of Magazines	%	Total Circulation Per Issue	%
10,000,000 & Over	3	0.8	47,891,703	17.8
5,000,000-9,999,999	8	2.0	51,019,075	19.0
2,000,000-4,999,999	11	2.8	33,593,596	12.5
1,000,000-1,999,999	30	7.7	43,883,339	16.4
500,000-999,999	65	16.6	46,895,273	17.5
150,000-499,999	115	29.4	31,099,810	11.6
Under 150,000	159	40.7	14,052,868	5.2
Total	391	100.0	268,435,664	100.0

(Source: ABC first six months of 1979 (excluding comics and newspaper supplements)/MPA. Printed in MPA Magazine Newsletter of Research (August 1980) 2.)

Magazines Grow Faster than Newspapers

Year	Magazines No.	Per-Issue Circulation (000)	Daily Newspapers No.	Per-Issue Circulation (000)	Sun. Newspapers No.	Per-Issue Circulation (000)
1950	250	147,260	1,772	53,829	549	46,582
1955	272	179,965	1,760	56,147	541	46,448
1960	273	190,432	1,763	58,882	563	47,699
1965	275	215,487	1,751	60,358	562	48,600
1970	300	244,164	1,748	62,108	586	49,217
1975	327	250,831	1,756	60,655	639	51,096
1976	336	255,421	1,762	60,977	650	51,565
1979	401	266,655	1,763	62,223	720	54,380
% Gain '50-'79		+81%		+16%		+17%

(Source: Magazines—ABC reports on General and Farm magazines (excluding comics and newspaper supplements) for the second six months of each year/MPA. Newspapers—Editor & Publisher Yearbooks. Printed in MPA Magazine Newsletter of Research (August 1980) 2.)

25

What's Ahead?

ANY STUDY of the past prepares one for a better comprehension of the future. Today there are a number of major obstacles from the past decade that will continue to plague publishers throughout the 80s. Most industry leaders would agree that costs will continue skyward and it will become more difficult to pass all of these added expenses on to the consumers.

In looking ahead, Norman R. Glenn, chairman of *Marketing & Media Decisions,* noted "the media explosion is busting out all over. Special-interest magazines, newspaper special-purpose sections, creative new out-of-home displays are examples of the all-media proliferation. Media buying habits aren't expected to change much in 1981." Glenn added that "There's more to write about and more to advertise."[1]

Among some other views from magazine leaders about the future are the following.

Edward T. Thompson, editor-in-chief of *Reader's Digest,* said "We might stop having printed magazines, and everything might appear on a screen someplace, but I don't think that's any less a magazine. If people prefer to read it sitting in front of a screen, fine, we'll create such an editorial product."

Helen Gurley Brown, *Cosmopolitan* editor, said "I don't think the satisfaction that comes from sitting down with the printed word is going to go away. And if magazines and books are going to become extinct in their present form, I hope to have a little cache, so I can sit down and read *Gone With The Wind* and *The Godfather* as I always have."

Otto Fuerbringer, former managing editor of *Time,* realized competition from television would continue as part of the electronic information explosion, yet he noted too that "television has had little effect on newsmagazines. There is some evidence that television helps the newsmagazines by whetting the appetite for more detailed and comprehensive coverage, especially of big events."[2] One notes a similar reaction in the sports world.

Postal Situation

First, the increase in postal rates has killed some periodicals, forced many to switch to a smaller format, and others to use lighter weight paper. And it has created the alternate delivery system in many communities.

However, the postal situation may become more stable in the 80s with increases not expected to be as high as those encountered throughout the 70s.

Computers, Information Systems

Second, the expanded use of computers, in-house typesetting and other refined composition work will affect the publishing mechanics. Readers seldom are aware of these changes but publishers will continue to seek faster and more economical methods for producing their periodicals.

Computers will continue to influence mass communications, as noted by Ralph E. Eary, Scripps-Howard Newspapers' director of engineering and production. Prices of advanced techniques will continue to drop. "Computers have become an integral part of all of our personal lives," he said. Advances continue in the development of mini-computers, communications satellites, facsimile mail and document transmission, touch-tone telephones, cable-television, and other areas.[3]

For the early 80s Eary predicted "rapid growth in communication networks results in dramatic data transmission-cost reduction. This gives rise to the development of international databanks; massive increases in directly accessible storage bring information Retrieval and Library Systems into common use; major advances occur in digitizing images, graphics, and logos." For the late 80s, Eary visualizes an expanded use of computers, world-wide television, video-terminals, and digital library systems. Automatic indexing would be available for using retrieval systems that will contain newspapers, magazines, technical and legal journals, government documents, etc. Although more concerned with newspapers, Eary's comments apply equally well to magazines.

In another study looking ahead to the 1990s, an Arthur D. Little Inc. report probed the potentials of the electronic information systems. Donald Sparrow, who directed the study, thought that media newspaper and magazine publishers who were willing to break with the tradition to become broad-based "information providers" would find expanded areas to utilize their news and information services. Others, too, have realized that this electronic revolution is underway and those leaders who utilize the benefits in the proper ways will benefit in the years ahead.

The study also observed that "Computerized pagination—systems that set copy, that lay out and paste-up text and art-work, pull proofs, and make printing plates all by using a single computerized system—will be widely available by

1985'' to help offset the continuing economic pressures on publishers and equipment manufacturers.

The Little study observed that the graphic scanner will be another link, allowing ''all pre-press work on photos and artwork to be done on a CRT. Color separations and screening of half-tones are achieved on the computer.''[4]

Paper and Production

Third, the 70s brought out a need for more stable and adequate supplies of paper. Hopefully, this problem is nearer a solution in the 80s, with increased capacity from American mills.

Publishers must counter rising paper expenses with higher per-copy costs, yet both the paper makers and the publishers must worry about the buyer's limit on his willingness to pay $2 or more for a magazine. Especially if the economic situation continues as it began in the 80s.

Some production costs may be saved by more advanced production equipment. Computerized binding will speed the individualization of copies, segmenting the audience even more. This could have benefits in some areas, such as attracting more advertising. On the other hand, it could also result in high production expenses.

Obviously the use of satellites to transmit text and photographs will continue. Related to production will be the expansion of research that will define more demographic splits, metro splits, executive and student editions, and the like.

Higher Per-Copy Costs

Fourth, with inflation an on-going problem, publishers will continue to seek a better balance between revenues generated from advertisers and from readers. This already has been demonstrated in the higher subscription rates and with more emphasis on per-copy sales at the newsstands.

This becomes more involved with the postal problems, with the alternate delivery systems, and with other areas of the publishing industry.

Competition With Television

Fifth, the competition with the television industry will continue as both compete for the advertisers' millions, as well as for the attention of the millions of readers and viewers/listeners. Especially significant is the expansion of television into more specialized areas, such as cable. With 24-hour sports programming, for example, some specialized sports magazines could suffer. And the same could happen in other areas of the magazine world.

Television will not disappear from the competitive arena. There obviously is the danger that libraries of books and collections of magazines may be replaced by libraries of videodiscs. And as the personalization of television continues it will compete more with the personalization seen in magazines, especially such as *People*. Obviously, with the splits expected from an increase in the number of magazines and the expansion of cable, individuals will encounter more decision-making on what to read or see.

The challenge will be placed before the magazine editors and publishers to better prepare their products for these highly competitive years ahead.[5]

Television leaders also predict a growth of viewing time as well as in the use of color receivers. More than 70 per cent of all homes will have more than one set by the mid-80s and the number of available channels by the end of the decade will be "mind-boggling, with more than 150 outlets in the home made possible through the technology of fiber optics," according to a Doyle Dane Bernbach media official, Michael Drexler. Such availability of material would compete with the special-interest magazines, with both sources battling for the limited markets. This could result in fewer newcomers among the specialized magazines, according to Drexler, who predicted "ad schedules in the next decade (the 80s) will be spread over more magazines with fewer insertions in each," making it necessary for the industry to "regroup and decide how to go about looking at other alternatives."[6] With the anticipated expansion of cable, pay television, super-stations, and the specialized channels for split audiences such as religion, sports, news, and the like, the segmented groups will be there for advertisers with their special audiences to tap. Logically, according to *Advertising Age* publisher Rance Crain, "magazines could complement such segmentation, providing more information for television viewers after the initial sales message had been put on the air."[7]

Since such splitting of the television audience was not seen as practical for five or ten years, magazines have some lead time to prepare. Meanwhile, some unexpected cooperation between television and magazines has been observed by an advertising executive, Neil Faber, who noted: "Oddly, television which helped in the demise of mass magazines, continues to help stimulate publications (*People, Us, Soap Opera Digest*)."[8] Some notice must be directed to the extensive use of television sets for video games, a factor advertisers need to consider.

When the 70s ended, Coen looked upon the industry as "more insulated from the recession than it had been in previous dips," despite anticipating some "bumpy shots" in the 80s. Among the plus factors for this decade would be the increase in discretionary spending as the result of the growth of two wage-earners households, together with the expansion of the senior citizen audience and their disposable money.

Other Competitive Factors

Although K. Robert Brink, Hearst Magazine vice-president, visualized "another outstanding five years in the magazine business," he recognized the need to hike per-copy income to offset assured hikes in paper, printing, and postage expenditures. Others were confident that the "industry's vitality" would be evident in the continuation of new publications. "The successful ones will more often than not come from the major, established houses, which are better able to deal with high energy costs and strong competition for both readers and advertisers," suggested the *American Printer and Lithographer.*[9] Such examples would include *Panorama,* sired by *TV Guide,* and *Inside Sports,* assured of millions of dollars from its owner, the *Washington Post.* No doubt the large conglomerates, seeking outside investment possibilities, will continue to probe the magazine industry as will foreign investors with their American dollars.

Closer to the readers are the projected personalized magazines, a further specialization of the geo-demo editions currently available. In late 1979, *Advertising Age* reported on the activities of U/Stat Inc., a Denver-based operation that seeks contracts to provide the first individualized magazine that would assemble pages, both editorial and advertising, for each name label. Non-smokers, for example, would receive publications without cigarette ads, thus furnishing "the ultimate marketing capability" to advertisers. More detailed profiles would be required of each reader, a process computers could handle.[10]

Meanwhile, Time Inc. moved closer to the first talking machine to go with their magazines. Research director Malcolm Ochs said, "There is technology available right now that can imprint grooves right on the page of the magazines. You then have a little box—scanner—that goes over these grooves and can actually pick up the voice that's impregnated in them." Similar sound could be added to the advertisements. Licensing agreements were being discussed between Time Inc. and Japanese manufacturers. Currently, talking storybooks are available in some toy stores. Another Time Inc. executive, Henry Grunwald, said "the great trick is not to get complacent" in looking ahead to the 80s.[11]

Mechanically, the 80s will witness more typesetting by in-house publishers and costs will decline as technical processes expand. The *American Printer and Lithographer* visualizes an increased use of "facsimile transmissions of electronically scanned four-color originals, which will generate fully screened color separations ready for image assembly and platemaking in major printing plants or color houses." Faster web offset equipment will be ready, some the result of European technology which will also supply speed-up rotogravure operations. Since such developments will demand heavy capital investments, their use will be limited initially to the major concerns handling long-run printing contracts. Letterpress operations will continue to decline as older plants are replaced with offset and gravure dominating about 90 per cent of the production of consumer magazines.

Technical advances also will provide better ink with "brighter colors, more gloss and smoother coverage on the paper." Bindery costs will continue to be high as will paper, as noted earlier.

Editorial Concerns

Often overlooked by publishers who tend to be more concerned with production methods and cost factors, is the editorial content. A major crisis has been predicted by John Mack Carter, *Good Housekeeping* editor-in-chief, who noted such issues facing editors as the "Southeast Asian problems, racism, sexism, consumerism, the environment, violence on television and freedom of the press." In other words, "Do we sit back and let people there (foreign nations) do anything they want to each other, or do we push in our editorial columns for renewed intervention?" Enormous responsibilities were seen for editors and producers who make the news "through that personal, subjective journalism we introduced a few years back." [12]

Added to this warning was a call by a Hearst executive, Frank A. Bennack, Jr., for geniuses to lead magazines into the 80s. "All the innovations and improvements and advances will go gurgling down the drain unless we're able to maintain a constant flow of bright, talented, dedicated people to give them meaning." Bennack was optimistic in his belief that teachers would stress again the three R's, thus overcoming some functional illiteracy. This would bring a "mini-renaissance in America with books and newspapers and magazines reaping the rewards." [13]

Carter also called upon editors to "stay pure. Not ignorant or naive, but pure in purpose and practice. The integrity of the magazine is, pragmatically, the exclusive responsibility of the editor." Carter wants editors to be "profit-minded, not for greed but for glory," fearless in battle, able and willing to speak out on not only editorial problems but also on promotion, circulation, and management challenges."

The University of Missouri School of Journalism made a study of what communication leaders visualized for the 1990s. The study was aimed, at least in part, to assist educators in the preparation of such personnel as Carter called for to handle the periodicals that survive to the end of this century.

One reply came from an unidentified retired editor who thought a student seeking a job in 1990 should be familiar with (a) the basics of the craft, i.e., reporting, research techniques, and lucid writing; (b) mechanical and technological know-how (which by 1990 may be rather sophisticated); (c) some inkling of how audiences respond to the various media and how to approach readers invitingly (this would include an overview of audience-survey techniques, plus some review of the psychological work done in this area). Then he added, "I should think most everything else will be learned by the candidate when he is on the job." The writer has been associated with the American Business Press, Inc.

Some others were critical of journalism schools that produce newspaper and news magazine graduates rather than generalists who can adapt to any or all media. Robert E. Kenyon, Jr., executive director of the American Society of Magazine Editors, called for basic liberal arts education with about 20 per cent journalism. He urged involvement with campus magazines or newspapers and summer internships at a magazine or newspaper. In addition, students looking to the magazine world need writing, reporting, and magazine editing and magazine publishing with emphasis on what the editor should know as a manager. Kenyon wants the all-around applicant, with knowledge about circulation, advertising, research, production and general management, "because the editor must also function as a manager." Kenyon, agreeing with others, thought "It is more important for young journalists to learn how to write, report and think" than to become too involved in the technology, which "might be obsolete even before graduation."[14]

Some Want Diversion

No doubt there will continue to appear many one-shot publications, notably those concerning personalities in the news and those involved in tragedies, such as John F. Kennedy, Elvis Presley, and John Lennon. Sales of these periodicals often reach into the millions.

"Readers want a pleasant diversion, an entertaining interlude," according to Doyle Dane Bernbach executive Robert M. Rees. Such a diversion is *People,* according to Rees. This weekly is successful because its contents feature "stories about ordinary people doing extraordinary things." He argues against those who feel one shouldn't stress the entertainment function of magazines. "All magazines are bought for and read for the entertainment value. Every magazine by definition generates the involvement of its readers, which means that a magazine's editorial content is the ultimate judgment of its readers. We shouldn't be afraid of that judgment and go solely with a book's numbers." To further support his claim, Rees concludes that "The diversion selected by a reader, for us in advertising, ought to be one good and acceptable measure of that reader. Nothing tells us more about a person than his diversions and entertainments."[15]

Rees' concepts certainly should become more answerable in the years ahead with the computerized, individualized editions which, obviously, will reveal the diversions and entertainment likes of the readers.

Another agency official, Larry Cole, of Ogilvy & Mather, predicted "Magazines will almost triple their rates by 1990 because of real increases, while pushing their ad/editorial ratios up to 60 per cent advertising. They'll become even more special-interest than they are now, with more single-subject specials within issues. The average adult will spend 27 minutes a day reading them.[16]

And More Questions?

Throughout these predictions for the years ahead, industry leaders need to continually ask themselves: Is my publication needed?

What of the 80s? Of the hundreds of newcomers each year, how many will survive the decade? What modifications will materialize among the traditional circulation leaders that will permit *TV Guide, Reader's Digest,* and *National Geographic* to retain their readership of millions? What will be the status of the conventional women's magazines, such as the *Ladies' Home Journal* and *McCall's,* as they compete with more recent arrivals such as *Ms., Self, Working Women,* and others with more liberal and specialized appeal? Will specialization trend continue, or will mass media publications, spurred by the success of *People,* make a comeback?

Studies reported by *Folio,* the voice of the magazine industry, have observed that publications undergo life cycles much as humans do, moving from infancy, to childhood, to adolescence, to manhood, to middle age, then old age, and, finally, death.[17] And, like humans, magazines often disappear before reaching the second or third stage. Also, like humans, magazines find it necessary to adapt to changing times to survive the later stages.

Theodore H. White noted the life-and-death cycle of magazines in his book, *In Search of History.* He could recall only six magazines with a history of a hundred years in America. His comments are appropriate here.

> The cycle usually depends on the vitality of one man or a succession of men who manage to capture and hold for a number of years the attention and mood of their time. To understand how very important the mood of the time is in the life cycle of magazines, one must distinguish between the different ancestors of the book and the magazine, for they are linked only by their use of printed words on paper pages. The ancestry of the book goes back to Greece and Rome and beyond. The book writer addresses himself to a reader, an audience of one. The magazine comes of entirely different ancestry—the ancient and medieval fairs, the Forum in Rome and the courtyard of the Temple in Jerusalem. A magazine is a fair, where merchants and peasants, townsmen and jugglers, bear-baiters and preachers, sex peddlers and elixir dispensers, offer their wares or entertainment . . . Nowhere, however, did the magazine form reach so high a peak of national influence as in America—and hold it for more than a half a century, starting in the 1890s.[18]

Here to Stay

John Mack Carter has no doubt about the future. "Magazines are here to stay," the *Good Housekeeping* chief firmly believes. "A magazine is not just a pound of paper. A magazine is a bunch of people with special interests and ideas communicating with a larger group who share the dedication to those interests. That equation promises permanence." But with increasing competition, Carter feels magazines will be forced to "do what they already do well but now must do far more wisely. Magazines will become more efficient for advertisers, first in the offering of new titles. The flow of 300 to 400 new consumer magazines each year seems destined to continue, fueled by (1) expanding reader interests that demand to be served; (b) less caution and skepticism on the part of advertisers, and (c) a fresh wellspring of capital from both within and without the publishing offices."

Carter is impressed by what he terms "reduced *reader* waste." Here he is concerned with the new computer-driven binders and their ability to select editions for individuals to meet their personal needs, a trend other publishers also have endorsed. "The reader in a sense is converted from a statistic to an individual with his or her interest-tailored copy . . . just the stuff editors' dreams are made of."[19]

Notes

NOTES TO CHAPTER I

1. Frank Luther Mott, *A History of American Magazines, 1741–1850* (Cambridge: Harvard University Press, 1957) Volume one of a five-volume history. See also Lyon N. Richardson, *A History of Early American Magazines, 1741–1789* (New York: Thomas Nelson and Sons, 1931). These are the most complete books for this phase of American magazine history.

2. Mott, *A History of American Magazines 1741–1850* I:75.

3. Theodore Peterson, *Magazines in the Twentieth Century.* (Urbana: University of Illinois Press, 1964) 448–451.

4. Theodore H. White, *In Search of History.* (New York: Harper & Row, 1978) 420.

5. Peterson, *Magazines in the Twentieth Century* 44. See also Wolseley's "The American Periodical Press and Its Impact," *Gazette*, Vol. 15, 1969.

6. Roland Wolseley, *The Changing Magazine* (New York: Hastings House, 1973).

7. C. Lennart Carlson, *The First Magazine, A History of the Gentleman's Magazine.* (Providence, R.I.: Brown University, 1938).

8. Mott, *A History of American Magazines 1741–1850* I:6.

9. *How and Why People Buy Magazines.* A national study of the consumer market for magazines. Completed by Lieberman Research Inc. of New York for Publishers Clearing House, Port Washington, N.Y., 1977.

10. Chris Welles, "Can Mass Magazines Survive?" *Columbia Journalism Review* (July/August 1971) 7–14.

11. *Magazine Industry Newsletter* (December 14, 1972).

12. Wolseley, *The Changing Magazine* 3.

13. Bob Donath, "Magazines hang hats on special interest," *Advertising Age* (November 18, 1974).

14. John Peter, "A Bicentennial Bonanza," *Folio* (December 1976) 38–44.

15. James L. C. Ford, *Magazines for Millions* (Carbondale: Southern Illinois University Press, 1969).

16. J. W. Click and Russell Baird, *Magazine Editing and Production* (Dubuque, Iowa: Wm. C. Brown Co., 1979).

17. *Consumer and Farm Magazine* and *Business Publication* rates and data books are issued monthly by Standard Rate & Data Service, Inc., Skokie, Ill. They are the most up-to-date record of thousands of magazines, containing founding dates, editorial profiles, and circulation/advertising data.

18. Barbara Love, "1980: the real test." *Folio* (September 1979)   45–50, 84.

19. *Advertising Age* (October 15, 1979)   1, 118.

20. "Futures," *Marketing & Media Decisions* (July 1980)   34.

21. Annual reports and other membership/promotional material published by the Magazine Publishers Association, Inc., New York.

22. See *A Study of Media Involvement,* conducted by Opinion Research Corporation for Magazine Publishers Association, 1980. This study contains detailed statistical results of opinions voiced by more than 2,000 men and women.

23. "Rhodes named to head MPA," *Advertising Age* (December 26, 1978)   1, 26.

24. "Business press needs comparability, BPA told," *Advertising Age,* (March 5, 1979)   79.

25. Thomas J. Campbell, *"Highlights of BPA History,"* four-page leaflet published by BPA, New York, 1976.

26. Material supplied by the International Association of Business Communicators.

Notes to Chapter 2

1. Jay S. Harris, ed., *TV Guide, The First 25 Years* (New York: Simon & Schuster, 1978). Also *Closed Circuit,* house organ for *TV Guide* employes, Special 25th Anniversary Issue, April 1978. Gaeton Fonzi, *Annenberg, A Biography of Power* (New York: Weybright and Talley, 1970).

2. John E. Cooney, *Wall Street Journal,* November 6, 1978.

3. *"Tv Guide* over takes *Time* in Revenue race," *Advertising Age* (January 7, 1980)   8. There are slight variations between this report and *Folio* (September 1980) summaries for 1979.

4. David M. Rubin, "Surprise: *TV Guide* Is No Longer a Toothless Wonder," *MORE* (October 1976)   32–36.

5. *Wall Street Journal,* (November 6, 1978).

6. "Triangle sets staff for *Panorama,*" *Advertising Age* (April 23, 1979)   1, 98.

7. "City magazines miffed by competition from the *Dial,*" *Folio* (August 1980)   5, 6; Also see "Senate threat to the *Dial* fizzles, controversy continues," *Folio* (December 1980)   6, 8.

8. On its 50th anniversary *Reader's Digest* reprinted the dummy copy and the first issue for promotional and historical purposes. The format remains basically that established in 1922. James Playsted Wood, *Of Lasting Interest* (Garden City, N.Y.: Doubleday & Co., Inc., 1958) is a favorable picture of *Reader's Digest.* On advertising see John W. Garberson, "A Limited Number of Advertising Pages," *Journalism Monograph* #25, November 1972, published by the Association for Education in Journalism.

9. On its 50th Anniversary in 1972, *Reader's Digest* reprinted Wallace's original specimen issue, dated January 1920, and the first issue quoted here. These were boxed for limited distribution.

10. For excellent "inside story" of *Reader's Digest* see *Time* (December 10, 1951)   64–75.

11. Warren Boroson, "The Pleasantville Monster," *Fact* (March–April 1966)   3–27.

12. John Mack Carter, comments in *Folio* (December 1976)   49.

13. *Changing Times* (September 1972)   44.

14. *Magazine Age* (February 1980) 14.

15. *National Geographic* (October 1966) 450–451, 476.

16. *Time* (August 14, 1967).

17. Frank Luther Mott, *History of American Magazines, 1885–1905* IV:620–632.

NOTES TO CHAPTER 3

1. Mott, *History of American Magazines, 1885–1905* IV:671–716.

2. Calvin E. Chunn, "History of News Magazines," Unpublished doctoral dissertation, University of Missouri, 1950 177–204.

3. Mott, *History of American Magazines, 1850–1865* II:469–487.

4. Mott, *History of American Magazines, 1885–1905* IV:569–579.

5. Robert T. Elson, *Time Inc. 1923–1941* (New York: Atheneum 1969) 77–78. See also his second volume, covering 1941–1960, published in 1973. For fuller development see David Halberstam, *The Powers That Be* (New York: Knopf, 1979) and W. A. Swanberg, *Luce and His Empire* (New York: Scribner's Sons, 1972).

6. David Shaw wrote a series on these periodicals for the Los Angeles Times Syndicate during mid-1980; See Merle Miller, "Why the Editor of *Newsweek* Is Not the Editor of *Time* and Vice Versa," *Esquire* (June 1973) 169–171, 225–232.

7. Chunn, "History of News Magazines" 349.

8. Letter from the Publisher, *Time* (July 16, 1945) 9.

9. "Bully for *Time*," *Nation* (March 8, 1958) 197–198; "Truer Words," *Nation* (January 10, 1959) 23.

10. Geoffrey T. Hellman, *"Time* Lumbers On," *The New Yorker* (April 16, 1955) 34–36.

11. Otto Friedrich, "There Are oo Trees in Russia," *Harper's* (October 1964) 59–65.

12. "G & W annual report ad trendsetter?" *Advertising Age* (February 19, 1979) 2, 91.

13. *"Newsweek* gets earful over 'Eyes On,' " *Advertising Age* (September 11, 1978) 41. Also, *Media Decisions* (November 1978) 16, 18.

14. David Lawrence, "U.S. News & World Report: A Two-Way System of Communication," speech before The Newcomen Society in North America, 1969.

15. *U.S. News & World Report* (September 5, 1977) 56–58.

16. *U.S. News & World Report* advertisement, *Advertising Age* (December 17, 1979) 15.

17. Julie Hover and Charles Kadushin, "Influential Intellectual Journals: A Very Private Club," *Change* (March 1972) 38–47. Kadushin, Hover and Monique Tichy also wrote "How and Where to Find Intellectual Elite in the United States," *Public Opinion Quarterly* (Spring 1971) 1–18.

18. Peterson, *Magazines in the Twentieth Century* 417.

19. John H. Schacht, *The Journals of Opinion and Reportage: An Assessment* (New York: Magazine Publishers Assn. Inc., 1966) A brief but informative picture of this category of magazines. Several are treated in fuller accounts by Mott.

20. James Brady, "A drink to the *'Nation'* " *Advertising Age* (May 21, 1979) 26, 28.

21. "Remarks on the occasion of this journal's 50th year: symposium," *New Republic* (March 21, 1964) 14.

22. *Christian Science Monitor* (March 27, 1974).

23. This statement was made by Buckley in his annual letter appealing for funds. Buckley said he didn't make a similar statement in 1981 "though the sentiments are correct."

24. "Spokesman for conservatism," *Time* (July 10, 1964)   74. Item notes that *National Review* set out to change the political face of America.

25. Schacht, *The Journals of Opinion and Reportage*   15.

26. "A Brief History of Harper's Magazine," undated, 4-page promotional material published by Harper & Row.

27. "Spur for *Harper's" Newsweek* (May 22, 1967)   68.

28. "Hang-Up at *Harper's," Time* (March 15, 1971)   41. Also, "What's Happened at *Harper's," Saturday Review* (April 10, 1971)   43–47, 56.

29. *"Harper's:* 1850–1980," *Newsweek* (June 30, 1980)   71.

30. *Kansas City Star* (June 29, 1980). See also, "Lewis H. Lapman, editor of Harper's," *Folio* (October 1980)   87–88.

31. "The *Atlantic* Makes Waves," *Time* (October 12, 1970)   73–74.

32. "New Cash for an Old Bostonian," *Time* (March 17, 1980)   97–98.

33. *"Saturday Review* Turns 40," *Advertising Age* (August 24, 1964)   51.

34. Cousins' introductory column, *Saturday Review* (March 16, 1940)   8. He used "Old Timer" as the speaker to carry on his story.

35. "Troubled Dream," *Time* (April 2, 1973)   65. See "Repositioning Saturday Review," *Magazine Age* (February 1981)   76–77.

36. Editorial, *Folio* (April 1978)   16.

37. Bob Greene, Chicago *Sun-Times* staffer, article reprinted in Los Angeles *Times* (November 26, 1978).

38. Michael Andrew Scully, "Would Mother Jones Buy 'Mother Jones' "? *Public Interest* (Fall 1978)   100–108.

39. "Mother's Call," *Time* (July 21, 1980)   62.

Notes to Chapter 4

1. Walter E. Botthof, talks, University of Missouri School of Journalism, January 12, 14, 1959.

2. Letter from Donald W. Altmaier, vice president/advertising and public relations, Chilton, February 26, 1980. Comments from William A. Barbour are from a talk in Milwaukee, July, 1979.

3. James L. C. Ford, *Magazines for the Millions*   113.

4. David P. Forsyth, *The Business Press in America, 1750–1865* (Philadelphia: Chilton Books, 1964). This is the best for early history. Also see Mott, *A History of American Magazines,* with the first four volumes providing useful data in this area.

5. Letter, G. Renfrew Brighton, Business Journals, Inc., February 15, 1980.

6. "The Survival Medium," a special report on American business press, *ADWEEK,* December 10, 1979   SR 3–32. An excellent source.

7. "New Dimensions of the Business Press." *Madison Avenue* (March, 1979)   20–25, 114.

8. From material supplied by *Forbes* as well as the *Playboy* interview, April, 1979. See also the 60th anniversary issue, September 15, 1977.

9. John Tebbel, *The American Magazine: A Compact History* (New York: Hawthorn, 1969)   230.

10. James Brady, "Henry Luce's improbable dream," *Advertising Age* (February 4, 1980)   28. In the same issue is a story on "A trimmer *Fortune* carries its weight well after 50 years."

11. Margaret Bourke-White, *Portrait of Myself* (New York: Simon and Schuster, 1963)   64.

12. "Forecast favorable for *Fortune* frequency facelift," *Advertising Age* (February 6, 1978)   28.

13. Brady, "Luce's improbable dream," 28.

14. "Business Week 'Aging Beautifully,' " *Advertising Age* (August 27, 1979) 10, 55.

15. Ibid, 55.

16. "Inc. sees niche as magazine for smaller companies," *Advertising Age* (October 2, 1978) 22.

17. Ford, *Magazines for Millions,* 141. See editorial profile in SRDS *Consumer Magazine and Farm Periodical* rate book.

18. James Brady, "Play ball with press . . . cautiously," *Advertising Age* (July 10, 1978) 98.

19. Letter from John M. Wehner, Jr., director of Medical Journals Division, J. B. Lippincott Co., March 4, 1979.

20. "ABC buys Chilton," *Advertising Age* (February 19, 1979) 1, 91.

21. Letter from Orvel H. Cockrel, February 21, 1980.

22. *"Quality* Magazine Makes a Sales Call," *Madison Avenue* (October 1979) 103–110.

23. "Business press braces for cold new year," *Advertising Age* (December 31, 1979) 1, 18.

NOTES TO CHAPTER 5

1. Wolseley, *Changing Magazines,* 109–110.

2. Nancy Yoshihara, writing for the Los Angeles Times Syndicate, December 23, 1979.

3. *Marketing & Media Decisions* (December 1979) 69.

4. "Magazines Focusing on the Working Woman," *Kansas City Star,* (October 22, 1978)

5. Edward W. Bok, "The Return of the Business Woman," *Ladies' Home Journal* (March 1900) 16.

6. Mott, *History of American Magazines, 1885–1905,* IV:555.

7. "Woman Power," *Time* (March 30, 1970) 59. Also, *Wall Street Journal* (August 3, 1970).

8. "LHJ cuts circulation, ad rates as Downe corporate revamping seen," *Advertising Age* (August 18, 1975) 1, 217. Also *Magazine Industry Newsletter* (August 15, 1975).

9. Helen Woodward, *The Lady Persuaders* (New York: Ivan Obolensky, Inc., 1960) 120, 141.

10. *Magazine Industry Newsletter* (January 14, 1970).

11. *Wall Street Journal* (August 3, 1970).

12. Nancy Yoshihara, Los Angeles Times Syndicate, from *Kansas City Times* (January 2, 1980).

13. From company's two-page history, dated September 1978.

14. *"Redbook'* new format an attack on clutter," *Advertising Age* (October 30, 1978) 143.

15. Mott, *History of American Magazines, 1885–1905* IV: 480–505.

16. Lana Ellis, sketch of Helen Gurley Brown, Louisville *Courier-Journal & Times Magazine* (December 6, 1970) 35–41.

17. *Madison Avenue Magazine* (April 1979) 38. Also see *"Family Circle* Makes a Sales Call," *Madison Avenue* (April 1981) 122–129 for fuller account.

18. Additional information from Rena Bartos, "What every marketer should know about women," *Harvard Business Review* (May–June 1978) 73–85.

19. *"Ms.* new tax status piques interest of other publishers," *Folio* (December 1979) 4.

20. Interview with Pat Carbine, *Folio* (April 1975) 30–34.

21. *Viva* (October 1973) 9.

22. "Death in the Family," *Newsweek* (November 27, 1978) 113–115. "Lack of identity, mismanagement, extravagant start-up costs, increasing postal rates and competition for advertising" were blamed for recent tragedies in the magazine field.

23. "Baker's dozen in women's magazines," *Marketing & Media Decisions* (October 1979) 64–65, 132, 138–140. Also see "Peter Diamandis," *Folio* (June 1980) 51, 56.

24. "Editor reveals struggle to find identity for *Self* magazine," *Folio* (June 1979) 33–34; "New *Self* captain sees calm seas ahead," *Advertising Age* (September 29, 1980) 18.

25. Columbia, Mo., *Tribune* (April 4, 1980) from Los Angeles *Times* Syndicate. See "Ira Ritter, Publisher of *Playgirl*," *Folio* (December 1980) 57–58, 60.

26. *Working Woman*'s news release (June 1978).

27. Columbia, Mo., *Tribune* (December 23, 1979) from Los Angeles Times Syndicate.

28. Julie Baymgold, "The Boss of 'Bazaar,' " *New York* (April 24, 1972) 48, 51. Also: "Make 'Bazaar' hot were orders, says publisher Brady," *Advertising Age* (September 13, 1971) 10.

29. Mott, *The History of American Magazines 1885–1905* IV: 756–762.

30. *Mademoiselle* (February 1960) 75–79.

31. Much of this material from a conference with Ruth Whitney sponsored by American Society of Magazine Editors and the Magazine Publishers Association, New York, May 1979.

Notes to Chapter 6

1. *Esquire* reprinted the initial issue in smaller-page size, apparently to satisfy the wide interest in its history.

2. Hannegan v. Esquire 327 U. S. 146 (1946)

3. Columbia University School of Journalism magazine awards for 1967–68, *Advertising Age* (November 4, 1968) 53–54.

4. "Brief," *Editor & Publisher* (December 20, 1975) 23. Additional comments in *Advertising Age* (December 22, 1975) 3, 37; *Editor & Publisher* (January 10, 1976) 48; and *Folio* (February 1976) 44–46.

5. "Felker Tells Plans for 'Esquire,' " *Advertising Age* (September 5, 1977) 3, 58.

6. "March 'Esquire' takes on the Clay Felker look," *Advertising Age* (January 9, 1978) 4. In a two-page advertisement in *Advertising Age* (November 21, 1977, 64–65) Felker and Glaser revealed many of their objectives.

7. "Now, Esquire Jr." *Newsweek* (May 14, 1979) 78, 83. Also, James Brady, "Deja vu over 'Esquire,' " *Advertising Age* (May 7, 1979) 100. The two men said their attitude was "to be truly human is to be truly hip." More on 13–30 Corp. in *Chronicle of Higher Education* (December 8, 1980) 17–18.

8. "Merchants of Raunchness," *Time* (July 4, 1977) 69.

9. Data from "The Folio 400," *Folio* (September 1980).

10. "The Skin-Book Boom: What Have They Done to the girl Next Door?" *Esquire* (November 1976) 91–97. See also in same issue, Roy Blount, Jr., "Where Will They Go From Here." 98–99.

11. "Skin Trouble," *Time* (September 22, 1975) 50.

12. "Playboy Heiress in Centerfold of Father's Work," by Marion Christy of Boston *Globe,* from *Kansas City Times,* April 1979.

13. "The Skin-Book Boom . . ." 91–97. See also Project '62, Playboy of the Modern World, a radio documentary on Canadian Broadcasting Company, copy supplied by Playboy Enterprises.

14. Charles Tannen, *"Folio* Talks With Hugh M. Hefner," *Folio* (February 1979) 47–52.

15. Gay Talese, "The Erotic History of Hugh Hefner," *Esquire* (November and December, 1979).

16. "Hugh Hefner of Playboy Enterprises, Inc." *Madison Avenue Magazine* (January 1979) 10–13.

17. *"Folio* Talk With Hugh M. Hefner,'' 47–52.

18. "Christie Hefner Planning to Keep *Playboy* Format,'' UPI story, Richmond *Times-Dispatch* (June 15, 1980).

19. *"Playboy* one-shots may yield new books," *Advertising Age* (November 19, 1979) 1, 92. Also see "How *Playboy* picks its new publication ventures," *Advertising Age* (January 16, 1978) 30.

20. *"Folio* Talks With Hugh M. Hefner,'' 47–52.

21. "Openers," *Oui* (October 1972) 5.

22. *"Playboy* one-shots may yield new books,'' 92.

23. "Skin Trouble," 50.

24. Robert Runde, "The Wages of Skin," *Money* (February 1980) 68–74.

25. "Merchants of Raunchness," 69.

26. "The Skin-Book Boom . . ." 91–97.

27. See "Hustling for the Lord," *Newsweek* (December 5, 1977) 6 for interesting details on this incident. Also see "Publisher's Statement. Fifth Birthday!'' *Hustler* (July 1979) 7.

Notes to Chapter 7

1. From special 24-page "Youth Marketing" supplement, *Advertising Age* (April 28, 1980).

2. William Brohaugh, ed., *1980 Writer's Market* (Cincinnati: Writer's Digest Books, 1979) 311–320.

3. Judith S. Duke, *Children's Books and Magazines: A Market Study* (White Plains, N.Y.: Knowledge Industry Publications, 1979).

4. Jack K. Lippert, *Scholastic, A Publishing Adventure* (New York: Scholastic Book Services, 1979). An excellent history of this organization. In the September, 1980, listing of the "Folio 400," *Scholastic Magazine* ranked 100th.

5. Interviews with publisher, editor-in-chief, and research director, *Seventeen* magazine headquarters, New York, May 1979; " 'Seventeen' Makes a Sales Call," *Madison Avenue* (November 1980) 85–96.

6. "Publisher drums up sales with not so new beat," *Advertising Age* ("Youth Marketing" supplement, April 28, 1980) S-2.

7. Double-page advertisement, *Advertising Age* (July 14, 1980) 22–23. Also see "Rolling Stone's 'College Papers'," *The Chronicle of Higher Education* (November 19, 1979) 18. Also, " 'Rolling Stone' going with magazine format," *Advertising Age* (September 22, 1980) 112.

8. Harland Manchester, "True Stories," *Scribner's* (August 1938) 26–27.

9. From *True Story* advertisements, such as *New York Times* (December 5, 1932).

10. Nona Cleland, "Confession Magazines Face Up to Sex Revolution," *More* (January 1977) 39–41.

11. From telephone conversation and correspondence between Michael Abrams, doctoral candidate, University of Missouri School of Journalism, and Ann White Segre, September 1979.

12. *New York Times* (January 17, 1952).

13. "The Customers Are Getting Older," *Business Week* (May 3, 1952) 40.

14. "Two retiree groups to begin ad sales for five publications," *Advertising Age* (July 23, 1979) 34.

15. " 'Modern Maturity' coming of age," *Advertising Age* (October 20, 1980) 46; "As demographics go, so go publications," *Advertising Age* (August 25, 1980) S-8–9.

16. Abrams, op. cit., interview/correspondence with Peter A. Dickerson, September 1979–January 1980.

17. Abrams, op. cit. correspondence with Roy Hemming (August 14, 1979).

18. George Rosenbranc, "Consumer Magazines" column, *Marketing & Media Decisions* (September 1979)   90. A discussion of specialty magazines for the 50–64 market.

19. "Market with a future, Retirement," *Marketing & Media Decisions* (December 1980)   74–76, 124–126.

Notes to Chapter 8

1. Ralph Ingersoll, "Notes About a Picture Magazine," (May 15, 1936) Time Inc. archives. Ingersoll loved to write memos. He served as general manager of the *Life* project.

2. Loudon Wainwright, *"Life* Begins," *Atlantic* (May, 1978)   56–73. The full prospectus has been published by Time Inc. At the time the original was prepared, the name *Life* had not been chosen. *Dime* was one of many possible titles considered.

3. *National Era* (March 24, 1859)   46, from Mott, *A History of American Magazines, 1850–1865*   II: 191.

4. Mott, *A History of American Magazines, 1850–1865*   II: 194; also see III: 186.

5. Mott, III: 191.

6. " '*Life*' expires after absorbing loss of $30,000,000 in last four years," *Advertising Age* (December 11, 1972)   1, 8. Also see "The End of the Great Adventure," *Time* (December 18, 1972)   46–55. Dun-Donnelley's advertisement appeared June 25, 1973   40–41.

7. Chris Welles, "Can Mass Magazines Survive?" *Columbia Journalism Review* (July–August 1971)   7.

8. Wolseley, *The Changing Magazines*   8.

9. "Making the consumer pay more," *Folio* (July 1976)   5–6.

10. "There Indeed Is *Life* After Death," *Folio* (April 1976)   13.

11. Howard Chapnick, "Markets & Careers" column, *Popular Photography* (August 1978)   34.

12. "Two Dreams come true, *Life, Look*," *Media Design* (November 1978)   68, 106.

13. "Back to *Life*," *Newsweek* (May 8, 1978)   93; "New '*Life*': More photos, lower numbers," *Advertising Age* (May 1, 1978)   1, 108.

14. Chapnick, "Markets & Careers"   143.

15. John G. Morris, "Should-and Could-There Be Another *Life?*" *Popular Photography* (November 1977)   202, 252.

16. "Records of the LOOK Years," summary report published by Cowles Communications, Inc., New York, n.d. Excellent, with statistical accounts.

17. "Daniel Filipacchi, The Frenchman behind the new LOOK," *Folio* (February 1978)   39.

18. "The New *Look*," *Newsweek* (February 12, 1979)   55–56.

19. "Gutwillig reacts to the mediocre start by '*Look*,' " *Advertising Age* (March 19, 1979)   12.

20. "New '*Look*' chief plots growth plans," *Advertising Age* (May 14, 1979)   3,96. Also see " 'Rolling Stone' confident third offshoot will grow,"   36, 40.

21. For a good summary see William P. Rankin, *Business Management of General Consumer Magazines* (New York: Praeger, 1980)   103–125.

22. *Popular Photography* (May 1937)   4.

23. Sean Callahan, *American Photography* (June 1978), introduction to the reader. Also see "Anatomy of a winner," *Folio* (May 1978)   78, 84.

24. "Introducing . . ." editor's comments, *People* (March 4, 1974)   2.

25. Nora Ephron, *Scribble, Scribble* (New York: Knopf, 1978)   13–18.

26. "Joining the *People* Parade," *Business Week* (May 16, 1977) 71.

27. Stephen Grover, "Grocery-Day Gossip Is Ringing Up Profits at *People* Magazine," *Wall Street Journal* (May 6, 1976).

28. "Richard Durrell of *People*," *Madison Avenue* (May 1979) 48, 51.

29. " '*People*'s' readers like it, *Time* says: ad jury is still out," *Advertising Age* (March 18, 1974) 3.

30. "Personality journalism; selling magazine for you," *IPDA Profit Ways* (May/June 1979) 33–34, 38.

31. " '*People*—5 going on 3,000,000," *Advertising Age* (February 26, 1979) 76.

32. John Mack Carter, "The pros said it couldn't be done, but *People*'s making it," *Folio* (February 1976) 58, 60.

33. "Why *People* Is on the Rise," *Advertising Age* (October 10, 1977) 45.

34. "Soft-news field grows with '*Us*' bow," *Advertising Age* (April 18, 1977) 8.

35. " '*Us*' denies sale rumor," *Advertising Age* (March 6, 1978) 10.

36. Double-page advertisement, *Advertising Age* (January 28, 1980) 32–33M.

37. "The Times Decides We Are Not '*Us*,' " *Newsweek* (March 17, 1980) 86. Also see "Peter J. Callahan," *Folio* (June 1980) 57–58.

NOTES TO CHAPTER 9

1. Ben L. Moon, "City Magazines, Past and Present," *Journalism Quarterly* (Winter 1970) 711–718. An excellent article.

2. John Peter, "The Rise of the city magazine," *Folio* (November/December 1973) 61–64.

3. "Can city books make it nationally?" (97–122) and "Directory of 165 city and state magazines (124–136), *Media Decisions* (April 1979).

4. "Special Report: City and Regional Magazines, two-parts, *Magazine Industry Newsletter* (May 9, 16, 1977).

5. "New magazine group tells local story," *Advertising Age* (November 27, 1978) 38; "City magazine group mulls tie with MPA," *Advertising Age* (April 7, 1980) 10; "City magazine group votes not to fold into MPA," *Advertising Age* (April 21, 1980) 10.

6. Much of early data from four-page announcement published by the *New Yorker*, n.d.

7. For more on financial status see "More than a magazine at 'The *New Yorker*.' " *Business Week* (April 14, 1980) 124, 126.

8. Dale Kramer, *Ross and the New Yorker* (New York: Doubleday, 1951) 91.

9. Comments from *News Workshop* (November 1972) published by New York University Department of Journalism, and lengthy interview with Shawn that appeared in a Dutch magazine, *Hollands Diep* (July 3, 1976). The *New Yorker* translated the article and made copies available. See also "The *New Yorker* at 40," *Newsweek* (March 1, 1965) 62–64.

10. "New Yorker 50th: Fete With Diffidence," *New York Times*, (February 22, 1975). Additional statistics in "The *New Yorker*, Mannerly Maverick at 50," (February 16, 1975).

11. "The *New Yorker* Turns Fifty," *Time* (March 3, 1975) 56–57.

12. Telephone interview with University of Missouri School of Journalism graduate student, Amy Hersh, November 20, 1980. See *Time* (January 12, 1981) 58–59; *Advertising Age* (Dec. 1, 1980) 28.

13. David Shaw, *Journalism Today* (New York: Harper's College Press, 1977) 187. Shaw has chapter on "City Magazines."

14. "Making It," *Time* (July 27, 1970) 77. Also "Edward Kosner," *Folio* (June 1980) 53, 56.

15. Lucian K. Truscott IV, "Requiem for a winner," *New Times* (March 4, 1977) 21–38.

16. David Shaw, "City Magazines Thrive in Era When National Publications Fold," *Los Angeles Times* (April 5, 1976).

17. Patricia Holt, "Lane Publishing Company Celebrates a Half-Century in the West," *Publishers Weekly* (March 12, 1979) 37–39; see also *"Sunset* 1929–1979," *Sunset* (February 1979) for special 16-page account. Additional data in *Sunset* (May 1978).

18. Interviews with Gary McCalla and Emory Cunningham in Birminghamn, spring, 1979, plus data from company's releases. McCalla's six-page history helpful.

19. Interview with Cunningham, *Madison Avenue Magazine* (July 1979) 98; also, "Sunbelt publishing part of good life," *Advertising Age* (September 26, 1977) 3, 88, 90, 92.

    See " 'Southern Living' turns regional image to gain," *Advertising Age* (March 3, 1981) 36M. More details about its trade publications and special sections.

20. For update review of *Yankee,* see Dick Gordon, "A Place To Be," *Advertising Age* (May 4, 1981) 55–56, 60.

21. Directory prepared from *Media Decisions* (April 1979) list; Standard Rate and Data's *Consumer Magazine and Farm magazine* rata book, plus other sources announcing starts/stops in the city magazine market. See *Advertising Age's* "City & Regional Magazines" section (March 30, 1981). This section appears regularly to update this fluid market. Ed Zotti's article provides excellent historical data.

NOTES TO CHAPTER 10

1. Jeff Sommer, "Sports magazines flourish," *Advertising Age* (May 19, 1980), S-2,S-4, from special section on "Sports Marketing."

2. Ibid, S-2.

3. *Magazine Industry Newsletter* (December 3, 1980).

4. Robert T. Elson, *The World of Time Inc., 1941–1960* (New York: Atheneum, 1973), II: 351–352.

5. " 'Newsweek' to test sports monthly," *Advertising Age* (July 9, 1979) 96.

6. Lee Lescaze, "John Walsh: The inside story on the 'Inside Sports' magazine," *Media People* (March 1980) 60–63.

7. " 'Sports Afield' Makes a Sales Call," *Madison Avenue* (September 1980) 70–75.

8. " 'Outdoor Life' Becomes a Movable Feast of Regional Targets," *Magazine Age* (August 1980) 60.

9. "Sports Marketing" section, *Advertising Age* (May 19, 1980).

10. "Bert Sugar gets title to 'Ring,' " *Advertising Age* (July 23, 1979) 86.

NOTES TO CHAPTER 11

1. "The Expanding Universe of Science Magazines," *Magazine Age* (August 1980) 23.

2. "The Science Boom," *Newsweek* (September 17, 1979) 104, 106.

3. "Expanding Universe of Science Magazines," 24–25.

4. "The Science Boom," 104, 106. See William Bennett, "Science hits the newsstands," *Columbia Journalism Review* (January 1981) 53–57.

5. "Science Magazines: A lively reaction to consumers' thirst for knowledge," *Madison Avenue* (July 1980) 30, 36.

6. *Scientific American* (December 1945) 328.

7. "Science Magazines: . . . ," 30, 36.

8. *Magazine Age* (August 1980)   30.

9. *Magazine Industry Newsletter* (May 7, 1980).

10. *Magazine Age* (August 1980)   30–31.

11. "Science Magazines: . . . ,"   30, 36.

12. Ibid.

13. "Chapter Two Begins at *GEO*," *Newsweek* (August 7, 1980)   57–58. Also see "GEO Magazines Makes a Sales Call," *Madison Avenue* (April 1980)   64, 68, 70, 72–73, 109, 112.

14. *Magazine Industry Newsletter* (March 19, 1980).

15. See Letter to Editor, *Folio* (October 1980)   4.

16. *Magazine Industry Newsletter* (February 6, 1980).

17. Ibid.

18. "Take off with the science fiction category," *IPDA Profit Way* (November–December 1979)   19–20, 22. This article noted that "The dedication of the science fiction and fantasy fan rivals that of the readers of any other category of books and magazines."

19. Henry R. Bernstein, "Energy books expand," *Advertising Age* (June 16, 1980)   S-40.

20. Edwin Diamond, "Take a Great Editor, Add Great Writers, Throw Caution to the Wind . . ." *Next* (February 1981)   54–57.

NOTES TO CHAPTER 12

1. From material supplied by Meredith Corp. *Imprint* (Meredith house organ, November, 1977) was devoted to the firm's 75th anniversary. See *Wall Street Journal* (July 10, 1953) for background data, plus more on its move into television "to stabilize its position."

2. Steve Weinberg, "Meredith adds to its house," *Des Moines Sunday Register* (February 26, 1978).

3. "Meredith to debut electronics 'BH&G,' " *Advertising Age* (September 1, 1980)   5.

4. " 'Apartment Life' studies new dwellings," *Advertising Age* (December 8, 1980)   80. Also see " 'Apartment Life' Sales Call," *Madison Avenue* (June 1979)   93–103.

5. Peterson, *Magazines for the Twentieth Century*,   217.

6. Peterson (240–242) says it was the *Bricklayer*; Robert T. Elson, *The World of Time Inc.*   II:322–326 calls it the *Brickbuilder*.

7. See Standard Rata and Data Service lists.

8. "Give them the simple life," *Marketing & Media Decisions* (January 1980)   74–76, 111.

9. Ibid.

NOTES TO CHAPTER 13

1. "Agrimarketing," *Advertising Age* (March 19, 1979)   S-1–24.

2. Mott, *A History of American Magazines 1794–1824*, I: 152–154.

3. Karl B. Raity and Stanley D. Brunn, "Geographic Patterns in the Historical Development of Farm Publication," *Journalism History* (Spring 1979)   14–15, 31–32.

4. "Meredith at 75: Multi-media expansion," *Advertising Age* (October 31, 1977)   3, 78, 80.

5. "*Successful Farming:* The Management Magazine Goes South," *Madison Avenue* (January 1979)   74–84, 110.

6. "*Progressive Farmer* Makes a Sales Call," *Madison Avenue* (January 1980)   98–105. Also see Emory Cunningham, "Eighty-Nine Years of Service in the South," address to Newcomen Society in North America, September 22, 1974.

7. "Farm Media," *Marketing & Media Decisions* (January 1980)   100, 102, 104–106.

8. *"Farm Journal* Makes a Sales Call," *Madison Avenue* (April 1980)   101–107.

9. Irene French Clipper, "The Curtis Publishing Company—Born Again in Indianapolis." Paper submitted to Association for Education in Journalism convention, August 23, 1977, Madison, Wis.

10. From background material supplied by *Mother Earth News*

11. "State Farm Publications," *Madison Avenue* (January 1980)   92, 94–95.

12. Earl L. Butz, "Agriculture—America's Biggest Business," *Madison Avenue* (September 1980)   79–80.

13. Letter from David S. Bennett, February 26, 1980.

NOTES TO CHAPTER 14

1. Lyon N. Richardson, *A History of Early American Magazines, 1741–1789,*   60.

2. Ibid., 345.

3. Research project, "Early American Religious Magazines," by Jeffery R. Hawkins, University of Missouri, 1975. See also his thesis, "The Northern Methodist Press and Slavery, 1844–1861," 1976.

4. Mott, *A History of American Magazines, 1741–1850*   I: 133.

5. Wolseley, *Understanding Magazines,* 354; Ford, *Magazines for Millions,*   63–77.

6. *Magazine Industry Newsletter* (May 20, 1970).

7. Information in part from *Consumer and Farm Rate and Data* reports supplied by publishers.

8. John Mack Carter, "The Power of Positive Publishing," *Magazine Age* (April 1980)   70.

9. "Exodus at *Quest,*" *Time* (January 12, 1981)   57.

10. Speech reprinted in full in *The Catholic Journalist* (June 1978)   4, 7–8.

NOTES TO CHAPTER 15

1. "Those sensational tabloids sales," *Profit Ways* (November/December 1979)   10, 12, 14; "The Biggest Numbers Are In The Sunday Supps," *Madison Avenue* (February 1981)   63–70.

2. Philip N. Schuyler, "American Weekly Leaves Many Ghosts," *Editor & Publisher* (July 20, 1963)   12, 57.

3. "Supps busting out all over," *Marketing & Media Decisions* (April 1980)   63, 172–180.

4. "The New York Times Magazine Makes a Sales Call," *Madison Avenue* (July 1980)   77–79, 82–87. Also, "Collision Course," *Marketing & Media Decisions* (September 1980)   114, 116.

5. Good early historical data available from John A. Haney, "A History of the Nationally Syndicated Sunday Magazine Supplements," unpublished doctoral dissertation, University of Missouri, 1953.

6. James Lardner, "The Man Behind the *Enquirer,*" Washington *Post* (April 2, 1978). A most detailed account of Pope and his publication. This story says Pope paid $25,000 for the *Enquirer* although the magazine's public relation releases use the $75,000 figure.

7. John Mack Carter, "You may not read it but millions do," *Folio* (April 1976)   43, 45–46.

8. "Writing guidelines from the *National Enquirer,*" *Folio* (August 1975)   68–70. The complete memo is reprinted.

9. "Scandal sheet or media pacesetter?" Kansas City *Star* (January 25, 1981). An unidentified former reporter tells of his experiences.

NOTES TO CHAPTER 16

1. Jane Levere, "Media on their marks in race for ad dollars," *Advertising Age* (April 2, 1979) S-10–11.

2. Frank Luther Mott, *The History of American Magazines 1865–1885* III: 139–143.

3. Mott, *The History of American Magazines 1741–1850* I: 215–217.

4. Ibid, 566–568.

5. Joseph Garland, "The New England Journal of Medicine, 1812–1968," *Journal of the History of Medicine* (April 1969) 126–139. Also see speech to Massachusetts Medical Society, Boston, May 20, 1952, reprinted in *New England Journal of Medicine* (May 22, 1952) 801–806.

6. Material concerning *The Lancet* furnished by the magazine's London offices, including several reprints.

7. Caroline Bird, "Gadfly of Medicine," *Esquire* (February, 1956) 42, 44.

8. Mott, *The History of American Magazines 1885–1905* IV: 524–535.

9. From interview with W. L. Chapman, son of founder, Lansing Chapman, to *MEDICUS*. Reprinted in booklet to provide early history of *Medical Economics*. n.d.

10. "How J. I. Rodale Founded *Prevention*," *Prevention* (June 1975) 56–59.

11. "Rodale patiently waiting for world to catch up with it," *Advertising Age* (July 21, 1980) 64, 72. See editorial, "The Rodale choice," in same magazine (August 4, 1980).

12. Letter to author, September 29, 1980.

13. Material supplied on each Mosby publication, by the company, for advertisers.

NOTES TO CHAPTER 17

1. "Minority Marketing," Special section, *Advertising Age* (April 16, 1979) S-1–36.

2. J. K. Obataka, "Black Journals Reflect Shift From Racialism," Los Angeles *Times* (April 27, 1975).

3. Highlights of *Ebony*'s first ten years are reported in the November 1965 edition, 121–132. This has been reproduced in pamphlet form.

4. "*Ebony* With Pictures," *Newsweek* (September 24, 1945) 86.

5. "White Man Turns Negro," *Life* (June 9, 1947) 131.

6. Paul M. Hirsch, "An Analysis of *Ebony:* The Magazine and Its Readers," *Journalism Quarterly* (Summer 1968) 261–270, 292.

7. Victoria L. O'Hara, "Black Consumer Magazines. *Black Enterprise, Ebony, Essence* (Northwestern University School of Journalism Study, 1974).

8. "John H. Johnson of *Ebony*," *Nation's Business* (April 1974) 854–860.

9. Question-answer interview with John H. Johnson, "Failure is a word I don't accept," *Harvard Business Review* (March–April 1976) 79–88.

10. "Of *Essence*," *Magazine Age* (January 1980) 98.

11. Bonnie Allen, "*Essence* & Other Thoughts on the 70's," *Essence* (May 1980) 94–96, 163.

12. Marjorie McManus, "*Essence* Magazine Success Story," *Folio* (December 1976) 27–29.

13. Herb Drill, "Backing black firms," *Philadelphia Bulletin* (March 13, 1979). Also see "Nine myths about the black market," *Marketing & Media Decisions* (September 1979) 104–108.

14. Hughes Jones, interview with Preston J. Edwards, *Black Collegian* (October–November 1980) 19–26.

15. " 'Main Man' arrives to fill a fashion void," *Advertising Age* (December 1, 1980) 81.

16. Paul Masserman and Max Baker, *The Jews Come to America* (New York: Bloch Publishing Co., 1932) 417.

17. Charles A. Madison, *Jewish Publishing in America* (New York: Sanhedrin Press, 1976) 243.

NOTES TO CHAPTER 18

1. "Proliferation, Localization, Specialization Mark Media Trend in Past Fifty Years," *Advertising Age* (April 30, 1980) 147–148, 155–156.

2. Mott, *A History of American Magazines, 1905–1903,* V: 59–71. Also, "Our 85th Milestone," *Editor & Publisher* (March 22, 1969) 6, and *Editor & Publisher's* 75th anniversary edition, June 27, 1959.

3. Edward D. Miller, "What's Wrong with *Editor and Publisher?*," *ASNE Bulletin* (April 1979) 3–14. Quotes from the magazine and reply from Robert U. Brown.

4. "Ad Age Marks Its 50th: Tells Steps Along the Way," *Advertising Age* (January 7, 1980) 49–57.

5. Early days recorded in "How's *Folio* doing: III" (September 1976) 9–11.

NOTES TO CHAPTER 19

1. Much of these data comes from Standard Rate and Data Service *Consumer and Farm Periodical* and *Business Periodical* rate and data books, especially from the profiles furnished by the magazines. Other material comes from *Ayer Directory of Periodicals,* which includes founding dates and current circulation figures.

2. Additional material on *Mad* may be found in Frank Jacobs, "William Gaines, *Mad* Magazine's Eccentric Publisher," *Hustler* (February 1980) 37–40, 52–54; Richard Reeves, *"Mad* Magazine—Witness for the People," *New York* (October 1, 1973) 40–42; *New York Times Magazine* (January 25, 1981) 17.

3. "National Lampoon Makes a Sales Call," *Madison Avenue* (December 1980) 81–87; Douglas C. Kenney talk to American Society of Magazine Editors, August 26, 1974.

NOTES TO CHAPTER 20

1. Nina Sadowsky, "Inflights: A Look at the Slick Magazines on Those Flying Machines," *Madison Avenue* (April 1980) 74–78; Mark Johnson, "In-Flight Magazines: They're Showing New Ability to Land Blue Chip Advertisers," *Magazine Age* (February 1980) 54, 56.

2. "Homechefs now have aid of magazine," A New York Times Service story printed in the Kansas City *Times* (July 11, 1980); "Feast for gourmet marketers," *Marketing & Media Decisions* (January 1981) 63, 150–152; and *"Cuisine* Makes a Sales Call," *Madison Avenue* (October 1980) 79–80, 84–88.

3. Leah Rozen, "New 'Rolling Stone' shakes off the moss," *Advertising Age* (January 26, 1981) 30; More data from " 'Rolling Stone' Tones Up," *New York* (January 26, 1981) 16–17; "Citizen Wenner," *New Times* (November 26, 1976) 16–52, and (December 10, 1976) 22–37, 54–61; " 'Rolling Stone' going with magazine format," *Advertising Age* (September 20, 1980) 112.

4. John Mack Carter, "Goodbye, Mr. Goodbar," *Magazine Age* (September 1980) 74; "Looking for a date or mate?" *Marketing & Media Decisions* (September 1980) 34; Daniel Machalaba, "High Times Magazine hated by Drug Foes, Suffers Hard Times," *Wall Street Journal* (July 29, 1980).

5. "High Times Magazine hated by Drug Foes, Suffers Hard Times," *Wall Street Journal* (July 29, 1980).

NOTES TO CHAPTER 21

1. Letter from Davis, February 7, 1980.

2. From Time Inc. annual reports.

3. *Gallagher Report* (July 11, 1977).

4. Magazine listings here and elsewhere in this chapter taken from appropriate Standard Rate & Data Service publications, trade advertisements, and materials supplied by the various publishers.

5. "Economy will test new M-H Publication Boss," *Advertising Age* (January 7, 1980)   14, 93.

6. Hearst material from these sources: Fred Danzig, "Hearst's top team shapes goals for next 25 years," *Advertising Age* (February 16, 1976)   3, 29–30, 55. Interview with Frank Herrera, *Folio* (June 1980), 55–56; "More expansion in Hearst plans," *Advertising Age* (October 8, 1979)   2.

7. Howard Ravis, "Gralla Publications" A successful brother act," *Folio* (August 1976)   88–93.

8. Letter to *Magazine Age* from Don Picard, manager of Corporate Advertising and Public Relations, The Webb Company, (September 1980)   8.

9. An excellent detailed study of this situation may be found in report by Edward J. Smith and Gilbert L. Fowler, Jr., "The Status of Magazine Group Ownership," *Journalism Quarterly* (Autumn 1979) 572–576. An update of this study would confirm a continuation of these trends. Additional worthwhile material is available from Christopher H. Sterling and Timothy R. Haight, eds., *The Mass Media: Aspen Institute Guide to Communication Industry Trends* (New York: Praeger Publishers, 1978).

10. Another good source is Benjamin M. Compaine, ed., *Who Owns the Media?* (White Plains, N.Y.: Knowledge Industry Publications, Inc., 1979). Many tables are provided along with data concerning group ownerships. Updated versions of some of these charts, prepared by the Magazine Publishers Association, are found in the appendix of this volume.

NOTES TO CHAPTER 22

1. Peterson, *Magazines for the Twentieth Century,* 30–32.

2. "A Guide Out of the Magazine Readership Mess," *Magazine Age* (January 1982)   8.

3. "Can you count on the numbers?" *Media Decisions* (April 1978)   59–63, 116–122.

4. David P. Forsyth, "A basic guide to magazine research," *Folio* (February 1981)   44–49, 54–61, 81. Each point is explained in details in this informative article.

5. Stephen Grover, "Magazine Industry Is Jolted by Lawsuits Challenging Audience-Survey Concerns," *Wall Street Journal* (March 10, 1975).

6. Bob Donath, "Simmons charges libel, conspiracy in countersuit on *Time,*" (April 21, 1975)   2, 100.

7. "*Time* study finds more readers than Simmons," *Advertising Age* (September 22, 1975)   1, 69.

8. "Controversial SMRB report boosts readership," *Advertising Age* (October 1, 1979)   6.

9. Bob Donath, "The new research monopolist: Frank Stanton," *Folio* (December 1978)   92, 94, 96.

10. "Simmons, Axiom merge operations," *Advertising Age* (July 10, 1978)   1, 115.

11. "SMRB report sparks anger, confusion; hope lies in ARF study," *Folio* (December 1979)   34; "Agencies tussle with research data," *Advertising Age* (October 22, 1979)   3, 105.

12. "Simmons study steams shops; seek split-sample," *Advertising Age* (October 30, 1978)   20.

13. "New Simmons report may stir research war," *Advertising Age* (September 8, 1980)   20, 76.

14. "Media Research," *Marketing & Media Decisions* (September 1979)   92.

15. "Top 23 Research leaders up 18%," *Advertising Age* (May 19, 1980)   3, 90.

16. "Dozen magazines study primary readers," *Advertising Age* (February 12, 1979)   2.

17. Barbara Love, "Folio survey of magazine research," *Folio* (February 1981)   54–61, 81. Another excellent picture of a complex situation with 23 charts and tables for added help.

18. "A publication marketing strategy for the 1980s," *Profit Way* (May/June 1980)   20, 25–26. In same issue see "Magazine sales: what's ahead for you," which includes material from the Knowledge Industry Publications "Consumer Magazines in the 1980s."

19. Ed Papazia, "Mediology column," *Media Decisions* (April 1979)   14, 16.

20. "Media Research," *Marketing & Media Decisions* (March 1980)   80, 82.

21. "Taking the Measure Of Magazine Audiences," The *New York Times* (February 3, 1981).

NOTES TO CHAPTER 23

1. Irving Herschbein and Bert Paolucci, "Which printing process should you use—letterpress, offset or gravure?" *Folio* (October 1975)   25–26.

2. "In 1980, rotogravure will hold 15 per cent of the printing market," *Folio* (May 1979)   36, 38.

3. "Everything you always wanted to know about in-plant photosetting in less than one hour." Wilmington, MA.: Compugraphic Corporation, 1977). An informative, well explained and profusely illustrated booklet for anyone considering this process.

4. Frank Romano, "Typesetting: Another decade of rapid change," *Folio* (February 1980)   46–48.

5. "Price plummets for digital CRT typesetting equipment," *Folio* (June 1980)   32, 41.

6. John Peter, "The Cover Story," *Folio* (August 1978)   44–48; David Merrill, "Why covers fail," *Folio* (March 1980)   68–78.

7. "Fourth Estate," *News-week* (September 28, 1935)   36.

8. Karlene Lukkovitz, "RDAs: Who's watching the stores?" *Folio* (July 1980)   67–75, 84.

9. "How 'Progressive Grocer' remains an industry staple," *Advertising Age* (May 12, 1980)   36.

10. "Publishers' paper requirements up despite recession," *Folio* (October 1980)   39.

11. "Why Postal Service Faces Black Future, *U.S. News & World Report* (December 1, 1980)   39.

12. Hearings before the U. S. House of Representatives Subcommittee on Postal Rates of the Committee on Post Office and Civil Service, April 21, 1970. Kennedy's quote, 166; Murray's 89.

13. "Publishers given conflicting advice on nine-digit Zip," *Folio* (August 1980)   12, 14; Charles L. Pace, "Understanding the new postal regulations," *Folio* (February 1980)   66–68, 84.

14. "Quality control sparks strong attraction to alternate delivery," *Folio* (June 1980)   24; see other related stories in the same magazine for April 1979 and September 1979. For additional data see Barbara Love, *"Folio's* first annual production survey," *Folio* (January 1981)   55–60; Barbara Love, "Five-year paper forecast," *Folio* (January 1981)   64–68. In the same issue, *Folio* published summaries of the responses to the MPA financial surveys for those publishers responding in each of the years 1977–1979, p. 26.

NOTES TO CHAPTER 24

1. Magazine Publishers Association *Newsletter of Advertising* (June 1980)   3–4.

2. Ibid., 3. This newsletter was edited by William H. Paul.

3. "Survey compares profits," *Advertising Age* (November 3, 1980) 70.

4. Statistics included in "Fast Facts," a Section 2 supplement, *Advertising Age* (February 16, 1981) S-4. *Advertising Age* provides the most accurate, up-to-date reports on changes in the allocations and totals spent for advertising.

5. Cahners Advertising Research Report, *Commentary,* No. 2000.1 (1979).

6. For the best guidelines see Henry Turner, "Sweepstakes," a chapter from *Handbook of Circulation Management,* Barbara Love, ed., New Canaan, Conn.: *Folio,* 1980. See another Turner article, "Sweepstakes: not just for giants anymore," *Folio* (September 1979) 73–74, 76.

7. "Magazine imitators cause of inefficiency, wholesaler claims," *Folio* (October 1978) 12, reprinted from an earlier *CPDA News.*

8. John D. Klingel, "How much is too much?" *Folio* (August 1979) 45–50.

9. "Consultant shares 10 circulation axioms," *Folio* (March 1979) 8.

10. Barry Green, "ABC and BPA compared," *Folio* (August 1976) 25–29, 104.

NOTES TO CHAPTER 25

1. Norman R. Glenn, "1981—an upper year," *Marketing & Media Decisions* (January 1981) 164. Also of interest is "Challenges of the '80s," a 32-page special section of *U.S. News & World Report* (October 15, 1979). With many helpful statistical tables.

2. Edwin Diamond, "Take a Great Editor, add Great Writers, Throw Caution to the Wind . . ." *Next* (January/February 1981) 54, 56–57. This issue featured a look into media's future with what *Advertising Age*'s columnist James Brady called "some of the prognostications fascinating, others clearly arguable."

3. "How computers will affect mass communication," *Editor & Publisher* (October 14, 1978) 30–32. Also see "Forecast 1981: making way for the coming electronic revolution," *American Printer and Lithographer* (December 1980) 43–58. This excellent study predicts "stable growth" for magazines yet notes "circulation could take a beating."

4. "Pagination systems will be widely available by 1985," *Folio* (August 1980) 16, 33. Also *ap Log* (Associated Press) (March 26, 1979) 4.

5. "Magazines versus television," *Folio* (November 1979) 77–79. This offers findings of a study by Opinion Research Corp.

6. Bernice Kanner, "Outlook brightens past '80: Coen," *Advertising Age* (December 17, 1979) 3, 71.

7. Barbara Love, "1980; the real test," *Folio* (September 1979) 48, and "Experts look at '81; Tough year ahead," *Folio* (December 1980) 62, 64–67, 92.

8. Neil Faber, "Consumer Magazines," *Media Decisions* (August 1978) 109.

9. Jeffrey R. Parnau, "Printing: The new technology comes of age," *Folio* (February 1980) 34–35, 38–40, 42, 85. This adds to the *American Printer and Lithographer*'s study.

10. "Personalized magazines near?" *Advertising Age* (November 12, 1979) 47.

11. "*Time* working on way to offer readers a talkie," *Advertising Age* (December 3, 1979) 1, 95.

12. "Major Crisis looms for editors," *Folio* (February 1979) 13, 17. Also see Carter's manifesto for editors in 1980s, *Folio* (September 1979) 25.

13. "Wanted: Geniuses to lead magazines into '80s," *Advertising Age* (November 19, 1979) 28.

14. *Communications 1990: A Report of the Future Committee,* School of Journalism, University of Missouri-Columbia, 1980.

15. Robert M. Rees, "Magazines: A Diverting Definition for Advertisers," *Magazine Age* (January 1981) 12–13.

16. "Newsmakers," *Marketing & Media Decisions* (April 1980)   24.

17. James B. Kobak, "A magazine's life cycle and its profits," *Folio* (October 1976)   48–55.

18. Theodore H. White, *In Search of History* (New York: Harper & Row, 1978)   419–420.

19. John Mack Carter, "The Last Word," *Magazine Age* (January 1981)   86.

Bibliography

No STUDY of the American magazine scene could be accomplished without serious attention to the following media-orientated periodicals. Each in its own way serves a segment of that audience and each provides the readers and the historians with material of significance. The material used from each source has been fully documented in the footnotes.

Advertising Age, with special attention to its regular supplements; *AD-WEEK; Columbia Journalism Review; Editor & Publisher,* since many newspaper owners are also in the magazine market; *Folio,* creator of the *Folio 400* and the interpreter of many topics of concern to publishers and editors; *Gallagher Report,* especially for statistical accounts; *Madison Avenue,* with emphasis on national advertising; *Magazine Age,* a newcomer for advertisers and agencies; *Media Industry Newsletter,* for its weekly accounts of the shape of the industry; *Marketing & Media Decisions; IPDA Profit Way* and *CPDA News* for data on distribution; and *Publishers Weekly.*

There are also the many associations that contribute to the growth and development of the industry. They have been identified in the text.

Ayer Directory of Publications. Published annually by Ayer Press, Bala Cynwyd, PA.

Brady, Frank. *Hefner.* New York: Macmillan, 1974.

Carlson, C. Lennart, *The First Magazine, A History of The Gentleman's Magazine.* Providence, R.I.: Brown University, 1938.

Click, J. W. and Russell N. Baird. *Magazine Editing & Production.* Dubuque, Iowa: Wm. C. Brown Co. 1979.

Citizens, consumers & communications, an interaction study of the climate for learning. New York: Magazine Publishers Association. n.d.

367

Compaine, Benjamin M. *Consumer Magazines at the Crossroads: A Study of General and Special Interest Magazines*. White Plains, NY.: Knowledge Industry Publications Inc. 1975.

Compaine, Benjamin M., ed. *Who Owns the Media?* White Plains, NY.: Knowledge Industry Publications Inc. 1979.

Cort, David. *The Sin of Henry R. Luce*. Secaucus, NJ.: Lyle Stuart Inc. 1974.

Cousins, Norman. *Present Tense*. New York: McGraw-Hill. 1967.

Directory of Business and Organizational Communicators. San Francisco, CA.: International Association of Business Communicators. Published annually.

Duke, Judith S. *Children's Books and Magazines: A Market Study*. White Plains, NY.: Knowledge Industry Publications. 1979.

Elson, Robert T. *Time Inc. The Intimate History of a Publishing Empire*. I: 1923–1941 (1968) and II: 1941–1960 (1973). New York: Athenean.

Emery, Edwin and Michael Emery. *The Press and America*. Englewood Cliffs, NJ.: Prentice-Hall Inc. 1978.

Garberson, John W. *A Limited Number of Advertising Pages, Journalism Monographs*, Association for Education in Journalism, No. 25, 1975. (Deals with *Reader's Digest*.)

Fielding, Raymond. *The March of Time 1935–1951*. New York: Oxford University Press. 1978.

Foley, Martha. *The Story of Story*. New York: W. W. Norton & Company. 1980.

Fonzi, Gaeton. *Annenberg: A Biography of Power*. New York: Weybright and Talley. 1970.

Ford, James L. C. *Magazines for Millions*. Carbondale: Southern Illinois Press. 1969.

Forsyth, David P. *The Business Press in America, 1750–1865*. Philadelphia: Chilton Books, 1964.

Friedrich, Otto. *Decline and Fall*. New York: Harper & Row. 1970.

Gill, Brendon. *Here at The New Yorker*. New York: Random House. 1975.

Goldberg, Joe. *Big Bunny: The Inside Story of Playboy*. New York: Ballantine. 1967.

Gordon, George N. *The Language of Communication*. New York: Hastings House, Publishers. 1969.

Halberstam, David. *The Powers That Be*. New York: Knopf. 1979.

Hamblin, Dora Jane. *That Was the Life*. New York: W. W. Norton & Co. Inc. 1977.

Harris, Jay S., ed. *TV Guide, The First 25 Years*. New York: Simon & Schuster. 1978.

How and Why People Buy Magazines. Compiled by Lieberman Research, Inc. for Publishers Clearing House. 1977.

Hulteng, John L. and Roy Paul Nelson. *The Fourth Estate*. New York: Harper & Row. 1971.

Hynds, Ernest C. *American Newspapers in the 1980s*. New York: Hastings House, Publishers. 1980. Second edition.

Kramer, Dale. *Ross and The New Yorker*. New York: Doubleday. 1951.

Lippert, Jack K. *Scholastic, A Publishing Adventure*. New York: Scholastic Book Services. 1979.

Love, Barbara, ed. *Handbook of Circulation Management*. New Canaan, Conn.: Folio Magazine. 1980.

MIMP (Magazine Industry Market Place), *Directory of American Periodical Publishing*. New York: R. R. Bowker Co. Annually.

Mott, Frank Luther. *A History of American Magazines*. Cambridge: Harvard University

Press. I: 1741–1850 (1957); II: 1850–1865 (1938); III: 1865–1885 (1938); IV: 1885–1905 (1957); V: 1905–1930 (1968).

Peterson, Theodore. *Magazines in the Twentieth Century*. Urbana: University of Illinois Press. 1964.

Podhoretz, Norman. *Making It*. New York: Random House. 1967. (*Commentary* magazine editor)

Rankin, William P. *Business Management of General Consumer Magazines*. New York: Praeger. 1980.

Records of the LOOK Years. New York: Cowles Communications, Inc., n.d.

Read, William H. *America's Mass Media Merchants*. Baltimore: Johns Hopkins University Press. 1976.

Richardson, Lyon N. *A History of Early American Magazines, 1741–1789*. New York: T. Nelson & Sons. 1931.

Schacht, John H. *A Bibliography for the Study of Magazines*. Urbana: University of Illinois. 1968. Published by the author.

Schacht, John H. *The Journals of Opinion and Reportage: An Assessment*. New York: Magazine Publishers Association, 1966.

Schreiner, J. *The Condensed World of The Reader's Digest*. New York: Stein and Day. 1977.

Shaw, David. *Journalism Today*. New York: Harper's College Press. 1977. Chapter on "City Magazines."

Smith, Anthony. *Goodbye Gutenberg*. New York: Oxford University Press. 1980.

Sokolov, Raymond. *Wayward Reporter, The Life of A. J. Liebling*. New York: Harper & Row. 1980.

Standard Periodical Directory. (For U.S. and Canada). New York: Oxbridge Publishing Co., Inc.

Standard Rate and Data Service *Consumer Magazine and Farm Publication* and *Business Publication* rate and data books, published monthly in Stokie, Illinois.

Sterling, Christopher H. and Timothy R. Haight, ed. *The Mass Media: Aspen Institute Guide to Communication Industry Trends*. New York: Praeger Publishers. 1978.

A Study of Media Involvement. Conducted by Opinion Research Corp. New York: Magazine Publishers Association. 1980.

Swanberg, William A. *Luce and His Empire*. New York: Scribner's Sons. 1972.

Tebbel, John. *The American Magazine—A Compact History*. New York: Hawthorn Books, Inc. 1969.

Ulrich's International Periodicals Directory. 19th edition. New York: R. R. Bowker Co. 1980.

Wolseley, Roland E. *Understanding Magazines*. Ames, Iowa: Iowa State University Press. 1969. Second edition.

Wolseley, Roland. *The Black Press*. Ames, Iowa: Iowa State University Press. 1971.

Wolseley, Roland. *The Changing Magazine*. New York: Hastings House, Publishers. 1973. (See its Supplementary reading list.)

Wolseley, Roland. *Magazine World*. Englewood Cliffs, N.J.: Prentice-Hall Inc. 1951.

Wood, James Playsted. *Magazines in the United States*. New York: Ronald Press Co. 1971.

Wood, James Playsted. *Of Lasting Interest*. Garden City, NY.: Doubleday & Co., Inc. 1958. (History of *Reader's Digest*. For another early book on *Reader's Digest* see John Bainbridge, *Little Wonder*. New York: Reynal & Hitchcock. 1946.)

Wood, James Playsted. *The Curtis Magazines*. New York: Ronald Press. 1971.

Woodward, Helen. *The Lady Persuaders*. New York: Ivan Obolensky, Inc. 1960.

Writer's Market, William Brohaugh, ed., Cincinnati: Writers Digest Books. Published annually.

Index

DATE DUE